KU-788-538

PROGRAMMING LANGUAGE CONCEPTS 2/E

PROGRAMMING LANGUAGE CONCEPTS 2/E

Carlo Ghezzi
Politecnico di Milano

Mehdi Jazayeri
Hewlett-Packard Laboratories

JOHN WILEY & SONS

New York   Chichester   Brisbane   Toronto   Singapore

Copyright © 1982, 1987 by John Wiley & Sons, Inc.

All rights reserved. Published simultaneously in Canada.

Reproduction or translation of any part of
this work beyond that permitted by Sections
107 and 108 of the 1976 United States Copyright
Act without the permission of the copyright
owner is unlawful. Requests for permission
or further information should be addressed to
the Permissions Department, John Wiley & Sons.

Library of Congress Cataloging in Publication Data:

Ghezzi, Carlo.
 Programming language concepts.

 Bibliography: p.
 Includes index.
 1. Programming languages (Electronic computers)
I. Jazayeri, Mehdi. II. Title.
QA76.7.G48 1987   005.13   86-18967

Printed in the Republic of Singapore.

10 9 8 7 6 5 4 3 2

Preface

This book introduces, analyzes, and evaluates the important concepts found in current programming languages. The book is based on two premises: programming languages exist for software production, and they are one of many, albeit very important, tools for this task. We thus evaluate a programming language or a programming language concept based on how it affects software production and how well it can be integrated with other software tools.

This book *is not* an introduction to any one programming language. It *is not* a feature-by-feature examination of programming languages. It *is* a study of programming languages *organized by concept*. We present and evaluate a few central concepts that can be used to understand the hundreds of programming languages in existence and to differentiate among them. We have taken a comparative approach: the concepts are illustrated by contrasting their appearance in different languages. Abstraction principles are emphasized throughout the book as the best way to understand and manage complex objects and phenomena. We also emphasize the fact that there are many programming styles or paradigms, such as imperative, functional, object-oriented, and declarative, each with its own strengths and weaknesses.

When discussing a particular concept, we emphasize the language that pioneered the concept, for example, class in SIMULA 67, strong-typing in ALGOL 68, type definition in Pascal, string and pattern-matching in SNOBOL4, functions as mathematical objects in LISP, and declarative specifications in PROLOG. To provide wide exposure, however, we draw examples from a variety of languages including Ada, ALGOL 60, ALGOL 68, APL, C, CLU, COBOL, Euclid, FORTRAN, FP, Gypsy, LISP, Mesa, Modula-2, SETL, SQL, and Smalltalk. Our purpose is to show the wide applicability of the concepts.

It *is not* our purpose to turn the reader into a proficient programmer in any of these languages. Rather, this book will improve the reader's ability to appreciate and evaluate programming languages (or language proposals). In addition, the reader will be able to identify the important concepts in programming languages and recognize their power as well as their limits. This ability is essential if one is to choose a language, design a language, extend an existing language, or even use a language to maximum advantage. Thus the book can be useful to software managers, professional programmers, and language designers, both as a study guide and as a reference text.

Prerequisites for the book are fluency in at least one programming language and an elementary knowledge of data structures. Reading knowledge of Pascal is helpful but not essential. The book's emphasis on systematic program design requires that the reader should have some software development experience. In particular, the reader should be aware of the need for a disciplined approach to programming and know how to use a language in a disciplined way—although this is not a prerequisite if the reader is willing to accept some of our assertions on faith.

PURPOSE AND CONTENTS OF THE BOOK

If any one notion distinguishes this work from other books on programming languages, it is the theme that programming languages should support software development. Indeed, our purpose is to evaluate programming language concepts in terms of their contribution to the software development process and to develop the criteria needed for such evaluation. These criteria are based principally on the relationship between programming languages and design methodologies and, to a lesser degree, on the relationship between programming languages and other software production tools. This point of view is developed in Chapter 1. In Chapter 2, we present four concepts—data types, control structures, program correctness, and programming in the large—that can be used to examine and evaluate programming languages. These concepts are also used to explain the evolution of the field over the past 30 years. Chapters 4 through 6 deal in detail with data types, control structures, and programming in the large. Program correctness issues are discussed in each chapter in relation to other concepts. An important point in these chapters is how various language features can be implemented. Chapter 3 provides the background in language processing that is necessary for the ensuing discussion in Chapters 4 through 6. Chapters 1 through 6 emphasize the conventional imperative languages. To provide a balanced view of programming languages, in the following two chapters we discuss two alternative programming paradigms. Chapter 7 is devoted to functional or applicative languages, with particular emphasis on FP, LISP, and APL. Chapter 8 is devoted to declarative and logic programming, with emphasis on PROLOG and references to SETL, SQL, and SNOBOL4. Exposure to the different styles of languages is essential for a thorough appreciation of the weaknesses and strengths, as well as the applicability—and indeed the *validity* and *viability*—of each style. We also feel strongly about semantics. Even though we use operational semantics throughout the book, we also introduce axiomatic and denotational semantics in Chapter 9. Formal semantics is an important and relevant topic to the study of programming languages—a topic that will grow in importance. We provide an introduction to the field, just enough to give the reader an appreciation of the needs and difficulties involved.

Finally, Chapter 10 discusses the subject of language design. Language design is an exciting and active area of computer science. The new languages being designed today are not merely minor improvements over previous ones but attempts at changing the very foundations on which our languages are built.

USE AS A TEXT

We have designed this book to be used as a textbook for a survey course on programming languages. Versions of this book have been used for several years in both undergraduate and graduate courses at several universities. Depending on the orientation of the course, the interests of the instructor, and the background of the students, different parts of the book can be emphasized. Chapters 1, 2, and 3 are introductory and should always be covered. They provide a perspective and the necessary background for the understanding of languages. Chapter 10 is a good way to conclude the course. In between, there are several alternatives. If the course is traditional and oriented towards imperative languages, Chapters 7, 8, and 9 can be treated lightly or not at all. If the instructor wants to emphasize the different paradigms, Chapters 7 and 8 should be covered at the expense of parts of Chapters 4 and 5. The material on concurrency in Chapter 5 is specialized enough so that it can be skipped without too much consequence. The student will see the same material in an operating systems course, although with a different orientation. In a more theoretical course, Chapter 9 should be covered, possibly right after Chapter 3. Chapter 10 may be treated at the beginning, at the end, or throughout the course. Having described the various alternatives, we mention that—as should be obvious from our choices for the contents of the book—we feel that all of the material in the book is important to a programming language student. We thus recommend that all chapters be covered, skipping sections if necessary, rather than eliminating entire chapters.

The book should be supplemented with manuals on specific languages. We have made a deliberate decision not to include in the text any detailed "summaries" of languages. A language summary can provide only a superficial view and therefore cannot be used as a reference document; only the language manual or the official definition can serve that purpose. Furthermore, one of the basic skills that the student should acquire in a programming languages course is the ability to learn and evaluate a language solely on the basis of its official definition. We have included a glossary of programming languages at the end of the book to direct the user to the required documents. Nevertheless, the book is a self-contained analysis of programming language concepts.

EXERCISES

For most students, the writing of programs seems to be an essential part of understanding the concepts of a language. One particularly good exercise is to try to write an "abstract data type" package in a language like Pascal or C that does not support abstraction, then have the student modify some internal fields of the data type and examine the needed changes, have the student do the same thing with Ada or Modula-2, and then try the same thing in LISP and PROLOG. The student will develop an appreciation for the importance of abstraction and the power of list structures.

Another good project is to have the student read the definition of an unfamiliar language and evaluate the language based on the concepts in this book. It is particularly educational for the student to try to identify issues that are not resolved or are ambiguous in the definition. Language comparisons are also good projects.

CHANGES FROM THE FIRST EDITION

The major development in the programming language field since the first edition of this book was written has been the gradual increase in importance of multiple programming paradigms. We have tried to reflect this trend by slightly deemphasizing the imperative languages, strengthening the coverage of material on functional languages such as LISP, and treating other paradigms. In particular, we have added Chapter 8 on declarative programming and PROLOG, and have expanded our treatment of object-oriented programming and Smalltalk in Chapters 4 and 6.

We have retained the book's emphasis on abstraction principles, as well as the use of the four concepts of data, control, correctness, and programming in the large for the analysis of languages. We have distributed the material of the old Chapter 6, which dealt with program correctness in isolation, to the other chapters, and discuss the issues in their proper context. Aside from many small changes throughout, we have made the following major changes:

- Chapter 8 on declarative programming. This is an entirely new chapter dealing with an area of growing importance. It complements the book's emphasis on multiple language paradigms.

- Chapter 9, on formal semantics, is another new chapter. We feel that knowledge of formal semantics is essential for the design of semantically sound languages. This is an area whose importance will grow with time.

- Chapter 3 is essentially rewritten. We have added an introductory section on syntax. We found that even though the book's emphasis is on semantics, most students need a treatment of syntax for completeness. We also have expanded the treatment of operational semantics in Chapter 3. The feedback we received from students was that the material was too terse. We have attempted to remedy this problem by defining an abstract machine and providing details in terms of this machine.

- The old Chapter 6, which dealt with program correctness issues, is gone. The material in that chapter is best discussed with other topics. Most of the old chapter has been distributed throughout the book.

- In the current Chapter 6, which deals with programming in the large, we have expanded the discussion of programming environments and added Ada and Smalltalk as examples.

- We have added many examples, explanations, and clarifications throughout the book. We have increased the number of examples in C, SNOBOL4, Smalltalk, and Modula-2.

- We have added many exercises.

- We have updated the bibliography extensively.

ACKNOWLEDGMENTS

The following people provided valuable comments for the first edition of this book: Jean-Pierre Banâtre, Dan Berry, Laurence Chan, Jon Cohen, Richard LeBlanc, Gyula Magó, Dino Mandrioli, David Moffat, and Kuo-Chung Tai. Edith Coon typed most of the manuscript. Vicki Baker typed early versions of several chapters.

For the second edition, we have had helpful comments from Walter Alvey, Bob Collins, Arthur Fleck, Ray Ford, Mariam Jazayeri, Jon Mauney, and

Dave Reisenauer. We would like to especially thank Ray Ford and Jon Mauney whose insightful, constructive, and detailed criticisms have been invaluable in improving the accuracy and coverage of the book.

Ada is a registered trademark of the U. S. Government, Ada Joint Program Office. UNIX is a trademark of Bell Laboratories.

CARLO GHEZZI
MEHDI JAZAYERI

Milano, Madesimo, Los Altos

Contents

Introduction

This book is concerned with programming languages. Programming languages, however, do not exist in a vacuum: they are tools for writing software. A comprehensive study of programming languages must take this role into account. We begin, therefore, with a discussion of the software development process and the role of programming languages in this process. This chapter provides a perspective from which to view programming languages and their intended uses. From this perspective, we will weigh the merits of many of the language concepts discussed in the rest of the book.

1.1 SOFTWARE DEVELOPMENT PROCESS

The software development process can be divided into five phases. These phases usually are followed as five sequential steps in software development. Each step, however, may identify deficiencies in the previous one, which then must be repeated. Each phase involves a distinct activity and results in a set of clearly identifiable products. These phases can be listed as follows.

i. *Requirements analysis and specification.* A software system is developed to meet a need perceived by a user community. User needs are stated in the form of a set of *requirements* that the system is expected to satisfy. These requirements are developed jointly by users and software developers. The success of a system is measured by how well the software mirrors these stated requirements, how well the requirements mirror the users' perceived needs, and how well the users' perceived needs reflect the real needs.

The result of this phase is a requirements document stating *what* the system should do, along with users' manuals, feasibility and cost studies, performance requirements, development plans, and so on. The requirements document does not specify *how* the system is going to meet its requirements.

ii. *Software design and specification.*   Starting with the requirements document, software designers design the software system. The result of this phase is a system design specification document identifying all of the modules comprising the system and their interfaces. Of the various approaches to software design and specification, none is universally accepted. The design methodology followed in this step can have a great impact on the choice of the programming language to be used in system implementation. We will come back to this point later in the chapter.

iii. *Implementation (coding).*   The system is implemented to meet the design specified in phase ii. This is the only step in which a programming language is used directly. The result is a fully implemented and documented system.

iv. *Certification.*   This step assesses the quality of the implemented system, which is then delivered to the user. Note that some certification activity occurs in every phase of software development to check that intermediate deliverables of the process satisfy their objectives. For example, one must check that the design specification document is consistent with the requirements which, in turn, must match the user's needs. According to Boehm (Boehm 1981) these checks are accomplished by answering the following two questions:

"Are we building the product right?"

"Are we building the right product?"

Two specific kinds of certification performed during implementation are module testing and integration testing. *Module testing* is done by each programmer on the module he or she is working on to ensure that it meets its interface specifications. *Integration testing* is done on a partial aggregation of modules; it is basically aimed at uncovering intermodule inconsistencies. Also included in the certification activity at this stage are any efforts aimed at formally verifying program correctness.

Careful checking during implementation does not eliminate the need for a separate certification phase, often called *quality assurance*. Very often the certification task at this stage is the responsibility of a group other than the development group. The main activities of this phase are running acceptance tests, stressing the software by generating heavy load conditions, checking programs and documentation for adherence to prespecified standards, and so on.

v. *Maintenance.*   Following delivery of the system, changes to the system may become necessary either because of detected malfunctions (errors) or a desire to add new capabilities or to improve old ones. These changes are referred to as maintenance. The importance of this phase can be seen in the fact that maintenance costs are typically at least as large as those of all the other steps combined.

We will next examine the role of the programming language in the software development process by illustrating the relationship between the programming language and other software development tools in Section 1.2 and the relationship between the programming language and design methodologies in Section 1.3.

1.2 THE PROGRAMMING LANGUAGE AS A COMPONENT OF A SOFTWARE DEVELOPMENT ENVIRONMENT

The work in any of the five phases of software development may be supported by computer-aided tools. The phase currently supported best is the coding phase, with such tools as text editors, compilers, linkers, and libraries. These tools have evolved gradually, as the need for automation has been recognized. In the early days of computing—and not even the earliest—one had to punch a program on cards, pick the necessary routines from a library of card decks, combine all the routines, and submit them to the compiler. The possibilities for clerical errors—let alone the possibility of wearing out the library decks—were great. Advances in many areas of computer science have led to the automation of many of these tasks. One can now use an interactive editor to create a program and a file manager to store it in a library for future use. When needed, several previously created and (possibly) compiled programs may be linked to produce an executable program. These computer-aided program development tools have increased programming productivity by reducing the chances of errors.

Yet, as we have seen, software development involves much more than programming. If we want to increase the productivity of software development, we must devise computer support for all of its phases.

By a *software development environment* we mean an integrated set of tools and techniques that aid in the development of software. The environment is used in all phases of software development: that is, requirements, design, implementation, certification, and maintenance.

An idealized scenario for the use of such an environment would be the following. A team of application and computer specialists interacting with the environment develops the system requirements. The environment keeps track of the requirements as they are being developed and updated, and guards against incompleteness or inconsistency. It also ensures the currency of the documentation as changes are being made to the requirements.

Following the completion of the requirements, system designers, interacting with the environment, gradually refine the design of the system, that is, they specify the needed modules and the module interfaces. Test data may also be produced at this stage. The implementers then undertake to implement the system based on the design. The tools provided by the software development environment at this phase are the most familiar. They include programming languages, editors, compilers, simulators, interpreters, linkers, debuggers, and others.

As far as the usefulness of the environment is concerned, it is important that these tools not only work well together but that they be compatible with tools used in the other phases. For example, the programming language must be compatible with the design methodology supported by the environment at the design stage. If the methodology is top-down design, the language must support this approach in the sense of allowing the hierarchical levels of the design to be apparent in the program. The next section is devoted to the effect of the design methodology on programming languages. The point we would like to impress upon the reader is that the environment must be viewed as consisting of tools and methodologies, and that these ought to be compatible, for maximum benefits.

In the certification phase, the help provided by the environment can be quite varied. The environment could be used to collect test data during the requirements, specification, and implementation phases. It could ensure that these tests are kept current (as changes are made to the specifications, for example). It could also support the use of formal specification and verification of modules. The results of tests could be collected and classified. Suitable measures could be used to determine the adequacy of the testing strategy.

The result of all this interaction with the ideal environment is a fully documented and certified system that corresponds to the requirements set down initially. If at any future time there is a need to modify the system—that is, the requirements—the environment must be capable of tracing the change to the design specification, code, test data, and documentation and to identify all affected areas.

The foregoing scenario provides a particularly simple and ideal illustration of the use of a software development environment. Although no such environment exists at present, current technology is not too far from making such a system possible. (In fact, all of the components of the environment exist; what is needed is the engineering job of integrating these components into a unified system.) In any case, the point of this discussion is to focus attention on the overall activity in which software developers are involved and the role that a programming language plays in this work. Whether or not these activities are supported by a computer system, they must be undertaken; the programming language is only one tool that software developers use. Because the usefulness of this tool can only be measured by its contribution to the software development process, it is necessary to examine the relationship of the programming language to other components of a software development environment.

We must mention that this view has not always been accepted. Certainly, the first programming languages were designed for "programming" rather than "software development." Nevertheless, even if a language was not designed with the goal of software production in mind, it must be evaluated on that criterion, since that is the desired end. This is the criterion used in this book.

1.3 SOFTWARE DESIGN METHODOLOGY AND PROGRAMMING LANGUAGES

As mentioned earlier, the relationship between software design methodologies and programming languages is an important one. This is so whether or not one views the programming language as a component of a software development environment. In trying to follow a certain design methodology, we will find that some languages are better suited than others.

Older languages, such as FORTRAN, were not designed to support specific design methodologies. For example, the absence of suitable high-level control structures in early FORTRAN makes it difficult to systematically design algorithms in a top-down fashion. Conversely, Pascal was designed with the explicit goal of supporting top-down design and structured programming. The developing trends in languages show that the idea that languages should support a design methodology is becoming increasingly accepted.

The fields of software design methodology and programming language design can converge, and in some cases, they already have. The most striking example of this trend is information hiding (as a design methodology) and data abstraction (as a language design principle).

Information hiding is a design technique for decomposing systems into modules. Each module hides a *secret*, often the format of a particular data structure (record, file, and so on). The module provides *access functions* that can be used to inquire or update the information contained in the data structure. Thus, users of the module (i.e., other modules) may access through function calls the information that the module is willing to provide. They cannot access the information by directly manipulating the module's data structure or by using global variables.

The goal of information hiding is to manage complexity by decomposing the system into highly independent pieces with clean interfaces. "Divide and conquer" and "separation of concerns" are the underlying philosophical principles. As a result, software becomes more readable, more amenable to independent development of parts, and most important, more easily modifiable and maintainable.

Languages with data abstraction facilities, such as SIMULA 67, CLU, Modula-2, Smalltalk, and Ada are quite capable of implementing this methodology. In fact, as we will see, a SIMULA 67 class, a CLU cluster, a Modula-2 module, a Smalltalk class, or an Ada package can directly represent an information-hiding module.

It is not clear if the concept of information hiding spawned the idea of the SIMULA class as a mechanism for describing abstractions. It is likely that the concepts of information hiding and the SIMULA class progressed independently and met in their maturation. The lesson is that the choice of design methodology can influence language design and should also influence the choice of the language to be used.

1.4 COMPUTER ARCHITECTURE AND PROGRAMMING LANGUAGES

Design methodologies influence programming languages in the sense of establishing requirements for the language to meet. Computer architecture has exerted influence from the opposite direction in the sense of restraining language designs to what can be implemented efficiently on current machines. Accordingly, languages have been constrained by the ideas of Von Neumann, because most current computers are very similar to the original Von Neumann architecture.

The Von Neumann architecture is based on the idea of a memory that contains data and instructions, a control unit, and a processing unit. The control unit is responsible for taking instructions out of memory, one at a time. Machine instructions are very low-level. Basically they require that data be taken out of memory, manipulated by the processing unit via arithmetic or logic operations, and that the results be copied back to some memory cells.

Conventional programming languages and Von Neumann architectures share at least two fundamental concepts: the sequential step-by-step execution of instructions and the modifiable repository of values. Sequential step-by-step execution of language instructions reflects the sequential fetch and execution of machine instructions performed by hardware. Also, the variables of conventional programming languages, which can be modified by assignment statements, reflect the behavior of the memory cells of the computer architecture. Therefore, many so-called high-level language-directed architectures are not being driven by real language needs, because the language motivating the architecture was itself motivated by the computer architecture in the first place.

Backus (Backus 1978) has strongly argued this point of view and has called for the use of a functional style of programming, because of both its simpler (and sounder) mathematical foundations and its higher expressive power. LISP is the best-known example of a language promoting such style, but many of LISP's original functional characteristics have been modified to make the language efficiently implementable on traditional machine architectures. Backus argues that we will abandon our traditional languages and adopt a radically different language only if the computers exist to execute these languages efficiently; he predicts that hardware technology will soon make this possible.

Backus attacks the concepts of assignment statements and variables as the roots of much evil and a curse passed on by the Von Neumann architecture. Although examples of functional programming languages, such as LISP, have been around for a number of years, they have succeeded in replacing the conventional programming languages only in certain application areas. Besides implementation problems, there are probably questions of the psychology and sociology of programming languages that favor the traditional approaches.

The debate in favor of and against different programming styles has become even more controversial since 1982 when the Japanese project for the development of a new generation of computers, known as the Fifth Generation Computer Project, announced the choice of logic programming as the basis for the new generation of machines. Whereas functional languages are based upon the mathematical notions of function, function composition, and function application, logic languages have their roots in logic, in particular, predicate calculus.

At present, there is much debate on foundational language concepts. In particular, the debate is

(a) Whether one should keep the various styles separate and choose among them depending on the application; or

(b) Use one style in all applications; or

(c) Try to integrate all styles into one uniform linguistic proposal.

A number of issues raised by this debate are still in the research stage.

This book considers the prevalent languages of the last 30 years and the issues that have influenced their design. The primary emphasis of chapters 2 through 6 is on the so-called statement-oriented languages. We cover the important issues in functional programming languages in Chapter 7 and logic languages in Chapter 8.

1.5   LANGUAGE DESIGN GOALS IMPOSED BY THE SOFTWARE DEVELOPMENT PROCESS

Returning to the theme of viewing a programming language as a tool for the development of software, this section identifies the requirements that this viewpoint places on the programming language.

i. *Software must be reliable.*   In other words, users should be able to rely on the software. They should feel comfortable in using it, even in the presence of infrequent or undesirable events such as hardware or software failures. This informal and hard-to-quantify property is strongly related to the more formal property of correctness. Software is correct if it behaves according to its specifications: the more rigorously and unambiguously the specifications are set down, the more convincingly program correctness can be proved. The reliability requirement has gained importance as software has been called upon to accomplish increasingly complicated tasks.

ii. *Software must be maintainable.*   Again, as software costs have risen and increasingly complex software systems have been developed, economic considerations have reduced the possibility of throwing away existing software and developing similar applications from scratch. Existing software must be modified to meet new requirements. Also, because it is almost impossible to get the real requirements right in the first place, for such complex systems one can only hope to gradually evolve a system into the desired one.

iii. *Software must execute efficiently.*   Efficiency has always been a goal of any software system. This goal affects both the programming language (features that can be efficiently implemented on present-day architectures) and the choice of algorithms to be used.

These three requirements—reliability, maintainability, and efficiency—can be achieved by suitable methodologies adopted during software development, appropriate tools in the software development environment, and certain characteristics of the programming language. We will now discuss language issues that directly support these goals.

1.5.1 Language and Reliability

The goal of software reliability is promoted by the following programming language qualities.

Writability.   This is an illusive property that is hard to quantify. Basically it refers to the possibility of expressing a program in a way that is natural for the problem. The programmer should not be distracted by details and tricks of the language from the more important activity of problem solving. Even though it is a subjective criterion, we can agree that higher-level languages are more writable than lower-level languages (e.g., assembly or machine languages). For example, an assembly language programmer is often distracted by the addressing mechanisms needed to access certain data, such as the positioning of index registers, and so on. The easier it is to concentrate on the problem-solving activity, the less error-prone is program writing and the higher is productivity.

Readability. It should be possible to follow the logic of the program and to discover the presence of errors by examining the program. Readability is also a subjective criterion that depends a great deal on matters of taste and style. However, the simpler the language is and the more naturally it allows algorithms to be expressed, the easier it is to understand what a program does by examining the code. For example, the **goto** statement has the potential of making programs hard to read, because it can make it impossible to read a program in one top-to-bottom pass and to understand it. One must jump around in the program in search of the targets of the **goto** statements. Although many programmers did not agree when it first was suggested that the **goto** statement is harmful, there is now a general consensus that the **goto** statement should be avoided in most cases.

As we will see, many of the qualities that make programs readable by humans also make them more easily checkable by a computer. Automatic checks performed by the computer contribute to program correctness very effectively.

Ability to deal with exceptions. The language should make it possible to trap undesired events (arithmetic overflows, invalid input, and so on) and to specify suitable responses to such events. In this way, the behavior of the system becomes totally predictable even in anomalous situations.

1.5.2   Language and Maintainability

The need for maintainable programs imposes two requirements on the programming language: programs written in the language must be readable, and they must be modifiable. Like readibility (discussed above), modifiability is somewhat subjective. It is possible, however, to identify features that make a program more modifiable.

A feature that makes programs more easily modifiable is *factoring*. By factoring we mean that there is one single place in the program where the description of a certain fact is concentrated. For example, an identical code segment repeated in several places can be factored in a subprogram and replaced by a subprogram call. In doing so, the program becomes more readable (if we give a meaningful name to subprograms) and more easily modifiable (a change to the fragment is localized to the subprogram's body).

As another example, several programming languages allow constants to be given symbolic names. Choosing an appropriate name for a constant promotes readibility of the program (e.g., we may use *pi* instead of 3.14). Moreover, a future need to change the value would necessitate a change only in the definition of the constant, rather than in every use of the constant.

Example (Pascal)

```
const no_of_words = 65536;
var memory: array [1..no_of_words] of integer;

         .  .  .

    if m > no_of_words then . . . . memory exhausted . . . .
```

The symbolic constant *no_of_words* represents the size of the memory. Each memory element is an integer and can be accessed by a subscript in the range 1 through *no_of_words*. If at any time the memory is expanded, all that needs to be changed is the first line of the program, even if the information that is changed is used in several places in the program.

1.5.3 Language and Efficiency

The need for efficiency has guided language design from the beginning. Many languages have had efficiency as a main design goal, either implicitly or explicitly. For example, FORTRAN originally was designed for a specific machine (the IBM 704). Many of FORTRAN's restrictions, such as the number of array dimensions or the form of expressions used as array indices, are based directly on what could be implemented efficiently on the IBM 704.

The issue of efficiency has changed considerably, however. Efficiency is no longer measured only by the execution speed and space. The effort required to produce a program or system initially and the effort required in maintenance can also be viewed as components of the efficiency measure. In other words, we are more concerned with productivity of software development than the performance of the resulting products. Once again, the programming language can have a great impact.

A language supports efficiency if it has the qualities of writability, maintainability, and optimizability. Writability and maintainability are discussed above. "Optimizability" refers to quality of allowing automatic program optimization.

Optimizability is important because much of the time traditionally spent in programming is devoted to trying to find efficient ways of doing things. However, the preoccupation with optimization should be removed from the early stages of programming. The ideal approach would be first to produce a program that is demonstrably correct and then, through a series of efficiency-improving transformations, to modify this program to obtain a correct and efficient one. A language is optimizable if it makes possible the automatic application of these transformations. For example, the existence of **goto** statements complicates automatic optimization. More generally, it has been shown that many features that reduce optimizability also hamper readability.

1.6 A BRIEF HISTORICAL PERSPECTIVE

This section examines briefly the developments in language design by following the evolution of ideas and concepts from a historical perspective.

The software development process originally consisted only of the coding phase. In the early days of computing, the computer was used mainly in scientific applications. An application was programmed by one person. The problem to be solved (e.g., a differential equation) was well-understood. As a result, there was not much need for requirements analysis or design specification or even maintenance. A programming language, therefore, only needed to support one programmer, who was programming what would be by today's standards an extremely simple application.

The desire to apply the computer in more and more applications led to its being used in increasingly less understood and more sophisticated environments. This, in turn, led to the need for "teams" of programmers and more formal approaches. The requirements and design phases, which up to then essentially were performed in one programmer's head, now required a team, with the results being communicated to other people. Because so much effort and money was being spent on the development of systems, old systems could not simply be thrown away when a new system was needed. Economic considerations persuaded people to enhance an existing system to meet the newly recognized needs. Also, program maintenance now became an important issue.

System reliability is another issue that has gained importance gradually, because of two major factors. One factor is that systems are being developed for users with little or no computer background; these users are not as tolerant of system failures as the system developers. The second factor is that systems are now being applied in areas such as nuclear power plants and patient monitoring, where system failures can be disastrous.

The shortcomings of programming languages has led to a great number of language design efforts. This book examines these influences on language design and assesses the extent to which the resultant languages meet their goals. Sections 1.6.1 through 1.6.6 describe the historical evolution of programming languages. Table 1 gives a genealogy of the major programming languages discussed in this book.

TABLE 1   Genealogy of Programming Languages

Language	Year	Originator	Predecessor Languages	Intended Purpose
FORTRAN	1954–57[a]	J. Backus (IBM)	—	Numeric computation
ALGOL 60	1958–60[b]	Committee	FORTRAN	Numeric computation
COBOL	1959–60[b]	Committee	—	Business data processing
APL	1956–60[b]	K. Iverson (Harvard)	—	Array processing
LISP	1956–62[a]	J. McCarthy (MIT)	—	Symbolic computation
SNOBOL4	1962–66[a]	R. Griswold (Bell Labs)	—	String processing
PL/I	1963–64[b]	IBM Committee	FORTRAN ALGOL 60 COBOL	General purpose
SIMULA 67	1967[c]	O.-J. Dahl et al. (Norwegian Computing Center)	ALGOL 60	General-purpose simulation
ALGOL 68	1963–68[b]	Committee	ALGOL 60	General purpose
Bliss	1971[c]	W. Wulf et al. (Carnegie Mellon U.)	ALGOL 68	Systems programming
Pascal	1971[c]	N. Wirth (ETH Zurich)	ALGOL 60	General and educational purpose. Supporting structured programming
PROLOG	1972[a]	A. Colmerauer (Marseille, France)	—	Artificial intelligence
C	1974[c]	D. Ritchie (Bell Labs)	ALGOL 68 BCPL[d]	Systems programming
Mesa	1974[b]	Xerox PARC	Pascal SIMULA 67	Systems programming
SETL	1974[a]	J. Schwartz (NYU)	—	Very high-level programming
Concurrent Pascal	1975[c]	P. Brinch Hansen (Cal. Tech)	Pascal	Concurrent programming
CLU	1974–77[a]	B. Liskov et al. (MIT)	SIMULA 67	Supporting a methodology based on abstraction
Euclid	1977[c]	Committee	Pascal	Verifiable systems programs

TABLE 1 (Cont.)

Language	Year	Originator	Predecessor Languages	Intended Purpose
Gypsy	1977[c]	D. Good et al. (U. of Texas—Austin)	Pascal	Verifiable systems programs
Modula-2	1977[c]	N. Wirth (ETH Zurich)	Pascal Mesa	Systems programming, real-time
Ada	1979[c]	J. Ichbiah et al. (CII Honeywell Bull)	Pascal SIMULA 67	General purpose, embedded applications, real-time
Smalltalk	1971–80[a]	A. Kay (XEROX PARC)	SIMULA 67	Personal computing environment

[a]Language design and initial implementation.
[b]Language design.
[c]First official language description.
[d]See (Richards 1969).

1.6.1 Early High-Level Languages: FORTRAN, ALGOL 60, and COBOL

The first attempts towards definition of high-level languages date back to the 1950s. Language design was viewed as a challenging compromise between the users' needs for expressiveness and the machine's requirements for efficiency. However, hardware was very expensive and execution efficiency concerns were the dominant design constraint.

The most important products of this historical phase were FORTRAN, ALGOL 60, and COBOL. FORTRAN and ALGOL 60 were defined as tools for solving numerical scientific problems, that is, problems involving complex computations on relatively few and simple data. COBOL was defined as a tool for solving business data-processing problems, that is, problems involving simple computations on large amounts of data (e.g., a payroll application).

These languages are among the major achievements in the whole history of computer science, because they have proven that the idea of a higher-level language was technically sound and economically viable. Besides that, each of these languages has brought up a number of important concepts. For example, FORTRAN introduced modularity via separately developed and compiled subprograms and possible sharing of data among modules via a global (COMMON) environment. ALGOL 60 introduced the notion of block structure and recursive procedures, and stimulated much research on formal language definition. COBOL introduced files and data descriptions, and the notion of natural language-like program description.

An even more convincing proof of the validity of these languages is that, apart from ALGOL 60, they are still among the most widely used languages in the application world. To be sure, there are other reasons for this long-term success, such as:

- The users' reluctance to move to newer languages, because of the need for remaining compatible with existing applications or just the fear of change.
- The fact that these languages have been evolving. For example, the present FORTRAN standard (FORTRAN 77) remains compatible with the previous standard (FORTRAN 66), but overcomes many of its major problems. A new standard (FORTRAN 8X) is presently under study.

1.6.2 Early Schisms: LISP, APL, and SNOBOL4

As early as in the 1960s there have been attempts to define programming languages with little concern for efficiency of implementation, but as notations for machine computations based on some well-characterized mathematical principles.

LISP is one such example. The language definition was based upon the mathematical concepts of function and function application, and gave foundation to a new class of languages called functional (or applicative) languages. Pure LISP is free from the Von Neumann concepts of modifiable variables, assignment statements, **goto** statements, and so on. LISP programs are exactly like general LISP data structures, and thus the LISP interpreter can be specified in LISP in a fairly simple manner.

APL is another language that supports a functional programming style. Its very rich set of operators, especially on arrays, relieves the programmer from using lower-level iterative, element-by-element array manipulations.

SNOBOL4 is a language providing string manipulation facilities and pattern matching. The programming style it supports is highly declarative.

LISP, APL, and SNOBOL4 are heavy consumers of machine resources (time and space). All of them require highly dynamic resource management that is difficult to do efficiently on conventional machines. Yet these languages have become very successful in specialized application areas. Also, they have been adopted by groups of very devoted users. For example, LISP has become *the* language for artificial intelligence research and applications; APL has been widely used for rapid prototyping and scientific applications involving heavy usage of matrix operations. SNOBOL4 has been used successfully for text manipulations. More recently, the principles behind these languages have received widespread attention both in research and industry.

An important contribution of LISP and SNOBOL4 was the emphasis on *symbolic computation*. As we mentioned, in the early stages of computing, computers were mainly used to solve numerical problems, such as systems of equations. This is why FORTRAN, ALGOL 60, and APL are mostly oriented towards numerical problem-solving. At present, however, only a small fraction of application developments are in the area of numeric computation. Major emphasis is on symbolic information processing, such as database queries and reporting, text processing, financial planning, and so on. COBOL can be seen as an initial step in this direction, because the language is more oriented towards formatting data than manipulating data through complex numeric computation. It is only with LISP and SNOBOL4 that symbolic computation became the central concern of the language.

1.6.3 Putting Them Together: PL/I

PL/I was designed in the mid 1960s with an ambitious goal: to integrate the most fruitful and original concepts of previous languages into a truly general purpose, universal programming language. Besides taking concepts from FORTRAN (such as separate modules), ALGOL 60 (block structure and recursive procedures), COBOL (data description facilities), and LISP (dynamic data structures), PL/I introduced less consolidated features, such as exception handling and some primitive multitasking facilities.

PL/I was probably too early. It incorporates different features, but does not really integrate them in a uniform manner. Also, newer features needed more research and experimentation before being incorporated in the language. As a result, the language is extremely large and complex, and its success is limited.

1.6.4 The Next Leap Forward: ALGOL 68, SIMULA 67, and Pascal

Other languages designed in the late 1960s brought up several interesting concepts that influenced later language designs. We refer to ALGOL 68, SIMULA 67, and Pascal.

ALGOL 68 was designed as a successor to ALGOL 60. It is based on the principle of *orthogonality*: language features can be composed in a free and uniform manner with predictable effects and without limitations. ALGOL 68 is a good case study to see how different language concepts can interact to provide computational power. Another important concept brought up by the ALGOL 68 effort is the need for formal language specification. The ALGOL 68 Report is probably the first complete example of a formal specification for a programming language. The "purity" of ALGOL 68, the intricacies that can result from an orthogonal combination of language features, and the absence of compromises with such mundane aspects as a user-friendly syntactic notation were responsible for the early decline of ALGOL

68. The language has been used in universities and research institutions, especially in Europe, but had only a few industrial applications.

SIMULA 67 was also a successor of ALGOL 60, designed to solve discrete simulation problems. In addition to *ad hoc* constructs for simulation and coroutines that provide a primitive form of parallel execution, the language introduced the concept of **class**, a modularization mechanism that can group together a set of related subprograms and a data structure. Classes can be organized as hierarchies of increasing specialization. The **class** concept has influenced most languages designed after SIMULA 67, such as CLU, Modula-2, Ada, and Smalltalk.

Pascal has been the most successful among these languages. Primarily conceived as a vehicle for teaching structured programming, there was an explosion of interest in Pascal in the late 1970s, along with the spread of microcomputers. The main appeal of the language is simplicity that does not sacrifice power. Distinctive features provided by Pascal are a modest but effective set of data-type definition facilities and structured control structures embedded in an ALGOL 60-like block structure.

BASIC is another language that was designed in the mid 1960s and is now used widely. The language has a simple algebraic syntax like FORTRAN and limited control and data structures. This simplicity, and the ease and efficiency of BASIC implementations, have made the language extremely popular with amateur programmers on personal computers. The language itself does not introduce any new linguistic concepts, but was among the first available tools supporting a highly interactive, interpretive programming style.

1.6.5   Experience and Experiments

In the 1970s, it became clear that the needs for supporting reliable and maintainable software imposed strong, *ad hoc* requirements on programming languages. This gave impetus to new research, experimentation, and language evaluations.

Among the most important language concepts investigated in this period were: abstract data types and access control to modules, strong typing and static program checking, relationship between language constructs and formal proofs of correctness, generic modules, exception handling, concurrency, and interprocess communication and synchronization. We will discuss these concepts in depth in the rest of this text. Among the most influential language experiments were CLU, Alphard, Mesa, Concurrent Pascal, Euclid, and Gypsy.

Other languages designed in the 1970s, which survived after their experimental stage and now are used extensively, are C and Modula-2. Both languages are mainly intended for use in systems programming.

1.6.6   Ada and the Future

The desire to unify the programming languages used in embedded computer applications, in particular, for computers embedded in weapon systems, and the need for more reliable and maintainable software led the U.S. Department of Defense in 1978 to set down the requirements for a programming language to be used as a common language throughout the D.O.D. Because no existing language met the requirements, the U.S. D.O.D. sponsored the design of a new language. The result of this process is the Ada programming language, which can be viewed as the synthesis of state-of-the-art concepts of conventional programming languages. Although there is only minimal experience with the use of Ada and thus little is known about its practical effect on the expected software qualities, much of the scientific debate is now on what lies beyond Ada.

In the world of applications that is the traditional domain of COBOL, we see an increasing availability of very high-level tools—the so-called fourth-generation languages—such as databases and query languages, spreadsheets, program generators that can be used by nonexpert programmers and even end-users for developing nontrivial, practical applications. Most current research efforts on programming languages have abandoned the traditional ground of Von Neumann concepts. Functional programming (exemplified by LISP), logic programming (exemplified by PROLOG), and object-oriented programming (exemplified by Smalltalk) are presently investigated both in light of the programming style they promote and the underlying theoretical and architectural aspects. The next decade promises to be an exciting period in which many different unconventional approaches to programming language design will be explored, resulting in a new generation of programming languages.

SUGGESTIONS FOR FURTHER READING
AND BIBLIOGRAPHIC NOTES

Numerous texts that discuss the entire life cycle of software have been published in recent years. The books (Fairley 1985) and (Sommerville 1985) give a comprehensive view of all aspects of software production. The book (Boehm 1981) is a classic on the managerial and economic aspects of software production.

The programming phase is discussed in depth in a special issue of the **ACM Computing Surveys** (ACM-CS 1974) with emphasis on programming style and systematic derivation of programs. In particular, Knuth discusses the uses and misuses of **goto** and Wirth discusses the writing of well-structured programs in Pascal. This language is suitable for supporting a top-down program design methodology—programming by stepwise refinement (Wirth 1971b). The origin of many ideas on systematic programming can be traced back to (Dijkstra 1968a), which is the starting point of the vast amount of research on "structured programming" of the early 1970s. An excellent reference on the topic is (Dahl et al. 1972). A more elementary view of structured programming is provided in the introductory programming textbook by N. Wirth (Wirth 1973).

The principle of "information hiding" has been proposed by (Parnas 1972b) as a basis for a design methodology supporting modularity, reliability, and modifiability of software. Further insight is provided in (Parnas 1972a) and (Parnas 1975). Other software design techniques are discussed in (Myers 1978), (Yourdon and Constantine 1978), (Jackson 1975), and (Jackson 1983).

Friendly programming environments that support program development with a large variety of tools are becoming increasingly popular. A comprehensive view of contemporary environments is provided by (Hünke 1980) and (Howden 1982). Many interesting papers dealing with the relationship between programming languages and environments are collected in (ACM-SIGPLAN 1985).

For a historical perspective on programming language developments, see (Wegner 1976) and (ACM-SIGPLAN 1978). Backus (Backus 1978a) argues that such developments display no real evolution and advocates a purely functional style of programming. The Turing lectures by Hoare (Hoare 1981) and Wirth (Wirth 1985) provide stimulating reflections on the evolution and state of the art of programming languages. New unconventional approaches to programming language design are surveyed in (IEEE Software 1986).

McCorduck and Feigenbaum (1984) give an overall view of the technical, social, and political issues behind the Japanese Fifth Generation Project.

EXERCISES

1.1 Write an essay on the costs of programming. Discuss both the costs involved in developing and maintaining programs, and the costs involved in running programs. Discuss the role of the programming language in both.

1.2. List the main features of your favorite programming language that can help make programs easily maintainable. Also discuss features that hinder maintainability.

Preview: Evolution of Concepts in Programming Languages

At the present time I think we are on the verge of discovering at last what programming languages should really be like. I look forward to seeing many responsible experiments with language design during the next few years; and my dream is that by 1984 we will see a consensus developing for a really good programming language (or, more likely, a coherent family of languages). Furthermore, I'm guessing that people will become so disenchanted with the languages they are now using—even COBOL and FORTRAN—that this new language, UTOPIA 84, will have a chance to take over. At present we are far from the goal, yet there are indications that such a language is very slowly taking shape. . . . A great deal of research must be done if we're going to have the desired language by 1984. (Knuth 1974)

We must recognize the strong and undeniable influence that our language exerts on our way of thinking, and in fact defines and delimits the abstract space in which we can formulate—give form to —our thoughts. (Wirth 1974)

*Language is the vehicle by which we express our thoughts, and the relation between those thoughts and our language is a subtle and involuted one. The nature of language actually shapes and models the way we think. . . . If, by providing appropriate language constructs we can improve the programs written using these structures, the entire field will benefit. . . . A language design should **at least** provide facilities which allow comprehensible expression of algorithms: **at best** a language suggests better forms of expression. But language* *is **not** a panacea. A language cannot, for example, prevent the creation of ob-scure programs: the ingenious programmer can always find an infinite number of paths to obfuscation. (Wulf 1977)*

Chapter 1 discussed the many facets of the relation between programming languages and the entire software production cycle. On the one hand, the language can favor the adoption of systematic program design methodologies; on the other, the language has a strong influence on the reliability, readability, and modifiability of programs. Rules and methodologies that have been found helpful in the development of reliable and high-quality software can be, and increasingly are, incorporated into programming languages in order to encourage users to apply these methodologies, or at least to make their application easier. A decade later, the quotation from Knuth is still quite descriptive of the current state-of-the-art in the field of programming languages. UTOPIA 84 is certainly not here yet. This book presents the important ideas that have influenced the evolution of language designs in order to outline how UTOPIA 84 is slowly taking shape. This chapter develops the criteria that will be used in the book to classify programming language concepts and explain their evolution.

The chapter is organized as follows. Section 2.1 introduces the concept of abstraction and shows its fundamental role in programming. Two particular instances of this concept in programming languages—data and control abstractions—are analyzed in Sections 2.2 and 2.3. Program correctness, another concept that has influenced the evolution of programming languages, is illustrated in Section 2.4. Finally, Section 2.5 shows the influence exerted on programming languages by the need for producing large programs.

This chapter is mainly introductory. Rather than examining language features in any detail, we will only motivate the concepts and criteria that will be used throughout the book in the presentation and evaluation of programming languages.

2.1 THE ROLE OF ABSTRACTION

Computers are increasingly replacing humans in applications, from business administration to process control. To replace a manual procedure, software designers must reproduce its behavior in a computer program. Computer programs can be thought of as models of these manual procedures.

Like any model, a computer program is an *abstraction* from reality. Abstraction is the process of identifying the important qualities or properties of the phenomenon being modeled. Using the abstract model, one is able to concentrate only on the relevant qualities or properties of the phenomenon and to ignore irrelevant ones. What is relevant depends on the purpose for which the abstraction is being designed. For example, someone learning to drive can represent a car simply by four properties: the gas, the brake, the clutch pedals, and the steering wheel. The engineer designing the car would use a model that also shows the relationship between the pedals and the engine. For the driver's abstraction, the engine is an irrelevant property; for the engineer, it is a crucial one.

Abstraction permeates the whole of programming. In particular, it has a twofold relationship with programming languages. On the one hand, programming languages are the tools by which software designers can implement the abstract models. On the other, programming languages are themselves abstractions from the underlying processor where the model is implemented.

The early programming languages, however, did not recognize the crucial role that abstraction plays in programming. For example, in the early 1950s the only abstraction mechanism provided by assembly languages over machine languages was symbolic naming. The programmer could use relatively self-explanatory terms to name operation codes and could symbolically name memory locations. Thus the programmer could abstract away from the machine representation of programs, and in particular, from the identity of memory locations and the particular bit-representation of operation codes.

The contributions of this facility to the readability and modifiability of programs are well known. The vast amount of bookkeeping required in machine language programming is automatically performed by the translator, which makes programming easier and less error-prone. For example, in a program for geometric modeling, the user can freely use self-explanatory names, such as VOLUME, AREA, SIZE, to denote the values of geometric entities, without keeping track of the memory locations where such values are actually stored. Moreover, some very simple correctness checks can be performed on the program at translation time. For example, undefined and multiply defined symbols can be caught by the assembler, which can help the programmer produce correct programs. Additional help can be provided by simple tools such as cross-reference tables. In our example, the source of an error in the evaluation of the volume of an object can be discovered by examining the list of statements that assign values to the variable VOLUME. Such a list may be provided by the cross-reference table.

Subprograms (and macros) also were introduced by assembly languages as a means for the programmer to name an activity described by a group of actions and to consider it as a single action. In our example, scale reductions, perspective views, planar projections, and so on might be drawn by suitable subprograms.

Subprograms are useful tools for methodical programming, because they are mechanisms for building abstractions. A subprogram is the implementation of an abstraction, whereas a subprogram call represents the use of the abstraction. When designing a subprogram, the programmer is concerned with *how* it works. Afterward, when the subprogram is called, the programmer can ignore the "how" and concentrate on *what* it does. This is another example of the use of abstraction in programming. The subprogram can be viewed as an extension of the programming language by a new operation. When using the operation, the programmer abstracts away from its actual implementation. The machine is viewed as an abstract, special-purpose processor whose instruction repertoire contains the new operation.

The late 1950s and early 1960s saw the design of the first higher-level languages, which provided a richer set of mechanisms for defining abstractions. These mechanisms can be used to define data abstractions and procedural or control abstractions. Data abstractions model the data manipulated by programs. Control abstractions model computations by combining elementary actions into patterns of arbitrary complexity. Sections 2.2 and 2.3 outline the evolution of data and control abstractions in programming languages.

2.2 DATA ABSTRACTION

2.2.1 Data Abstraction in Early Languages

Machine-level languages view stored data as strings of bits that can be manipulated by the machine's instructions. The instruction repertoire includes shifts, logical operations, fixed-point arithmetic, and several other operations.

A first step toward introducing abstractions on data was taken by FORTRAN, COBOL, and ALGOL 60. In these languages, the information stored in memory locations is viewed not as a sequence of anonymous bits, but as an integer value, a real, a boolean, or something else. The decision about the particular data abstractions to be included in a programming language was mainly dictated by the machines for which the languages were intended (e.g., the machine-provided fixed- and floating-point arithmetic) and the spectrum of applications the languages were supposed to cover (e.g., the language was intended to cover scientific applications).

As a result, no language turns out to be appropriate for all applications, because the programmer is limited by the expressive power of the fixed set of abstractions provided by the language. For example, FORTRAN is not the appropriate language for string manipulation problems, nor is COBOL for solving a system of differential equations; neither one is particularly suitable for matrix manipulation or applications requiring highly dynamic data structures with a variety of access paths.

PL/I tried to overcome these problems by collecting many of the abstractions provided by the previous programming languages—namely, FORTRAN, ALGOL 60, and COBOL. However, many data-related features of the language turned out to be difficult to master and often unsafe. Examples will be given in Chapter 4. Moreover, the proliferation of built-in abstractions, as opposed to mechanisms for defining new abstractions, has the principal effect of making the language large without exhausting all the needs that may arise in different applications.

2.2.2 Data Abstraction in ALGOL 68, Pascal, and SIMULA 67

The approach followed by the languages of the next generation—SIMULA 67, ALGOL 68, Pascal—is in some sense less ambitious, but has proved to be more effective. Such languages try to achieve generality not by providing an exhaustive set of built-in abstractions, but by providing flexible and easy-to-use mechanisms by which the programmer can define new abstractions. Such an approach quite naturally fits in with a design methodology based on the recognition of abstractions. Moreover, the abstractions identified for the design of the software become mirrored, at least to some extent, by the resulting structure of the program. Consequently, programs are more easily understandable and modifiable, and have a higher likelihood of being correct.

ALGOL 68 and Pascal allow the programmer to use the built-in data types and constructors (arrays, records, and so on) to define new types. For example, using the Pascal notation, the following definitions and declarations define two new types (*student* and *course*) and three variables (*comp_sci_15, comp_sci_140, comp_sci_240*) of type *course*.

```
type student = record first_name: array [1..10] of char;
                      mid_init: char;
                      last_name: array [1..15] of char
            end;
     course = record no_of_students: 0..20;
                     attendants: array [1..20] of student
            end;
var comp_sci_15, comp_sci_140, comp_sci_240: course;
```

The newly defined type *student* is a data structure with three components used to store a student's identification. Type *course* is defined as a table of students (*attendants*), together with the number of students (*no_of _students:* an integer between 0 and 20) who are registered for the course. Thus, any of the above variables (*comp_sci_240*, say) can be viewed as shown in Figure 2.1

A natural question is why did we choose to represent students and courses as described above? More basically, why do we need a data structure for students and courses? The answers to these questions lay in the motivations of the program and the abstractions that are identified during design;

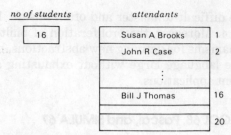

FIGURE 2.1   Data structure for variable *comp_sci_240*.

it is impossible to find them by looking at the program. It would be helpful to have a language that allows the clarification of such issues as part of the program.

For example, we may imagine that the program solves an application for a computer science professor who teaches *comp_sci_15, comp_sci_140*, and *comp_sci_240*. This professor receives from the registration office a deck of cards containing data on the students who signed up for these courses and wants to produce a sorted listing of the students, grouped by course taken.

We may also imagine that type *course* has been introduced because it is necessary to operate on data objects, such as *comp_sci_15*, by inserting a new student (in the appropriate order) and printing the names of the enrolled students. The initial abstract version of the program could be

```
for each card of the card deck do
        let S be the student's identification and let C be the
        course name;
        insert S into the table for course C in appropriate
        order
end-of-do;
print table for comp_sci_15;
print table for comp_sci_140;
print table for comp_sci_240;
```

The (imaginary) approach followed by the designer consists of characterizing a set of *logical* operations on course tables before deciding on how to implement such tables in the computer. Any specific way of implementing course tables must provide a *representation* for the tables as well as *concrete operations*, that is, algorithms expressed in the programming language corresponding to the logical operations on the course tables. However, the decision as to how to represent course tables and how to implement the operations is at a lower level of abstraction than the decision that course tables are needed to store the students' identification.

In Pascal (and similarly, in ALGOL 68) these decisions lead to the declaration of the new types described above, and to the implementation of the following procedures, one for each logical operation.

- *Insert:* takes a parameter of type *course* and a parameter of type *student* and inserts the value of student in *course.*
- *Print:* takes a parameter of type *course* and prints its contents.

Procedures *insert* and *print* are related very closely to type *course.* They are exactly the concrete operations that manipulate objects of type *course.* However, this logical relationship is not apparent from the Pascal (or ALGOL 68) program.

On the other hand, SIMULA 67 provides a construct (the **class**) that allows both the representation and the concrete operations to be specified in a single syntactic unit. This construct considerably improves program readability, because related entities implementing a certain abstraction are grouped together.

2.2.3 Toward Abstract Data Types

There are similarities between the user-defined types of Pascal, ALGOL 68, and SIMULA 67 and the built-in types of these languages. Consider the built-in type *integer* and the user-defined type *course* of Section 2.2.2. Both types are abstractions built upon an underlying representation—a bit string for *integer* and a record for *course.* Both types have an associated set of operations—arithmetic operations and comparisons for *integer, insert* and *print* for *course.*

In one important point, however, built-in types and user-defined types differ from one another. Built-in types hide from the programmer the underlying representation; it cannot be directly manipulated. For example, the programmer cannot access a particular bit of the bit string representing an *integer.* Procedures *insert* and *print,* on the other hand, are not the only means to manipulate a *course.* The programmer can operate directly on the components of objects of type *course* and is not forced to call the operations defined for the new type. For example,

```
comp_sci_240.no_of_students: = 17
```

would be a legal—but quite possibly undesirable—operation that modifies the number of students enrolled in *comp_sci_240.* In other words, there is no language-enforced distinction between two abstraction levels: the level at which one can use courses as new objects, and the level at which one implements courses in terms of lower-level abstractions. At the same time, the programmer can view courses as abstract objects manipulable via *insert* and *print* operations and as particular data aggregates whose components can be accessed and modified individually.

This confusion between levels of abstraction can lead to the production of programs that are hard to read. Even more important, it reduces program modifiability. Suppose that we decide to change the representation of tables to a sequential list structure or a binary tree. The change is not localized within the declarations of data and the concrete operations. It is also necessary to check out all direct accesses to the representation of data, which may be spread throughout the program.

In conclusion, to define new data types in a program, one would like to have language features that allow (a) the association of a representation to the concrete operations in a suitable language unit that implements the new types, and (b) the hiding of the representation of the new type from the units that use the new type.

User-defined types that satisfy properties (a) and (b) are called *abstract data types*. Property (a) makes the final version of the program reflect the abstractions discovered during program design. The resulting structure of the program becomes self-explanatory. Property (b) enforces the distinction between levels of abstraction and favors program modifiability. Traditional languages have somewhat severe deficiencies with respect to (a) and (b). The SIMULA 67 **class** satisfies point (a), but not point (b). Recent languages, such as CLU and Ada, provide facilities for defining abstract data types that satisfy both properties (a) and (b).

The concept of an abstract data type derives from the more general principle of information hiding; a program part implementing an abstract data type is an example of an information-hiding module (Section 1.3). Abstract data types hide representation details and route accesses to abstract objects via procedures. The representation is *protected* from any attempt to manipulate it directly. A change in the implementation of an abstract data type is confined within the program part that describes the implementation and does not affect the rest of the program.

2.3 CONTROL ABSTRACTION

Control structures describe the order in which statements or groups of statements (*program units*) are to be executed. Just as with data abstraction facilities, control abstraction mechanisms can determine the suitability of a language for particular application areas. Control structures can be classified as either *statement-level* control structures—that is, those that are used to order the activation of individual statements—and *unit-level* control structures—that is, those that are used to order the activation of program units. The evolution of control abstractions according to this classification is outlined below.

2.3.1 Evolution of Statement-Level Control Structures

Conventional hardware provides two very simple mechanisms to govern the flow of control over individual instructions: sequencing and branching. Sequencing is implemented by automatically incrementing the program counter after executing each instruction. This mechanism allows instructions stored in consecutive memory locations to be fetched and executed one after the other. The program counter can also be explicitly altered by branch instructions to accomplish control transfer to a specified location other than the next one in the sequence.

In assembly languages, instructions to be executed consecutively are written one after the other. Branching is represented by a **jump** instruction. For example, looping N times over a certain set of instructions requires initializing, modifying, and testing a counter value (often stored in a register), as in the following scheme (many machines include an instruction to modify, test, and branch in one instruction).

```
          set register to N;
loop :    if the value in register is zero jump to after;
          < loop body>;
          restore the counter value in register (if necessary)
          and decrease it by one;
          jump to loop;
after :   . . . . . .
```

Machine-level control structures are difficult to use and error-prone. The resulting programs are difficult to read and maintain, because these structures are not natural for humans. Humans organize their computational processes according to some standard patterns, such as repetition or selection among different choices. For example, a more natural way to describe the above programs would be

```
do the following N times
< loop body>
```

User-oriented control structures have been incorporated in higher-level languages in order to facilitate programming and to promote a better programming style. However, most higher-level languages retain branching, in the form of **goto** statements, and therefore also support a low-level programming style. **Goto** statements are a source of obscurity in programming (see Section 1.5.1). The **goto** controversy of the early 1970s did not provide a definitive solution to the problem of which control structures should be included in a programming language. Nevertheless, there is general agreement that **goto** statements should be used only as a technique to synthesize "legitimate" control structures if the language does not include those control structures.

2.3.2 Evolution of Unit-Level Control Structures

2.3.2.1 Subprograms and Blocks

Programming languages provide facilities for grouping statements implementing an abstract action into a suitable program unit. The most common and useful example is the subprogram, which has been present since the first assembly languages were formulated. A subprogram definition gives a name to a certain program unit. A subprogram call *invokes* a program unit—that is, forces control to transfer to the called unit, which upon completion of its task *returns* control to the calling point. *Parameter passing* conventions allow units explicitly to exchange information.

A simpler example of a program unit is the ALGOL 60 or C block, which provides for the grouping of actions, but not for the naming of the group. A block, therefore, cannot be invoked explicitly and is executed when it is encountered during the normal progression of execution.

Subprograms and, to a lesser extent, blocks are useful tools for program structuring. In particular, subprograms support the distinction between the definition of an abstract action (the subprogram body) and its use (the subprogram call). There are cases in which the control regime of subprogram call and return unduly constrains the programmer. Several recent programming languages recognize this constraint and provide additional unit-level control structures.

2.3.2.2. Exception Handling

The events or conditions that a program unit encounters during its execution can be classified as either usual or exceptional. Examples of exceptional conditions include the following: a subprogram discovers that some values of parameters can cause the execution of an illegal division by zero; a storage allocator runs out of storage to allocate; a protocol error is caught during reception of a message on a transmission line.

To increase the readability of the program and to indicate the programmer's assumptions about the expected and unexpected events, it is desirable to be able to divide the program into several units. Some units handle the usual events and can detect the occurrence of anomalous or exceptional conditions (called *exceptions*). The occurrence of an exception implicitly transfers control to an appropriate unit, called an *exception handler*, that deals with the exception.

Conventional programming languages provide little help in dealing with exceptions. A subprogram that may raise the exception could be coded by introducing an additional return parameter (e.g., an integer) denoting an exception code (e.g., 0 = no exception, 1 = exception number one, and so on). The calling unit would explicitly test the exception code after each call and then transfer control to the appropriate exception handler, if necessary. This limitation of the expressive power of the language forces programmers to state their intentions and assumptions in an awkward way that obscures the logic of the program.

PL/I was the first higher-level language to provide (*ad hoc*) features for exception handling. Other exception handling facilities have been adopted by later language designs (e.g., Bliss, Mesa, CLU, and Ada).

2.3.2.3   Coroutines

Conventional subprograms cannot describe program units that proceed concurrently, as happens in discrete simulation. For example, the simulation of a four-player card game could be done by designing four program units, one for each player. After each move, a unit should activate the unit that corresponds to the next player. When activated, a unit should resume execution wherever it left off when it last transferred control to another unit. Several programming languages provide a facility—the *coroutine*—to implement this form of interleaved execution. Each coroutine representing a player of the card game would have the following general structure.

coroutine for player *i*
declarations of local data (e.g., the cards of player i);
while *game_not_finished* **do**
   select card;
   play card;
   resume execution of the coroutine corresponding to the next
      player
end-of-do

Conventional subprograms are subordinate to their caller and upon termination, return to the caller. In most programming languages the return operation causes the deletion of the subprogram's local data. In our example, this means that the information about the cards of the player would be lost. Unlike subprograms, coroutines are symmetric units that explicitly activate each other; they do not return, but *resume* each other. When coroutine *A* resumes coroutine *B*, *A*'s local data are retained. A later resumption of *A* allows *A* to continue its execution from wherever it last left off. In the example, the information about the cards held by a player is retained when another player is resumed.

2.3.2.4   Concurrent Units

Coroutines are quite adequate to model activities that are executed in an interleaved fashion. In many applications, however, it is useful to model a system as a set of units, called *concurrent units*, whose execution proceeds in parallel (whether or not they are actually executed in parallel). This facility is particularly important in areas such as operating systems. In describing concurrent units, it is necessary to abstract from the physical architecture of the underlying machine, where the units are executed. The machine might be a multiprocessor, with each processor dedicated to a single unit, or it might be a multiprogrammed uniprocessor. Allowing for the possibility of different machines means that the correctness of a concurrent system cannot be based on an assumption of the speed of execution of the units. Indeed, the speed can differ greatly if every unit is executed by a dedicated processor, or if a single processor is shared by several units. Moreover, even if the architecture is known, it is difficult to design a system in such a way that its correctness depends upon the speed of execution of the units.

Coroutines are a low-level language construct for describing concurrent units. They can be used to simulate parallelism on a uniprocessor by explicitly interleaving the execution of a set of concurrent units. Therefore, they do not describe a set of concurrent units, but a particular way of sharing the processor to simulate concurrency. Many recent programming languages provide specialized features to deal with concurrency.

Even though concurrency is becoming an important aspect of programming languages, its main motivations and principles have traditionally arisen from the area of operating systems. The following example should help clarify the basic problems and concepts of concurrent programming.

Suppose that a certain system contains two concurrent activities: a producer and a consumer. The producer produces a stream of values and places them into a buffer of a certain size, N; the consumer reads these values from the buffer in the same order as they are produced. This model represents many operating system functions, such as file input and output. In the sample solution to this example shown below, the units implementing the two activities are described by cyclic and, ideally, nonterminating program units.

unit producer	unit consumer

repeat *produce an element;*
      append the element to
      the buffer
forever
	repeat *remove one item from*
	      the buffer;
	      perform some
	      computation on the
	      item
	forever

The two units represent activities that cooperate to achieve a common goal. The common goal is to transfer data from the producer (which could be reading it from an input device) to the consumer (which could be storing it in a file). It is desirable to make the units insensitive to the variations in speed of the two activities (e.g., the speed of the input device). The buffering mechanism does precisely that, by smoothing such variations. To guarantee the correctness of the cooperation, however, the programmer must assure that no matter how quickly or slowly the producer and the consumer progress, there will be no attempts to write into a full buffer or to read from an empty buffer. Concurrent programming languages provide *synchronization statements* that allow the programmer to delay a unit whenever necessary for correct cooperation with other concurrent units. In the example, the producer must be delayed if it tries to append an element when the buffer is full until the consumer removes at least one element. Similarly, the consumer must be delayed if it tries to remove an item when the buffer is empty until the producer appends at least one new element.

Another, more subtle, need for synchronization may arise when both activities can legally have access to the buffer. For example, suppose that operations *append* and *remove* update value of t, the total number of buffered items, by performing (1) $t := t + 1$ and (2) $t := t - 1$, respectively. Also suppose that (1) and (2) are implemented as

```
read t into a private register;
update the value stored in such register;
write the value stored in the private register into t
```

where *update* is "increment by one" and "decrement by one," respectively, for (1) and (2). The actions that form (1) and (2) are indivisible machine instructions, in the sense that if one such action starts to execute, it is guaranteed to finish before any other machine operation is started. This is in contrast with the operations (1) and (2) themselves: because they are not indivisible, the execution of their constituent actions may be interleaved. One of many possible sequences of interleaved actions could be as follows: the first action of (1), the first action of (2), the second action of (1), the second action of (2), the third action of (1), and finally, the third action of (2).

Given that (1) and (2) are not indivisible actions, it is easy to verify that if m is the value of t before the concurrent execution of a pair (*append, remove*), the value of t after the execution can be m, $m + 1$, or $m - 1$—the first value being the only correct result. To guarantee correctness, the programmer must assure that (2) does not start while (1) is in progress, and vice versa. We say that (1) and (2) must be executed in *mutual exclusion*, as if they were "indivisible" operations.

We are now in a position to state some requirements for the abstractions we need to deal with concurrency, as well as for the language constructs that can be used to define such abstractions.

A concurrent system should be viewed as a set of *processes*, each process being represented by a program unit. Processes are *concurrent* if their executions can be (conceptually) overlapped in time, that is, if the start of a process can occur when the previously executing process is not terminated. Processes $P_1, P_2, \ldots P_N$ are *disjoint* if they describe activities that never interact with one another, that is, if they do not access any shared objects. The result of the execution of one process is independent of the other processes; in particular, processes can have arbitrary speeds. Very often, however, processes are *interacting*. Interaction results from one of the following two reasons.

Competition Processes compete for access to a certain shared resource, which is to be used in mutual exclusion (e.g., a line printer).

Cooperation   Processes cooperate to achieve a common goal.

Processes interact correctly only if a certain precedence relation holds among their elementary actions, that is, certain actions must precede certain other actions. Such a relation defines a *partial ordering* among actions. For example, in the producer/consumer example, if $P_j(C_j)$ denotes the production (consumption) of the jth element, correct cooperation requires ("→" should be read as "precedes")

$$C_j \rightarrow P_{j+N} \text{ and } P_j \rightarrow C_j \text{ for all } j$$

Correct competition requires that no two updates of shared variable t be executed at the same time. If $IT_j(DT_j)$ denotes the jth increment (decrement) of variable t performed by the producer (consumer), correct competition requires

$$IT_j \rightarrow DT_k \text{ or } DT_j \rightarrow IT_k \text{ for all } j \text{ and } k$$

Concurrent programming languages provide language facilities for the definition of processes and suitable synchronization statements to enforce the required partial ordering of actions. Coroutines, as mentioned above, can be used to implement concurrency on a uniprocessor, but they provide an inadequate level of abstraction for this task. They overspecify the system by explicitly showing when a process resumes another. In other words, they impose a total ordering on actions even when a partial ordering is a completely adequate description of the system.

2.4   PROGRAM CORRECTNESS

Correctness and reliability have become prominent software production goals. In the early days of computing, these were only implicit and obvious goals. Today that view is regarded as quite naïve. It is now recognized that if one hopes to come close to achieving such goals, special care and painstaking measures must be taken. The evolution of correctness considerations from tangential to central concerns has affected the development of both software methodologies and programming languages. The effect on programming languages also has been felt indirectly through the new methodologies. In this section, we will trace the development of correctness ideas in programming languages.

Our first task is to define precisely the terms we have been using informally so far. A program is *correct* if it meets its specifications. In contrast, a program is *reliable* if it is highly probable that when we demand a service from the system, it will perform to our satisfaction. As such, reliability is hard to quantify, because it is related to the quality of the system as perceived by the user. Often, situations in which the service from the system is needed urgently weigh more in this perception than those in which demands are routine. Moreover, a system is often considered reliable, even if the strict notion of correctness is not satisfied. This can happen because

1. The error does not impair the usability of the system and is easily detected and corrected by the user. For example, a spelling error in a message such as

PRAMETER N. 3 OUT OF RANGE

does not impair the reliability of the system. In contrast, signaling an incorrect parameter number might impair reliability.

2. The error does not manifest itself very often or does not occur in critical cases. For example, in a message switching system, in peak situations, the (infrequent) loss of a packet of characters belonging to a long text, received on a certain input line, may be tolerated. In contrast, the loss of data can be unacceptable if the data are used to monitor a nuclear plant in real-time, and emergency situations are to be handled as soon as critical data are received by the computer.

On the other hand, software whose correctness has been rigorously assessed can be unreliable. In fact, correctness is defined relative to the specification, so that a program may be correct even if it does not achieve the user's needs. The basic reasons for this situation are:

1. The specifications incorrectly or incompletely reflect the requirements. For example, the requirements may specify that a certain authorization is required for reading the amount of deposits of each customer of a bank, but the specifications fail to specify how and when such authorization is to be checked.

2. The specifications do not state what the system is supposed to do in "anomalous" cases such as failures of the underlying hardware/software or input data errors. Therefore, the system behaves correctly if several assumptions about the environment hold, but unexpected (and undetected) input data might cause serious violations of system correctness, because no exception handlers are provided.

Although reliability is the ultimate goal, it is hard to quantify, and correctness is often used as an approximation in the hope that the specifications adequately capture the desired properties of the system. Moreover, correctness can be stated in precise terms, and suitable methodologies have been devised for proving program correctness.

There are two different approaches to the production of correct programs. The first, *error correction*, consists of modifying an already written program every time the symptom of an error is discovered. The second, *error prevention*, consists of trying to develop programs that are correct in the first place.

Obviously, no programs are developed with complete disregard for correctness, and no programs are developed so carefully as to be free of all possible errors. Much of the cost of software production results from error correction, but the adoption of suitable systematic approaches to software design can help prevent the introduction of errors.

One way to favor the production of correct programs is to make the design and coding effort easily manageable, so that we can be confident of the desired behavior of the system. Abstractions on data and control, as discussed in Sections 2.2 and 2.3, are powerful ways of mastering the complexity of program design. Language constructs that allow the mapping of design abstractions into program structures promote the production of well-structured, correct programs. Such programs structures make it possible to break down the complex task of reasoning about a large object—the entire program—to reasoning about smaller, manageable, largely autonomous, abstract objects. Also, individual program units must be easy to write and understand, so that possible errors can be located and fixed easily. A number of harmful features—that is, features that make it difficult to reason about programs—have been identified in programming languages, starting with the well-known case of the **goto** statement. (A review of such features and a number of alternative solutions proposed by language designers is presented in Chapters 4, 5, and 6.)

Even systematically designed programs can contain errors, so it is still necessary to devise strategies for isolating and removing such errors. A solid basis for a systematic certification of programs—at different levels—is provided by the programming language itself. At the lower level are *consistency checks*, which verify that programs adhere to the language definition. For example, programs must be syntactically well-formed (i.e., consistent with the syntactic rules of the language); program variables must be used in a way that is consistent with their type; subprograms must be called with actual parameters that are consistent in number and type with the formal parameters that appear in the subprogram's heading.

Consistency checks performed before executing the program are called *static checks*; those performed during execution are called *run-time* (or *dynamic*) *checks*. *Syntax checks* performed by the translator are an example of static checks. *Type checks* are another example of consistency checks that most languages require, and that often can be done statically. The following Pascal program fragment illustrates these points.

```
var x, y: integer;
    z: char;
    .
    .
    .
x:= (((x+y)*5+x*y);
if x< 0 then y:= z;
```

The assignment statement contains a syntax error, because of a missing closing parenthesis. The **if** statement contains a type error because a character-valued variable (*z*) is assigned to an *integer*. Both errors can be caught statically.

Although any statically detectable error could also be detected at run-time, it would be unwise to delay such error checking to run-time for two reasons. First, potential sources of error would only be detected at run-time by providing input data that cause the error to be raised; for example, the above-cited incorrect program fragment would signal the type error only if the value of *x* is negative. Second, dynamic checking slows down the program execution.

Not all languages allow programs to be type-checked completely before run-time. For example, in APL the type of a variable is determined by the variable's current value and thus can change during program execution, as the following fragment shows.

```
A ← 'STRING'
    .
    .
    .
A ← 3.77
    .
    .
    .
```

As a consequence, adding a numeric value to *A* is correct only if the current value of *A* is a number and not a character string. But, in general, this can only be ascertained at run-time.

We can conclude that correctness can be enhanced by a language whose definition requires extensive checks on programs, and all the more so, if the checks can be done statically. Early programming languages did not recognize the need for language features supporting program correctness. Most recent languages, on the other hand, have been designed with the goal of supporting extensive program checking.

Even in the presence of extensive static checking, the programmer can still produce a program that does not meet its specifications. The program is therefore gradually modified until it can be certified. The traditional approach to program certification consists of *testing* the program by submitting a sample of inputs taken from the program specification documents, and observing whether the output produced by the program adheres to the specified behavior of the program. Incorrect results are symptoms of errors that must be removed from the program. Correct results, however, do not imply the correctness of the program, because all that can be said is that the program behaved correctly for those particular input data. Thus, following a remark by Dijkstra, we can say that testing can be used to prove the presence of bugs, not their absence!

This intrinsic deficiency of program testing has stimulated a large amount of research in *program verification*. Verification aims at verifying correctness of a program independently of its execution. Program verification in the strict sense means proving that a program *implementation* is consistent with its *specification*. Specification, in turn, is intended here as a formal and precise description of what the program is to do.

Program verification can be done manually, but in such a case the confidence in the correctness of the program depends on the confidence in the correctness of the proof itself. Automatic systems for program verification have also been implemented, but there is limited experience with their use in the verification of large, practical systems. One example is reported in (Walker et al. 1979). The authors of this experiment come to the conclusion that "there appears to be no technical reasons, other than the necessity for engineering a suitable (computer assisted) verification system . . . that program proving methods could not be employed for the development of software where correct operation is critical. . . . Current techniques, however, are still not suitable for general use." Program verification is only possible if the semantics of the language has been defined formally. An introduction to formal semantics is the subject of Chapter 8.

Neither testing nor verification are likely to provide the exclusive, final answers to the need of proving programs correct. Program verification is theoretically sounder than testing. However, in the early stages of program development, when many errors are likely to be present in the program, testing can be more economical than proving. In other words, the techniques complement one another and together provide greater assurance of correctness than either one alone. Unfortunately, a practically usable and theoretically well-founded methodology that embodies a blend of the two approaches is still to be found.

2.5 PROGRAMMING IN THE LARGE

The production of large software systems often requires coordination of the activities of a large number of people. Programs are assembled as collections of individual modules, possibly written by different persons and coded in different languages. Very large programs—"nearly impossible programs," according to (Yourdon 1975)—may be up to 10^6 source statements long, written by hundreds of programmers over a period of several years, and consist of several hundred modules with complex interactions among themselves and other separately developed systems. Systems software for large computers, government and military applications, large banking projects, management information systems, and several other applications fall into this category. Successful management of the design, production, certification, and maintenance of such software systems is a formidable task, involving problems ranging from the sociology of human relations to software production methodologies.

At a lower level of size and complexity, projects that require production of large programs (several thousands of source statements long, written by 5 to 20 programmers over a period of two to three years) are becoming increasingly common. Managing the design and production of such large systems requires suitable methodologies and tools to keep the complexity under control.

The entire life cycle of software production in large software systems can be rather different from small-sized programs. In (DeRemer and Kron 1976) it is argued that *"programming in the large* is an essentially distinct and different intellectual activity from that of constructing the individual modules"—that is, *programming in the small*. Consequently, they conclude that "essentially distinct and different languages should be used for the two activities."

We have implicitly assumed that large systems are made up of individual components called *modules*. Modularity, in fact, is generally recognized as the only guideline available for mastering the complexity of design and implementation of large and complex systems. However, "modularity" is a buzz-word that often is used to denote several properties of software. In many cases, modularity is defined in terms of size of the program units that comprise a system. Thus, for example, there are organizations that adopt production standards such as "Each FORTRAN subroutine must be contained in a page of printout." Restrictions that apply only to the size of modules do not improve the quality of programs in any real sense: chopping the long text of a program into a sequence of smaller pieces does not make the program any better.

A more helpful notion of modularity is in terms of independence. This means that each module should be understood and, possibly, implemented independently of the other modules of the system. Each module should realize a single and simple conceptual function of the system; consequently, restrictions on module size result automatically as a by-product of the design process. Information hiding as a design principle favors the production of highly independent modules. In fact, design decisions internal to a module are hidden and do not affect the correctness of the cooperation among the modules. Once the module interfaces have been (carefully) designed, modules can be developed independently of each other, stored in a library, and later assembled to construct a unique program.

The goal of modular software design exerts a strong influence on programming languages. Languages should provide facilities for the definition of modules and for information hiding. They should also provide facilities for structuring a collection of modules in a unique system. Finally, it should be possible to develop and certify modules separately. Some recent language designs (e.g., Ada) have been strongly influenced by these concepts.

The need for producing large, complex, and reliable software systems has also influenced the development of a number of tools that can assist the programmer in designing, coding, certifying, and maintaining individual programs. As we argued in Chapter 1, programming languages and program development methodologies in isolation are not enough to significantly increase programmer productivity. The combination of a suitable programming language with a number of powerful, integrated, easy-to-use, language-sensitive tools—that is, a software development environment—can become the key factor in improving the quality of programs. The first step in this direction has been taken with systems such as UNIX, which was developed by Bell Laboratories for the DEC family of computers. The development of a consistent and complete program-development system, however, is still an open research problem.

SUGGESTIONS FOR FURTHER READING AND BIBLIOGRAPHIC NOTES

The book by Sammet (1969) is a compendium of a large number of programming languages and provides a comprehensive view of the early evolution in the field. Wegner (1976) surveys the evolution of programming languages until 1975. The proceedings of the ACM SIGPLAN Conference on the History of Programming Languages (ACM-SIGPLAN 1978) puts earlier successful language design efforts into a historical perspective. Several papers of (ACM-SIGPLAN 1978) explicitly point out the strong influence exerted by hardware upon the abstractions provided by languages (see, for example, Backus's paper on FORTRAN). The evolution of the concept of abstraction in programming languages is discussed in (Guarino 1978). Wegner's paper in (Wegner 1979) presents an overview of research directions in programming languages until 1978.

A solution to Exercise 2.6 can be found in (Conway 1963), which is the origin of coroutines.

This chapter has emphasized programming language concepts and their evolution. A detailed analysis and a critical evaluation of the solutions adopted by several programming languages will be presented in Chapters 3 through 8. Suggestions for further reading and bibliographic notes on the topics outlined in Sections 2.2 through 2.5 are given in the Further Reading sections of Chapters 4 through 8.

EXERCISES

2.1 Programming language abstractions can be classified according to how naturally they support program writing. Often, the more natural they are, the more difficult it is to implement them on a computer. Give examples of this from the languages you know.

2.2 Because only a finite number of values can be represented in a computer, the hardware-supported integer data type does not fully correspond to the mathematical notion of integer. What happens on your computer when the result of an integer expression is out of the acceptable range of values?

2.3 As part of a large programming project, you are asked to design and implement a queue data structure called STORE for storing and retrieving integer values. Values are extracted from the queue in first-in/first-out order. The queue must be able to detect attempts at insertion into a full queue or retrievals from an empty one. Because the requirements for the project are not quite firm yet, you must design your program to be easily modifiable. For example, the maximum size or the storage organization of the queue might need to be changed later.

(a) Specify the requirements for STORE as abstractly as you can, and then produce a concrete implementation.

(b) Code your concrete implementation in your favorite programming language.

(c) Discuss the modifiability of your solution and the ways in which the language helped or hindered in achieving it.

2.4 The ALGOL-like program fragment

while $a > b$ **do**

.
.
.

end-of-do

can be rewritten by using (conditional and unconditional) jumps. Briefly compare the two approaches in terms of readability and writability.

2.5 A program reads an integer value in the subrange 1..10 and performs a different action for each possible input. Write a solution using FORTRAN and one solution using Pascal. Compare the two solutions in terms of readability.

2.6 This exercise illustrates the use of coroutines. Design a program to read characters from cards and print them out. Every occurrence of a pair of asterisks ("**") in the input must be replaced with the single character "↑" in the output. All other characters simply are copied. Your solution should consist of two coroutines: an input coroutine to provide the next character and an output coroutine to print characters.

2.7 The values of two variables, **v1** and **v2**, are interchanged by each one of two concurrent processes, *P*1 and *P*2. The interchange is accomplished by the following sequence of indivisible machine-level operations.

Load **v1** into register R1.
Load **v2** into register R2.
Store value from register R1 into **v2**.
Store value from register R2 into **v1**.

What is the effect of concurrent execution if *P*1 and *P*2 do not execute the interchange in mutual exclusion?

2.8 Give examples of static and dynamic checks supported by your favorite programming language.

2.9 *Exhaustive testing* is the testing of a program for all possible values of its input variables. Give arguments (and examples) to show that exhaustive testing is impractical.

2.10 What are the criteria you follow to select data for testing your programs? How confident are you of the correctness of your program after testing?

2.11 Which of the languages familiar to you is more supportive of programming in the large, and why?

2.12 Have you ever been a member of a team working on a program of substantial size? If so, what difficulties did you face that you would not face when writing a simpler program by yourself?

The Structure of Programming Languages

A programming language is a formal notation for describing algorithms for execution by computer. Like all formal notations, a programming language has two major components: *syntax* and *semantics*. The syntax is a set of formal rules that specify the composition of programs from letters, digits, and other characters. For example, the syntax rules may specify that each open parenthesis must match a closed parenthesis in arithmetic expressions, and that any two statements must be separated by a semicolon. The semantic rules specify "the meaning" of any syntactically valid program written in the language. Such meaning can be expressed by mapping each language construct into a domain whose semantics is known. For example, one way of describing the semantics of a language is by giving a description of each language construct in English. Such a description, of course, suffers from the informality, ambiguity, and wordiness of natural language, but it can give a reasonably intuitive view of the language.

In this chapter, we will take the *operational* approach to semantics, that is, the semantics of a programming language will be described by specifying the behavior of an abstract processor that executes programs written in the language. This semantic characterization of a language could be presented using a rigorous and formal notation. Instead, we will follow a more traditional and informal approach, because it is more easily and intuitively understood by computer programmers and provides a high-level view of the problems found in implementing the language.

This chapter is organized as follows: In Section 3.1, we will discuss how the syntax and semantics of a language can be defined. In Section 3.2 we

41

will discuss language implementation. We then will define three fundamental semantic concepts in Sections 3.3, 3.4, and 3.5, namely, *binding, variables*, and *program units*. In Section 3.6 we will introduce a convenient method for classifying programming languages according to their run-time memory requirements and describe the structure of various languages according to this classification. In Section 3.7 we will discuss parameter passing. Finally, we will end the chapter by discussing language standardization and "official" language definitions.

3.1 LANGUAGE DEFINITION

When you read a program, how do you know what it means? How does a compiler know how to translate the program? Any programming language must be *defined* in enough detail to enable these kinds of issues to be resolved. More specifically, a language definition should enable a person or a computer (program) to determine (1) whether a purported program is in fact valid, and (2) if the program is valid, what is its meaning or effect.

In general, two aspects of a language—programming or natural language—must be defined: syntax and semantics.

3.1.1 Syntax

The syntax rules of a language define the *form* of the language: they define how *sentences* may be formed as sequences of basic constituents called *symbols*. Using these rules we can tell whether a sentence is legal or not. The syntax does not tell us anything about the *content* (or *meaning*) of the sentence—the semantic rules tell us that. As an example, Pascal symbols are keywords (such as **begin**, **end**, **if**, **while**, . . .), identifiers, numbers, operators, and so on. The Pascal syntax tells us how to combine such symbols to form legal programs.

The set of characters that constitutes the alphabet of the language and the way such characters can be combined to form valid symbols is specified by the *lexical rules* of the language. For example, Pascal considers lowercase and uppercase characters to be identical, but C considers them to be distinct. Thus, according to the lexical rules, "Memory" and "memory" refer to the same variable in Pascal, but to distinct variables in C. The lexical rules also tell us that < > is a valid operator in Pascal but not in C, where the same operator is represented by !=.

The distinction between syntax and lexical rules is somewhat arbitrary. They both contribute to the "external" appearance of the language. We will use the terms "syntax" and "syntax rules" in a wider sense that includes lexical issues as well.

How does one define the syntax of a language? Because there are an infinite number of legal and illegal programs in any useful language, we clearly can not enumerate them all. We need a way to define an infinite set using a finite description. FORTRAN was defined by simply stating some rules in English. ALGOL 60 was defined with a context-free grammar developed by John Backus. This method has become known as BNF or Backus Naur form (Peter Naur was the editor of the ALGOL 60 report.) It allows us to provide a compact and clear definition for the syntax of a language.

3.1.1.1. BNF

BNF is a syntax *metalanguage*. A metalanguage is a language that is used to describe other languages. The English language rule that a sentence may consist of a subject, verb, and object followed by a period is described in BNF in this way:

$$\langle sentence \rangle \ \rightarrow \ \langle subject \rangle \ \ \langle verb \rangle \ \ \langle object \rangle$$

The symbols "$<$", "$>$", and "$\rightarrow$" are symbols of the metalanguage and not the language being described. The symbol "$\rightarrow$" stands for "is defined as". Thus, the above *rule* states that a *<sentence>* is defined as a *<subject>*, a *<verb>*, an *<object>*, and a "." placed next to one another in order. In this rule the entities inside the metalanguage brackets "$<$", and "$>$" are called *nonterminals*; an entity such as the "." above is called a *terminal*. Terminals are what we have previously called symbols, whereas nonterminals are linguistic entities that stand for sets of strings of symbols. The syntactic rules state which subset of these strings are valid. In the above rule, the nonterminal *<sentence>* appears on the *left-hand side* and is defined by the definition on the *right-hand side* of the rule (everything to the right of $\rightarrow$). Nonterminals on the right-hand side must be defined with other BNF rules; terminals must be valid symbols of the language. A complete syntactic description of a language—called a *grammar*—consists of a set of such rules in which every nonterminal is defined. A particular nonterminal is designated as the *start symbol*. In programming languages this is usually a nonterminal that is given the name *<program>*.

A string consisting of only terminal symbols is a valid *sentence* in the language if it can be *derived* (or *generated*) from the start symbol. We derive a string from the start symbol by replacing the start symbol with one of its definitions. This yields a string consisting of terminals and nonterminals. Each nonterminal in the string then is replaced by one of its definitions. This step is repeated until no nonterminals remain and we are left with a string consisting of only terminal symbols. For example, let us complete our grammar for English sentences by defining the following additional rules:

$\langle verb \rangle \ \rightarrow \ see \ | \ hit \ | \ grab$
$\langle subject \rangle \ \rightarrow \ I \ | \ we$
$\langle object \rangle \ \rightarrow \ him \ | \ her \ | \ you$

and assume that $<sentence>$ is the start symbol. The symbol "|" is read "or" and is used to provide alternative definitions for the same nonterminal. Given this grammar, we can derive the sentence "I hit you." by the following sequence of steps (we will use the symbol $\Rightarrow$ to separate the different steps): $<sentence> \Rightarrow <subject> <verb> <object>. \Rightarrow I <verb> <object>. \Rightarrow I$ hit $<object>. \Rightarrow$ I hit you. Note that in each step of the derivation, we have a choice as to which nonterminal to replace next. In this example derivation, we have always replaced the leftmost nonterminal. Instead, we could have derived the same string with the following steps: $<sentence> \Rightarrow <subject> <verb> <object>. \Rightarrow <subject>$ hit $<object>. \Rightarrow <subject>$ hit you. $\Rightarrow$ I hit you.

This derivation process can be best modelled with a *derivation tree*, where the root is the start symbol and the leaves are the terminals in the string. For example, our two derivations can be shown with the tree below:

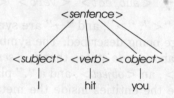

Now we can say that a string of symbols is valid in the language if we can build a derivation tree for it. The derivation tree also is called a *parse tree*. Deriving the parse tree is called *parsing*. The task of determining whether a string is valid is called *recognition*. As we have seen, recognition can be accomplished by parsing.

Parsing is an essential step of language processing, and many efficient parsing algorithms have been developed. There are two basic classes of parsers: top-down parsers and bottom-up parsers. Top-down and bottom-up refer to the direction in which the tree is built, that is a top-down parser starts at the root of the tree and builds the tree down and a bottom-up parser starts at the leaves of the tree and builds the tree up.

A *bottom-up parser* starts with a string of terminal symbols and uses some strategy to repeatedly replace sequences in the string—corresponding to the right-hand side of some grammar rule—with a nonterminal—corresponding to the left-hand side of the same rule. The process is repeated until the terminal string is reduced to the grammar's start symbol. A *top-down parser* uses some strategy to derive the given terminal string starting from the grammar's start symbol, and repeatedly rewriting nonterminals according to the rules.

Note that our example grammar is an oversimplified model of English. It is possible to make this grammar more powerful and more realistic by adding rules that will allow it to describe an infinite number of English sentences. But BNF is inadequate for completely describing a complicated language such as English—or any other natural language. BNF is capable of defining *context-free grammars*, and English is not describable with a context-free grammar. Intuitively, a context-free grammar can describe the syntax of a language if valid senences in the language can be derived by simply replacing a nonterminal for its right-hand side. In a *context-sensitive grammar*, on the other hand, whether a nonterminal can be rewritten using a particular rule may depend on the context, that is, on other symbols in the string. Context-sensitive grammars are needed to describe natural languages. For example, in deriving an English sentence, we may use "does" only if we have used a "third person singular" subject.

A similar problem arises in the description of programming languages. For example, in Pascal the use of a variable in an expression must be consistent with the type of the variable, as stated in the variable's declaration. A constraint of this kind can only be handled by a context-sensitive grammar. On the other hand, the solution that is usually adopted in the definition of programming languages is to use strict BNF to describe the syntax. Thus, there are infinitely many incorrect programs that can be derived legally according to the BNF definition. They are exactly those programs that do not satisfy the additional, context-sensitive requirements. Often, context-sensitive requirements are verified after the program has been checked syntactically. It is conventional to call context-sensitive requirements the *static semantics* of the language.

Let us return to syntax for a more relevant example. Consider the following grammar which defines how to form arithmetic expressions in a hypothetical, but realistic language:

```
<expression>  →  identifier |
                 (<expression>) |
                 <expression>  <operator>  <expression>
<operator>  → + |  −  |  /  |  *
```

In this grammar, *identifier* is being treated as a terminal but somewhat differently from the way that "(" is. We are relying on the lexical rules to define an *identifier*. In fact, we intend it to stand for many different symbols. Most languages define an identifier to be "a letter followed by any number of letters and digits," although some languages have simpler or more complicated rules.

Note that in this example, the nonterminal *<expression>* is used in its own definition. Such definitions are called *recursive*. It is these recursive rules that allow a finite set of rules to define the structure of an infinite number of programs. In particular, the above rules for expressions allow us to recognize valid expressions of any length. For example, the rule

```
<expression>  →  (  <expression>  )
```

allows us to derive an arbitrary nesting of an expression, whereas the rule

< expression > → *< expression > < operator > < expression >*

allows us to combine an arbitrary number of expressions to form a new expression. Obviously, it is exactly through the the following nonrecursive rule

< expression > → identifier

that derivation from the nonterminal *< expression >* can terminate. For example, assuming that A is an identifier, the following derivations are possible starting from an *< expression >* nonterminal: *< expression >* ⇒ *< expression > < operator > < expression >* ⇒ *< expression > < operator > < expression > < operator > < expression >* ⇒ (*< expression >*) *< operator > < expression > < operator > < expression >* ⇒ (A) *< operator > < expression > < operator > < expression >* ⇒ . . . and so on.

3.1.1.2. Syntax Diagrams

The original Pascal definition uses *syntax diagrams*, a pictorial technique for syntax description that is equivalent to BNF but somewhat more intuitive. The expression rules may be shown as:

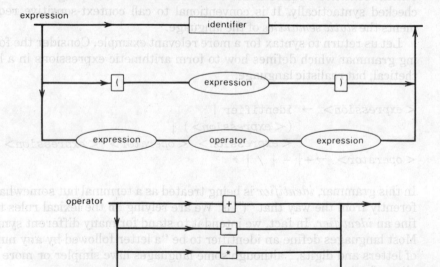

Nonterminals are represented by circles and terminals by boxes. The nonterminal symbol is defined with a transition diagram having one entry and one exit edge. A string is valid if it can be generated by traversing the syntax diagram from the entry to the exit edge. In this traversal, if a terminal (box) is encountered, that symbol must be in the string being recognized;

if a nonterminal (circle) is encountered, then that nonterminal must be recognized by traversing the transition diagram for that nonterminal. When a branch in the path is encountered, any one edge may be traversed. Syntax diagrams are similar enough to BNF to allow you to understand the rules.

In conclusion, the syntactic description of a language has two primary uses:

(a) It helps the programmer know how to write a syntactically correct program. For example, if one is unsure about the syntax of **if-then-else** statements, a look at the BNF or syntax diagrams can quickly settle any doubts.

(b) It can be used to determine whether a program is syntactically correct. This is exactly what a processor for the language (i.e., a compiler) does. The compiler writer uses the grammar to write a *syntactic analyzer* or *parser*, that is capable of recognizing all valid programs. This process is now largely automated. In fact, there are programs ("compiler generators") that can use the grammar of the language as input and produce the analyzer as output. LEX and YACC are two well-known UNIX tools that generate lexical and syntax analyzers, respectively, starting from a description of the lexical and syntactic rules of the language.

As we saw, these two uses of grammars are referred to as *derivation* and *recognition*.

3.1.2 Semantics

The semantic rules of a language define the meaning of valid sentences in that language. For example, the semantics of Pascal help us determine that the statement

var s: **set of** (red, white, blue)

causes space to be reserved for a variable named *s*; further, the values that this variable may hold are constrained to be elements of the powerset of the set {*red, white, blue*}. As another example, the semantics of C state that the statement

if (a>b) then max=a; else max=b;

means that the expression $a > b$ must be evaluated, and depending on its value, one of the two given assignment statements is executed. Note that the syntax rules tell us how to form this statement—for example, where to put a ';'—and the semantic rules tell us what is the effect of the statement.

Although syntax diagrams and BNF have become standard tools for syntax description, no such tool has become widely accepted and standard for semantic description. Many different approaches to semantic definition exist (see Chapter 9), but none is entirely satisfactory.

In this chapter and throughout this book, we are taking an operational approach to describing the semantics of programming languages. In this approach, the behavior of an abstract processor is used to describe the effects of each language construct. We will describe such a machine in the next subsection. We will then describe the semantics of programming language constructs in terms of the operations of this machine.

Our machine is *abstract*. This means that it is not a real machine such as the IBM 370 or the HP 3000. It is designed to show the run-time requirements of programming languages simply, rather than to execute them efficiently. It also can be used as a model for language implementation in the sense that one can derive straightforward, simple implementations by applying the concepts that we discuss here. The resulting implementation, however, probably would be inefficient. To achieve efficiency, any real implementation will have to differ from the model in important ways, for example, in how data structures are arranged and accessed. The purpose of the model is simply to state the effects of the language, given the structure of the abstract machine. A particular implementation of the language on a given real machine is in no way obligated to implement the structure of the abstract processor used to define the semantics of the language; it is only required to implement the same effects, given the restrictions and structure of the implementation machine.

It is very important to separate the semantic issues of the language from the implementation issues (we will come back to this point later). This can be done by keeping in mind which part of the description is a description (or restriction) of the machine and which is of the language.

3.1.2.1 SIMPLESEM: A Simple Abstract Semantic Processor

We will describe the basic structure of a simple abstract processor that we will call SIMPLESEM. In later sections, we will define further characteristics of SIMPLESEM as we need to define more complicated semantic constructs.

SIMPLESEM allows us to define and understand the semantics of programming language constructs. In its basic form, SIMPLESEM consists of an *instruction pointer* and a *memory*. The memory is divided into separate sections for code and data. The instruction pointer is always pointing to a location in code memory that contains an instruction. We will refer to the instruction pointer by ip. We will refer to the two memory sections as C (for code) and D (for data), and to memory location i as $C[i]$ or $D[i]$, depending on to which memory we are referring. We will use the symbol ":=" to denote assignment. For example

$$ip := ip + 1$$

means "increment the instruction pointed by 1."

The machine operates by executing the following steps repeatedly until it executes a special *stop* instruction:

1. Execute the instruction pointed at by the *ip*.
2. If the instruction does not explicitly modify the instruction pointer, then the instruction pointer is incremented to point to the next instruction to be executed ($ip := ip + 1$).

To start the machine, a program is loaded into memory (by a special loader program) and the instruction pointer is made to point to the first instruction of the program. We will assume that SIMPLESEM has instructions for all the usual operations such as $+$, $*$, $>$, and so on that are required by various programming languages. Figure 3.1 shows the structure of SIMPLESEM. As we examine different kinds of languages in the next three subsections, we will complete the description of SIMPLESEM.

We define the semantics of a programming language construct by defining the construct in terms of operations of SIMPLESEM. This approach is based on the assumption that we "know" or "understand" the semantics of our machine and, therefore, once we understand the effect of the construct in terms of the operations of SIMPLESEM, we know the meaning of the construct. This is somewhat analogous to defining the meaning of the Italian verb "pensare" as "to think" because we assume we know the meaning of "to think." Note that for this approach to be successful, it is important to keep the semantics of SIMPLESEM itself as simple as possible so that we can concentrate on the programming language semantics rather than the intricacies of the machine, which is simply a modelling tool.

We can view a machine such as SIMPLESEM in two ways. Ideally, one might think that high-level language programs are stored in their source form, and SIMPLESEM is capable of decoding and executing such high-level instructions. Alternatively, one might think that the source program is

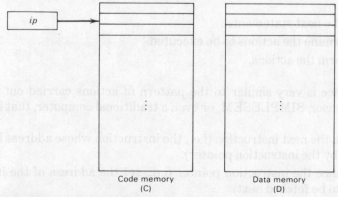

ip

Code memory
(C)

Data memory
(D)

FIGURE 3.1 SIMPLESEM structure.

first translated to the (lower-level) machine language of SIMPLESEM. The two choices can have an equivalent effect as far as semantics of the high-level language is concerned, but can affect the efficiency of the implementation. We discuss this problem in the next section with respect to real machines. The issues hold for the implementation of a high-level language, both on real machines and abstract machines such as SIMPLESEM.

3.2 LANGUAGE PROCESSING

Although in theory it is possible to build special-purpose computers to execute directly programs written in any particular language, present-day computers directly execute only a very low-level language, the *machine language*. Machine languages are designed on the bases of speed of execution, cost of realization, and flexibility in building new software layers upon them. On the other hand, programming languages often are designed on the basis of the ease and reliability of programming. A basic problem, then, is how a higher-level language eventually can be executed on a computer whose machine language is very different and at a much lower level.

There are generally two alternatives for an implementation: interpretation and translation.

3.2.1 Interpretation

In this solution, the actions implied by the statements of the language are executed directly. Usually, for each possible action there exists a subprogram—written in machine language—to execute the action. Thus, interpretation of a program is accomplished by calling subprograms in the appropriate sequence.

More precisely, an interpreter is a program that repeatedly executes the following sequence.

1. Get the next statement.
2. Determine the actions to be executed.
3. Perform the actions.

This sequence is very similar to the pattern of actions carried out by our model processor, SIMPLESEM, or even a traditional computer, that is:

1. Fetch the next instruction (i.e., the instruction whose address is specified by the instruction pointer).
2. Advance the instruction pointer (i.e., set the address of the instruction to be fetched next).

3. Decode the instruction.
4. Execute the instruction.

This similarity shows that interpretation can be viewed as a simulation, on a host computer, of a special-purpose machine whose machine language is the higher level language.

3.2.2 Translation

In this solution, programs written in a high-level language are translated into an equivalent machine-language version before being executed. This translation is performed in several steps. Subprograms might first be translated into assembly code; assembly code is translated into relocatable machine code; units of relocatable code are linked together into a single relocatable unit; finally, the entire program is loaded into main memory as executable machine code. The translators used in each of these steps have specialized names: compiler, assembler, linker (or linkage editor), and loader, respectively.

In some cases, the machine on which the translation is performed (the *host machine*) is different from the machine that is to run the translated code (the *target machine*). This kind of translation is called *cross-translation*. Cross translators offer the only viable solution when the target machine is too small to support the translator.

Pure interpretation and pure translation are two ends of a continuous spectrum. In practice, many languages are implemented by a combination of the two techniques. A program may be translated into an intermediate code that is then interpreted. The intermediate code might be simply a formatted representation of the original program, with irrelevant information (e.g., comments and spaces) removed and the components of each statement stored in a fixed format to simplify the subsequent decoding of instructions. In this case, the solution is basically interpretive. Alternatively, the intermediate code might be the (low-level) machine code for a virtual machine that is to be later interpreted by software. This solution, which relies more heavily on translation, can be adopted for generating portable code, that is, code that is more easily transferable to different machines than machine language code.

In a purely interpretive solution, executing a statement may require a fairly complicated decoding process to determine the operations to be executed and their operands. In most cases, this process is identical each time the statement is encountered. Consequently, if the statement appears in a frequently-executed part of a program (e.g., an inner loop), the speed of execution is strongly affected by this decoding process. On the other hand, pure translation generates machine code for each high-level statement. In so doing, the translator decodes each high-level statement only once. Frequently-used parts are then decoded many times in their machine language representation; because this is done efficiently by hardware, pure translation can save processing time over pure interpretation. On the other hand, pure interpretation may save storage. In pure translation, each high-level language statement may expand into tens or hundreds of machine instructions. In a purely interpretive solution, high-level statements are left in the original form and the instructions necessary to execute them are stored in a subprogram of the interpreter. The storage saving is evident if the program is large and uses most of the language's statements. On the other hand, if all of the interpreter's subprograms are kept in main memory during execution, the interpreter may waste space for small programs that use only a few of the language's statements.

3.3 THE CONCEPT OF BINDING

Programs deal with *entities*, such as variables, subprograms, statements, and so on. Program entities have certain properties called *attributes*. For example, a variable has a name, a type, a storage area where its value is kept; a subprogram has a name, formal parameters of a certain type, certain parameter-passing conventions; a statement has associated actions. Attributes must be specified before an entity is processed. Specifying the exact nature of an attribute is known as *binding*. For each entity, binding information is contained in a repository called a *descriptor*.

Binding is a central concept in the definition of programming language semantics. Programming languages differ in the number of entities with which they can deal, in the number of attributes to be bound to entities, and in the time when such bindings occur (*binding time*).

Some attributes may be bound at language definition time, others at program translation time (i.e., compile time), and others at program execution time (i.e., run-time). For example, in FORTRAN and Ada, the type INTEGER is bound at language definition/implementation time, that is, the language definition states that the type INTEGER must be supported and the language implementation determines the set of values that are contained in the type. Pascal, on the other hand, allows the programmer to redefine the type *integer*, that is, the type *integer* is bound to a representation at translation time. A binding is *static* if it is established before run-time and cannot be changed later; it is *dynamic* if it is establishd at run-time and can be changed according to some language-specified rules.

The concepts of binding and binding time help clarify many semantic aspects of programming languages. In the next section we will use these concepts to illustrate the notion of a variable.

3.4 VARIABLES

Conventional computers are based on the notion of a main memory consisting of elementary *cells*, each of which is identified by an address. The contents of a cell comprise its *value*. The value of a cell can be read and/or modified. Modification implies replacing a value with a new value. Furthermore, hardware allows for access to cells on a one-at-a-time basis. With a few exceptions, programming languages can be viewed as abstractions, at different levels, of the behavior of such conventional computers. In particular, they introduce the notion of variables as an abstraction of the notion of memory cells and the notion of assignment statements as an abstraction of the destructive modification of a cell.

In most of this and the following chapters we basically will restrict our considerations to these conventional, "assignment-based" programming languages. Alternative languages that support functional and declarative styles of programming will be discussed in Chapters 7 and 8.

A variable is characterized by a *name* and four basic attributes: scope, lifetime, value, and type. The name is used to identify and refer to the variable. Some languages allow variables that do not have names; examples of these so-called *anonymous* variables are given later in the chapter. Discussed below are each of these four attributes and the different policies adopted by programming languages for binding attributes to variables.

3.4.1 The Scope of a Variable

The *scope* of a variable is the range of program instructions over which the variable is known, and thus manipulable. A variable is *visible* within its scope and invisible outside it. Variables can be bound to a scope either statically or dynamically. *Static scope binding* defines the scope of a variable in terms of the lexical structure of a program, that is, each reference to a variable is statically bound to a particular (implicit or explicit) variable declaration. Static scope rules are adopted by most traditional languages.

Dynamic scope binding defines the scope of a variable in terms of program execution. Typically, each variable declaration extends its effect over all the instructions executed thereafter, until a new declaration for a variable with the same name is encountered. APL, LISP, and SNOBOL4 are examples of languages with dynamic scope rules.

Dynamic scope rules are rather easy to implement but have disadvantages in terms of programming discipline and efficiency of implementation. Programs are hard to read because the identity of the particular declaration to which a given variable is bound depends on the particular point of execution, and so cannot be determined statically.

3.4.2   The Lifetime of a Variable

The lifetime, or *extent*, of a variable is the interval of time in which a storage area is bound to the variable. This area is used to hold the value of the variable. We will use the term *data object* (or simply, *object*) to denote the storage and the value together.

The action that acquires a storage area for a variable is called *allocation*. In some languages, allocation is performed before run-time (*static allocation*). In other languages, it is performed at run-time (*dynamic allocation*), either upon explicit request from the programmer via a *creation statement* or automatically upon the entering of the variable's scope. Section 3.6 presents an extensive analysis of these issues.

3.4.3   The Value of a Variable

The value of a variable is represented in coded form in the storage age bound to the variable. The coded representation is then interpreted according to the variable's type.

In some programming languages, the value of a variable can be a *reference* (*pointer*) to an object. In such languages, an object can be made accessible via a chain of references (or *access path*) of arbitrary length. Two variables *share* an object if each has an access path to the object. A shared object modified via a certain access path makes the modification known to all possible access paths. Sharing of objects is used to conserve storage, but it can lead to programs that are hard to read, because the value of variables can be modified even when they are not referenced. References are the primary means for accessing anonymous variables.

The binding between a variable and the value held in its storage area is usually dynamic; the value can be modified by an assignment operation. An assignment such as $b := a$ causes a copy of a's value to be made into the storage area bound to b.

Some languages, however, allow for freezing of the binding between a variable and its value once it is established. The resulting entity is, in every respect, a user-defined *symbolic constant*. For example, in Pascal one can write

const *pi = 3.1416*

and in ALGOL 68

real *pi = 3.1416*

and then use *pi* in expressions such as

`circumference:= 2 * pi * radius`

Variable *pi* is bound to value 3.1416 and its value cannot be changed, that is, the translator reports an error if there is an assignment to *pi*.

Pascal and ALGOL 68 differ in the time of binding between the variable and its unchangeable value. In Pascal the value is either a number or a string of characters, and thus it is possible to establish binding at translation time. The translator can legally substitute the value of the constant for its symbolic name in the program. In ALGOL 68 the value can be given as an expression involving other variables and constants: consequently, binding can only be established at run-time, when the variable is created. A *manifest constant* is a symbolic constant whose value can be bound at translation time.

A subtle question concerning the binding between a variable and its value is: What is the value immediately after the variable is created? There are a number of possible approaches. Unfortunately, most language definitions fail to specify the answer to this question. As a result, the problem is solved differently by different implementations of the same language. This fact makes it difficult to prove the program correct, because correctness may depend on the implementation. Furthermore, moving an apparently correct program to a different installation may produce unforeseen errors or unexpected results.

One obvious and frequently adopted solution to the problem is to ignore it. In this case, the bit string found in the area of storage associated with the variable is considered its initial value. Another solution is to provide a system-defined initialization strategy: for example, integers are initialized to zero, characters to blank, and so on. Yet another solution consists of viewing an uninitialized variable as initialized with a special *uninitialized value* and forbidding any read accesses to such variables until a meaningful value is assigned to the variable. This solution, by far the cleanest, can be enforced in different ways. Its only drawback could be the cost associated with the run-time checks necessary to ensure that an uninitialized value is never used in the program.

3.4.4 The Type of a Variable

The type of a variable can be viewed as a specification of the class of values that can be associated with the variable, together with the operations that can be legally used to create, access, and modify such values.

When the language is defined, a type name is usually bound to a certain class of values and a set of operations. For example, type *boolean* is bound to the values *true* and *false* and the operations **and, or,** and **not**. Values and operations are bound to a certain machine representation when the language is implemented. For example, *true* might be bound to the bit string

00 . . . 001, *false* might be bound to 00 . . . 000. Operations **and, or,** and **not** might be implemented via suitable machine instructions that operate on the bit strings representing booleans.

In some languages, the programmer can define new types by means of a type declaration. For example, in Pascal one can write

type *t*= **array** [1..10] **of** *boolean*

This declaration establishes a binding—at translation time—between the type name *t* and its implementation (i.e., an array of 10 booleans, each accessible via an index in the subrange 1 to 10). As a consequence of this binding, type *t* inherits all the operations of the representation data structure (the array); thus, it is possible to read and modify each component of an object of type *t* by indexing within the array.

In languages that support the definition of abstract data types there is no default binding between a new type and the set of operations; the operations must be specified as a set of subprograms in the declaration of the new type. The declaration of the new type has the following general form.

type *t*= data structure representing objects of type *t*;
        procedures to be used for manipulating data objects of
        type *t*
end

Types can be bound to variables either statically or dynamically. The static solution is adopted by most traditional languages, such as FORTRAN, ALGOL 60, COBOL, Pascal, ALGOL 68, SIMULA 67, CLU, and Ada. In these languages, the binding between a variable and its type is usually specified by a *variable declaration*. For example, in Pascal one can write

var *x,y: integer;*
    z: boolean;

However, in some languages (such as FORTRAN) the first occurrence of a new variable name is taken as an implicit declaration. The advantage of explicit declarations lies in the clarity of the programs and improved reliability, because such things as spelling errors in variable names can be caught at translation time. For example, in FORTRAN the declaration of variable ALPHA followed by a statement such as ALPA = 7.3 intended to assign a value to it, would not be detected as an error. "ALPA" would not be considered as an incorrect occurrence of an undeclared variable (i.e., as a misspelled, ALPHA), but as the implicit declaration of a new variable, ALPA.

Note that the issue of implicit type declarations is not a semantic one. Semantically, Pascal and FORTRAN are equivalent with respect to the typing of variables because they both bind variables to types at translation time.

FORTRAN has default rules to determine the particular binding but the time of binding is the same in the two languages.

APL and SNOBOL4 are two languages that use a dynamic binding between variables and types. For example, in APL a variable name may denote at different points during execution a simple variable, a one-dimensional array, a multidimensional array, or even a label. Actually, APL variables are not explicitly declared; their type is implicitly determined by the value they currently hold. For example, after executing the assignment statement

$$A \leftarrow 5$$

A is an integer variable holding "5" as its value. A later statement

$$\rightarrow A$$

would treat A as a label variable and jump to the statement whose number is the value of A. Still later, A may be modified by the following assignment:

$$A \leftarrow 1 \ 2 \ 51 \ 0$$

Now A denotes a one-dimensional array of length 4. The lower bound of the index is implicitly set to 1.

Dynamic binding provides great flexibility in creating and manipulating data structures. However, it has disadvantages in terms of programming discipline, program correctness, and efficiency of implementation. Programs are hard to read because the type of a variable that occurs in a statement is not immediately known, but depends on the paths of execution of a given program invocation. As a consequence, an APL statement such as

$$A[2;3] \leftarrow 0$$

intended to assign zero to the component in row 2, column 3, of a two-dimensional array, is correct only if, at that particular point of execution, A is a two-dimensional array. For example, it would be incorrect if $A \leftarrow 0$ were the latest assignment to A. In other words, APL requires *dynamic type checking* to verify that the use of each variable is consistent with its type. In contrast, static binding is the basis of static type checking, whose benefits to program correctness were discussed in Section 2.4.

As another example, consider the APL statement

$$A \leftarrow B + C$$

This statement is correct if either one or both of the variables B and C are simple variables, but also if B and C are arrays with the same number and size of dimensions. Moreover, the actions necessary to execute the statement depend on the types of B and C. If B and C are simple variables, the implied actions are a simple addition and an assignment. If B and C are one-dimensional arrays, the implied actions comprise a loop of additions and assignments.

This example shows that information about types of APL variables must be used at run-time not only to perform dynamic type checking, but to choose the appropriate actions for executing statements. To use type information, descriptors must exist at run-time and must be modified every time a new binding is established. This is precisely the reason that other languages (such as Pascal) are designed so that type information is known at translation time. Consequently, descriptors need to exist only at translation time.

Programming languages that adopt dynamic binding between variables and types are processed more naturally by interpretation. As the example shows, there generally is not enough information before run-time to generate code for the evaluation of expressions involving variables of unknown type. The choice between translation and interpretation in the implementation of a language is therefore heavily influenced by the binding rules between variables and types. Languages with dynamic binding are interpretation-oriented, whereas languages with static binding are translation-oriented.

3.5 PROGRAM UNITS

Programming languages allow a program to be composed of a number of *units*. Program units can be developed in a more or less independent fashion and can sometimes be translated separately and combined after translation. Variables declared within a unit are *local* to the unit. A unit can be *activated* at execution time. Assembly language subprograms, FORTRAN subroutines, and ALGOL 60 procedures and blocks are well-known examples of program units. The next section reviews some elementary mechanisms that control the flow of execution among program units and the bindings established when a unit is activated. Subprogram parameter passing is discussed in Section 3.7.

The representation of a program unit during execution is called a *unit instance*. A unit instance is composed of a *code segment* and an *activation record*. The code segment, whose contents are fixed, contains the instructions of the unit and is stored in the instruction memory of SIMPLESEM. The contents of the activation record, which is stored in the data memory, are changeable. The activation record contains all the information necessary to execute the unit, including, among other things, the data objects associated with the local variables of a particular unit instance. The relative position of a data object in the activation record is called its *offset*.

Units may be named or unnamed. Procedures in Pascal and C are examples of named units; ALGOL 60 and C blocks are examples of unnamed units. A unit is not a self-contained, completely independent piece of program. If it is a subprogram, it can be activated by a subprogram call issued by another unit, to which control is returned after execution. Therefore, the *return point* is a piece of (changeable) information that must be saved in the activation record at subprogram invocation time. Moreover, units can reference variables (*nonlocal variables*) other than those declared locally, if the scope rules of the language allow this. Nonlocal variables that can be referenced by every unit in the program are called *global variables*.

The *referencing environment* of a unit instance U consists of U's local variables, which are bound to objects stored in U's activation record (*local environment*), and U's nonlocal variables, which are bound to objects stored in the activation records of other units (*nonlocal environment*). Two variables of a unit's referencing environment that denote the same data object are called *aliases*. The modification of a data object bound to a nonlocal variable is called a *side-effect*.

Units can often be activated recursively, that is, a unit can call itself either directly or indirectly through some other unit. In other words, a new activation can occur before termination of a previous activation. All the instances of the same unit are composed of the same code segment but different activation records. Thus, in the presence of recursion, the binding between an activation record and its code segment is necessarily dynamic. Every time a unit is activated, a binding must be established between an activation record and its code segment to form a new unit instance.

Some languages, such as FORTRAN, do not support recursive unit activations, that is, they allow a maximum of one instance for each unit. Thus the binding between the code segment and the activtion record can be static, and the creation (and initialization) of the data objects for the local variables of a unit can be done before program execution. The following sections discuss these issues in more detail.

3.6 RUN-TIME STRUCTURE OF PROGRAMMING LANGUAGES

One way to classify languages is according to their run-time behavior. We can identify three classes of languages. This is a semantic classification and we will use SIMPLESEM to explain the differences between the classes.

Static languages. Exemplified by FORTRAN and COBOL, these languages guarantee that the memory requirements for any program can be determined before program execution begins. Therefore, all the needed memory can be allocated before program execution. Clearly, these languages cannot allow recursion because recursion would require an arbitrary number of unit instances and thus the memory requirements could not be determined at translation time. (As we will see later, the implementation is *not required* to do the memory allocation statically. The semantics of the language, however, give the implementer the freedom to make that choice.)

Stack-based languages. These languages, exemplified by ALGOL 60, allow more poweful programs whose memory requirements cannot be computed at translation time. However, their memory usage is predictable and follows a last-in-first-out discipline; therefore we can use a stack on SIMPLESEM to model their behavior (see Section 3.6.2). Once again, note that a particular implementation of these languages *need not* use a stack. We use a stack for our model because it is sufficient and its semantics is known. A stack is not part of the semantics of the language; it is a part of our semantic model.

Dynamic languages. These languages, as the name implies, have unpredictable memory usage. These languages, which include LISP, PROLOG, APL, and SNOBOL 4, cannot be modelled by a stack-based SIMPLESEM because they allow the programmer to create data objects at arbitrary points during program execution.

Most current languages, including Pascal, C, ALGOL 68, and Ada, are primarily stack-based with some dynamic features. In the following sections, we will examine these classes more closely.

3.6.1 The Structure of FORTRAN

A FORTRAN program is composed of a set of units: a *main* program and a (possibly empty) set of subprograms (*subroutines* and *functions*). The amount of storage required to hold each local variable is fixed; it is known at translation time and cannot be changed during the execution of the unit. Each unit is compiled separately and is associated with an activation record that can be allocated before execution, that is, variables can be created before run-time and their lifetimes extend over the entire program execution (*static variables*). The scope of a variable, however, is limited to the unit in which it is declared.

Units can access global variables declared via COMMON statements. These variables can be viewed as belonging to a system-provided activation record, global to all program units. A view of a FORTRAN program on SIMPLESEM is illustrated in Figure 3.2.

A FORTRAN program must go through three steps of transformation before it takes on the form in Figure 3.2. In the first step—the *compile* step—each unit is translated (by a compiler) separately without knowledge of other units. As the result of this step, all statements are translated to the machine language of SIMPLESEM, except that all memory references (data as well as code) are translated to a pair (unit name, offset). In the second step—the *link* step—the units that comprise the program are linked together (by a linker). As a result of this step, all units are assigned to specific memory locations and therefore all memory references are translated to

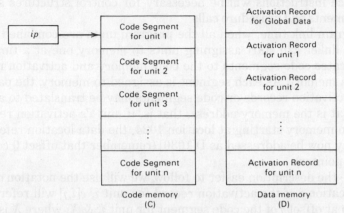

FIGURE 3.2   A FORTRAN program in the SIMPLESEM environment.

specific memory addresses.* The third step—the *load* step—simply consists of loading the program into the memory of SIMPLESEM and setting up *ip* to point to the first program instruction. This step is performed by a loader. We will describe these steps in detail with an example below.

We describe the semantics of each FORTRAN statement in terms of the specific actions that it implies on our abstract processor. The semantically interesting statements are those that cause transfer of control, especially between units, because they effect a change in the environment. We will review only these statements here (others will be found in exercises).

The first location of each activation record (offset 0) is reserved for a return pointer. For an instance of unit *A*, the return pointer will contain the address of the instruction that should be executed after the unit *A* is finished. The only other information in the activation record is for the local variables. (Later, when we discuss parameter passing, we will see that the activation record must also contain information about the parameters.) During the translation step for a unit, consecutive locations of the unit's activation record are reserved for local variables as variable declarations are processed, that is, offsets are bound statically to variables. Each variable reference is thus translated into the pair (unit name, offset), mentioned above. Note that if we knew where in memory each activation record would be stored, then we could translate each variable reference to a memory address and would not need to keep the unit name. In general, however, because an activation record is bound to a particular memory area at load/link time, the translator cannot assign memory addresses.

Similarly, each instruction also can be referenced using a pair: the unit name and the offset of the instruction within the code segment. The ability

---

*Note that an actual linker can produce relocatable code—as discussed in Section 3.2.2. For our purposes, however, we do not care about relocatability.

to reference instructions will be necessary for control structures such as **goto** statements and procedure calls.

At program link time, when all the program units are combined by the linker, the linker can start assigning units to memory one at a time. The linker allocates code segments to the code memory and activation records to the data memory. As each segment is assigned to memory, the pair that refers to activation records or code segments may be translated to a single number that is the memory address, that is, if unit i's activation record is assigned to memory starting at location 1024, the data location referenced by $(i,6)$ may now be addressed as D[1030] (remember that offset 0 contains the return pointer).

To make the description easier to follow, we will use the notation $d[i,j]$ to refer to location j of the activation record for unit i; $c[i,j]$ will refer to the instruction at offset j of the code segment for unit i; & X, where X is either $c[i,j]$, or $d[i,j]$, stands for the address of X. The linker will translate these quantities to particular values (i.e., memory addresses), that is, the translator translates a variable name to either a $c[i,j]$ or $d[i,j]$, and the linker will translate the result to a $C[m]$ or $D[m]$.

You should now once again refer to Figure 3.2 which shows a conceptual view of a typical FORTRAN program in the memory of our abstract machine. A program is executed by first loading it into the memory (as described above). Then the instruction pointer is made to point to the first instruction of the main program.

The semantics of a **goto** statement can now be seen to be simply: replace the contents of the instruction pointer with the target address of the **goto** statement. Note that the translator has translated the label into a pair and that the linker has translated the pair into an actual address. In other words:

goto x means *ip:= &c[i,j]*, where *i* is the unit being
                  translated and *x* is the label of instruction
                  located at offset *j* of code segment for unit *i*.

Procedure call and return are the most interesting constructs semantically. A call to procedure P is translated to the following sequence of instructions:

1. Store the address of the next instruction in $d[P,0]$—location 0 of activation record for unit P {store the return point}.
2. Replace the contents of the instruction pointer with &$c[P,0]$—the first instruction of unit P {transfer control to unit P}.

Or

d[P,0]:= ip+2 {*ip+2* because a call is translated into two
                        instructions}
ip:= &c[P,0]

After linking, these instructions will turn into:

$$D[m] := ip + 2 \ \{m \text{ is the address assigned to } P\text{'s}$$
$$\text{activation record}\}$$
$$ip := n \ \{n \text{ is the address assigned to } P\text{'s}$$
$$\text{code segment}\}$$

A procedure return in unit P is translated to:

1. Replace the instruction pointer with contents of $d[P,0]$, where P is the current unit.

Or

$$ip := d[P,0]$$

which, after linking, will turn into:

$ip := D[m]$ {again, m is the address assigned to P's activation record}

To give you a better understanding of SIMPLESEM and our approach to semantics, let us go through a complete example of a FORTRAN program, its various stages of translation, and its execution on SIMPLESEM. It is important for you to understand this example completely so that you will be able to follow the more complicated languages that we will discuss in the next sections. The program (which performs no useful task) consists of the following main program.

```
     INTEGER I,J
     COMMON I
     CALL X
     GOTO 10
10   CONTINUE
     END
```

and the following subroutine:

```
     SUBROUTINE X
     INTEGER K,J
     COMMON I
     K=5
     I=6
     J=I+K
     RETURN
     END
```

(CONTINUE is a FORTRAN statement that has no effect. We will translate it to *noop*, which stands for *no operation*.)

The translator performs the following bindings for the main program:

```
I ↔ d[COMMON,0]
J ↔ d[MAIN,1]
10 ↔ c[MAIN,3]
X ↔ c[X,0]
```

and the following bindings for the subroutine:

```
I ↔ d[COMMON,0]
K ↔ d[X,1]
J ↔ d[X,2]
```

The linker then performs a further binding of addresses by combining the main program and the subroutine X. It assigns the data memory to the COMMON activation record, activation record for MAIN, and activation record for X, in order; it assigns the code memory to MAIN and then X. As a result, it produces the following bindings in the main program:

```
I ↔ D[0]
J ↔ D[2]
10 ↔ C[3]
X ↔ C[5]
```

and the following bindings for X:

```
I ↔ D[0]
K ↔ D[4]
J ↔ D[5]
```

Note how the common I is being referred to by the same address in both MAIN and X, while the two distinct J's have been assigned different addresses. Figure 3.3 shows this program as loaded into the SIMPLESEM memory.

Figure 3.4 shows snapshots of execution of the FORTRAN program of our example on the SIMPLESEM machine. Note that changes occur in ip and the data memory while the code memory stays unchanged throughout execution of the program. Also note that in this example, the contents of the return point location in MAIN's activation record are not used because MAIN does not "return" to a caller. On a real computer, however, MAIN is "called" by the operating system and this location can be used to return to the operating system.

3.6.2 The Structure of ALGOL-Like Languages

Most of the languages discussed in the following chapters are descendants of ALGOL 60 and often are called ALGOL-like languages. The most distin-

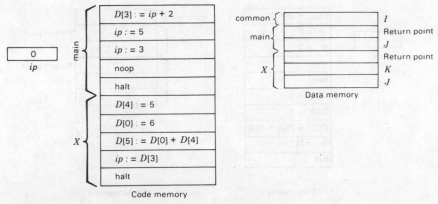

FIGURE 3.3   A FORTRAN program loaded in SIMPLESEM.

guishing characteristic of ALGOL-like languages is a feature—the *block structure*—that is used to control the scope of variables and to divide the program into units. Any two units (or *blocks*) in the program text can be either *disjoint* (i.e., they have no portion in common) or *nested* (i.e., one unit completely encloses the other.)

The structure of the program can thus be viewed as a *static nesting of units* (Figure 3.5(a)). Such a static nesting also can be represented by a tree structure. The tree structure in Figure 3.5(b) for the program of Figure 3.5(a) clearly shows that units B and E are statically enclosed within unit A; units F and G are statically enclosed within E; C within B; and D within C. A variable declared at the outermost unit—at the root of the nesting tree—is said to be at level 0; variables in the units enclosed by the outermost unit are at level 1; and so on. We will use the notation *level(u)* to refer to the nesting level of unit u.

If an entity such as a variable is locally declared in a unit U, it is visible in U, but not in the units that enclose U. However, it is visible (with one exception) to all the units that are statically nested within U. In Figure 3.5, a variable declared in unit B is not visible to A, E, F, and G; it is visible to B, C, and D. It is local to B and global to C and D.

The exception to the rule occurs when a variable local to a given unit is given the same name as a variable declared in an enclosing unit. In such a case, the same name denotes both the locally declared object and the global object declared in the outer unit. The convention in ALGOL-like languages is that local declarations mask nonlocal declarations. This implies that in Figure 3.5, if variable v is declared both in A and C, any references to v within A, B, E, F, and G refer to the variable v local to A, whereas any references to v within C and D refer to the variable v local to C.

In general, in determining the variables visible to a unit, it is necessary to proceed from that unit outward through all the enclosing levels of static

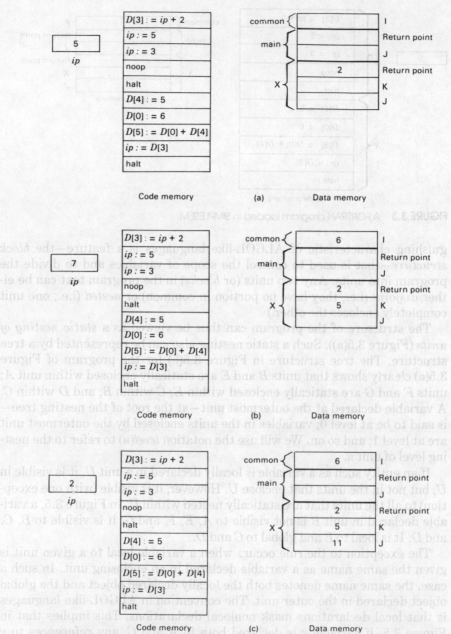

FIGURE 3.4 The FORTRAN program of Figure 3.3. **(a)** After execution of the CALL X; **(b)** after execution of I=6; and **(c)** after execution of RETURN.

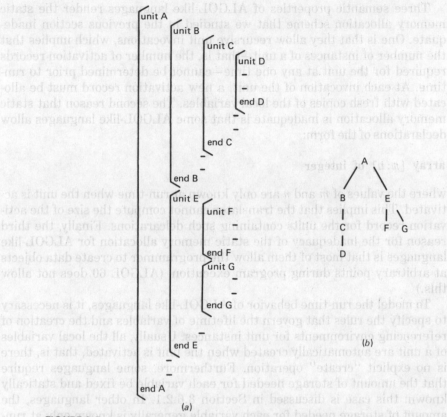

FIGURE 3.5   (a) Static nesting of ALGOL-like units, and (b) the corresponding nesting tree.

nesting. Every declaration of a variable that was not previously encountered defines a name visible to the unit.

In ALGOL-like languages, units fall into one of two categories: blocks and subprograms. Blocks are unnamed units; they are activated when they are encountered during the normal progression of execution and only serve to define a new environment by means of local declarations. Subprograms, on the other hand, are named units activated only when they are called explicitly. The scope rules of subprogram names are the same as those described for variables.

For example, in Figure 3.5, the names F and G are local to unit E. The names B and E are local to unit A. The names F and G are not visible in units B, C, or D and thus B, C, or D cannot activate (i.e., call) F or G directly. It is interesting to note that the name B, for example, is local to A and therefore can be used in A; it may also be used in B itself—recursively—but its use then is as a nonlocal symbol. This point is sometimes confusing to beginners but is consistent with the scope rules for variables.

Three semantic properties of ALGOL-like languages render the static memory allocation scheme that we studied in the previous section inadequate. One is that they allow recursive unit invocations, which implies that the number of instances of a unit—that is, the number of activation records required for the unit at any one time—cannot be determined prior to run-time. At each invocation of the unit, a new activation record must be allocated with fresh copies of the local variables. The second reason that static memory allocation is inadequate is that some ALGOL-like languages allow declarations of the form:

array $[m:n]$ **of integer**

where the values of m and n are only known at run-time when the unit is activated. This implies that the translator cannot compute the size of the activation record for the units containing such delcarations. Finally, the third reason for the inadequacy of the static memory allocation for ALGOL-like languages is that most of them allow the programmer to create data objects at arbitrary points during program execution. (ALGOL 60 does not allow this.)

To model the run-time behavior of ALGOL-like languages, it is necessary to specify the rules that govern the lifetime of variables and the creation of referencing environments for unit instances. Usually, all the local variables of a unit are automatically created when the unit is activated, that is, there is no explicit "create" operation. Furthermore, some languages require that the amount of storage needed for each variable be fixed and statically known: this case is discussed in Section 3.6.2.1. In other languages, the amount of storage needed for each variable generally is known only at run-time when the unit is activated; this case is discussed in Section 3.6.2.2. In still other cases, local variables may be explicitly created by the programmer. Consequently, the amount of storage required by an activation record is not even known when the unit is activated, but grows dynamically when new creation statements are executed. This case is discussed in Section 3.6.2.3. A final important aspect—how ALGOL-like unit instances can access their nonlocal environment—is discussed in Section 3.6.2.4.

In Sections 3.6.2.1 through 3.6.2.3 we make two assumptions: there is no separate compilation and there are no nonlocal references to symbols. These assumptions allow us to simplify our discussion: First, we can bypass the link step and translate a program to a SIMPLESEM program with no relocatable symbols directly in one step. Second, each code reference—labels or procedures—can be directly translated to absolute addresses in the code memory. Third, references to variables can be translated to a single number rather than a pair: their offset within the activation record. The underlying assumption is that the full address will be evaluated by SIMPLE-SEM at run-time, as we will show in the sequel.

3.6.2.1   Activation records with statically known size

In this case, local variables are implicitly created when the unit is activated, and the amount of storage required to hold the value of each local variable is known at translation time. Pascal (if we ignore pointers) and C are two languages in this class.

As in the case of FORTRAN, the size of the activation record and the offset of each local variable within it are known at translation time. However, the activation record cannot be bound to the unit's code segment statically—before execution—because there may be several recursive activations of the unit at the same time. The activation record must therefore be allocated and bound dynamically for each new activation. Consequently, at translation time a variable can be bound only to its offset within the activation record; the binding to physical storage requires knowledge of the address of the activation record and can only be done at run-time. Variables of this class will be called *semistatic variables*.

For example, suppose that the following declaration appears in a unit:

a: **array** [0..10] **of** integer

(i.e., a is an array of integers with subscripts in the range 0 to 10). Also suppose that each integer occupies one location in the activation record and that consecutive storage cells are allocated to the array. At translation time, a's address, *offset (a)*, is known relative to the address of the first location of the activation record, which will become known at execution time. If x is this address, a reference to $a[i]$ is evaluated as a reference to location $x + offset(a) + i$.

Dynamic allocation of activation records has two major effects: it allows the implementation of recursive unit activations and, as we will see, it allows more efficient utilization of data storage. To make return from an activation possible, activation records must contain enough information to identify the instruction to be executed and the activation record to become active upon return. We have already seen the use of the return pointer at offset 0 in the case of FORTRAN; we will now also reserve the location at offset 1 of each activation record for a pointer to the activation record of the calling unit—this pointer is called the *dynamic link*. The chain of dynamic links originating in the currently active activation record is called the *dynamic chain*. The dynamic chain represents the dynamic nesting of unit activations.

When a unit U completes its current instance, its activation record is no longer needed. The lifetime rules specify that each instance of U must have a new activation record. The local variables of U can be visible only to units that are nested within U and activated after the current activation of U. Hence, such activations are completed before U's current instance. Therefore, after a unit completes its current instance, it is possible to free the space occupied by the activation record and make it available to store new activation records. For example, if A calls B which then calls C, the activation records for units are allocated in the order A, B, C. When C returns to B, C's activation record can be discarded; B's activation record is discarded next, when B returns to A. Because the activation record that is freed is the one that was most recently allocated, activation records can be allocated with a last-in/first-out policy on a stack-organized storage.

We will now turn to the operational semantics of unit activations in the case of ALGOL-like languages. We will modify SIMPLESEM slightly to allow it to manage stacks of activation records. We will assume that SIMPLESEM has two more pointers in addition to ip. The first is called *free* and will always point to the next available location in data memory. The second is called *current* and will always point to the start of the current activation record. (In the implementation of a language on a real machine, this information is usually kept in machine registers.) Every time a location in the data memory is accessed, SIMPLESEM automatically adds the value of *current* to its offset, that is, we will now use $d[i]$ to refer to location $D[current + i]$.

We can use these two pointers to illustrate the effect of unit activations. For example, a call to procedure "p", is equivalent to:

```
D[free]:= ip+5 {set the return point; there are 5 SIMPLESEM
                instructions corresponding to a call}
D[free+1]:= current {set the dynamic link for the new
                     activation record}
current:= free {set current to base of activation record to be
                allocated}
free:= free+S {update free; S is the size of the activation
               record for p}
ip:= starting address of p's code segment
```

A procedure return, or **end**—that is, unit termination—corresponds to:

```
free:= current {remove the current activation record}
current:= D[current+1] {reset current using the dynamic link}
ip:= D[free] {use the return point to set ip}
```

For example, if units F and G of the program shown in Figure 3.5 are mutually recursive subprograms, Figure 3.6 represents a partial description of the state of SIMPLESEM (only the dynamic chain, *current* and *free* are shown) after the following sequence of calls:

Call E issued by A
Call F issued by E
Call G issued by F

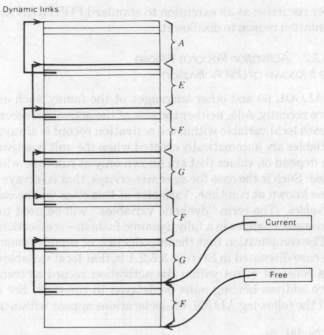

FIGURE 3.6   Activation record stack for program of Figure 3.5.

Call F issued by G
Call G issued by F
Call F issued by G

A stack-based storage management for ALGOL-like languages is an implementation choice and is not strictly implied by the semantics of the language. The semantics of the language only requires that local variables be bound to a new activation record for each new activation, and conceptually, the local objects of previous activations can continue to exist forever. However, thanks to the scope rules of the language, an activation record becomes inaccessible as soon as the instance terminates. This is why we can choose to allocate activation records on a stack. The possibility of reusing the storage released by activation records is why dynamic storage allocation is in principle more efficient in the use of storage than is static allocation.

We note at this point that this stack-based scheme also can be used in implementing FORTRAN. Even though we discussed FORTRAN in terms of static memory allocation, it is not a requirement that it be so implemented. The stack-based scheme has more power than is necessary. It is up to the implementer whether to employ the technique. In fact, some implementations of FORTRAN do use a stack-based scheme. These implementations often offer recursion as an extension to standard FORTRAN as there is no implementation reason to disallow it.

3.6.2.2   Activation Records Whose Size Is Known at Unit Activation

In ALGOL 60 and other languages of the family, such as ALGOL 68 and, more recently, Ada, neither the size of the activation record nor the position of each local variable within the activation record is always known statically. Variables are automatically created when the unit is activated, but their size can depend on values that are known only at run-time when the unit is activated. Such is the case for *dynamic arrays,* that is, arrays whose bounds become known at run-time. Variables of this class will be called *semidynamic variables.* (The term "dynamic variables" will be used to denote variables whose size changes in a fully dynamic fashion—see Section 3.6.2.3.)

The complication that the introduction of semidynamic variables adds to the case discussed in Section 3.6.2.1 is that local variables cannot be bound to a constant offset within the activation record at translation time, and more address binding must be delayed to run-time. For example, suppose that the following ALGOL 68 declarations appear within unit U.

```
[1:n] int a;
[1:m] real b;
```

(That is, a is an array of integers with subscripts in the range 1 to n, and b is an array of reals with subscripts in the range 1 to m.) Let m and n be two nonlocal variables. Because the values of n and m are not known at translation time, the amount of storage needed for a and b, and therefore for U's activation record, cannot be determined statically. However, the language semantics require that the values of m and n (and therefore the size of the activation record) be known at unit activation time. This provides the basis for a rather efficient implementation as described below.

At translation time, we can reserve, within the activation record, storage for the descriptors of the dynamic arrays a and b. The descriptor includes one cell in which a pointer to the storage area for the dynamic array will be stored and one cell each for the lower and upper bounds of each array dimension. As the number of dimensions of the array is known at translation time, the size of the descriptor is known statically. All accesses to semidynamic variables are translated as indirect references through the pointer in the descriptor, whose offset is determined statically.

At run-time, the activation record is allocated in several stages. First, the storage required for semistatic variables and descriptors of semidynamic variables are allocated. When the declaration of a semidynamic variable is encountered, the dimension entries in the descriptors are entered, the actual size of the semidynamic variable is evaluated, and the activation record is expanded to include the variable. (This expansion is possible because, being the active unit, the activation record is on top of the stack.) Finally, the pointer in the descriptor is set to point to the area just allocated.

More specifically, we now need to associate some run-time actions with declarations of semidynamic variables. In the case of the previously declared array a we will maintain a descriptor for it at some offset m. The descriptor will contain the starting address of a, the lower bound, and the upper bound on a's index at locations m, $m+1$, and $m+2$, respectively. At entry to unit U, we need to have some code to allocate space for a (by incrementing *free*), and update the contents of a's descriptor since all the needed information is known at this time.

Any access to elements of a are translated to indirect references. Assuming each integer occupies one location in the data memory and i is stored at offset s

$a[i]$ *means* D[D[current + m] + D[current + s]]

The reader should contrast the SIMPLESEM operations for semidynamic variables with those required for static variables to appreciate the semantic differences.

3.6.2.3 Activation Records with Dynamically Variable Size

The languages described in the previous sections are characterized by having all local variables implicitly created at unit activation time. Moreover, the size of the activation records either is known statically or, at worst, known when units are activated. Languages of the ALGOL family—except for ALGOL 60—from PL/I and Pascal to ALGOL 68 and Ada, also allow programmers to deal with data objects whose size can vary during execution. Consequently, the amount of storage required by an activation record is not known when the unit is activated. Such variables will be called *dynamic variables*.

One notable example of dynamic variables is the *flexible array* provided by ALGOL 68 and a few other languages. A flexible array is an array whose bounds can vary during program execution to accommodate the size of the object assigned to it. Consider the following ALGOL-like program structure.

begin Unit A;
    begin Unit B;
    end B;
end A;

Let x be a flexible array declared locally in unit A, and let x be assigned within unit B. Storage for holding the value of x cannot be reserved on the stack within A's activation record, because the amount of space necessary to hold the value assigned by unit B is known only when B is executed (i.e., when B's activation record is on top of the activation record stack). At that point of execution, A's activation record is farther down in the stack, and changing its size to accommodate the object newly assigned to x would require restructuring the stack—an obviously infeasible solution.

Another example of dynamic variables is provided by variables that are allocated under program control. These exist in PL/I, Pascal, and other languages, and allow the creation of data structures that can be expanded and contracted. Such a data structure can be modeled as consisting of a set of nodes; nodes may be added to and deleted from the structure dynamically. Examples of these data structures are linked lists and trees. The nodes are often connected via pointers. Since the nodes are allocated while the program is executing and their numbers are not known at the time of writing the program or at translation time, it is impossible to name them explicitly. They are accessed indirectly through pointers. For example, in Pascal, every pointer is qualified such that it is able to point to objects of only one type. Assuming that p has been declared to be a pointer of type t, then the statement

```
new (p)
```

creates an object of type t and assigns its address to p. The lifetime of the object created in this way, unlike that of semistatic and semidynamic variables, does not end when the block containing the allocation statement is exited. Instead, some languages (e.g., PL/I) provide statements for deallocating such objects explicitly. Other languages (e.g., Pascal) state that the object lives as long as a reference (i.e., a pointer) to it exists. Furthermore, it is possible to create several such objects without deallocating any of them. It is easy to see, therefore, that such objects cannot possibly be allocated on the stack.

Consider again, for example, the above-mentioned program structure. Let p be a pointer declared in unit A, and let B contain the allocation statement "new (p)." When the allocation statement is executed, the activation record on top of the stack is that of unit B. The object cannot be allocated on top of the stack, because when B is exited the object would be deallocated (while p still points to it). Allocation in A's activation record is also infeasible, because, as we saw in the case of flexible arrays, it would require restructuring the stack.

In summary, dynamic variables denote data objects whose size and/or number can vary dynamically during their lifetimes. This fact prohibits the allocation of these variables on a stack; instead, they are allocated in a memory area called a *heap*. The term "heap" is meant to indicate freedom from the last-in/first-out connotation of the stack. For this reason, dynamic variables are called *heap variables*, as opposed to semistatic and semidynamic variables, which are called *stack variables*.

On SIMPLESEM, because the activation record stack is being allocated at the low addresses and grows towards high addresses, we can allocate the heap at the other end of memory, starting with high addresses and growing towards low addresses. In fact, this is the way most actual implementations are done. Further discussion of heap variables and hints on the run-time management of the heap are given in Sections 4.6.2.6 and 4.6.4.

3.6.2.4 Accessing Nonlocal Environments

So far we have only examined how a unit activation can reference its own local environment. We will now discuss how unit activations can refer to their global environment; the problem of parameter passing will be discussed in the next section.

In a language such as FORTRAN, global variables can be considered as belonging to a system-provided activation record that is global to all units, and all bindings between global variables of a unit and storage allocated to such global variables can be established statically.

In ALGOL-like languages, the activation records that are on the stack at any given time represent the dynamic chain of unit activations. Figure 3.6 shows the stack of our abstract processor after the sequence of calls described in Section 3.6.2.1 for the program shown in Figure 3.5. Suppose that the integer variable x is declared within both E and G, and that the integer variable y is declared within G, B, and A. Moreover, let z be an integer variable locally declared within F. Suppose that the execution on SIMPLE-SEM reaches the assignment $z := x + y$ when the activation record stack is that shown in Figure 3.6. As we have seen, the appropriate binding to a stack location for z is partially established at translation time by translating each occurence of z into a reference to $current + offset$ (z) ($offset(z)$ is a statically known value), and is completed at run-time when the value of $current$ (the starting address of F's activation record) becomes known. But what about x and y? Note that the binding between x (or y) and the stack location allocated to it is *not* the most recently established binding. In fact, the most recent binding to a stack location for variable x has been established by the latest activation of unit G, but the scope rules of the language require variable x referenced within F to be the one declared within E. Similarly, variable y referenced within F is the one declared within A, and not the one most recently allocated by the latest activation of G. In other words, the sequence of activation records stored in the stack represents the sequence of unit instances dynamically generated at run-time. But what determines the nonlocal environment are the scope rules of the language, based on the static nesting of unit declarations.

3.6.2.4.1. Static Chain. One way to make access to nonlocal variables possible is for each activation record to contain a pointer (*static link*) up the stack to the activation record of the unit that statically encloses it in the program text. Figure 3.7 shows the static links for Figure 3.6. The sequence of static links that can be followed from the active activation record is called the *static chain*. Referencing nonlocal variables can be explained intuitively as a search that traverses the static chain. To find the correct binding between a variable and a stack location, we search along the static chain until a binding is found. In our example, a reference to x is bound to a stack location within E's activation record, whereas a reference to y is bound to a stack location within A's activation record—as indeed it should be.

In practice, searching, which would entail considerable run-time overhead, is never necessary. A more efficient solution is based on the fact that the activation record containing a variable named in a unit U is always a fixed distance from U's activation record along the static chain. In terms of the nesting tree in Figure 3.5(b), this distance attribute is the number of tree branches you need to traverse up to get from the variable reference to the variable declaration. If the variable is local, the distance is obviously zero (this is why we only needed an offset in the previous sections, because we were assuming only local variables); if it is a variable declared in the immediately enclosing unit, the distance is one; and so on. This distance attribute can be evaluated and bound to the variable at translation time. Consequently, variables may be statically bound to a pair (*distance, offset*) within the activation record. If the variable is semidynamic, the offset is the rela-

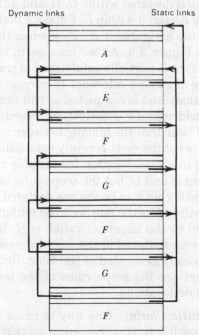

Dynamic links   Static links

FIGURE 3.7 Figure 3.6 with static links.

tive position of a descriptor that contains a pointer to a stack location where the object is stored. If the variable is dynamic, the offset is the relative position of a pointer to a heap area where the object is stored.

The pair (*distance, offset*) is used at run-time as follows. If *d* is the value of the distance, starting from location *current*, we traverse *d* steps along the static chain. The value of the offset is then added to the address so found, and the result is the actual run-time address to the nonlocal data object. In the case of semidynamic and dynamic variables, this process leads to a location through which an extra level of indirection is required to reach the actual data object.

We can define this formally in terms of a recursive function *fp*(*d*), that stands for the *frame pointer*—a pointer to an activation record—that is *d* static links away from the active activation record. *fp*(*d*) can be defined as:

```
fp(d)=if d=0 then current else D[fp(d-1)+2]
```

For example, *fp* (0) is simply *current* and *fp*(*1*) is *D*[*current* + 2]. Notice that function *fp* can be easily translated into SIMPLESEM instructions; we leave this to the reader as an exercise.

Using *fp*, access to a variable *x*, with (*distance, offset*) pair (*d,o*), can be defined with the following table:

VARIABLE TYPE	SIMPLESEM SEMANTICS FOR VARIABLE ACCESS
Semistatic	$D[fp(d)+o]$
Semidynamic	$D[D[fp(d)+o]]$
Dynamic	$D[D[fp(d)+o]]$

We also need to modify our procedure call semantics to install static link entries in activation records. This can be done quite easily. Consider unit *A* calling unit *B*. Because *B* is visible to *A*, it must be either at the same nesting level or at a shallower level, or it must be nested directly in *A*. If *a* = *level*(*A*) and *b* = *level*(*B*), then the static link to be installed for *B* should be set to point to the activation record that is *a* − *b* + 1 steps along the static chain originating from *A*. For example, if *B* is immediately nested within *A*, then the static link for *B* is set to point to *A*'s activation record. If *A* and *B* are at the same level, then the static link for *B* is set to point to the activation record of the unit that immediately encloses both *A* and *B*.

In other words:

```
call B in unit A means
    D[free]:= ip+6 {set return point}
    D[free+1]:= current {set dynamic link}
    D[free+2]:= fp(d), where d=level(A)-level(B)+1 {set static
    link}
```

```
current:= free {set the current frame pointer}
free:= free+size of B's activation record {allocate room
    for activation record}
ip:= starting address of B in code memory {transfer
    control}
```

Note that these semantics do not work in the presence of procedure parameters. We will cover that case in Section 3.7. Procedure return has exactly the same semantics as before and no special treatment is needed for static links.

The main drawback to the use of static links is the need for following the static chain for each reference to a nonlocal variable. The time required to locate a nonlocal data object is not constant and depends on the number of steps traversed along the static chain. There are other implementation techniques that avoid this problem. We will not discuss them here because we are interested primarily in semantics rather than efficiency of implementation.

3.6.3 The Structure of Dynamic Languages

The term "dynamic languages" implies many things. In general, it refers to those languages that adopt dynamic rather than static rules. For example, APL, LISP, and SNOBOL4 use dynamic typing and dynamic scope rules. In principle, of course, a language designer can make these choices independently of one another. For example, one can have dynamic type rules but static scope rules. In practice, however, dynamic properties are usually adopted together.

In this section, we will examine how the adoption of dynamic rules changes the semantics of the language in terms of run-time requirements. In general, a dynamic property implies that more of the bindings are carried out at run-time and cannot be done at translation time. We will examine dynamic typing and dynamic scoping.

In a language that uses dynamic typing, the type of a variable and therefore the method of access or even the allowable operations cannot be determined at translation time. In Section 3.6.2, we saw that we needed to keep a run-time descriptor for semidynamic variables, because we could not, at translation time, determine the size of or starting address of such variables. In that case, the descriptor had to contain the information that could not be computed at translation time, namely, the starting address and the array bounds. It was possible to keep the descriptor in the activation record because the size of the descriptor was fixed and known at translation time. In the case of dynamically typed variables, we also need to maintain the type of the variable in the descriptor. If the type of a variable may change at run-time, then the size and contents of its descriptor may also change. For example, if a variable changes from a two-dimensional array to a three-dimensional array, then the descriptor needs to grow to contain the values of the bounds for the new dimension. This is in contrast to the descriptors of semidynamic variables whose contents were fixed at unit activation time (see Section 3.6.2). Every access to a dynamic variable must be preceded by a run-time check on the type of the variable followed by appropriate address computation, depending on the current type of the variable.

What is maintained for each variable in the activation record for a unit? As we have seen, not only the variable's size may change during program execution, but so may the size of its descriptor. Therefore, we cannot maintain the descriptors in the activation records (as we did for semidynamic variables). For each variable, we will maintain a pointer in the activation record that will point to the variable's descriptor in the heap that, in turn, may contain a pointer to the variable itself in the heap.

We now turn our attention to dynamic scope rules. We will use APL as an example, although the discussion applies to other dynamically scoped languages such as LISP and SNOBOL4.

An APL program usually consists of a number of subprograms and a sequence of statements, which can be viewed as the main program (Figure 3.8). The first line of a subprogram definition declares the formal parameters (I in the case of SUB, N in the case of FUN). Function subprograms also indicate the result parameter (R in the case of *FUN*). Local variables (X in the case of FUN, Y in the case of SUB) are also declared. Subprograms may not be nested textually.

Global variables are implicitly declared by an assignment to an identifier that has not been declared as local. A variable declaration does not specify the variable's type. Subprogram names are considered as global identifiers.

APL scopes rules are dynamic, that is, the scope of a name is totally dependent on the run-time call chain (i.e., on the dynamic chain), rather than the static structure of the program. In the example shown in Figure 3.8, consider the point when the call SUB 2 is issued. The nonlocal references to X and Z within the activation of SUB are bound to the global X and Z defined by the main program. When function FUN is activated from SUB, the nonlocal reference to Y is bound to the most recent definition of Y, that is, to the data object associated to Y in SUB's activation record. The next instruction of the main program calls function FUN again. In this case, the nonlocal reference to Y from FUN is bound to the global Y defined in the main program.

The implementation of the APL global-referencing mechanism can be very simple. Activation records are allocated on a stack and joined together by dynamic links. Each entry of the activation record explicitly records the name of the variable and contains a pointer to a heap area, where the value can be stored. Allocation on a heap is necessary because the amount of storage required by each variable can vary dynamically (see Sec-

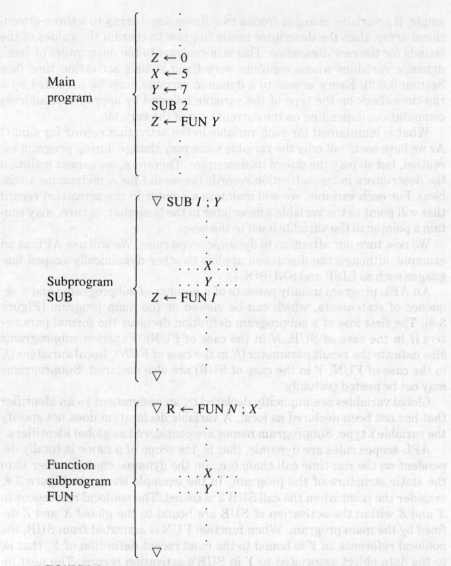

Main program

$$Z \leftarrow 0$$
$$X \leftarrow 5$$
$$Y \leftarrow 7$$
$$\text{SUB } 2$$
$$Z \leftarrow \text{FUN } Y$$

Subprogram SUB

$$\nabla \text{ SUB } I \; ; \; Y$$
$$. \; . \; . \; X \; . \; . \; .$$
$$. \; . \; . \; Y \; . \; . \; .$$
$$Z \leftarrow \text{FUN } I$$
$$\nabla$$

Function subprogram FUN

$$\nabla \text{ R} \leftarrow \text{FUN } N \; ; \; X$$
$$. \; . \; . \; X \; . \; . \; .$$
$$. \; . \; . \; Y \; . \; . \; .$$
$$\nabla$$

FIGURE 3.8   Structure of an APL program.

tion 3.3.1). For each variable—say, T—the stack is searched by following the dynamic chain. The first association found for T in an activation record is the proper one. Figure 3.9 illustrates the stack for the program of Figure 3.8 when FUN is called by SUB, which is, in turn, called by main.

Although simple, this accessing mechanism is inefficient. Another approach is to maintain a table of currently active nonlocal references. Instead of searching along the dynamic chain, a single lookup in this table is suffi-

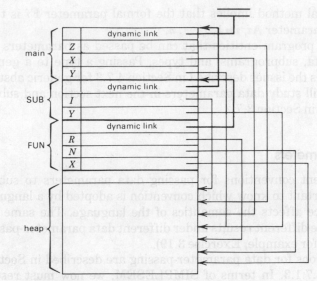

FIGURE 3.9 SIMPLESEM data memory at a particular point of execution of the program of Figure 3.8.

cient. We will not discuss this solution any further but the reader should note that this technique speeds up referencing nonlocal variables at the expense of more elaborate actions to be executed at subprogram entry and exit. These additional actions are necessary to update the table of active nonlocal references.

3.7 PARAMETER PASSING

Parameter passing allows for the communication of data among program units. Unlike communication via global environments, parameters allow for the transfer of different data at each call and provide advantages in terms of readability and modifiability.

Most programming languages use a positional method for binding actual to formal parameters in subprogram calls. If the procedure is declared as

subprogram S $(F1, F2, \ldots Fn)$;

.
.
.

end S

and the subprogram call is

call S $(A1, A2, \ldots An)$

then the positional method implies that the formal parameter Fi is to be bound to actual parameter Ai, $i = 1, 2, \ldots n$.

We can divide program entities that can be passed as parameters into three classes: data, subprograms, and types. Passing a type to a generic procedure involves the issues described in Section 4.7.3 for generic abstract data types. We will study data parameters in the next section and subprogram parameters in Section 3.7.2.

3.7.1   Data Parameters

There are different conventions for passing data parameters to subprograms. It is important to know which convention is adopted by a language, because the choice affects the semantics of the language. The same program may produce different results under different data parameter-passing conventions (see, for example, Exercise 3.19).

Three conventions for data parameter-passing are described in Sections 3.7.1.1 through 3.7.1.3. In terms of SIMPLESEM, we now must reserve space in the activation record for parameters as well as local variables. A detailed description of semantics in terms of SIMPLESEM is left to the reader as an exercise.

3.7.1.1   Call by Reference (or by Sharing)

The calling unit passes to the called unit the address of the actual parameter (which is in the calling unit's environment). A reference to the corresponding formal parameter in the called unit is treated as a reference to the location whose address is so passed. A variable that is transmitted as an actual parameter is thus shared, that is, directly modifiable by the subprogram. If an actual parameter is anything other than a variable, for example, an expression or a constant, the subprogram receives the address within the calling unit's activation record of a temporary location that contains the value of the actual parameter. Some languages treat this situation as an error.

3.7.1.2   Call by Copy

In call by copy—unlike in call by reference—formal parameters do not share storage with actual parameters; rather, they act as local variables. Thus, call by copy protects the calling unit from inadvertent modifications of actual parameters. It is possible further to classify call by copy into three modes, according to the way local variables corresponding to formal parameters are initialized and the way their values ultimately affect the actual parameters. These three modes are call by value, by result, and by value-result.

In *call by value*, the calling unit evaluates the actual parameters, and these values are used to initialize the formal parameters, which act as local variables in the called unit. Call by value does not allow any flow of information back to the caller, as assignments to formal parameters do not affect the calling unit.

In *call by result*, local variables corresponding to formal parameters are not set at subprogram call, but their value, at termination, is copied back into the actual parameter's location within the environment of the caller. Call by result does not permit any flow of information to the called unit.

In *call by value-result*, local variables denoting formal parameters are both initialized at subprogram call (as in call by value) and delivered upon termination (as in call by result).

Call by value-result and call by reference can have different effects; this counterintuitive result will be discussed in Chapter 5. Also, note that call by result or by value-result requires that we modify the semantics of the SIM-PLESEM return statement so that it is preceded by an assignment to actual parameters. Further insights into call by copy can be found in Exercise 3.22.

3.7.1.3   Call by Name·

As in call by reference, a formal parameter, rather than being a local variable of the subprogram, denotes a location in the environment of the caller. Unlike with call by reference, however, the formal parameter is not bound to a location at the point of call; it is bound to a (possibly different) location each time it is used within the subprogram. Consequently, each assignment to a formal parameter can refer to a different location. Basically, in call by name each occurrence of the formal parameter is replaced textually by the actual parameter. This apparently simple rule can lead to unsuspected complications. For example, the following procedure, which is intended to interchange the values of a and b (a and b are by-name parameters)

```
procedure swap (a,b: integer);
var temp: integer;
begin temp:= a;
      a:= b;
      b:= temp
end swap;
```

can produce unexpected and incorrect results when invoked by the call

```
swap (i,a[i])
```

The replacement rule specifies that the statements to be executed are

```
temp:= i;
i:= a[i];
a[i]:= temp
```

If $i = 3$ and $a[3] = 4$ before the call, $i = 4$ and $a[4] = 3$ after the call ($a[3]$ is unaffected)!

Another trap is that the actual parameter that is (conceptually) substituted into the text of the called unit belongs to the referencing environment of the caller, not to that of the called unit activation. For example, suppose that procedure *swap* also counts the number of times it is called and it is embedded in the following fragment.

```
procedure x . . .
var c: integer;
. . . . .
    procedure swap (a, b: integer);
    var temp: integer;
    begin temp:= a; a:= b;
          b:= temp; c:= c + 1
    end swap

    procedure y . . .
    var c, d: integer;
        . . . . . .
        swap (c, d);
        . . . . . .
    end y;

end x;
```

When procedure *swap* is called by procedure *y*, the replacement rule specifies that the statements to be executed are

```
temp:= c; c:= d;
d:= temp; c:= c + 1
```

However, the location bound to name *c* in the last statement belongs to procedure *x*'s activation record, whereas the location bound to the previous occurrences of *c* belong to *y*'s activation record. Notice that the problem is not the identification of the actual parameter—that can be done easily at translation time. The problem is the difficulty encountered by the programmer in foreseeing the run-time binding of actual and formal parameters.

Call by name, therefore, can easily lead to programs that are hard to read. It is also hard to implement. The basic implementation technique consists of replacing each reference to a formal parameter with a call to a subprogram (traditionally called *thunk*) that evaluates a reference to the actual parameter in the appropriate environment. One such thunk is created for each actual parameter. Obviously, the burden of run-time calls to thunks makes call by name costly.

Call by reference is the standard parameter passing mode of FORTRAN. Call by name is standard in ALGOL 60, but, optionally, the programmer can specifiy call by value. SIMULA 67 provides call by value, call by reference, and call by name.

Pascal allows the programmer to pass parameters either by value or by reference. For example, the heading of the procedure.

procedure x (y: integer; **var** z: newtype)

specifies that y is passed by value, whereas z (of type *newtype*) is passed by reference (indicated by the keyword **var**).

3.7.2 Subprogram Parameters

Many languages allow procedures to be passed as parameters. This facility is useful in many practical situations. For example, a subprogram S that evaluates analytic properties of functions of a single variable in a given interval a..b can be written without knowledge of the function and can be used for different functions, if the values of the function are produced by a subprogram that is sent to S as a parameter. As another example, if the language does not provide explicit features for exception handling (see Chapter 5), one can transmit the exception handler as a subprogram parameter to the unit that may raise the exception.

Subprogram parameters behave very differently in statically scoped and dynamically scoped languages because of the different ways that these languages determine the referencing environment for a unit. In Section 3.7.2.1 we will consider languages with static scope rules—the ALGOL family. In Section 3.7.2.2 we will consider dynamically scoped languages.

3.7.2.1 Procedure Parameters in Statically Scoped Languages

In this section, we will discuss the semantic requirements of procedure parameters in statically scoped languages such as Pascal, C, and FORTRAN, all of which support this feature. Consider the program in Figure 3.10. In this program, b is called in procedure *main* (line 14) with actual parameter a; inside b, the formal parameter x is called (line 11), which in this case corresponds to a. When a is called, it should execute normally just as if it had been called directly, that is, there should be no observable differences in the behavior of a procedure called directly or through a formal parameter. In particular, the invocation of a must be able to access the nonlocal environment of a (in this case the variables u, and v in *main*. Note that these variables are not visible in b because they are masked by b's local variables with the same name). This introduces a slight difficulty because our current scheme does not work. As you recall (Section 3.6.2.4), the call to a procedure is translated to several instructions, one of which is intended to set up the static link for the called procedure. In the case of "call x" in b, this is impossible at translation time because we do not know what procedure x is, let alone its enclosing unit. This information, in general, will only be known at run-time. We can handle this situation by passing the needed static link at the point of call.

```
1  procedure main . . .
2  var u,v: integer;
3      procedure a . . .
4      var y: integer;
        . . . .
5      end a;
6      procedure b (procedure x);
7      var u,v,y: integer;
          procedure c . . . .
            . . . . . .
9              y: = . . . . .;

10         end c;
11         x;
12         b(c);
           . . . . .
13     end b;
           . . . . . . . . . . . .
14     b(a);
           . . . . .
15 end main;
```

FIGURE 3.10 Program with procedure parameters

How do we know this static link to pass? From the scope rules, we know that in order for a unit (in this case, *main*) to pass procedure *a* to procedure *b*, *main* must either:

(a) Have procedure *a* within its scope, that is, *a* must be nonlocally visible or local (immediately nested); or

(b) *a* must be a formal parameter in *main*, that is, some actual procedure was passed to *main* as a procedure parameter.

The two cases can be handled in the following way:

Case (a): The static link to be passed is a pointer to the activation record that is *d* steps along the static chain originated in the calling unit, where $d = level \ (main) - level(a) + 1$; this is the same as function *fp* of Section 3.6.2.4.1.

Case (b): The static link to be passed is the one that was passed to *main* for *a*.

We leave the task of formulating these rules in terms of SIMPLESEM as an exercise for the reader.

What about *calling* a procedure parameter? The only difference from calling a procedure directly is in the way the static link must be set. The value of the static link is simply copied from the parameter area.

The program in Figure 3.10 shows another subtle point: that when procedure parameters are used in a program, nonlocal variables visible at a given piont are not necessarily those of the latest allocated activation record of the unit where such variables are locally declared. For example, after the recursive call to b when c is passed (line 12), the call to x in b (line 11) will invoke c recursively. Then the assignment to y in c (line 9) will not modify the y in the latest activation record for b but in the one allocated prior to the latest one. Figure 3.11 shows this point.

Let us review the impact of procedure parameters. First, our semantic description is more complicated because the basic mechanism now has been extended. Procedure calls, in particular, have become considerably more complicated because they have to deal with different cases of objects. Both the procedure call's semantic description and its implementation have increased in complexity. Contrast this with, say, adding a new arithmetic operator to a language that requires hardly any changes to our semantic description at all. We can say that the ability to pass procedures as parameters adds to the semantic power (and complexity) of a language.

3.7.2.2 Procedure Parameters in Dynamically Scoped Languages

Procedure parameters sometimes cause a peculiar problem in languages with dynamic scope rules, such as LISP. If we consider the program in Figure 3.10 under dynamic scope rules, when procedure a is called through x, references to u and v in a will be bound to the u and v in b and not to those in *main*. This is certainly difficult to use and confusing since when the procedure a was written, it was quite reasonable to expect access to u and v in *main* but because b happens to contain variables with the same names, they mask out the variables that were probably intended to be used.

Simply stated, the problem is that the nonlocal environment, and therefore the behavior of the procedure, is dependent on the dynamic sequence of calls that have been made before it. Consider several programmers working on different parts of the same program. A seemingly innocuous decision, what to name a variable, can change the behavior of the program entirely. Because LISP is a dynamically scoped language, it exhibits this problem.

The problem, however, was discovered very early in the development of LISP and a solution to it was devised. The solution is to precede a function definition with the word FUNCTION before passing it as a parameter. Procedures passed this way are passed along with their nonlocal environment at the point of call, that is, they follow static scoping.

Of course, a different solution to the problem would have been to adopt static scope rules for the entire language. Indeed, several dialects of LISP have been devised recently that follow static scoping. The Common LISP language that is emerging as the LISP standard has adopted static scoping, but allows dynamic scoping if desired by the programmer.

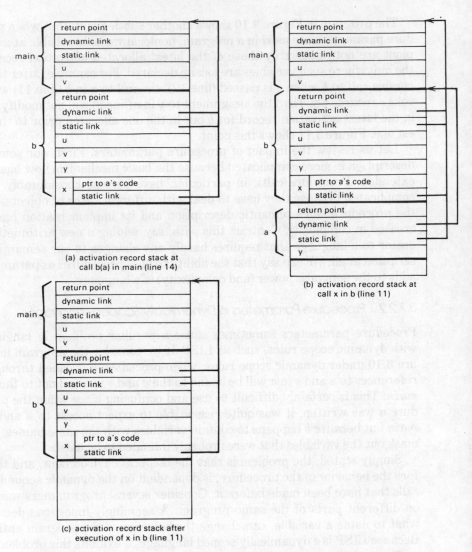

FIGURE 3.11 Activation record stack (in data memory) at various points in the execution of program in Figure 3.10.

3.8   OFFICIAL LANGUAGE DEFINITIONS

We started this chapter by discussing precise methods for defining languages. We then discussed the many different semantic properties of languages and attempted to give precise definitions for them. We now turn our attention to a more practical matter as far as language definitions are concerned, namely, what happens in practice and how is a language definition

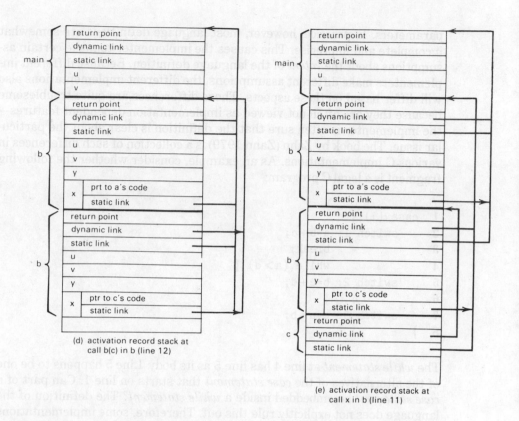

(d) activation record stack at
call b(c) in b (line 12)

(e) activation record stack at
call x in b (line 11)

FIGURE 3.11 cont.

related to a language implementation. In other words, how does a language definition help you use the language on a particular machine/compiler.

First, *a language definition defines the requirements that every implementation must satisfy.* A language definition also specifies a number of issues that must be determined by the implementation. For example, the definition of Pascal states that every implementation must support a type called *integer*, but it does not state what the maximum value for integers should be; it is left to the implementation to define this value. Thus, if you know a language, you should be able to use its different implementations. You may sometimes need to refer to a particular implementation manual to learn some implementation-dependent facts. But, in general, implementation issues such as whether activation records are allocated from a heap or a stack are irrelevant to the user because they do not affect the semantics of the language.

Ideally, to use a language, you would only need to study the language definition and consult the implementation manual for implementation-defined parameters. In practice, however, most language definitions are somewhat incomplete and imprecise. This causes the implementer to make certain assumptions about the *intent* of the language definition. Because different implementers make different assumptions, the different implementations also will differ based on these aspects. These differences are quite troublesome because they are often not viewed as implementation-dependent features— the implementer is often sure that the definition is clear about the particular issue. The book by Zahn (Zahn 1979) is a collection of such differences in various C implementations. As an example, consider whether the following fragment is a legal C program:

```
1    case (i) {
2        switch 1: a=b+c;
3                  break;
4                  while (a>d) {
5        switch 2: b=c+d;
6                  }
7        switch 3: c=a+b;
8    }
```

The *while statement* at line 4 has line 5 as its body. Line 5 happens to be one of the alternatives of the *case statement* that starts on line 1. Can part of a *case statement* be embedded inside a *while statement*? The definition of the language does not explicitly rule this out. Therefore, some implementations allow it and others do not because they just assume it is illegal.

The problem with differences in implementations of the same language is that they inhibit program portability. The only way to avoid this problem is to have precise language definitions and ensure that all implementations are faithful to the definition. This is often not practical, however, if we consider the reality of how a language definition comes into existence. Usually, the designer(s) publishes the definition or makes an implementation available. Once the language achieves widespread use and enough of a following, it becomes a candidate for standardization.

There are several organizations whose charter it is to produce standards. A language definition is such a standard. For example, the American National Standards Institute (ANSI) has produced standards for various areas of information processing, such as data communication and magnetic tape labels, and standards for FORTRAN (FORTRAN 1966 and FORTRAN 1977), COBOL (COBOL 1974), BASIC (BASIC 1978), and Ada (ADA 1983). There are current efforts at producing standards for Pascal and C. Other organizations that produce language standards are ISO and IEEE.

In the past, a language standard was produced after the language had existed for some time and the negative consequences of the lack of a standard became severe. Most recently, to avoid those problems completely, an Ada standard was produced before the language had been subjected to much use.

There are both advantages and disadvantages to early standardization. For example, by the time a committee was formed to produce the ISO standard for Pascal, a number of the problems in original Pascal had become well-known through actual use of the language. This knowledge enabled the committee to produce a standard that was free of these problems. Had the standard been done earlier, these problems would probably have become part of the standard and every implementer would have had to implement them. Because standards are slow—sometimes even impossible—to change, these problems would have become permanent features of the language. On the other hand, the disadvantage of producing a standard for a language that has been in use for many years is that by the time the standard is developed, many implementations of the language exist and these implementations each extend and interpret the language rules in their own way. It is almost impossible (and even unwise) to have a standard that will cover all these implementations. Therefore, the main goal of a standard—having compatible implementations on different machines—may be impossible to achieve!

The Ada language evolution has followed a course very different from other languages. Ada was defined and standardized before any real implementations existed and certainly before the language had received extensive use. The goal of the Ada group was to ensure that all implementations would have a chance to conform to the standard and the usual implementation differences would not exist for Ada. They tried to discover most of the language problems—which are usually found through use of the language—by extensive and widespread reviews of the language. Also, a validation center has been established whose charter it is to certify that compilers that claim to compile Ada do indeed meet that claim. It remains to be seen whether or how well they succeed. Clearly, if it is possible to detect most of a language's problems without using the language, it is best to standardize the language as soon as possible.

The inevitability of language standardization has touched even the LISP language which is known for its many different implementations. There have been essentially two main branches of LISP—MACLISP and INTERLISP—each having spawned many subdialects of its own. In 1981, representatives from the various MACLISP factions met and decided to define a language, called Common LISP, containing all the best known features of LISP. The INTERLISP community subsequently joined this effort. All the LISP variants are expected to work towards this common language. Each is free, however, to make extensions to Common LISP.

Standard language definitions are written very carefully and precisely. However, the use of natural language in the defining document introduces the possibility of inconsistencies and ambiguities that are difficult to detect regardless of the amount of care and precision. In Chapter 9, we will discuss the role that formal definitions of languages can play in alleviating this problem.

SUGGESTIONS FOR FURTHER READING AND BIBLIOGRAPHIC NOTES

We have studied programming language semantics in this chapter rather informally by describing the behavior of a processor. Formal approaches to the definition of semantics are introduced in Chapter 9. Our view here is oriented towards language implementation. We have emphasized the important concepts of binding and binding time. This viewpoint also is taken by other textbooks on programming languages, such as (Pratt 1984). Additional details on language implementation as well as on syntax and parsing can be found in compiler textbooks such as (Gries 1971), (Barrett and Couch 1979), (Waite and Goos 1984), and (Aho et al. 1985). Johnston (Johnston 1971) presents another operational model (called Contour Model) for describing programming language semantics.

The results of the experiments reported in (Gannon and Horning 1975) and (Gannon 1977) support the assertion that languages that statically bind a type to variables lead to more reliable programs.

EXERCISES

3.1 In section 3.1.1.1 we gave a very simple grammar for English sentences.

(a) Suppose you wish to introduce a new start symbol < paragraph > that will allow you to generate any number of sentences. How would you modify the grammar?

(b) Suppose you wish to be able to generate sentences with all possible pronouns as subjects (e.g., you, he, she, it, they). What problems do you encounter? How can you solve these problems?

3.2 A simple way to write a parser for a context-free language is to write a procedure for each syntax rule. Thus, to recognize an expression, we can call the procedure *expression*. In writing the procedure, if we expect a terminal, we read the input and look for that terminal; if we expect a nonterminal, we call the procedure for that nonterminal. Write a parser, in Pascal or C, for arithmetic expressions based on the grammar in Section 3.1.1.1. Assume identifiers are of length 1. They may be any lower or uppercase letter.

3.3 Write a program, based on the grammar of Section 3.1.1.1, to *generate* arithmetic expressions (see previous exercise).

3.4 A program unit is history-sensitive if it can produce different results when activated twice with the same values of parameters and accessible nonlocal variables. Explain why a language with static allocation scheme can be history-sensitive.

3.5 Explain how you could write a history-sensitive FORTRAN subprogram (see previous exercise). Is this behavior approved by the standard (ANSI 1978)? Devise an experiment to check whether your FORTRAN implementation allows you to write history-sensitive subprograms.

3.6 Consider the following ALGOL-like program:

```
program A;
    procedure B;
        procedure C;
            .
            .
            call B;
            .
            .
        end C;
        .
        .
        call C;
    end B;
    procedure D;
        .
        .
        call B;
    end D;
    .
    .
    call D;
end A;
```

Describe each stage in the life of the stack until *B* is called within procedure *C*. In particular, show the dynamic and static links before and after every call.

3.7 Explain why the static and dynamic links have the same value for ALGOL-like blocks.

3.8 Nonlocal referencing for a language with dynamic scope rules can be implemented via a table that keeps track of the referencable nonlocal variables (Section 3.6.3). Detail the actions that must be executed at subprogram entry and exit in order to keep this table up-to-date.

3.9 "Early binding supports efficient implementation and favors reliable programming; late binding provides flexibility." Give examples that support this statement. Give counterexamples.

3.10 Explain why APL requires more run-time support than ALGOL-like languages and why ALGOL-like languages require more run-time support than FORTRAN. Is this phenomenon a function of the compiler/interpreter, or is it inherent in the language? Draw some conclusions about the comparative run-time efficiency of these languages. How about space efficiency? Programming efficiency?

3.11 In ALGOL 60, a variable may be declared to be **own**. An **own** variable is allocated storage the first time that its enclosing unit is activated, and its storage remains allocated until program termination. Normal scope rules apply, so that the variable is known only within the unit in which it is declared. In essence, the effect of the **own** declaration is to extend the lifetime of the variable to cover the entire program execution.

(a) **own** variables are *not* automatically initialized to certain default values. This, in practice, turns out to limit their usefulness greatly. To appreciate this weakness, write a function that keeps track of the number of times it has been called. This value is kept in an **own** variable and returned each time the function is called.

(b) Outline an implementation model for **own** variables. For simplicity, assume that **own** variables can only have simple (unstructured) type.

3.12 Design an interpreter for a mini-language (a language consisting of five types of statements or less).

3.13 Design a translator for a mini-language.

3.14 Write a Pascal procedure called x in which it is not possible to call x.
(Hint: take advantage of scope rules to make the procedure invisible).

3.15 Describe the SIMPLESEM semantics of two-dimensional semidynamic variables.

3.16 In various sections of this chapter, we have given SIMPLESEM semantics for procedure calls under different assumptions (e.g., no nesting, no parameters, no procedure parameters, and so on) Combine all these rules into one definition that covers all the cases.

3.17 Discuss the difficulties in a language that adopts static typing and dynamic scoping.

3.18 Give SIMPLESEM semantics for APL procedure call and return. Pay special attention to maintaining the nonlocal environment.

3.19 Manually execute the following ALGOL-like program by assuming (**a**) call by reference, (**b**) call by value, (**c**) call by result, (**d**) call by value-result, (**e**) call by name. Show the results produced by each call in array a and variable i.
Assume that integer variables are automatically initialized to zero.

```
program parameter_passing;
   var i: integer;
       a: array [1..3] of integer;
   procedure mess (v: integer);
      begin v:= v+1;
            a[i]:= 5;
            i:= 3;
            v:= v+1
```

```
    end mess;
    for i:= 1 to 3 do a [i]:= 0;
    a [2]:= 10;
    i:= 2;
    call mess (a[i])
end parameter_passing
```

3.20 The following subprogram is supposed to interchange the contents of two integer variables.

```
subprogram swap (a,b: integer),
var temp: integer;
begin temp:= a; a:= b; b:= temp
end swap
```

If a and b are parameters called by name, swap may not be commutative (i.e., the effect of swap (c,d) can be different from that of swap (d,c)). Prove this fact by examining the effect of swap $(i,a[i])$, where a is an integer array.

What happens if a and/or b are passed by value? By value-result?

3.21 An implementation technique for referencing the nonlocal environment in ALGOL-like languages—instead of the static links that we used—is based on the use of a *display*. The display is an array of variable length that contains, at any point during program execution, pointers to the activation records of the units that form the referencing environment—that is, exactly those pointers that would be in the static chain. Let an identifier be represented as a pair (d,o) where d is the number of steps along the static chain and o is the offset. The display is set up such that *display* $[d]$ yields the address of the activation record which contains the identifier (d,o).

  (a) Show (pictorially) the equivalent of Fig. 3.11 when displays are used instead of static links. Assume that, like *free* and *current*, the display is kept outside the data memory.

  (b) Show the SIMPLESEM actions that are needed to update the display when a procedure is called and when a procedure returns. Pay special attention to procedure parameters. How are variables accessed?

  (c) Displays and static chains are two implementation alternatives for the same concept. Discuss the relative advantages and disadvantages of each solution.

3.22 Our definition of call by copy contains one ambiguous point, because it is not clear when the addresses of parameters passed by result should be evaluated. The effect can be different if the address is evaluated at the call point or at the return point, as Tai (Tai 1982) points out. In the same paper, the author proposes to use the term call by copy (or copy-out if there are not value parameters) in the former case and call by value-result (or call by result) in the latter. Give a sample program supporting Tai's argument.

Data Types

Computer programs can be viewed as functions that are applied to certain input to produce certain desired results. In conventional programming languages, this function is evaluated through a sequence of steps that produce intermediate data that are stored in program variables. Languages differ in the kinds of data they use, the available kinds of operations on data, and the way data can be structured and used.

Programming languages usually provide a fixed, built-in set of elementary data types, and mechanisms for structuring more complex data types, starting from the elementary ones. We will concentrate on languages that establish a static binding between a variable and its type. In particular, we will review and discuss the data type features provided by ALGOL 68, Pascal, SIMULA 67, CLU, Modula-2, and Ada. We also will look briefly at the dynamic type features of Smalltalk.

This chapter is organized as follows. Section 4.1 discusses built-in types. Section 4.2 classifies the basic mechanisms provided by programming languages to combine elementary data into complex data structures. Section 4.3 discusses how such mechanisms can be used to define new data types in ALGOL 68, Pascal, and Ada. Section 4.4 presents an assessment and evaluation of several interesting type issues. Section 4.5 presents language features for defining abstract data types, with emphasis on SIMULA 67, CLU, Modula-2, and Smalltalk. Section 4.6 discusses implementation models.

4.1 BUILT-IN TYPES

Programming languages provide a fixed set of built-in types that, as mentioned in Sections 2.1 and 2.2, in most cases reflect the behavior of the underlying hardware. At the programming-language level, built-in types identify the abstract behavior of a set of data objects with a common set of operations. For example, the integer data type denotes a set of data objects that can be manipulated by the well-known operators $+, -, *$, and $/$. The translator for the programming language maps this abstract view into a concrete implementation. For example, the implementation maps the abstract object "25" into a certain bit string, such as, 00011001 in two's-complement representation. Similarly, the addition of two integers is mapped into the machine's fixed-point addition operation.

Based on some of the points already raised in Sections 2.2 and 2.4, we can say that built-in types introduce four useful properties. The first of these properties holds for both static and dynamically typed languages, and the other three hold only for statically typed languages.

1. *Invisibility of the underlying representation.* The programmer does not have access to the underlying bit string that represents a value of a certain type. Such a bit string may be changed as a result of the application of operations, but the change is visible to the programmer as a new value of the built-in type, not as a new bit string. Invisibility of the underlying representation has the following two benefits.

- **Programming style.** The abstraction provided by the language increases program readability by protecting the representation of the objects from undisciplined manipulation. This contrasts with the underlying conventional hardware, which does not enforce protection. Any object is viewed as an uninterpreted bit string that can be manipulated by any machine instruction. For example, a location containing an instruction can be added to a location containing a string of characters or even another instruction.

- **Modifiability.** The implementation of abstractions can be changed without affecting the programs that make use of the abstractions. Consequently, *portability* of programs also is improved, that is, programs can be moved to machines that use different internal data representations.

Programming languages provide instructions to read and write values of built-in types. Most languages also provide features for formatting the output. Machines perform input/output by interacting with peripheral devices in a complicated and machine-dependent way. High-level languages hide these complications and the physical resources involved in machine input/output (registers, channels, and so on). We will ignore these issues in this text.

2. *Correct use of variables can be checked at translation time.* If the language requires the declaration of variables, then illegal operations on a variable can be caught by the translator, that is, protection of variables can be enforced at translation time.

We already have mentioned, however, that static type-checking does not exhaust all the checks that can be done on a program. For example, the expression i/j might be statically checked as correct (e.g., i and j are both *real*) and yet might require a run-time check if a division by zero is to be trapped. Another example is given in point 4.

3. *Disambiguation of operators can be done at translation time.* There are languages in which a few operator symbols can be used to represent a large number of operators. For example, the symbol "+" can represent both addition of reals and addition of integers. In a statically typed language (Section 3.4), the machine operation to be invoked for executing $A + B$ can be chosen by the translator, because the types of the operands are known. This makes the implementation more efficient than in a dynamically typed language such as APL, in which it is necessary to keep track of types in run-time descriptors. An operator whose meaning depends on the types of its operands is called *overloaded, polymorphic,* or *generic.* The "+" operator is overloaded because it is defined for both integers and reals (and implemented by different machine instructions on the underlying representation). A judicious use of overloading can contribute to the simplicity and usability of a programming language. For example, having two different symbols for integer and real addition would make programming more tedious. However, excessive use of overloading can generate programs that are hard to understand, because a unique name denotes completely different entities.

4. *Accuracy control.* In some cases, the programmer can explicitly associate a specification of the relative accuracy of the representation with the type. For example, FORTRAN allows the user to choose between single and double-precision floating-point numbers. ALGOL 68 allows one to specify the required (relative) precision by declarations such as **long real**, **long long real** (for floating-point values) and **long int**, **long long int**, (for fixed-point values). The number of **long** (or **short**) prefixes supported is determined by the implementation and is available in constants *int lengths, int shorts, real lengths,* and *real shorts.* Accuracy of numeric data types also can be controlled in Ada. Accuracy specification can be viewed both as a space optimization directive to the translator and as a request to the translator to insert run-time checks to monitor the values of variables. The latter provides an effective aid for the programmer in assessing the correctness of programs. Finally, programs with accuracy specifications are more easily adaptable to different installations with different memory word lengths, because source program changes are localized to declarations.

4.2 DATA AGGREGATES

Programming languages allow the programmer to specify aggregations of elementary data objects and, in turn, aggregations of aggregates. A well-known example is the array constructor, which constructs aggregates of homogenous-type elements. An aggregate object has a unique name. Manipulation can be done on a single elementary component at a time, each component being accessed by a suitable *selection* operation. In many languages, it is also possible to assign and compare entire aggregates. Sections 4.2.1 through 4.2.6 classify the basic structuring mechanisms provided by programming languages.

4.2.1 Cartesian Product

The Cartesian product of n sets A_1, A_2, A_n, denoted by $A_1 \times A_2 \times \ldots A_n$, is a set whose elements are ordered n-tuples $(a_1, a_2, \ldots, a_n)$, where each a_i belongs to A_i. For example, regular polygons might be characterized by an integer—the number of edges—and a real—the length of an edge. Any polygon thus would be an element in the Cartesian product

```
integer × real
```

Examples of Cartesian products in programming languages are *records* in COBOL and Pascal, and *structures* in PL/I and ALGOL 68.

Programming languages view Cartesian product data objects as composed of a number of symbolically named fields. In the previous example, variables of type *polygon* could be declared as composed of an integer field (*no_of_edges*) holding the number of edges and a real field (*edge_size*) holding the length of each edge. The fields of Cartesian products are selected by specifying, in an appropriate syntactic notation, the *selectors* (or *field names*) *no_of_edges* and *edge_size*. For example, using Pascal syntax, to make the polygon *t1* an equilateral triangle of edge 7.53, one should write

```
t1.no_of_edges:= 3;
t1.edge_size:= 7.53
```

In ALGOL 68 and Ada, this could be done in one statement.

```
t1:= (3,7.53)
```

4.2.2 Finite Mapping

A finite mapping is a function from a finite set of values of a domain type DT onto values of a range type RT. Programming languages possess an *array* constructor that allows one to define finite mappings. The Pascal declaration

var a: **array** [1..50] **of** char

can be viewed as a mapping from integers in the subrange 1 to 50 to the set of characters.

An object of the range can be selected by *indexing*, that is, by providing as an index an appropriate value in the domain. Thus, the Pascal notation a[k] can be viewed as an application of the above mapping to the argument k. Indexing with a value not in the domain results in an error that usually only can be caught at run-time.

In some languages, such as APL, ALGOL 68, and Ada, indexing can be used to select more than one element of the range. For example, in Ada, a [3..20] specifies a one-dimensional subarray of a containing 18 elements. This operation is sometimes called *slicing*, that is, it selects a *slice* of the array.

SNOBOL4 provides two interesting examples of finite mappings. The ARRAY construct does not require that the elements of the range set be all of the same type. For example, one element of the array may be an integer, another a real, and yet a third a string. In other words, the range set is the *union* of all the SNOBOL4 types. The SNOBOL4 TABLE construct extends this notion to the index type as well, that is, it provides a finite mapping from the domain set that is a union of all SNOBOL4 types to the range set that is a union of all SNOBOL4 types. For example, the following statements create a TABLE and assign values to some of its elements:

```
T = TABLE ( )
T< 'RED' > = 'WAR'
T<6> = 25
T<4.6> = 'PEACE'
```

The TABLE construct is quite powerful because it provides the capability of associative retrieval.

The strategy for binding the domain of the function to a specific subset of values of type *DT* varies according to the language. Basically, there are three possible choices.

1. *Compile-time binding.* The subset is fixed when the program is written and frozen at translation time. This restriction was adopted by FOR-TRAN, C, and Pascal. It supports static and semistatic variables.

2. *Object creation-time binding.* The subset is fixed at run-time, when an instance of the variable is created. This choice (*dynamic arrays*) initially was used by ALGOL 60 and has been adopted by SIMULA 67 and Ada. Following the terminology introduced in Chapter 3, such array variables are called semidynamic.

3. *Object manipulation-time binding.* This is the most flexible and the most costly choice in terms of run-time execution. For these so-called *flexible arrays*, the size of the subset can be changed at any time during the object's lifetime. This is typical of dynamic languages such as SNOBOL4 and

APL. Of compiled languages, ALGOL 68 was the first to allow it in the form of **flex** arrays, followed by CLU. According to the terminology introduced in Chapter 3, such array variables are called dynamic.

4.2.3 Sequencing

A sequence consists of any number of occurrences of data items of a certain component type CT. This structuring mechanism has the important property of leaving unspecified the number of occurrences of the component; therefore, it requires the underlying implementation to be able to store objects of arbitrary size (at least in principle).

Strings provide a well-known example of sequences in which the component type is character. The concept of sequence also captures the familiar data-processing idea of a sequential *file*.

It is difficult to abstract a common behavior from the examples of sequences provided by existing programming languages. For example, SNO-BOL4 views strings as data objects with a rich set of operations. Conversely, Pascal and C view strings simply as arrays of characters, with no special primitives for string manipulation. Taking somewhat of a middle ground, PL/I and Ada provide string manipulation primitives but, to reduce the problem of dynamic storage allocation, require that the maximum size of a string be specified in the declaration of the string. Files present more serious problems in that they often have peculiar, system-dependent aspects as a result of the necessary interface with the operating system.

Conventional operators on strings include the following.

1. *Concatenation.* The concatenation of *THIS_IS_* and *AN_EXAMPLE* gives *THIS_IS_AN_EXAMPLE*.
2. *Selection of the first (last) component.* Selection of the last component of the above string yields *E*.
3. *Substring.* A substring can be extracted from a given string by specifying the positions of the first and last desired characters.

Simple primitives are usually provided for files. For example, a Pascal file only can be modified by appending a new value to the end of an existing file. Reading is possible only by sequential scanning.

4.2.4 Recursion

A recursive data type T can contain components that belong to the same type T. To define a recursive type, one can use the type name in the type's definition. For example, type *binary_tree* can be defined as either empty or a triple composed of an atomic element, a (left) *binary_tree* and a (right) *binary_tree*.

Recursion is a structuring mechanism that can be used to define aggregates whose size can grow arbitrarily and whose structure can have arbitrary complexity. As opposed to sequencing, it allows the programmer to create arbitrary access paths for the selection of components.

Pointers are the most common mechanism provided by programming languages for building recursive data objects. Each component of the recursive type is represented by a location containing a pointer to the data object, rather than the data object itself. This indirection is because data objects may be an arbitrary size. For example, each node of a binary tree has two associated locations: one containing a pointer to the left subtree (if any) and the other containing a pointer to the right subtree (if any). (We ignore other information being kept at each node.) The tree itself is identified by another location containing a pointer to the root node of the tree. Starting from this location, it is possible to access each node by following a suitable chain of pointers. A null pointer corresponds to an empty (sub)tree. Sections 4.3.1.2.3, 4.3.2.3, and 4.3.3.3 illustrate how binary trees can be defined in ALGOL 68, Pascal and Ada, respectively. LISP's list type is an example of a recursive type that does not use pointers.

4.2.5 Discriminated Union

The discriminated union is a structuring mechanism that specifies that a choice should be made between different, alternative structures. Each alternative structure is called a *variant*.

COBOL supports discriminated unions with its REDEFINES clause. This construct supports the common data-processing situation in which the structures of some stored records are identical for the most part, differing only for some fields. In a payroll program, a field may refer either to the employee's monthly salary or the hourly pay, depending on how he or she is paid. In the following example, SALARY and HOUR_RATE refer to the same record-field, but each has a different PICTURE (which, in COBOL, is analogous to the concept of type).

```
01 EMPLOYEE_RECORD.
    05 NAME                          PIC X(20).
    05 SALARY                        PIC 9999.
    05 HOUR_RATE REDEFINES SALARY    PIC 99V99.
```

Most modern programming languages allow the programmer to define—to a more-or-less general degree—the type of a variable as a discriminated union. Two examples are the *union* of ALGOL 68 and C, and the *variant record* of Pascal and Ada.

4.2.6 Powerset

It is often useful to define variables whose value can be any subset of a set of elements of a certain type T. The type of such variables is *powerset* (T), the set of all subsets of elements of type T. Type T is called the *base type*. For example, suppose a language processor accepts the following set O of options.

LIST_S: produce listing of source program.
LIST_O: produce listing of object program.
OPTIMIZE: optimize object code.
SAVE_S: save source program on backup storage.
SAVE_O: save object code on backup storage.
EXEC: execute object code.

A command to the processor can be any subset of O, such as

{LIST_S,LIST_O}
{LIST_S, EXEC}
{OPTIMIZE,SAVE_O,EXEC}

The type of command is *powerset (O)*.

Variables of type *powerset* (T) represent sets. The operations permitted on such variables are set operations such as union and intersection. It is also possible to test whether a given object of type T is in the set. Pascal's use of this concept is shown in Section 4.3.2.2.3. In the absence of a language-supported set type, programmers use arrays of booleans, linked lists, or other means for representing powersets.

4.3 USER-DEFINED TYPES

The constructors reviewed in the previous sections allow the programmer to define complex data objects as aggregates of elementary items. An example of a structured variable declaration in Pascal is

```
var a: record x: integer;
             y: array [1..101] of char
         end
```

The type of variable a has no explicit name, but is described in terms of its representation (a Cartesian product, one of whose fields is a finite mapping).

Several modern programming languages, such as ALGOL 68, Pascal, and Ada, also provide a facility for defining a new type name. The programmer can define data types by renaming existing types or aggregating a number of elementary and/or user-defined types via some of the constructors discussed in Section 4.2. The notion of type is used in these languages in a limited framework just to capture a uniform mechanism to access the components of structured objects. A type declaration defines a prototype data structure (a *template*) that can be instantiated by declaring as many variables of that type as are necessary.

For example, in Pascal one can declare the following Cartesian product type.

```
type complex= record radius: real;
                      angle: real
            end
```

All variables of type *complex* are composed of two fields—*radius* and *angle*—for holding the absolute value and argument of a complex number. The declaration

```
var c1, c2, c3: complex
```

instantiates three *complex* variables named *c1*, *c2*, and *c3*.

The basic advantages of providing facilities to give explicit names to types are

1. *Readability.*   Appropriate choice of the new type names can improve the readability of programs. Used properly, the stepwise refinement process that leads to the definition of a class of data can be mirrored by the hierarchical structure of type definitions.

For example, after the previous declaration of *complex*, one could declare the following types.

```
voltage= complex;
voltage_table= array [1..10] of voltage
```

These declarations show quite explicitly that variables of type *voltage_table* can represent the values of *voltage* in a space of 10 points, a *voltage* being represented by a *complex* number.

2. *Modifiability.*   A change of the data structures that represent the variables of a given type requires a change only in the type declaration, not in the declarations of all the variables (i.e., it is localized to small portions of the program). However, it still may require a change to the instructions of the program that manipulate variables whose type is changed.

3. *Factorization.*   The definition of a complicated data structure prototype is written only once and then is used as many times as necessary to declare variables. This removes the need for repeating the same definition for each variable and reduces the possibility of clerical errors. The idea of factorization was only applied to procedures in early languages.

4. *Consistency checking.* The possibility of defining new types allows the programmer to extend the application of a simple, but effective validation tool such as type checking, from the limited class of built-in types to any class of user-defined types. The amount of type checking that can be done depends on the notion of type compatibility (or equivalence) specified by the language. The type-checking mechanism treats two compatible types as the same type. This topic will be discussed in Section 4.4.3.

Sections 4.3.1, 4.3.2, and 4.3.3 will review user-defined types as provided by ALGOL 68, Pascal, and Ada. More powerful mechanisms that allow the programmer to define abstract data types are discussed in Section 4.5.

4.3.1 The Type Structure of ALGOL 68

The type structure of ALGOL 68 is rich and elaborate. One of the design goals of the language, carried through and clearly visible in its type structure, is *orthogonality*. To achieve simplicity, the language provides a small number of independent primitive concepts; to achieve expressive power, it allows these concepts to be applied orthogonally (i.e., independently or in any combination).

ALGOL 68 uses a precise but unusual terminology. For the sake of uniformity, we will describe the language using the terms and concepts developed in Chapter 3. The reader should be aware that some of our terms (e.g., "name") may have a different meaning in the official ALGOL 68 terminology.

ALGOL 68 uses the term "mode" for "type." A variable declaration has the form

type *variable_name*

where **type** may be a user- or language-defined type. There are five primitive types (*plain modes*) and five ways of constructing new types. The language-defined types also include some nonprimitive types that have been defined by the language in terms of primitive types and the type construction facilities.

4.3.1.1 Primitive Types (Plain Modes)

Of the five primitive types, four are quite usual: **int, real, bool,** and **char.** Whole numbers are represented by **int,** rational numbers by **real.** Two implementation-defined constants, *max int* and *max real* give the largest (respectively) integer and real number representable. Booleans are represented by **bool,** which consists of the two values, **true** and **false.** Single characters are represented by **char.**

The fifth mode is **void**, whose only value is **empty**. The purpose of the mode **void** is to add consistency to the language. Every statement has a mode, including assignment statements and procedure-call statements. The mode of an assignment statement is the mode of the returned value; if the procedure does not return a value, the call has the mode **void**.

4.3.1.2 Nonprimitive Types (Nonplain Modes)

The language provides five ways to construct new modes from the plain modes. The new mode may be given a name or used in variable declarations without a name.

For example, if **X** stands for the definition of a new mode, we could give it the name **newmode** with the following definition:

mode newmode = **X**

and then use **newmode** to declare variables:

newmode *x, y, z*

Or we could say

X *x, y, z*

without giving the mode a name. Notice that when a new mode is defined, it becomes part of the language (for this program) and its name appears in boldface.

Presented below are the type construction mechanisms of ALGOL 68.

4.3.1.2.1 References. Two attributes of a variable are the value and the reference to the area of storage where the value is kept (Section 3.3). Most languages do not emphasize the distinction between these two concepts. For example, in the Pascal statement

x:= *x* + 2

assuming *x* has been declared as an *integer*, the right-hand side *x* stands for the value of the variable, and the left-hand side *x* stands for the reference to the storage area where the value is kept. In the declaration

var *x*: *integer*

integer qualifies the values that may be assigned to variable *x*. It is not quite right to say "the type of *x* is *integer*"; it is more correct to say "the type of values assigned to *x* is *integer*." In most languages, however, the two quoted phrases can be used interchangeably.

ALGOL 68 makes this distinction between value and reference to a data object quite explicit. A variable always stands for a reference to a data object. The effect of the following ALGOL 68 declaration

int x

is to declare x as a *reference* to data objects of type **int**, that is, the type of x is **ref int**.

For a statement

x:= x+2

ALGOL 68 states that the x on the right-hand side is *"dereferenced"* to yield the value needed for " + "; on the left-hand side, a reference to a data object is needed and no dereferencing takes place. Whether or not dereferencing is needed is determined from context.

Notice that the effect of the declaration or the assignment statement is the same as in Pascal. The difference is in ALGOL 68's clear definition of the difference between references and values, and the dereferencing operation.

The concept of a reference is used as a mechanism for defining new modes. Preceding a previously defined mode with the symbol **ref** results in a new mode. For example, the declaration

ref int ri

creates ri of mode **ref ref int**, that is, the value stored in the area referenced by ri is of mode **ref int**—a reference to an integer. In other words, ri is what other languages call a pointer. We can assign to ri names of mode **ref int**, such as x above:

ri:= x

Here, ri requires a value of mode **ref int**, which x is. Therefore, no dereferencing on x is necessary—ri will simply hold the reference to the data object bound to x.

The general rule for an assignment statement is that the mode of the left-hand side is used to determine whether dereferencing (or any other conversion) is necessary on the right-hand side. In fact, the left-hand side variable should be a **ref** to some mode **x**. If the right-hand side is not of the mode to which the left-hand side can refer (i.e., **x**), dereferencing is applied automatically until the assignment can be done.

Using a pointer such as ri, we can access both a **ref int** value and an **int** value (the value held by the object referenced by the **ref int** value). For example.

int x, y;
ref int ri;
x:= 2;
ri:= x;
y:= ri

will assign 2, the value of *x*, to *y*. In the last assignment, *y* requires a value of mode **int**; *ri* is dereferenced twice to get such a value; in this case, this value is the one most recently assigned to *x*.

The assignment

```
ri:= 1
```

is not valid because *ri* requires a value of mode **ref int** and 1 is of mode **int**. In general, the right-hand side must be of a mode with one less **ref** than the left-hand side, or must be dereferenceable to such a mode (which 1 is not).

We can assign a value to the object currently pointed to by *ri* by explicitly dereferencing *ri*. Explicit conversion is called *casting* in ALGOL 68.

The statement

```
(ref int) ri:= 1
```

causes the retrieving of a **ref int** object from *ri* and then the assigning of 1 to that object. In this case, casting *ri* to **ref int** will yield a reference to the same data object referenced by *x* as *ri:= x* is the most recent assignment to *ri*. The value of this object is changed to 1.

Casts also can be used on the right-hand side. For example

```
(ref int) ri:= (int) ri+1
```

adds 1 to the value of the object pointed to by *ri*. The cast on the right-hand side, however, is not required in this case, because the dereferencing would have been determined from context and applied automatically.

Because any mode may be preceded by **ref**, all the following modes (as well as others) are valid in ALGOL 68.

ref int
ref ref int
ref ref ref real

We can create as many levels of indirection as we like. This is an example of the orthogonality of design. There are no exceptions such "only one **ref** may precede a mode."

A problem associated with the use of pointers in most languages is the *dangling reference* problem. A dangling reference is a pointer (i.e., reference) that points to a storage area that has been deallocated. Such problems can occur if we allow pointers to refer to program variables. Program variables are deallocated upon exiting from the unit where they are locally declared; consequently, a pointer to them may remain dangling.

ALGOL 68 has a simple-looking rule that prevents the occurrence of dangling references: in an assignment to a reference variable, the scope of the value being assigned must be the same as, or enclose, the scope of the reference variable. The following program fragment shows some legal and illegal assignments.

begin ref int *ri*; **int** *i*;

    . . . .

    begin ref int *rx*; **int** *x*;

        . . . .

```
        rx:= x; ¢ legal   ¢
        rx:= i; ¢ legal   ¢
        ri:= i; ¢ legal   ¢
        ri:= x ¢ illegal ¢
```
    end

```
        ¢ at this point, rx and x have disappeared, no
        pointers to them should exist; ri and i, however,
        still exist ¢
```
    . . . .

   end

As discussed in Chapter 3, pointers in programming languages can be used to point to anonymous objects. In ALGOL 68, such objects may be created via *generators*. A generator creates a data object of a given mode and yields a reference to the data object. There are two kinds of generators: one creates stack variables (**loc**); the other, heap variables (**heap**).

The statement

```
ri:= heap int
```

creates an integer data object on the heap and assigns its address to *ri* (which should be a **ref int**).

The statement

```
ri:= loc int:= 2
```

creates a local variable (on the stack), assigns the value 2 to it, and makes *ri* (a **ref int**) point to it. As usual, this object will cease to exist upon exiting from the scope in which it is declared. It differs from program variables only in that it does not have an explicit name.

4.3.1.2.2 Multiples.

Multiple, the ALGOL 68 term for "array," can be used to create finite mappings. The domain of the finite mapping is a subrange of integers. The new modes are called rows. For example, "[] int" is the mode "row of integers" (a one-dimensional array). "[,]int" is a "row row of integers" (two-dimensional array), and so on. We also can have the mode "[][]int," which is the mode "row of row of integers." The difference between values of mode "row row of integers" and "row of row of integers" is that the former is a two-dimensional array, but the latter is a one-dimensional array, each of whose elements is itself a one-dimensional array.

We may have multiples of values of any mode. For example

[] ref [,] int

is a valid mode: row of references to row row of integers, or an array of pointers to two-dimensional arrays of integers.

Note that although the number of dimensions of an array is part of its type, the size of an array, that is, the number of elements in each dimension, is not. Any variable declared to be a multiple, however, must indicate this size—at least in terms of variables.

[m:n] int ri

declares the data object referenced by ri to be a semidynamic array with indexes in the range $m..n$. When this declaration is encountered at execution time, the array is allocated according to the current values of m and n; ri preserves this size until it disappears at exit from its scope.

On the other hand, arrays may be declared to be flexible, in which case their size may be changed when an assignment is made to them. These are an example of dynamic variables.

flex [1:0] int a

declares the data object referenced by a to be a row containing (initially) no integers.

```
a:= (2,3,49)
```

changes the bounds to [1:3] and assigns values to all its elements. The bounds may be changed only by assignment to the whole array.

The mode **string** is predefined by the language as a flexible array of characters.

mode string = flex [1:0] char

The actions allowed on strings, which are the same as for arrays, are subscripting, with which one element is retrieved, and trimming, with which a cross-section (or "slice") of the array is retrieved.

4.3.1.2.3 Structures. Rows allow the creation of a finite mapping, that is, a mode consisting of homogenous elements. A new mode also may be constructed from inhomogeneous elements by a Cartesian product. This can be done by the ALGOL 68 *structure*. A structure (or *structured value*) consists of a set of values, called *fields*, which may have different modes.

mode person= struct (string *name,* **int** *age*)

creates a new mode consisting of the two fields *name* and *age*. Having created variables of this mode, for example, we may assign values to them.

person *mom, dad;*
mom:= (*"helen"*, *35*);
dad:= (*"tom"*, *36*)

Individual fields also can be accessed for retrieval or assignment by using the selector **of**, as illustrated in the following example:

age **of** *dad:=* *age* **of** *dad+1*

Again, structures may be made of any modes.

struct (**ref ref** [,] **int** *one*, **flex** [1:0] **real** *two*, **int** *three*, **person** *four*)

is an allowable (although not obviously useful!) mode.

Recursive data structures can be created by combining references and structures. For example, the mode of nodes of a binary tree can be declared as

mode binary_tree_node= struct (**string** *info*, **ref binary_tree_node** *left, right*)

The predefined modes **compl**, **bits** and **bytes**, and **sema** have been defined using the following structures.

mode compl= struct (**real** *re, im*);
mode bits= struct ([1:*bits width*] **bool** *x*);
mode bytes= struct ([1:*bytes width*] **char** *x*);
mode sema= struct (**ref int** *x*)

The implementation-defined constants *bits width* and *bytes width*, respectively, indicate the number of bits and bytes in a machine word. The mode **sema** is the semaphore (see Section 5.2.4) and can be used for parallel programming. The operations **up** and **down** are defined for **sema**. The names of the fields of the **bits**, **bytes**, and **sema** structures are not available to the programmer, so, for example, one cannot use indexing with a **bits** value. Mode bits may be used to implement powersets, which are not directly supported by the language (see Exercise 4.17).

4.3.1.2.4 Unions. In a sharp departure from previous ALGOL-like languages, ALGOL 68 allows discriminated unions—in the form of *united modes*.

mode ib= union (**int**, **bool**)

defines the new mode **ib**, whose values may be *integers* or *booleans*. Notice that variable x declared as

ib x

at any moment holds a value of type **int** or **bool**, but the type of x is always **ref ib**.

Assignments to a variable x of type **ib** are like other assignments:

ib x,y;
y:= 5;
x:= y;
x:= **true**

Accessing the value of x, however, cannot be done so easily, because the type of the value must be established before the value can be used. The determination of the type is done with the use of a *conformity clause*. The conformity clause ensures that no type mismatch may occur at run-time, that is, the programmer is forced to anticipate all such events.

case x **in**
    (**int** x1):. . . .x1. . . .
    (**bool** x2):. . . .x2. . . .
esac

is an example of such a clause. Within each alternative of the **case** clause, the type of x is established and a new name is used to refer to x. More precisely, x1 and x2 are constants "initialized" with the value of x at entry to the conformity clause; their types are, respectively, *integer* and *boolean*, and therefore, type checking on the use of x1 and x2 can be done statically.

United modes may be derived from any other mode, including **void**:

union (**int**, **ref** [] **int**, **void**)

United modes often are used in procedures that may take parameters of different types. They present the introduction into a programming language of an important, but possibly dangerous, concept—discriminated union—in an elegant, systematic, and safe way.

4.3.1.2.5 Procedures. The final method of constructing new types in ALGOL 68 is through the use of procedures. The concept of mode in ALGOL 68 is more general than type in other languages. For example, a procedure is an object of mode **procedure** with specified modes for its parameters and its result.

mode p1= **proc** (**bool**, **real**) **int**

defines a new mode **p1**, which is a procedure accepting a boolean and a real parameter and returning an integer result. Just as with other modes, variables of mode **p1** may be declared and assigned (in contrast to most other languages).

```
p1 x,y;
x:= proc(bool b, real r) int:. .body of procedure. . .;
. . .
y:= x;
```

With procedures, the full generality of ALGOL 68 modes and the systematic application of orthogonal design can be seen clearly. Procedure modes may be made up of any other modes, for example, unions, references, or other procedures. Thus, the following is a valid definition.

mode funnyproc=
    proc (int, ref [] bool) proc([] ref int, proc(real)int)void

It defines a mode that is a procedure that happens to return another procedure as its result; the returned procedure takes a procedure as its second parameter and returns a value of type **void**.

Orthogonality of design makes the rules of the language simple and uniform. It does not, and is not intended to, prevent the coding of complicated constructs. The type structure of ALGOL 68 is summarized in Figure 4.1.

4.3.2 The Type Structure of Pascal

In this section, we review the type structure of Pascal. Here and in what follows, we will always implicitly refer to the language as originally defined in the Report. Whenever appropriate, we will also mention the major modifications made by the ISO standard.

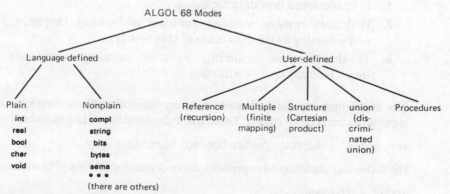

Figure 4.1 ALGOL 68 type structure.

4.3.2.1 Unstructured Types

As in ALGOL 68, data types in Pascal must be ultimately built from unstructured components belonging to primitive, unstructured types. Some of these unstructured types are built-in; others are user-defined. The built-in unstructured types are *integer, real, boolean,* and *char.* A value of type *integer* is an element of an implementation-defined ordered subset of whole numbers. The implementation-defined standard identifier *maxint* denotes the largest integer value that can be handled by the given Pascal implementation. A value of type *real* is element of an implementation-defined subset of rational numbers. Both the maximum magnitude and the precision of real values are implementation-dependent, the limits being imposed by the underlying floating-point arithmetic of the machine. A value of type *char* is an element of a finite, ordered set of characters. Both the set of characters and their ordering relations are implementation-defined. Booleans can have one of two values, *true* and *false*; they can be compared (*false* is considered to be less than *true*) and manipulated by the boolean operators **and, or**, and **not**.

Integers, Booleans, and characters can be collectively called *ordinal types,* because each element of the type has a unique predecessor and a unique successor. For booleans, *true* is defined to be the successor of *false*. The successor and the predecessor of an ordinal value are evaluated by the built-in functions *succ* and *pred*. Such functions are examples of overloaded operators, because they can accept a parameter of any ordinal type.

Pascal programmers can define new ordinal types in two ways. The first is by enumeration of the possible values. For example,

type *day*= (*sunday, monday, tuesday, wednesday, thursday, friday, saturday*)

This declaration has the following effects.

1. It introduces a new data type *day*.
2. It defines *sunday, monday, tuesday, wednesday, thursday, friday,* and *saturday* as the constants of this new type.
3. It defines an ordering relation among constants: *sunday < monday < . . . < saturday.*

The only implicitly defined operations on variables of this new type are assignments and comparisons. Thus, after declaration of the variables

var *today, tomorrow, yesterday, my_birthday: day*

the following statements represent correct manipulations of the variables.

today:= thursday;
tomorrow:= succ(today);

```
yesterday:= pred(today);
my_birthday:= tomorrow
```

Unfortunately, values of enumerated types cannot be read or written by a program. Although we can say that type *day* includes all weekday names, we must read the value of a day in some coded form, say, *integer,* and then explicitly convert it to a value of type *day.*

The second way of defining new ordinal types is by specifying the subrange of an ordinal type (the *associated ordinal type* or *base type*). For example, having defined the type *day,* we may define *work_day* as the subrange *monday* through *friday.* The following fragment illustrates this feature.

```
type work_day= monday..friday;
     age= 0..120;{subrange 0 through 120 of integers}
var my_age: age;
    class_day: work_day;
```

New types may be used without being given an explicit name, for example

```
var course_taught: (comp_sci_15, comp_sci_240);
```

which specifies the (anonymous) type of *course_taught* as the enumeration of the values *comp_sci_15* and *comp_sci_240.*

The above declarations legally can be followed by the statements

```
course_taught:= comp_sci_240;
my_age:= 33;
if course_taught = comp_sci_15
   then class_day:= tuesday
   else class_day:= wednesday
```

Variables of subrange type have the same behavior as variables of the subrange type's base type, except for the set of values they may assume, which is a subset of the set of values of the base type. A verification of this property in general requires a run-time check. For example, execution of *class_day:= succ(class_day)* would raise a run-time error if *class_day* is equal to *friday,* because *succ(friday)* is *saturday* and *saturday* does not belong to type *work_day.*

4.3.2.2   Aggregate Constructors

4.3.2.2.1   *The Array Constructor.* The **array** constructor allows the programmer to define finite mappings. The general form of an array structure is

array [*t1*] **of** *t2*

where *t1*, the *index* (or domain) *type*, is an ordinal type, and *t2*, the *compo-nent* (or range) *type*, is the type of each component of the array.

For example,

```
type flavor= (chocolate, mint, peach, strawberry, vanilla,
              bluecheese, catsup, garlic, onion);
     icecream_flavor= chocolate..vanilla;
     icecream_order= array [icecream_flavor] of boolean;
var my_order, your order: icecream_order;
     choice: icecream_flavor;
```

can be followed by

```
for choice:= chocolate to vanilla do
    my_order[choice]:= false;
my_order [mint]:= true;
your_order:= my_order
{both my_order and your_order are mint}
```

Note that the legality of an array access such as

```
my_order [succ(choice)]
```

requires a run-time check to verify that the index is within the bounds. In fact, if *choice = vanilla*, then *succ* (*choice*) would generate *bluecheese*, that is, a value that does not belong to type *icecream_flavor*.

Pascal regards arrays with different index types as different types. For example, *a1* and *a2* below are different types.

```
type a1= array [1..50] of integer;
     a2= array [1..70] of integer
```

This was a serious problem in Pascal as originally defined. Because proce-dures require formal parameters to have a specified type, it was not possi-ble, for example, to write a procedure that sorted both arrays of type *a1* and type *a2*.

During the standardization of Pascal by ISO, a new feature was added to solve this problem. This feature, called the *conformant array*, allows the formal array parameter of a procedure to *conform* to the size of the actual array parameter. The actual and formal parameters are required to have the same number of indexes and the same component type. The following exam-ple illustrates the use of conformant arrays:

```
procedure sort (var a: array[low..high: integer] of Ctype);
var i:integer;
    more: boolean;
begin {sort}
```

```
    more:= true;
while more do begin
    more:= false;
    for i:= low to high−1 do begin
      if a[i] > a[i+1] then begin
          move_right (i);
          more:= true
      end;
      end;
  end;
end {sort};
```

When the procedure *sort* is called with a one-dimensional array parameter, *low* and *high* assume the values of the lower and upper bounds of the actual parameter, respectively.

Conformant arrays, however, are only a partial solution. For example, it is still not possible to declare in *sort* a local dynamic array of size *low..high*, because subrange bounds must be compile-time constants. For exactly the same reason, we cannot declare variable *i* of type *low..high*.

Multidimensional arrays can be defined in Pascal as arrays whose elements are themselves arrays. For example,

type *row*= **array** [−5..10] **of** *integer*;
var *my_matrix*= **array** [3..30] **of** *row*

However, the abbreviation

var *my_matrix*: **array** [3..30, −5..10] **of** *integer*

also is allowed.

4.3.2.2.2 The Record Constructor. The **record** constructor can be used to define Cartesian products. The general form of a record structure is

record *field_1*: *type_1*;
       field_2: *type_2*;
       . . .
       field_n: *type_n*
end

where *field_i*, $1 \le i \le n$ is a field identifier and *type_i*, $1 \le i \le n$ is a field type. The record can be accessed as a whole or individual fields can be accessed by using the symbol "." as a selector (dot notation). For example, the declarations

type *reg_polygon*= **record** *no_of_edges*: *integer*;
                           edge_size: *real*

```
                          end;
     var t,q,p: reg_polygon,
```

can be legally followed by

```
t.no_of_edges:= 3; t.edge_size:= 7.53;
   {t is an equilateral triangle. The length of the edge is
    7.53}
q.no_of_edges:= t.no_of_edges+1;
q.edge_size:= 2*t.edge_size;
p:= q
```

A record type can also have a variant part, in which case it is possible to define discriminated unions. For example

```
type dept= (houseware, sports, drugs, food, liquor);
     month= 1..12;
     item= record price: real;
                  case available: boolean of
                     true: (amount: integer;
                            where: dept);
                     false: (month_expected: month)
           end
```

The field identifier *available* is the discriminating component (the *tag field*) of the above record structure. If the value of *available* is *true* then an item is characterized by the available amount and the name of the department in which it is kept. If it is *false*, then an item is characterized by the month of its expected delivery. In both cases, the item has an associated price.

Pascal allows the programmer to access all fields of a record structure, including the tag field. Therefore, if *i1* and *i2* are declared and manipulated as follows

```
var i1, i2: item;
    . . .
    i1.price:= 5.24;
    i1.available:= true;
    i1.amount:= 29;
    i1.where:= liquor;
    i2.price:= 324.99;
    i2.available:= false;
    i2.month_expected:= 8
```

the resulting structures can be illlustrated as in Figure 4.2.

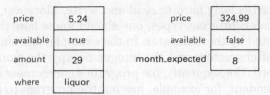

price	5.24
available	true
amount	29
where	liquor

price	324.99
available	false
month_expected	8

Figure 4.2 An example of Pascal variant records.

Type checking for variant records generally can be done only at run-time. For example, if *i* is of type *item*

`i.amount`

is a correct field selection only if the current variant has a true value in its tag field.

If we change the tag field of a variant record, it is as if a new record has been created (conceptually) and all its fields are uninitialized. For example, if after the above statements we write:

`i1.available:= false`

then we have a new variant of *i1*. We should not be able to access the value of the field *i1.month_expected* at this point because it has not been initialized. Most Pascal implementations allow this kind of access, however, for two primary reasons. One reason is that the run-time checks to disallow the access can be quite expensive and sometimes not even possible. The second reason is that this way of using variant records allows an escape from the strict type checking of the Pascal langauge. Actually, this is only true because the conventional implementation of variant records consists of overlapping all variants over the same storage area. Therefore, variant records allow the programmer to interpret the string of bits stored in this area under the different views provided by the types of each variant. In our example, after setting fields *amount* and *where* of variable *i1* under one variant, it is possible to change the variant by setting *available* to *false* and then to interpret the value previously stored into field *amount* as the value of *month_expected*.

This is an insecure—although practical—use of variant records. Viewing the same storage area under different names and types can be useful in modeling some practical situations. For example, a program unit that simulates an input device might view a variable as a sequence of characters, but a program unit that simulates a special-purpose processor might view the same variable as an integer to be read. In general, however, giving different names (and types) to the same data object is a dangerous programming practice. The fact that an object can be modified under one name and the effect of the modification become visible under a different name makes programs particularly hard to read and write. Moreover, to view a certain bit string under different types, one should know how the different types are represented by the translator. In the example, one should know that the sequence of characters and the integer occupy the same amount of storage, say, a word. Consequently, the program's correctness becomes implementation-dependent, for example, moving the program to a computer system in which both integers and single characters occupy an entire word would make the program incorrect.

Making Pascal variant records even less secure is the fact that the tag field of a variant record is optional. The above type *item* could be declared as

```
record price: real;
     case boolean of
          true: (amount: integer;
                 where: dept);
          false: (month_expected: month)
end
```

In this case, the variant record construct is intrinsically insecure. Either *amount* and *where* or *month_expected* can be used when they are not present; there is no way to catch the error, even at run-time, because there is no field of the record to denote the currently applicable variant. The solution of making the compiler insert an appropriate tag field, although feasible, has no real justification, because the absence of the tag field is a deliberate choice provided to the programmer to save storage.

It is interesting to contrast the insecurities of the Pascal discriminated union with the conceptual soundness of the ALGOL 68 counterpart (union modes). This shows how the apparent simplicity of Pascal, which is responsible for much of its popularity, sometimes hides unsuspected problems.

4.3.2.2.3   The Set Constructor.
The **set** constructor is a restricted version of the powerset constructor, in that the base type only can be an ordinal type. Consequently, it is not possible to define sets of reals, sets of tables, sets of sets, and so on. Also, every implementation must impose a practical limit on the size of the base type. Most implementations, for example, do not support "**set of** integer."

The following declaration defines an enumerated type and two set variables.

```
type vegetable= (bean, cabbage, carrot, celery, lettuce, onion,
                 mushroom, zucchini);
var my_salad, leftover: set of vegetable {variables may contain
     any set of vegetables; their type is powerset of vegetable};
```

The following statements are legal.

```
leftover:= . . .;
my_salad:= [carrot..onion] {assigns a set value with four
                                members to my_salad};
if not bean in leftover {membership test}
  then my_salad:= my_salad+leftover {"+" stands for "union of
                                            sets"}
```

4.3.2.2.4 The File Constructor
A Pascal file is a sequence of elements of any type. The following sample declarations define *t1* and *t2* as file variables.

```
type pattern= record. . .end;
     tape= file of pattern;
var t1, t2: tape
```

Automatically associated with each file is a *buffer variable* that contains the next element of the file. The program can read from or write to this buffer variable. The operations *get* and *put* read the next element into the buffer and append the contents of the buffer to the end of the file, respectively. Pascal files can be processed only sequentially: the current position within a file is implicitly updated by the operations *get* and *put*.

4.3.2.3 Pointers
Pointers form a third class of data types in Pascal. Pointers are unstructured but they can be used to build structured (recursive) data.

Pointers allow reference to anonymous data objects allocated in the heap. Heap data objects are allocated by the explicit creation statement *new* (see Section 3.6.2.3). The following example illustrates the use of Pascal pointers in the building of recursive types such as binary trees.

```
type tree_ref= ↑binary_tree_node;
     binary_tree_node= record info: char;
                              left, right: tree_ref
                       end
var my_tree: tree_ref
```

my_tree is defined as a pointer (↑) to the root node of a binary tree of characters. An empty binary tree can be constructed by the following assignment.

```
my_tree:= nil
```

The value **nil** can be held by any pointer (independent of the type of the object to which it points) and points to no element at all. If p is a pointer not equal to **nil**, the object pointed to by p is denoted by $p\!\uparrow$. Unlike ALGOL 68, dereferencing must always be written explicitly.

A binary tree consisting of one node can be created by writing

```
new (my_tree);
my_tree↑.info:= symbol;
my_tree↑.left:= nil;
my_tree↑.right:= nil
```

The first instruction allocates a record of type *binary_tree_node* and makes *my_tree* refer to it. The next three instructions initialize the field *info* with the value of a character valued variable *symbol,* and the two pointer fields to **nil.** The result is illustrated in Figure 4.3, assuming *symbol* is equal to "*a.*"

Appending a left tree to *my_tree* can be done as follows.

```
new (node_ref) {node_ref must be of type tree_ref};
node_ref↑.info:= 'b';
node_ref↑.left:= nil;
node_ref↑.right:= nil;
my_tree↑.left:= node_ref
```

The result is shown in Figure 4.4.

Pointers can be manipulated by assignment and comparison for equality and inequality. Such manipulations, however, are only legal if the operands point to objects of compatible type (see Section 4.4.3 for a definition). Unlike ALGOL 68, Pascal pointers can point only to unnamed data objects; in particular, they cannot point to the location associated with a variable that is allocated on the stack. Pascal's type structure is summarized in Figure 4.5.

4.3.3 The Type Structure of Ada

The type structure of Ada is largely based on Pascal, but is richer and more systematic, and solves several of the problems and insecurities of the original Pascal definition. In this section we give a comprehensive overview of the Ada type system, with two notable exceptions: private types and task types will be discussed later on (see Section 4.5.2.2 and Section 5.2.4.3, respectively). We will first review Ada's data types and constructors, and then turn to a discussion of some general properties of the Ada type system.

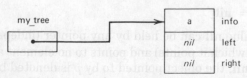

Figure 4.3 A binary tree with one element.

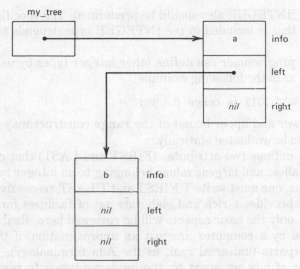

Figure 4.4   Binary tree of Figure 4.3 after adding a left subtree.

4.3.3.1   Scalar Types: Numeric Types and Enumerations

Scalar types define unstructured data objects. They can be divided into two classes: numeric and enumeration types. The first class can be further decomposed into integer and real types; integer and enumeration types also are called discrete types. The set of values of any scalar type is ordered; thus, all relational operators are defined on them.

All integer types comprise a set of consecutive integer values. The Ada language predefines one such type called INTEGER. It is left to the implementation whether other integer types, such as SHORT_INTEGER or

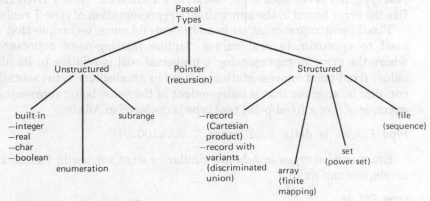

Figure 4.5   Pascal type structure.

LONG_INTEGER also should be predefined. The specific subset of integer values that is included in the INTEGER type depends on the implementation.

The programmer can define other integer types by using the **range** construct, as in the following example:

type TWO_DIGIT **is range** 0..99;

The lower and upper bound of the **range** construct may be any expression that can be evaluated statically.

Ada defines two attributes (FIRST and LAST) that can be used to get the smallest and largest values belonging to an integer type. If T is an integer type, one must write T'FIRST and T'LAST, respectively.

Ada provides a rich and elaborate set of facilities for dealing with real values; only the basic aspects will be reviewed here. Real values that can be handled by a computer are just an approximation of their mathematical counterparts (universal real, in the Ada terminology). In fact, the fixed number of bits set apart by the implementation to represent real values makes it possible to store the exact value of only a limited subset of the universal reals.

The Ada language predefines one real type, called FLOAT. It is left to the implementation whether additional real types, such as SHORT_FLOAT or LONG_FLOAT, should be provided. The programmer can define additional real types, such as:

type FLOAT_1 **is digits** 10;

Both FLOAT and FLOAT_1 are floating-point real types, for which the minimum number of significant decimal digits is specified. For user-defined reals, the minimum number is fixed by the type declaration (it is 10 for FLOAT_1). For FLOAT, it is predefined. Ada defines an attribute (DIGITS) that gives the minimum number of digits associated with a floating-point real type; if T is one such type, one writes T'DIGITS. Thus T'DIGITS specifies the error bound in the approximate representation of type T reals.

Fixed-point representation is another well-known technique that can be used to approximate real values. Unlike floating-point representation, where the error in representing a universal real is relative to its absolute value, fixed-point representation results in an absolute representation error, that is, an error that is independent of the value being represented. An example of how a fixed-point real type is declared in Ada is:

type FIX_PT **is delta** 0.01 **range** 0.00..100.01

Enumeration types in Ada are similar to what we saw in Pascal. For example, one can write:

type DAY **is**
(SUNDAY,MONDAY,TUESDAY,WEDNESDAY,THURSDAY,FRIDAY,SATURDAY);

Characters and booleans are provided by Ada as specific examples of enumeration types:

type CHARACTER **is** (*the ASCII character set*);
type BOOLEAN **is** (FALSE,TRUE);

4.3.3.2   Composite Types

Ada's composite (or structured) types comprise arrays and records.

4.3.3.2.1   Arrays.

Arrays in Ada can have fixed index bounds, as in Pascal. For example

type MONTH **is** (JAN,FEB,MAR,APR,MAY,JUN,JUL,AUG,SEP,OCT,NOV,DEC);
type YEARLY_PAY **is array** (MONTH) **of** INTEGER;
type SUMMER_PAY **is array** (MONTH **range** JUL..SEP) **of** INTEGER;

YEARLY_PAY and SUMMER_PAY are called *constrained* array types, because their index bounds are statically known.

Unlike Pascal, Ada supports the declaration of dynamic arrays. For example

type SOME_PERIOD_PAY **is array** (MONTH **range** < >) **of** INTEGER;
type INT_VECTOR **is array** (INTEGER **range** < >) **of** INTEGER;
type BOOL_MATRIX **is array** (INTEGER **range** < >, INTEGER **range**< >)
of BOOLEAN;

Symbol < > (the *box*) stands for an unspecified range, and SOME_PERIOD_PAY, INT_VECTOR, and BOOL_MATRIX are called *unconstrained* array types.

In Ada, array types are characterized by the types of the components, the number of indices, and the type of each index; the values of the bounds are not considered a part of the array type and thus may be left unspecified at compile-time. In the previous example, array indices have type MONTH (in the case of SOME_PERIOD_PAY) and INTEGER (in the case of INT_VECTOR and BOOL_MATRIX). The "**range** < >" clause specifies that the actual bounds are left unspecified. The values of the bounds, however, must become known when an object comes into existence. For example, one can declare the following variables:

SPRING_MONEY : SOME_PERIOD_PAY (APR..JUN);
Z : INT_VECTOR (−100..100);
W : INT_VECTOR (20..40);
Y : BOOL_MATRIX (0..N, 0..M);

Notice that the values of the bounds need not be given by a static expression. It is only required that the bounds be known when the object declarations are processed.

An even more interesting way of instantiating the bounds is by parameter passing. For example, the following function receives an object of type INT_VECTOR and sums its components:

```
function SUM (X : INT_VECTOR) return INTEGER;
RESULT : INTEGER := 0;
begin
    for I in X'FIRST..X'LAST loop
            RESULT := RESULT + X(I);
    end loop;
    return RESULT;
end SUM;
```

Variable RESULT is local to SUM, and it is initialized to zero when it is declared. Loop variables (e.g., *I*) are considered to be implicitly declared. The formal parameter (*X*) has, automatically, the same bounds as the actual parameter, and such bounds can be accessed by concatenating the attribute names FIRST or LAST to the name of the array. Consequently, the function can be called with arrays of different sizes as actual parameter. For example

```
A := SUM(Z) + SUM(W);
```

It is also possible to declare, local to the procedure, an array whose bounds depend on the parameters; for example

```
TEMPORARY : INT_VECTOR (X'FIRST..X'LAST);
```

As in Algol 68, strings are viewed as arrays of characters and they are predefined as follows:

```
type STRING is array (POSITIVE range < >) of CHARACTER;
```

where POSITIVE is the integer subrange 1..INTEGER'LAST.

Besides conventional selection of individual array components through indexing, Ada provides a way to select consecutive components (called *slice*) of a one-dimensional array. This facility is especially valuable in string manipulation, because it supports the concept of substring. For example, the following fragment defines a variable LINE (a string of 80 characters). A slice of LINE is then assigned a one-dimensional array of characters.

```
LINE : STRING (1..80);
. . .
LINE (1..11):= ('D','e','a','r',' ','f','r','i','e','n','d');
```

4.3.3.2.2 Records. Similar to Pascal, records in Ada can support both

Cartesian products and discriminated unions. An example of a Cartesian product is:

```
type COORDINATE is
    record
        X : INTEGER range 0..100;
        Y : CHARACTER;
    end record;
```

It is interesting to examine how Ada handles discriminated unions and, in particular, how it solves several of the insecurities we have seen in original Pascal. For example, the Pascal declarations shown in Section 4.3.2.2.2. in the discussion of variant records, can be written in Ada as follows.

```
type DEPT is (HOUSEWARE, SPORTS, DRUGS, FOOD, LIQUOR);
type MONTH is range 1..12;
type ITEM (AVAILABLE: BOOLEAN:= TRUE) is
    record
        PRICE: REAL;
        case AVAILABLE of
            when TRUE => AMOUNT: INTEGER;
                         WHERE: DEPT;
            when FALSE => MONTH_EXPECTED: MONTH;
        end case;
    end record;
```

Type ITEM has a discriminant AVAILABLE that defines the possible variants of ITEM. The default initial value of the discriminant is declared above to be TRUE. Thus an object declared as

```
PEACH : ITEM
```

is available by default.

It is possible to declare an object whose variant is frozen, for example

```
ORANGE : ITEM (FALSE);
```

In such a case the amount of space to be reserved by the translator for ORANGE is exactly what is needed by the variant; the variable cannot change its variant at run-time.

Variables of a discriminated-union type are handled safely by Ada. In fact, the discriminant is mandatory and cannot be assigned directly. In the absence of default initial values for the discriminants, a discriminant constraint must be given for any object declaration.

The value of a discriminant can be changed only for objects that have not been explicitly constrained (e.g., it can be changed for PEACH but not for

ORANGE). Moreover, the discriminant can be changed only by assignment to the record as a whole, not by assignment to the discriminant alone. This forbids the producing of inconsistent data objects. For example, after the declaration

```
COCA_COLA : ITEM; --AVAILABLE has the default initial value TRUE,
```

we can write the following statement:

```
COCA_COLA := ORANGE; --gets the value of ORANGE, thus sets
                        --variant to FALSE
```

or the statement:

```
COCA_COLA := (PRICE => 1.99, AVAILABLE=> TRUE, AMOUNT=> 1500,
              WHERE=> FOOD);
                   --the right-hand side of the assignment is a
              record value
              --specified field by field
```

```
COCA_COLA.WHERE
```

is automatically converted by the compiler into the run-time test

if not `COCA_COLA.AVAILABLE` **then raise** `CONSTRAINT_ERROR`
`--raises a run-time error`
end if;

that precedes the required manipulation of COCA_COLA.WHERE.

4.3.3.3   Access Types

Access types (pointers) are used to allocate and deallocate data dynamically. Their use in Ada is quite similar to what we have seen in Section 4.3.2.3 for Pascal. For example, the following declarations define a binary tree:

```
type BINARY_TREE_NODE; --incomplete type declaration
type TREE_REF is access BINARY_TREE_NODE;
type BINARY_TREE_NODE is
record
     INFO : CHARACTER;
     LEFT, RIGHT : TREE_REF;
end;
```

(Note that Ada requires an incomplete type declaration when recursive types are being defined).

If P and Q are two pointers of type TREE_REF, then the INFO component of the node referenced by P is P.INFO. The node itself is P.**all.** Thus, assignment of the node pointed to by P to the node pointed to by Q is written as

```
Q.all := P.all;
```

4.3.3.4   Subtypes and Derived Types

Ada carefully distinguishes between the *static* and *dynamic* properties of types. Static properties are those that can (and must) be checked by an analysis of the program at translation time. Dynamic properties are those that can, in general, be checked only at run-time. Static properties of types are the applicable operations; dynamic properties are, for example, **range** constraints on integers or index constraints on arrays. To make the distinction clear, Ada allows the programmer to specify a dynamic property on a type by defining a **subtype**. For example,

```
type FLAVOR is (CHOCOLATE, MINT, PEACH, STRAWBERRY, VANILLA,
                BLUECHEESE, CATSUP, GARLIC, ONION);
subtype ICE_CREAM_FLAVOR is FLAVOR range CHOCOLATE..VANILLA;
subtype SMALL_INT is INTEGER range -10..10;
subtype SMALL_POS_INT range 1..10;
subtype MY_INT_SET is INTEGER range A..B;
```

A variable of a subtype such as ICE_CREAM_FLAVOR inherits all the properties from type FLAVOR, but has values that satisfy a certain constraint (they belong to the subset CHOCOLATE through VANILLA). The last example (MY_INT_SET) shows that constraints may involve expressions that cannot be evaluated statically; they are assumed to be evaluated when the subtype declaration is elaborated at the entry of the scope where the declaration appears.

The subtype mechanism also can be used to constrain an array type, as in the following example:

```
type MY_ORDERS is array (INTEGER range < >) of
                                ICE_CREAM_FLAVOR;
subtype MONTHLY_ORDERS is MY_ORDERS (1..31);
subtype ANNUAL_ORDERS is MY_ORDERS (1..365);
```

In the example, future declarations of objects of types MONTHLY_ORDERS and ANNUAL_ORDERS generate arrays whose bounds are 1..31 and 1..365, respectively.

Also, one can use the subtype mechanism to freeze the variant of a discriminated union type. For example

```
subtype OUT_OF_STOCK is ITEM (FALSE);
```

where ITEM is the variant record type illustrated in Section 4.3.3.2.2. Any variables of type OUT_OF_STOCK are thus frozen to the specific variant where AVAILABLE is FALSE.

In conclusion, the subtype mechanism allows the programmer to constrain a certain given type; constraints may be static or dynamic. The mechanism does not define a new type, but simply places some constraints upon the set of values an object may assume.

Unlike subtypes, *derived types* define new types. The general form of a derived type declaration is defined here in terms of extended BNF, where brackets [and] enclose optional parts.

type <new_type> **is new** <parent_type> [<constraint>]

For example

type POSITIVE **is** 1..INTEGER'LAST;
type WEIGHT **is new** POSITIVE **range** 1..100;
type LENGTH **is new** POSITIVE;

The new type inherits all properties (values, operations, and attributes) from its parent type, but is considered a different type.

4.3.3.5 Attributes

Ada make extensive use of *attributes*. Attributes are used to designate properties of data objects, types, and program units. As we saw in the previous examples, the value of an attribute is retrieved by writing the name of the entity whose attribute is being sought, followed by a ' and the name of the attribute. Ada predefines more than 40 attributes; in addition, an implementation may provide implementation-dependent attributes.

Attributes are a powerful programming tool and support disciplined programming practices. For example, as we saw in Section 4.3.3.2.1, array attributes FIRST and LAST allow the programmer to write subprograms that manipulate arrays of any size. Also, the programmer can write statements that explicitly choose among different alternative elaborations in response to the value of some attributes. The type structure of Ada is illustrated in Figure 4.6.

4.4 EVALUATION AND ASSESSMENT OF SOME TYPE ISSUES

We have stressed that programming languages are not important in themselves, but as tools that help in the production of software. Therefore, we are interested not in features that make a language "more clever" or fancier than another, but in how such features can support the production of quality software.

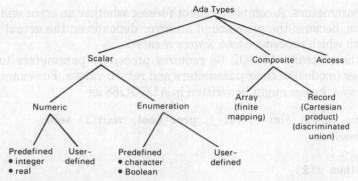

Figure 4.6 Ada type structure.

In this section, we will review the central concepts dealing with data type issues in programming languages. We will see how these concepts are treated in the languages we have discussed and show how the discoveries of flaws have stimulated the definition of different and—one hopes—better features.

4.4.1 Static vs. Dynamic Type Checking

We have seen that languages fall into two general classes: statically typed or dynamically typed. One major effect of the introduction of types is the possibility of static type checking. The resulting programs are more likely to be correct and efficient, because it is not necessary to have run-time type descriptors or to execute checks on them. A language is said to be strongly typed if it allows all type checking to be done statically.

By examining Pascal and ALGOL 68, we can conclude that Pascal, as defined in the Report, is not strongly typed, but that ALGOL 68 is, for the following reasons.

1. The type of a procedure or function parameter, that is, a procedure or function that is itself a parameter, is not determinable for Pascal at translation time. For example, the Pascal procedure

```
procedure who_knows (i,j:integer; procedure f);
    var k: boolean;
begin k:= j < i;
    if k then f(k) else f(j)
end
```

might contain one or two incorrect calls to the actual parameter associated with the formal *f*, because of type mismatch and/or differences in the number of parameters. A compiler cannot foresee whether an error will arise at run-time, because the presence of an error depends on the actual parameters with which procedure *who_knows* is called.

On the contrary, ALGOL 68 requires procedure parameters to specify the types (modes) of their parameters and return values. For example, procedure *who_knows* might be written in ALGOL 68 as

```
proc who_knows= (int i, int j, proc(bool) void i) void;
begin bool i;
   k:= j< i;
   if k then f(k)
      else f(j) ¢ illegal call, caught by compiler ¢
   fi
end
```

2. In Pascal, subranges cannot be checked statically. For example, in $a := b + c$ where the variables are all declared to belong to the subrange 1..10, it is not possible to state *a priori* whether the value of $b + c$ belongs to the subrange type; this can be done at run-time. Because the index type of an array is part of the type of the array, every time the index belongs to the base type of the index type, access to an array element requires a run-time check to verify that the index lies within the bounds. ALGOL 68, on the other hand, considers the array bounds as part of the value, not the type. Subscripts of subscripted variables are ignored at translation time, and checks on values are inserted for run-time evaluation.

3. It is not possible to check the correct use of Pascal's variant records statically; run-time checking is seldom provided, because of execution efficiency considerations. Therefore, variant records provide a loophole that allows the programmer to shortcut the protection of the type structure of the language. In contrast, the ALGOL 68 union is completely safe, that is, the syntax of the language is such that all improper accesses can be caught at compile-time. As any run-time checks are explicitly specified by the programmer, the costs are not hidden in the implementation.

4. There were no rigorously specified type-compatibility rules in the Pascal Report, but ALGOL 68 takes great pains to define the notion of compatibility precisely (see Section 4.4.3). Consequently, Pascal type checking was often based on shaky grounds, and its effect can vary on different implementations. The ISO Pascal has defined the notion of type compatibility, but it will take some time before implementations can comply with it.

Similar conclusions can be derived by comparing Pascal with Ada. A detailed analysis is left to the reader as an exercise.

4.4.2 Type Conversion

It is often necessary to *convert* a value of one type to a value of another, as, for example, when we want to add the integer variable *v* to the real constant 3.753. In most languages, such conversion is implicit. For example, the evaluation of the above addition usually implies a conversion of *v* from integer to real and then the execution of the floating-point addition. Implicit conversion is made explicit by the translator, which generates conversion code based on the type of the operands and the type hierarchy of the language. For example, FORTRAN's hierarchy is COMPLEX > DOUBLE PRECISION > REAL > INTEGER. Given the operation *a op b,* the operand with a type lower in the hierarchy is converted to the type of the other operand before the execution of *op.*

ALGOL 68 consistently applies the principle of implicit conversions (*coercions* in the ALGOL 68 jargon) to the extreme. The type of the value required at any point in an ALGOL 68 program can be determined from the context. For example, if the mode of *a* is **ref t**, the type of the value yielded by the right-hand side of an assignment *a:* = . . . must be **t**. A set of rules is defined that effect the implicit coercion of values from a given type to the desired type. We already have seen the coercion of dereferencing, which causes a value to be automatically stripped of one **ref**. *Deproceduring* effects a procedure call and uses the returned value; *rowing* converts a single value to a row of a single value; *voiding* yields **empty** and discards the original value; *uniting* changes the mode to a desired united mode that must include the original mode; *widening* converts an **int** to a **real** and a **real** to a **compl**. There is no coercion from **real** to **int**. This conversion must be explicitly performed using a cast by the programmer. Examples of these coercions are shown in the following program segment.

```
int i; real r; [1:1] int rowi; ref int refi;
union (int,real) ir; proc int p;
. . .
r:=i/r;      ¢ widening of i ¢
ir:=i;       ¢ uniting ¢
ir:=r;       ¢ uniting ¢
i:=p;        ¢ deproceduring ¢
i:=refi;     ¢ dereferencing (twice) ¢
p;           ¢ deproceduring followed by voiding ¢
rowi:=5;     ¢ rowing ¢
```

It is interesting to consider the interaction of coercion rules with other constructs of the language. For example, united modes such as

mode wrong= **union** (**int, ref int**)

are not allowed, because for a variable *v* of this mode, it sometimes cannot be determined whether or not dereferencing is needed. For example, consider:

wrong *w*;
ref int *v*;
w: = *v*

Should *v* be dereferenced or not? A united variable can take on values of different modes. But whether a value is dereferenced is determined by the mode of the value that is desired, for example, on the left-hand side. In the above assignment, these two rules conflict, because the left-hand side can accept either an **int** or a **ref int**. Thus, such united modes are not allowed (they are mnemonically called *incestuous*).

These elaborate notions of coercion in ALGOL 68 can be criticized on the ground that they lead to rather obscure programs. Automatic conversions weaken the ability of the translator to type-check the program, because they override the declared type of a variable with default automatic transformations. In general, the more the translator can perform implicitly, the less error-checking service it can provide, because the compiler may assume actual errors to be implicit requests for conversions.

Ada takes the opposite approach. Whenever a type conversion is allowed according to the Reference Manual, it must be stated explicitly. A typical case is the conversion from an expression of a derived type to its parent type. For example, if P and L are variables of types POSITIVE and LENGTH, as defined in Section 4.3.3.4, we can write:

P := POSITIVE (2*L + 35)

This means that the expression 2*L + 35 must be converted into POSITIVE.

4.4.3 Type Compatibility

So far, we have been deliberately informal in our discussion of compatibility (or type-equivalence) rules. Such rules should give an exact specification of how the type checking mechanism should be applied. More specifically, two types T1 and T2 are compatible if any value of type T1 can be assigned to a variable of type T2, and vice versa and actual parameters of type T1 can correspond to formal parameters of type T2, and vice versa. Consider the following Pascal declarations.

```
type t= array [1..20] of integer;
var a,b: array [1..20] of integer;
    c: t;
    d: record a: integer;
              b: t
       end
```

It is possible to define the following two notions of type compatibility.

1. *Name equivalence.* Two variables have compatible types if they have the same user-defined or built-in type name. Thus, *c* and *d.b* have compatible types—but not *a, b,* and *c.* The term "name equivalence" reflects the fact that two variables have compatible types only if their type name is the same.*

2. *Structural equivalence.* Two variables have compatible types if they have the same structure. According to this definition, user-defined type names are used just as an abbreviation (or as a comment) for the structure they represent and do not introduce any new semantic features. To verify structural equivalence, user-defined type names are replaced by their definition. This process is repeated until no user-defined type name remains. The types are then considered to be structurally equivalent if they have exactly the same description. In the above example, *a, b, c, d.b* have compatible types. This definition of structural equivalence can lead to an infinite loop when pointers are used to create recursive type definitions. Languages adopting structural equivalence take care of this problem by providing an appropriate rule (see Exercise 4.19). Type compatibility is defined in ALGOL 68 via structural equivalence. The Pascal Report, on the other hand, did not specify the adopted notion of type compatibility and thus left this important issue to be decided by the implementation. An unfortunate consequence is that a Pascal program accepted by one compiler might be rejected by another.

In most cases, the original Pascal implementation used structural equivalence. The choice of name equivalence would have made it illegal, for example, to assign an integer value to a variable that is specified as a subrange of integers, unless appropriate conversions are defined by the language. Name equivalence is used for parameter passing. The ISO Pascal has defined type compatibility rigorously, mainly based on name equivalence (see Exercise 4.20).

Type compatibility in Ada is defined via name equivalence. Objects belonging to different subtypes of the same type are compatible. Constraints must be checked during translation wherever possible; otherwise, at run-time.

The concept of type compatibility based on structural equivalence adopted by ALGOL 68 goes to the extreme of completely ignoring user-defined names. Consequently, ALGOL 68's strong typing is based on a rather

---

*Some authors consider two variables equivalent also if they appear in the same declaration. According to this definition, *a* and *b* are equivalent. The definition we have given is the one adopted by Ada.

poor, purely syntactic notion of type. For example, the ALGOL 68 type declarations

mode celsius= **int**

and

mode fahrenheit= **int**

cause **celsius** and **fahrenheit** to be compatible types. Consequently, the value of a variable representing a temperature in celsius degrees can legally be assigned to a variable representing a temperature in fahrenheit degrees, even though, this would most likely be a programming error. The Ada solution to this problem consists of defining both CELSIUS and FAHRENHEIT as derived types of INTEGER:

type CELSIUS **is new** INTEGER;
type FAHRENHEIT **is new** INTEGER;

Name equivalence is closer than structural equivalence to the concept of abstract data types. Although it does not associate operations with the type, it does prevent considering two data types compatible just because their structures happen to be identical. Commonality of properties thus can be specified by using the same type name, which would enhance the readability of programs. Name equivalence also is simpler to implement. In fact, implementing structural equivalence requires a pattern-matching procedure that can be quite complicated.

Both notions however, can be regarded as mostly syntactic, rather than semantic. From a semantic point of view, what should be expressed is the notion of identical behavior under application of the same operations, rather than that of compatible representation structures; however, this requires language facilities that support the definition of abstract data types.

4.4.4 Problems with Pointers

Pointers came under criticism in the mid 1970s. Just as unrestricted **goto**s broaden the context from which a labeled statement can be executed, unrestricted pointers broaden the context from which a data object can be accessed.

Pointers comprise the basic tool for representing recursively defined data objects. As a lower-level language construct, they can be used for purposes other than those originally intended. They make programs less understandable and, often, unsafe, for the following reasons:

(a) In some languages the use of pointers can lead to serious type violations, if pointers are not qualified by the type of data objects to which they may point. For example, pointers in PL/I are declared simply as pointers, rather than as pointers to a certain type. Variables declared as BASED are accessed only through pointers. For example, the declarations

```
DECLARE P POINTER,
    X FIXED BASED, /* INTEGER */
    Y FLOAT BASED; /* REAL */
```

declare P as a pointer, X as an integer, and Y as a real. Access to X is made through a pointer, that is, P→X indicates access to an integer data object X through a pointer P. A pointer to a based variable is set when the variable is (explicitly) allocated, as in

```
ALLOCATE X SET P;
```

Because P is not qualified to point only to integers, we may also try to access Y through the same P, as in P→Y. At translation time, it is impossible to guarantee that the pointer being supplied is pointing to a variable of the correct type. In many implementations, dynamic checking is considered quite costly. The usual solution is for the translator to assume that accesses are being made correctly. This can result in run-time errors that are very hard to find.

(b) A pointer may be left dangling, that is, it can refer to a location that is no longer allocated for holding values. A classic PL/I example is the following:

```
BEGIN;
  DCLP POINTER;
  BEGIN; DCL X FIXED;/*ALLOCATE NEW X*/
    P= ADDR(X);/*P NOW POINTS TO X*/
  END;
/*AT THIS POINT, X IS DEALLOCATED BUT*/
/*P STILL POINTS TO ITS LOCATION! THE*/
/*REAL CULPRIT IS THE FUNCTION ADDR*/
/*WHICH ALLOWS THE ADDRESS OF ANY VARIABLE*/
/*TO BE USED AS A VALUE*/
END;
```

As we pointed out, both ALGOL 68 and Pascal bind each pointer value to a specific data type, and thus they overcome problem **(a)**. In terms of problem **(b)** both languages have a number of insecurities.

(b.1) The ALGOL 68 restriction that in an assignment to a pointer, the scope of the object being pointed to be at least as large as that of the pointer itself, can only be checked at run-time. For example, consider a procedure p with two formal parameters: x, an integer, and y, a pointer to integers. Whether the assignment $y: = x$ in the procedure is legal depends on the actual parameters and obviously is unknown at translation time. As usual, checking the error at run-time slows down the execution of the program; not checking the error leaves dangling references uncaught. Pascal pointers do not give rise to such problems, because they can only be bound to unnamed, heap-allocated data objects.

(b.2) The amount of heap storage allocated during execution of a program can become exceedingly large. As soon as an area of heap storage becomes unreferenced, it could be released and later allocated to new heap variables. To make this possible, Pascal provides the standard procedure *dispose*, which explicitly deallocates heap storage. Unfortunately, the programmer can request deallocation of a heap variable while there are still pointers to it, which creates a dangling reference. This error is difficult to check and therefore checks are not included in most Pascal implementations. A similar problem arises in Ada, which provides a built-in procedure UNCHECKED_DEALLOCATION to deallocate unused storage explicitly. Both ALGOL 68 and SIMULA 67 avoid this problem by not allowing explicit deallocation of heap variables. Instead, they rely on a garbage collector that automatically reclaims unused heap storage. Garbage collection will be discussed in Section 4.6.4.

(c) Uninitialized and **nil**-valued pointers can cause uncontrolled access to storage, because the bit string found in the location bound to the pointer is interpreted as a pointer value. To make run-time checking possible, pointers can be automatically initialized to **nil**, with the value of **nil** being an illegal address; accordingly, addressing with a **nil** value can be detected automatically by the hardware at run-time.

(d) If the use of Pascal variant records is not checked at run-time, a field might be assigned an integer under one variant and be interpreted as a pointer under another. Consequently, the program could randomly modify the contents of storage in an absolutely uncontrolled way. The following example illustrates this point.

```
type harmful= record. . .
            case tag: boolean of
                true: (i: integer);
                false: (ref:↑integer)
        end;
```

```
    var trouble_maker: harmful; . . .
    begin . . .
        while b do
        begin trouble_maker.tag:= true;
              trouble_maker.i:= 0;
              trouble_maker.tag:= false;
              trouble_maker.ref↑:= 0
              . . .

        end
        . . .
    end
```

An additional problem with Pascal pointers arises as a consequence of the undefined notion of type compatibility. For example, after the declarations

```
type ptr= ↑node; ref= ↑node;
     node= record item: integer;
                   next: ptr
            end
```

it is not clear whether it is legal to assign a variable of type *ref* to a variable of type *ptr,* and vice versa.

Euclid solves this problem by introducing *collections.* Collections are special programming variables that denote a set of data objects of the same type. When a pointer is declared, it is bound to a collection. Several collections can have elements of the same type. Several pointers can point into the same collections, but each pointer can only refer to a specific collection. For example

```
type nodes= record . . . end
var my_nodes: collection of nodes;
type my_ref= ↑my_nodes;
var my_ref1, my_ref2: my_ref;
```

declare *my_ref1* and *my_ref2* as references into the collection of nodes *my_nodes.* Variables *my_ref 1* and *my_ref 2* can point to nodes of the collection *my_nodes,* but no other pointers can, unless they are declared as bound to the same collection. There are no operations defined for collections; collections only can be passed as parameters, but cannot be assigned. This view of pointers has strong analogies to array indices. A pointer is an index within the collection, and dereferencing is equivalent to indexing within the array. As with arrays, a pointer cannot be dereferenced within a given scope unless its collection is visible within that scope, that is, the collection is a global variable or it is passed as a parameter.

Pointers in Ada are defined in a way similar to that used in Pascal. Moreover, two pointers can refer to the same data object only if their types are compatible. Using the Euclid terminology, each pointer type has an implicitly associated collection. Two pointers of compatible types are associated with the same implicit collection, two pointers with noncompatible types are guaranteed not to point into the same collection.

4.5   ABSTRACT DATA TYPES

The concept of type, as defined in Pascal and ALGOL 68, has been a major step toward achieving a language capable of supporting structured programming. However, these languages do not fully support a methodology—such as information hiding—in which programs are developed by problem decomposition based on the recognition of abstractions. The data abstraction useful for this purpose should not merely classify objects according to their representation structure; rather, they should be classified according to their expected behavior. Such behavior is expressible in terms of the operations that are meaningful on those data, and the operations are the only means for creating, modifying, and accessing the objects.

Starting with SIMULA 67, many programming languages, such as Concurrent Pascal, CLU, Mesa, Euclid, Modula-2, Smalltalk, and Ada, allow the programmer, to a varying degree, to define an abstract data type by providing special language constructs for encapsulating both the *representation* and the *concrete operations* that implement the abstract view. As we saw in Section 2.2, the existence of an encapsulating mechanism to enclose in a textual unit both the structure that represents the objects and the procedures that represent the operations improves the localization of modifications. A change to the data structure is likely to require a change in the access procedures, but the effect of these changes is confined within the boundaries of the encapsulating mechanism. Similarly, a change to the program that uses the data abstraction has no effect on the correctness of the program part enclosed within the encapsulating mechanism.

The possibility of *parameterizing* user-defined abstractions provides a still more flexible and powerful tool for expressing abstractions in a programming language. For example, the abstract data types "integer queue" and "customer queue" may display the same abstract behavior independently of the (abstract) type of the items that are enqueued. A natural way of expressing this is by defining a *generic type* (or *polymorphic type* or *type generator*) "queue," where the type of storable items is a parameter.

Section 4.5.1 reviews the concept of **class** as originally proposed in SIMULA 67, and evaluates its power and flexibility in defining abstract data types. A modification of the SIMULA 67 class mechanism will be justified and further detailed in Section 4.5.2 along with a presentation of the features provided by CLU, Ada, Modula-2, and Smalltalk.

4.5.1 The SIMULA 67 Class Mechanism

SIMULA 67, a general-purpose programming language, was defined as an extension to ALGOL 60 for systems description and simulation. Its most important addition to ALGOL 60 is the concept of **class**, which, initially inspired by the particular requirements of discrete simulation, was later recognized as a general tool for designing programs organized in levels of abstractions. Its generalization to concurrent programming led to the Concurrent Pascal concept of *monitor.* Similarly, classes originated the idea of *abstract data types,* as provided by Concurrent Pascal (with the **class** construct) and CLU (with the **cluster** construct). More generally, they suggested how to provide language constructs for information-hiding modules and object-oriented programming, which resulted in the Ada and Smalltalk languages.

SIMULA 67 has a conventional ALGOL-like nested structure. A class can be declared in the declaration list that appears in the heading of a block, together with procedures and variables. A class declaration has the general form

⟨*class_heading*⟩ ; ⟨*class_body*⟩

⟨*class_heading*⟩ contains the name of the class and the formal parameters. ⟨*class_body*⟩ is a conventional block, that is, it can contain local declarations of variables, procedures, and classes, and executable statements.

For example, the concept of complex numbers in polar form can be described by the following class declaration. Parameters x and y denote the components of the complex number in Cartesian form, and local variables *angle* and *radius* denote the components in polar form. Functions *sqrt* and *arctan* are built-in, and *error* (which is left unspecified) is a procedure accessible from the class. Global variable *epsilon* denotes a positive real value that is used as an approximation of zero. Global real variable *pi* represents the value of π.

```
class complex (x,y); real x,y;
begin real angle, radius;
    radius:= sqrt(x**2+y**2);
    if abs(x) < epsilon
       then begin if abs(y) < epsilon
                     then error
                     else begin if y > epsilon
                                  then angle:= pi/2;
                                  else angle:= 3*pi/2
                           end
              end
       else angle:= arctan (y/x)
end complex;
```

As with the type declarations of ALGOL 68 and Pascal, a class declaration defines a *prototype* or *template* of a class of data objects. Each instance of the class is a manipulable data object.

Class instances (called *objects* in SIMULA terminology) can be created dynamically in an arbitrary number and individually referred to only via a pointer. For example, in the following pair of statements, *c* is declared to be a pointer to a *complex* in the first statement and is made to point to a newly created object in the second statement.

```
ref (complex) c;
c:- new complex (1.0, 1.0)
```

(":-" is the reference assignment symbol and is read "denotes.") The effect of these statements is illustrated in Figure 4.7.

The *attributes* of a class instance are the variables declared local to the class body and the parameters listed in the class heading. Like the fields of a Pascal record, the attributes of a class instance are accessible from outside the class through the use of dot notation. For example, after the above-listed statements have caused the generation of the class instance pointed by *c*, the execution of the statements

```
my_angle:= c.angle;
my_radius:= c.radius;
my_x:= c.x;
my_y:= c.y
```

yields the following values:

```
my_angle= 0.78, my_radius= 1.42, my_x= 1.0, and my_y= 1.0.
```

Class declarations resemble the ALGOL 68 or Pascal record type declarations. Actually, SIMULA 67 does not have an explicit Cartesian product constructor; the class can be used for this purpose. Unlike ALGOL 68 or Pascal, however, access in SIMULA 67 is available only via reference varia-

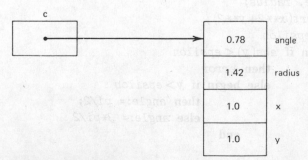

Figure 4.7   An instance of class complex.

bles; class instances have no name. Also, each instance of the class must be generated explicitly via a **new** statement. Finally, an instance of a class is an initialized object, because the class body is automatically executed by the **new** statement.

More generally, classes are encapsulating mechanisms that support the definition of abstract data types. A class may enclose the procedures that implement the operations on data. For example, procedures *add* and *multiply*, for adding and multiplying complex numbers, can be enclosed within the body of the class *complex*. These operations also are attributes accessed via the dot notation—*c.add, c.multiply*—and they may take parameters. For example, the headings of procedures *add* and *multiply* enclosed within class *complex* are

procedure *add* (*operand*); **ref** (*complex*) *operand*;

and

procedure *multiply* (*operand*); **ref** (*complex*) *operand*;

Addition between the complex numbers referenced by $c1$ and $c2$ can be expressed as

c1.add (*c2*)

That is, $c2$ is passed as a parameter to the *add* procedure associated with $c1$. This notation is rather awkward for binary operations on variables of an abstract type, because the same operation also can be expressed as

c2.add (*c1*)

That is, $c1$ is passed as a parameter to the *add* procedure associated with $c2$.

A more serious problem is that the dot notation provides access to all attributes of an object, and so, for example, one is not forbidden from writing

c1.angle:= *c2.angle*;
c1.radius:= *c2.radius*+ *c3.radius*

to make $c1$ denote the result of the addition of the complex numbers denoted by $c2$ and $c3$, if the angles of $c2$ and $c3$ are known to be equal. In other words, *add* and *multiply* are not the only operations that can manipulate *complex* data objects, because direct access to the representation also is permitted.*

SIMULA 67 contains a special feature that allows the programmer to specify both discriminated unions of types and generic abstract data types. The particular feature used for this purpose, the *subclass*, has a more general applicability and is intended to provide a general tool in the organiza-

---

*Constructs to enforce protection were later added to the language.

tion of systems in levels of abstraction. It is achieved by *prefixing* a class with the name of another class.

Suppose we want to define the abstraction "stack of elements" (of possibly nonhomogeneous type). The operations on a stack should allow the programmer to reference the first element (*top*), to insert a new element in the first position (*push*), to eliminate the first element (*pop*), and to check whether the stack is empty (*empty*). Such operations are independent of the particular types of the elements that are stacked together. We first describe the class of items that can be stacked.

```
class stack_member;
begin ref (stack_member) next_member;
    next_member:- none
end
```

This specifies that the only property shared by all stackable objects is the existence of an attribute that is a reference to the next item in the stack. Each instance of *stack_member* has the attribute *next_member* initialized to **none**, the null pointer value. The class *stack* can be described separately, specifying only the operations applicable to all stackable objects.

```
class stack;
begin ref (stack_member) first;
    ref (stack_member) procedure top;
        top:- first;
    procedure pop;
      if ⌐empty then first:- first.next_member;
    procedure push(e); ref (stack_member)e;
    begin if first =/= none
            then e.next_member:- first;
        first:- e
    end push;
    boolean procedure empty;
        empty:= first==none;
    first:- none
end stack
```

Procedure *top* returns the topmost element, that is, a **ref** (*stack_member*), of a nonempty stack. Symbol "⌐" in procedure *pop* stands for "not." Symbol "=/=" in procedure *push* stands for "not equal." Procedure *empty* returns a **boolean**; symbol "==" stands for "equal." Each instance of class stack is initialized as an empty stack, because attribute *first* is set to **none**.

Having defined the two classes *stack_member* and *stack*, we can now create stackable objects of a particular type, for example, *complex,* by prefixing class *complex*

```
stack_member class complex (. . .);
                  . . .
            end complex
```

specifies that the objects generated by

new *complex*

have all the attributes of *stack_member,* as well as the attributes of *complex.* In other words, they are complex numbers that can be stacked. *Complex* is called a subclass of *stack_member*—it is more specialized than *stack_member* and *inherits* properties from it.

If *s* is declared to be of type **ref** (*stack*), we can create a stack of complex numbers by doing

```
s:- new stack;
```

Stack *s* currently contains no elements, so that *s.empty* returns **true**. If we have several complex objects, *c1, c2, c3,* we may insert them in the stack in the following way.

```
s.push (c1);
s.push (c2);
s.push (c3).
```

We can look at the top element by doing *s.top,* which returns a reference; we can remove the top element by *s.pop.*

Note that because *first* is available for access by users of the class, the user is not protected from accidentally modifying *s.first* and thus losing the entire stock (see Exercise 4.10).

Class *stack_member* can be viewed as a union of the types corresponding to all its subclasses. For example, if the following declaration appears in the program

```
stack_member class vector (. . .);
                  . . .
            end vector;
```

a variable of type **ref** (*stack_member*) can reference both a *complex stack_member* and a *vector stack_member.*

In fact, vector objects and complex objects may be inserted in the same stack. All that *stack* cares about is that an attribute *next_member* of type *ref* (*stack_member*) exists in the object it is manipulating. All subclasses of *stack_member* include such an attribute.

This freedom also causes insecurities. For example, if we insert two vector objects, *v1* and *v2,* in the above stack, that is, *s.push(v1); s.push(v2),* a future *pop* may yield either a *vector* or a *complex* object. It is therefore possible to try to access an attribute in an object that does not have that attribute, for example, *v.angle*. Although SIMULA 67 provides facilities for examining the type of an object (**if** *v* **is** *vector* **then**. . .), the programmer is not forced to use them. In other words, the language does not automatically enforce protection. In particular, if the goal is to define *stack* as a truly generic type, one must be careful not to push stack members of different types onto the same stack instance.

Another interesting feature of the SIMULA **class** is the ability to create class instances that work in quasiparallel, that is, in an interleaved fashion. The class bodies can be activated as coroutines. This subject is treated in Chapter 5.

In conclusion, the SIMULA 67 class combines many interesting concepts:

(a) It allows grouping of related, highly dependent programming objects into an encapsulating construct (*class*).

(b) It provides a useful linguistic construct (*subclass*) for hierarchical system decomposition through inheritance.

(c) It views abstract objects as entities that can only be accessed via references and provides explicit facilities to manipulate references.

(d) It allows the specification of quasiconcurrent execution of class instances.

4.5.2 Abstract Data Types in Modern Languages

The initial design of SIMULA 67 did not provide any form of protection for classes, whose attributes could be (perhaps inadvertently) manipulated by users of the class. Invisibility of the representation of abstract data types is a major issue of newer languages, such as Concurrent Pascal, CLU, and Smalltalk. In other languages, such as Mesa, Euclid, Modula-2, and Ada, the encapsulating construct is not restricted to hiding the implementation of one abstract data type, but, more generally, acts as a filter that makes possible explicitly to control which internal details of the encapsulated unit are made visible to users (i.e., are *exported*). In some cases, it also is possible to specify the external information that is made visible within the module (i.e., *imported* by the module). This view of modules as information-hiding devices provides a powerful system-structuring language tool that can be especially valuable for large, complex programs. Sections 4.5.2.1 through 4.5.2.4 review the constructs provided by CLU, Ada, Modula-2, and Smalltalk for describing data abstractions.

4.5.2.1 CLU

CLU provides the *cluster* construct for defining abstract data types. The following example illustrates the use of clusters, along with some other features of the language.

We want to define the abstract data type *complex* number with the following operations:

- *create*: receives a pair of real numbers as parameters and generates a complex number with the two parameters as real and imaginary parts, respectively (CLU data objects must be created explicitly).
- *add*: receives a pair of complex numbers as parameters and delivers the result of their addition.
- *equal*: receives a pair of complex numbers as parameters and if they are equal, delivers a **true** result; otherwise, a **false** result.

The cluster implementing the data type is described below.

```
complex= cluster is create, add, equal
    rep= record [x,y: real]
    create= proc (a,b: real) returns (cvt)
            return (rep $ {x:a, y:b})
    end create
    add= proc (a,b: cvt) returns (cvt)
            return (rep $ {x:a.x+ b.x, y:a.y+b.y})
    end add
    equal= proc (a,b: cvt) returns (bool)
            return (a.x = b.x and a.y = b.y)
    end equal
end complex
```

The cluster heading (**cluster is . . .**) lists what operations are available on the data type *complex*. The data structure chosen to give a concrete representation to objects of the abstract type is specified by the **rep** clause. In the example, it is a record with two fields—one for the real part and the other for the imaginary part. The procedures that implement the operations (as well as other possible local procedures not listed in the cluster heading) follow the **rep** clause. In the example, they are procedures *create*, *add*, and *equal*.

The keyword **cvt**, which only can be used within a cluster, denotes a change of viewpoint. For example, in procedure *add* the parameters *a* and *b* are of type *complex* when viewed from outside the cluster, but are "converted" to their representation type (here, **record . . .**) inside the *add* procedure. Consequently, it is legal to write *a.x* within procedure *add*. Similarly, the returned data object of the representation type that holds the result of the addition is "converted" to the abstract type *complex* at procedure exit. The meaning of **return (rep** $. . .) is that an object of the representation type (i.e., a **record**) is returned; the value stored in the record is specified within curly brackets in a self-explanatory notation. The **cvt** in the **returns** clause causes a change to the abstract representation after return to the caller.

An important semantic issue that makes CLU somewhat unusual is how the language views variables and data objects. First, scope and lifetime are disjoint issues, that is, variables are declared within units, as

```
p: complex
```

but they are explicitly created, as

```
p:= complex$create(h,k)
```

The symbol "$" is similar to the dot notation of Simula 67. Therefore, operation *create* enclosed within cluster *complex* is invoked with *h* and *k* as actual parameters. The **return** statement executed by procedure *create* generates an object (a complex number whose real and imaginary parts are *h* and *k*, respectively). The returned object is assigned to *p*.

Second, CLU variables are uniformly viewed as references to data objects. An assignment such as

```
x:= e
```

causes *x* to refer to the data object resulting from the evaluation of *e*. Therefore, the assignment does not modify the data object referenced by *x*, but makes *x* refer to a different data object and leaves the original data object unmodified. The original data object still may be referenced by other variables, or, if no such variables exist, becomes inaccessible. This form of assignment is called *assignment by sharing*.

Parameter passing in CLU is defined in terms of assignments. For example, the call

```
. . . complex $ add (x,y) . . .
```

assigns *x* and *y* to the formal parameters *a* and *b*, respectively, that act as local variables. Consequently, the same data object becomes shared by *x* and *a*, and *y* and *b*, respectively.

CLU procedures and clusters can be *generic* (or *polymorphic*), that is, they may be parameterized by a type. A generic procedure or cluster must explicitly state which procedures the parameter type must provide. For example, a cluster implementing sets of components of type *t* might have the following heading.

set= **cluster** [*t*: **type**] **is** *create, insert, delete, is_in*
       where *t* **has** *equal*: **proctype** (*t, t*) **returns** (**bool**)

This means that type *set* is characterized by the operations *create, insert, delete,* and *is_in* (membership test); type *t* must have an operation *equal,* which returns a boolean when applied to two parameters of type *t.* Operation *equal* is needed in the body of *set,* for example, in the implementation of the membership test. The information about parameters of type **type** that must be provided in the cluster heading allows the type-checking mechanism to verify that only the listed operations are used on objects of the parameter type within the cluster.

Declaration of a set variable must specify the type of the components as a parameter, for example

s: set[**integer**]
t: set[**bool**]

Similarly, operations on such sets must be written as

set [**integer**] $ *create* (. . .)
set [**bool**] $ *create* (. . .)

4.5.2.2 Ada

An Ada program is a collection of program units, among which are subprograms and packages. The *packages* is the Ada encapsulating mechanism. Like other program units, the package has a typical Algol-like nested structure. As in Pascal, nesting is achieved through declarations, that is, a declaration of a subprogram or a package can contain a declaration of local variables, subprograms, and packages.* Nesting also can be achieved by defining new blocks, as in ALGOL 60.

Packages can be used for a variety of applications, ranging from the declaration of a set of common entities—variables, constants, or types—to grouping a set of related subprograms (e.g., a mathematical package for the solution of differential equations) or describing abstract data types.

An example of the first case is

```
package COMPLEX_NUMBERS is
    type COMPLEX is
        record
            RE: INTEGER;
            IM: INTEGER;
        end record;
    TABLE: array (1..500) of COMPLEX;
end COMPLEX_NUMBERS;
```

*Tasks are another kind of unit that can be hierarchically nested (see Section 5.2.4.3).

The above declaration is processed as if it were the declaration of the enclosed variables and types; therefore, such variables and types have the same scope and lifetime as the variables and types declared in the declarative part, where the declaration of package COMPLEX_NUMBERS appears. The names declared within the package can be used within the scope of the package by using the dot notation (à la SIMULA 67), as in

COMPLEX_NUMBERS.TABLE(K)

When grouping a set of related subprograms or describing an abstract data type, it is often necessary to hide some local entities within the package. For the set of related subprograms, the hidden local entities might be local variables and/or local procedures; for abstract data types, they will include the concrete representation and perhaps some internal auxiliary variables and procedures. The lack of this capability, as we have seen, is a weakness in other languages. Ada has overcome this problem.

The general structure of a package is composed of two parts: the *package specification* and the *package body*. The package specification contains exactly all the information that is exported by the module; the package body contains all the hidden details of the implementation and an initialization section that is executed upon activation of the unit that contains the package declaration.

The following package exports the following two related functions.

• BELONGS_TO (*X*): gives a boolean result if *X* belongs to a certain (ordered) set of integers;
• POSITION (*X*): gives the ordinal position of *X* in the set.

The structure and the contents of the ordered set of integers is hidden within the package; the operations BELONGS_TO and POSITION are the only available manipulations on integer sets.

```
package INT_SET_PACK is
    function BELONGS_TO (X: INTEGER) return BOOLEAN;
    function POSITION (X: INTEGER) return INTEGER;
end INT_SET_PACK;
package body INT_SET_PACK is
    STORED_INT: array (1..10) of INTEGER;
    function BELONGS_TO (X: INTEGER) return BOOLEAN;
        . . .
    end BELONGS_TO;
    function POSITION (X: INTEGER) return INTEGER;
        . . .
    end POSITION;
```

```
--now comes the initialization of array
--STORED_INT, i.e., the initialization of the set
    . . .
end INT_SET_PACK;
```

The following package defines the abstract data type *complex* number that we have already described in CLU.

```
package COMPLEX_NUMBERS is
    type COMPLEX is private;
private
    type COMPLEX is
        record R, I: REAL;
        end record;
end COMPLEX_NUMBERS;
package body COMPLEX_NUBMERS is
    procedure INITIALIZE (A,B: in REAL; X: out COMPLEX) is
    begin X.R:= A;
        X.I:= B;
    end INITIALIZE;
    function ADD (A,B: in COMPLEX) return COMPLEX is
    TEMP: COMPLEX;
    begin TEMP.R:= A.R+B.R;
        TEMP.I:= A.I+B.I;
        return TEMP;
    end ADD;
end COMPLEX_NUMBERS;
```

In the example, type COMPLEX exported by the module is **private**, that is, the details of representation enclosed within the portion **private . . . end** COMPLEX_NUMBERS of the package specification are not visible outside the package. Variables of type COMPLEX only can be manipulated by using the subprograms INITIALIZE and ADD exported by the package. The predefined operations of assignment and test for equality/inequality also are permitted.

Exported variables also can be described as **limited private**. In such a case, assignemnts and tests for equality/inequality would not be automatically defined for the type. If they are needed, they must be explicitly provided by the package as additional procedures.

One difference from CLU is that no explicit *create* operation must be provided by the Ada package, because it is automatically performed when the units that declare variables of type COMPLEX are activated. Package COMPLEX_NUMBERS, however, provides an explicit procedure for initialization.

In the example, parameters to procedures are specified as either **in** or **out**. The specification **in** denotes an unmodifiable input parameter. The specification **out** specifies an output parameter whose value is set by the procedure. Parameter passing in Ada is discussed in Section 5.2.1.

Packages (and procedures) can be **generic**, in which case they must be instantiated before use, as shown below. For example, a package describing sets of a predefined maximum cardinality may have the following specification part.

```
generic
    type COMPONENT is private;
package SET_MANIPULATION is
    type SET is limited private;
    procedure INSERT (S: in out SET; ELEM: in COMPONENT);
    procedure DELETE (S: in out SET; ELEM in COMPONENT);
    procedure IS_IN (S: in SET; ELEM: in COMPONENT) return
    BOOLEAN;
private
    type SET is
        record STORE: array (1..MAX_CARDINALITY) of COMPONENT;
               CARDINALITY: INTEGER range
                                   0..MAX_CARDINALITY:= 0;
        end record;
end SET_MANIPULATION;
```

Procedure INSERT (DELETE) can be used to insert a new element into (delete an existing element from) a set. Function IS_IN returns a boolean value that is true if an element ELEM is in a set, and false otherwise. The data structure used to represent sets comprises an array whose component type is a parameter specified in the **generic** clause that prefixes the package. The size of sets is fixed by the value of global variable MAX_CARDINALITY.

Type COMPONENT is **private**, that is, the only operations permitted on components within the package are assignments and tests for equality and inequality. Additional operations, if necessary, can be provided as other generic parameters. The field CARDINALITY of type SET is used to record the number of elements that are stored in a set; it is initialized to zero.

Instantiation of a generic module requires a specification of the actual generic parameters. For example

```
package INTEGERS is new SET_MANIPULATION (INTEGER);
package FLAVORS is new SET_MANIPULATION (FLAVOR);
```

where type FLAVOR is the one defined in Section 4.3.3.4. Semantically, the two instantiations can be viewed as declarations of two distinct packages, which happen to have the same internal structure (and thus are described by the same generic module). In the scope of such instantiations, it is possible to write the declarations

```
A,B: INTEGERS.SET --A and B are of type SET instantiated by
                  --INTEGERS
C: FLAVORS.SET    --C is of type SET instantiated by FLAVORS
```

4.5.2.3   The Modula-2 Module

The module is the most notable construct that distinguishes Modula-2 from its predecessor, Pascal. This construct provides all of the basic features provided by the Ada package, but is embedded in a language that is much simpler than Ada.

A Modula-2 program is a collection of modules. Each module has a Pascal-like nesting structure, in which nesting is achieved through declarations. The declaration of a subprogram or module can contain declarations of local subprograms and/or modules.

Modules can import and/or export entities by listing their identifiers in the **import** and/or **export** clause, as in the following example:

```
. . . .
var a,b : integer;
module x;

    import a;
    export e,f;
    var e,g : integer;
        h : boolean;
    procedure f (. . . .);

    . . . .
    end f
end x;
```

Module x imports a variable a from the outside and exports variable e and procedure f. Imported entities must be a subset of those that are visible at the lexical point where the module appears in the program, based on the scope rules of the language. Exported entities must be a subset of those that are locally declared in the module. They become visible outside as if the module construct did not exist.

The module construct can be used to encapsulate a set of related subprograms that can be used to access a hidden protected data structure. The Ada example of INT_SET_PACK that was sketched in Section 4.5.2.2 is coded in Modula-2 as follows:

```
module IntSetpack;

    export BelongsTo, Position;
    var Stored_Int: array [1..10] of integer;
    procedure BelongsTo (X : integer) : boolean;
```

```
    . . . .
end BelongsTo;
procedure Position (X : integer) : integer;
    . . . .
end Position;
```

{procedures may return values in Modula-2}

{modules may have a body; the body is executed when the
    module scope is entered}

{Here the body may be used to initialize Stored_Int}

Modula-2 modules can export any kind of entity including types. When a type is exported, the details of its structure also are automatically exported. Modula-2 provides a solution to the problem of hiding the structures of encapsulated data types, but this works only if the modules that implement abstract data types appear at the outermost level of the nesting structure. In fact, outermost level modules that export entities are split into two parts: a definition module (DM) and an implementation module (IM). Basically, a DM lists all items exported by the module that might be used by the *client modules*, that is, modules that import those items. To hide the details of an exported type, Modula-2 provides a so-called *opaque export*. Opaque export means that only the name of the type is listed in the DM, and all details are given in the corresponding IM. To allow efficient implementation, opaque export is restricted to pointers; thus, to hide the details, abstact data objects must be defined as accessible via pointers.

The following example defines the abstract data type complex number that we have already described in CLU and Ada.

```
definition module ComplexNumbers;
    export qualified Complex, Initialize, Add;
    {the attribute qualified means that exported names are
    accessed by the client using the dot notation: module_name.
    imported_entity.}

    type Complex; {This is opaque export because no detail about
    the type is given here. The details are only given in the
    corresponding implementation module}
    procedure Initialize (A,B : real; var X : Complex);
    procedure Add (A,B : Complex) : Complex
end ComplexNumbers.

implementation module ComplexNumbers;
    type C= record
                R, I : real
            end;
```

```
type Complex=pointer to C;
procedure Initialize (A,B : real ; var X : Complex);
begin
    new (X);
    X↑.R := A ; X↑.I := B
end Initialize;
procedure Add (A,B : Complex) : Complex;
    var T : Complex;
begin
    new (T);
    T↑.R := A↑.R+B↑.R;
    T↑.I:= A↑.I+B↑.I;
    return (T)
end Add
end ComplexNumbers.
```

4.5.2.4   Abstract Data Types in a Dynamic Language: Smalltalk

Smalltalk is an interesting language and supports an original programming style. It incorporates the concepts underlying abstract data types—data encapsulation, protection, inheritance, and instantiation—in a highly dynamic binding structure. Also, the language is strongly integrated with its support environment, as we will see in Section 6.4.2. For these reasons, Smalltalk has gained popularity as the best-known example of *object-oriented programming languages*.

The Smalltalk encapsulating mechanism is the *class*, based on SIMULA 67's class. A class describes an abstract data type; class instances are called *objects*. A class contains a description of the *instance variables*, which represent the date structure to be allocated at each instantiation, and a description of the operations to be used to instantiate and manipulate objects. Such operations are called *instance methods*. A method responds to a *message* sent to the object. Apart from syntactic niceties (the so-called syntactic sugar), a method is just a procedure; message-sending is like a procedure call, and response to a message is like procedure execution. Because the Smalltalk syntax is rather unusual, we will concentrate on the concepts rather than distract the reader with syntactic details.

Classes can be organized in a *hierarchy,* where each class has at most one superclass; because the superclass is exactly as any other class, it can have a superclass, and so on. Thus, the resulting structure can be represented by a tree (Figure 4.8). The hierarchical structure is such that a class *inherits* all properties of its superclass(es), as we will see shortly.

Smalltalk variables are uniformly viewed as references to objects. Unlike previous languages however, references are not typed: a variable is not statically bound to a class, but can refer to any class instance. Thus, type check-

Figure 4.8   Class hierarchy.
c is a superclass of c1, c2, c3;
c3 is a superclass of c31, c32, c33.

ing is necessarily delayed to run-time. A message sent to "x" is *type-correct* if the class of the object currently bound to "x" provides a method for it. A class provides a method either because such a method appears in the class definition, or because it appears in its superclass, or its superclass's superclass, and so on. The first method encountered in this search represents the response to the message.

Objects are allocated dynamically under the programmer's control via the **new** statement. Deallocation of unused objects is done automatically by the implementation (see garbage collection in Section 4.6.4).

Dynamic binding of variables to their types makes it easy to write generic code, and thus to implement generic abstract data types. Following the CLU and Ada examples, suppose one wishes to implement a generic abstract data type *set of T* providing operations *insert, delete,* and *is_in,* which require the equality test operator to be defined on the components of parameter type *T*. In Smalltalk one needs to define a class, say, *AnySet* implementing the *set of T* concept. To implement the methods of *AnySet* it is necessary to use the equality operator, for example, the equality operator is a message sent to the parameter of *insert* to compare the value to be inserted with the values already stored in the set. The only thing that Smalltalk requires is that the object to which the message is sent during execution does indeed provide a method to respond to such message. For example, if *complex* is another class implementing type "complex" and the equality test on complex numbers is defined by *complex*, then one can create sets of complex numbers by instantiating an object of class *AnySet,* say, *cSet,* and sending it messages like *insert c1, insert c2,* . . . (*c1* and *c2* being complex objects). The equality operator invoked within *insert* will automatically be bound exactly to the equality test method provided by *complex*.

As the reader might suspect, these highly dynamic binding policies and the requirements to provide an interactive environment to support Smalltalk programming, make the language amenable to an interpretation-oriented implementation.

Except for dynamic binding of variables to types, Smalltalk is heavily based upon SIMULA 67; in particular, it incorporates the concepts of class, prefixing, and access to objects via pointers. However, Smalltalk consciously takes the spirit of SIMULA 67 to its extreme consequence.

The primary concept of Smalltalk is that of an object. Actually, everything in Smalltalk is an object, including classes and control structures. A class is an object of predefined class "class" and, in particular, it provides a method to respond to messages requesting an instantiation. A control structure is described as a message passed to an instance of predefined class "block." Such an instance represents the statements to be executed under supervision of the control structure.

Similarly, run-time Smalltalk entities, such as activation records, also are viewed as Smalltalk objects. Thus, most of the Smalltalk language is described in terms of Smalltalk itself. Consequently, not only the language is easy to understand, but it can be extended or modified by the programmer.

In conclusion, many of the principles upon which Smalltalk is based date back to SIMULA 67; they also can be traced to other languages, in particular, CLU. However, the extreme and uniform approach taken by Smalltalk makes the language the champion of a new programming paradigm: object-oriented programming.

We can see the object-oriented philosophy in action at three levels. First, the language itself is intrinsically object-oriented. Second, the Smalltalk programming support environment provides an interactive, object-oriented user interface (see Chapter 6). Third, the language enforces an object-oriented programming methodology. In fact, in a conventional approach, design decomposes a system into *active* functions that operate upon *passive* objects (data). Conversely, an object-oriented methodology decomposes a system into objects—instances of classes—that model real-world entities. Objects are viewed as active components that respond to messages sent by other objects. Also, objects can be organized in a hierarchy by inheritance.

Apart from purely linguistic issues, Smalltalk has brought up several innovative and influential concepts upon which the design of modern interactive workstations is heavily based. We will discuss them in Section 6.4.2.

4.6 IMPLEMENTATION MODELS

This section reviews the basic implementation models for data objects. The description is intended to be rather language-independent, but the examples given and the emphasis of the discussion are Pascal-oriented. Our representation models are not intended to provide a detailed description of efficient techniques for representing data objects within a computer, which can be highly dependent on the hardware structure. Rather, the most straightforward solutions will be presented, along with some comments on alternative, more efficient representations.

Following the discussion of Chapter 3, data will be represented by a pair consisting of a descriptor and a data object. Rather than use a concrete data structure, we will describe the descriptor abstractly as a set of attributes of

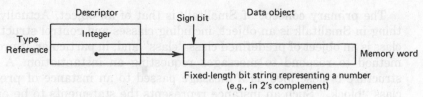

Figure 4.9 Representation of an integer variable.

the data object. The main reason for doing this is that descriptors are usually kept in a table during translation, and, as we have seen, only a subset of the attributes stored there needs to be saved at run-time. Therefore, the format of descriptors—free versus fixed format, number of fields, and so on—is highly dependent on the overall structure of the table, and the number of attributes stored in a descriptor can vary from translation-time to run-time.

4.6.1   Built-in Types and User-Defined Unstructured Types

Integers and reals are hardware-supported on most conventional computers that provide fixed and floating-point arithmetic. Integer and real variables are often represented as shown in Figures 4.9 and 4.10.

Values in a subrange can be represented as if they were in the base type, so that transfer of values between the subrange and the basic type does not require any conversion, only run-time checks. The descriptor must contain the values of the subrange bounds; such values are needed at run-time to make bounds checking possible.

Values of an enumeration type t can be mapped into the integer values 0 to n-1, n being the cardinality of t. This mapping does not introduce any possibility of mixing up values of type t with values of any other enumeration type, if all run-time accesses are routed via a descriptor containing the type information. The use of descriptors is of course not necessary for typed languages.

Booleans and characters can be viewed as enumeration types and implemented as above. To save space, characters can be stored in storage units

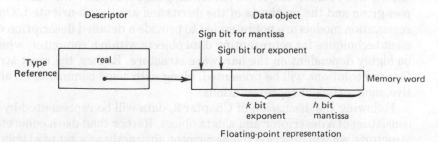

Figure 4.10   Representation of a real variable.

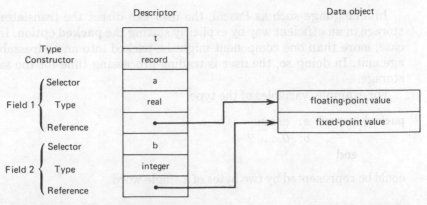

Figure 4.11   Representation of a Pascal record.

smaller than a word (e.g., bytes), if such units are addressable by the hardware directly. It is also possible to pack several booleans declared in the same unit into the same word (or byte), each boolean being represented by a particular bit. In this case, accessing an individual boolean (i.e., a bit) within the collection (i.e., a word or a byte) would be less efficient on machines that do not have bit addressing.

4.6.2 Structured Types

4.6.2.1 Cartesian Product

The standard representation of a data object of a Cartesian product type is a sequential layout of the components. The descriptor contains the Cartesian product type name and one set of triples (name of the selector, type of the field, reference to a data object) for each field.

Figure 4.11 illustrates this representation for a variable of the Pascal type

type t= **record** a: *real*;
              b: *integer*
       end

Each component of the Cartesian product occupies an integral number of addressable storage units (e.g., words), and can be referenced within the program by giving the field name. Field names cannot be used as values of variables. In a strongly typed language, therefore, descriptors need not be saved at run-time, and the reference to each field within the activation record of the unit to which the Cartesian product is local can be evaluated by the translator.*

---

*This is true for Pascal records. For simplicity's sake the possibility of having dynamic arrays as components of a Cartesian product (as in ALGOL 68) is ignored here.

In a language such as Pascal, the user can direct the translator to use storage in an efficient way by explicitly stating the **packed** option. In such a case, more than one component might be packed into an addressable storage unit. In doing so, the user is trading processing time for the saving in storage.

For example, variables of the type

packed record a: *char*;
     b: *0 .. 7*
  end

could be represented by two bytes of a single word.

4.6.2.2 Finite Mapping

A conventional representation of a finite mapping allocates an integral number of addressable storage units (e.g., words) for each component. The descriptor contains the finite-mapping type name; the name of the base type of the domain type, along with the values of the bounds; the range type name, along with the number of locations necessary to store each element; the reference to the first location of the area where the data object is stored. For example, the Pascal declaration

type a= **array** [0 .. 10] **of** *real*

could be represented as in Figure 4.12.

Because indexing into the array can be done by subscripting with a variable, the array bounds should be saved in a run-time descriptor to perform bounds checking at run-time.

A reference to $a[i]$ is computed as an offset from the address (b) of the first component of the array (within the activation record of the unit in

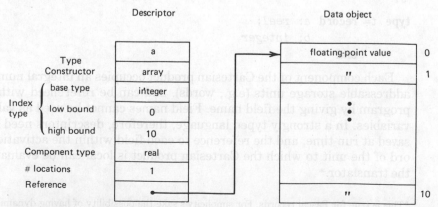

Figure 4.12 Representation of a Pascal array.

which the array is local). If the domain type is a subrange $m \mathinner{\ldotp\ldotp} n$ and the number of words occupied by each element is k, then the offset to be evaluated for accessing $a[i]$ is $k(i - m)$. Thus, a reference to $a[i]$ can be expressed as $b + k(i - m) = (b - km) + ki = b' + ki$, where b' is a constant that can be evaluated at compile-time.

As in the discussion presented in Section 3.6.2.2, in a language that supports dynamic arrays, the descriptor can be split into a static part and a dynamic part. The static part contains the information that is used only at translation time (such as the type of the array components) and a reference to the dynamic part. The dynamic part is allocated at run-time within the activation record of the unit that declares the array at an offset known at translation time. It contains a reference to the array data object (which, in general, can only be evaluated at run-time) and the values of the bounds. Any access to a dynamic array is translated as an indirect address through the dynamic descriptor (which is called a *dope vector*).

4.6.2.3 Sequences

Both sequences of characters (strings) and sequences of records on a backup storage (i.e., files) are represented in a variety of ways, depending both on the semantics of the language and—especially in the case of files—on certain aspects of the machine architecture.

In Pascal, strings are nothing more than a packed array of characters; therefore, their lengths are statically determinable and cannot be changed. In Ada, strings are nothing more than dynamic arrays of characters; therefore, the length generally is unknown at translation time, and becomes known upon entry to the unit in which the string variable is declared. In both languages, strings can be represented as other arrays (Section 4.7.2.2).

In other languages, such as SNOBOL4 and ALGOL 68, strings may vary arbitrarily in length, having no programmer-specified upper bound. As we have seen, strings of this kind are dynamic variables and must be allocated on a heap. Figure 4.13 shows an example of a possible representation for a string of length 5. As before, the descriptor is split into a static part and a dynamic part; the dynamic part is allocated on the activation record stack and contains the current string length (useful for dynamic type checking) and a reference to the head of the string. The string is allocated on the heap as a linked list of words, each word containing one or more characters. The number of characters stored in a word depends on the word size; Figure 4.13 assumes that each word contains two characters.

4.6.2.4 Discriminated Union

A variable of discriminated union type is not bound to any particular variant, but the variant can vary as a result of assignments. Therefore, the amount of space to be allocated for the variable should be sufficient to hold values of the variant requiring the most space.

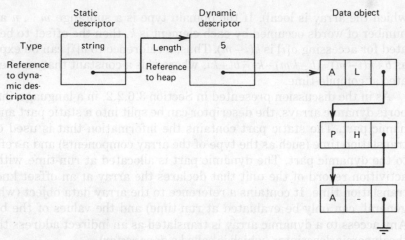

Figure 4.13   Representation of a variable-length string.

Ada provides the option of binding a variable to a specific variant. In such a case, the amount of space to be allocated can be exactly that required by the variant.

Figure 4.14 shows the representation of a variable of the following discriminated union type.

type *v*= **record** *a*: *integer*;
                   case *b*: *boolean* **of**
                           true: (*c*: *integer*);
                           false: (*d*: *integer*;
                                        e: *real*)
                   end

The tag field has an entry in the descriptor that points to a case table. For each possible value of the tag, the case table contains a reference to a descriptor for the associated variant.

4.6.2.5 Powerset

It is possible to implement powersets efficiently, in terms of access, manipulation time, and storage space, provided that a machine word has at least as many bits as there are potential members in the set (i.e., the number of elements in the base type). The presence of the ith element of the base type in a certain set S is denoted by a "1" as the value of the ith bit of the word associated with S. The empty set is represented by all zeros in the word. The union between two sets is easily performed by an *or* between the two associated words, and the intersection by an *and*. If the machine does not allow

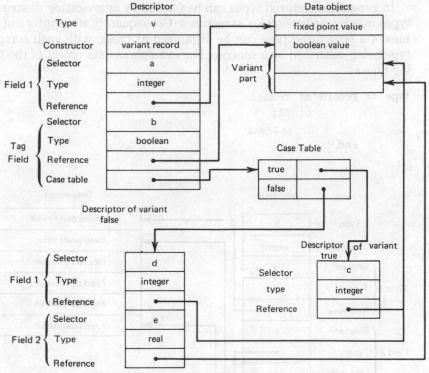

Figure 4.14 Representation of a discriminated union.

bit-level access, test for membership requires shifting the required bit into an accessible word position (e.g., the sign bit), or using a mask.

The existence of such an appealing representation for powersets is responsible for the implementation-defined limits for the cardinality of sets, which is usually equal to the size of a memory word.

4.6.2.6 Pointers

A pointer variable holds as a value the absolute address of an object of the type to which the pointer is bound. The description of such type appears in the descriptor of the pointer. The pointer value **nil** can be represented by an address value that causes a hardware-generated error trap to catch an inadvertent reference via a pointer with value **nil**. For example, the value might be an address beyond the physical addressing space into a protected area.

Pointer variables are allocated on the activation record stack, like any other varaible. In Pascal, data objects that are referred to via a pointer variable are allocated in the heap.

In general, structured types can be formed by aggregating unstructured types in arbitrarily complex structures. Consequently, descriptors of variables of a structured type can be organized as trees, with each component type being described by a subtree. For example, a data object of the following type t

type t= **record** a: *real*;
$\qquad\qquad\quad$ b: *t1*;
$\qquad\qquad\quad$ c: *integer*
$\qquad$ **end**

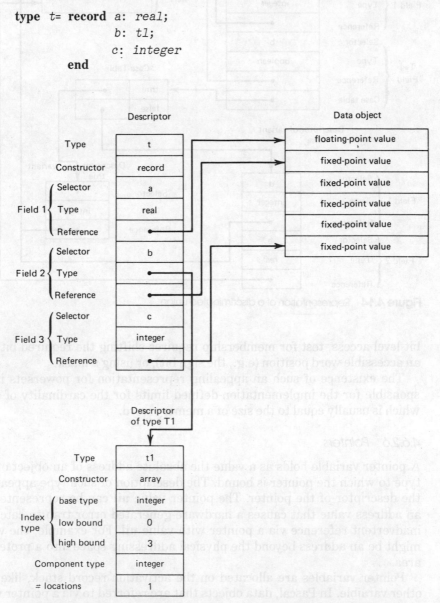

Figure 4.15 An example of representation of a hierarchically structured data object.

where

$t1 =$ **array** $[0 .. 3]$ **of** *integer*

can be represented as in Figure 4.15.

Similarly, a two-dimensional array variable of the type

type $t2 =$ **array** $[0 .. 3]$ **of** $t4$

where

$t4 =$ **array** $[0 .. 5]$ **of** *integer*

can be represented as in Figure 4.16.

Each component of type $t4$ of an array of type $t2$ is represented by six consecutive integer values. Each elementary component of the array can be indexed by a pair (i,j)—i being a value in the subrange $0 .. 2$ that selects a component of type $t4$ and j being a value in the subrange $0 .. 5$ that selects an integer within this component. If b is the starting address of the array within its activation record, the reference to the component is given by the expression $b + 6i + j$.

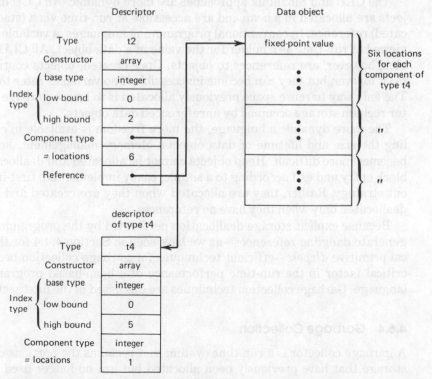

Figure 4.16   An example of representation of a hierarchically structured data object.

4.6.3 Classes and Abstract Data Types

The implementation of SIMULA 67 classes can be rather straightforward, if we do not consider the possibility of class instance bodies to run quasiconcurrently. Class references, like ALGOL 68 or Pascal reference variables, are allocated on the stack; variables that correspond to attributes of a class are allocated on the heap (see Exercise 4.11).

Other programming languages that contain constructs derived from the SIMULA 67 class have a different behavior as far as the generation of encapsulated data objects is concerned. Two opposite approaches are briefly mentioned below.

The first approach is the more static approach followed by Modula-2 and Ada. The basic idea is that the encapsulating mechanism (**module** in Modula-2, **package** in Ada) should simply package a set of highly related declarations and provide suitable initialization. The encapsulating mechanism does not introduce a new template of a unique, structured object to be dynamically created, but only a set of (partially visible) declarations. Among the exported entities can be types, but the variables of such types behave like other program variables.

The CLU and Smalltalk approaches are more dynamic. All CLU data objects are allocated in a heap and are accessible at run-time via a (stack-allocated) reference. In conventional programming languages, a variable can be viewed at run-time as a holder for the value of a data object. All CLU variables, however, are references to objects. Once created, objects continue to exist forever, but they can become inaccessible if no variables refer to them. The only way to reuse space previously allocated is to have a garbage collector reclaim storage occupied by unreferenced data objects.

The more dynamic a language, the more freedom is available in controlling the size and lifetime of data objects. Memory management, however, becomes more difficult. Heap objects cannot be allocated and deallocated at block entry and exit according to a simple, easily implemented, first-in/first-out strategy. Rather, they are allocated when they are created and can be deallocated only when they have no references.

Because explicit storage deallocation performed by the programmer can generate dangling references—as we have seen in Section 4.4.4 for the Pascal primitive *dispose*—efficient techniques for garbage collection become a critical factor in the run-time performance of a heap-based programming language. Garbage collection techniques are discussed in the next section.

4.6.4 Garbage Collection

A garbage collector is a run-time system that reclaims the portions of heap storage that have previously been allocated but are no longer used by the program. Usually, the garbage collector is automatically invoked when the space set aside for the heap is nearly full. Garbage collection is needed for languages that support dynamic variables; it is vital for languages like LISP that cause a large amount of dynamic memory activity. In fact, garbage collection was invented for implementing the first LISP systems.

Garbage collection is reasonably easy when

  i. The heap data objects have fixed size.
 ii. It is known *a priori* which fields of a heap object contain pointers to other heap data objects.
iii. It is possible to find all the pointers into the heap.

Free fixed-size storage elements can be chained together in a *free list*; the garbage collector is automatically called when a request for a new heap element is issued and the free list is empty.

The following two-step method for garbage collection can be implemented easily.

1. Mark all reachable heap data objects, starting from the references stored in the stack. To do so, a temporary stack T may be used. Initially, T contains the heap references in the stack. Every time the top element E is popped, the object referenced by E is marked, and E is replaced by the references to the node(s) referenced by E, if they are not marked. When T becomes empty, all reachable heap data objects have been marked.

2. Insert all unmarked data objects into the free list.

This simple method presents a number of problems in practice.

(a) Heap objects are of variable size and contain pointers to other heap objects in different positions. As a result, the identification of unreferenced data objects can proceed in a way similar to the homogeneous-size case outlined above, provided that the heading of each data object contains coded information (i.e., a run-time descriptor) about the fields of the data object that contain references to other heap objects and about the size of the object.

(b) As we did for SIMPLESEM, the stack and the heap are often implemented as growing from the two sides of a fixed-size main memory area. In such a case, the garbage collector is called when the two areas meet, because the heap must be compacted to allow the stack to grow. Implementation of this method, however, requires that some space be set aside for the additional stack used by the marking algorithm. This stack can be implemented in an area within the heap, but its size is very critical. If it is large, space for the heap is lost; if it is small, there is a chance of overflow during execution of the marking algorithm.

An alternative method that does not require an additional stack is described in (Schorr and Waite 1967). Starting from a reference into the heap stored into the stack, a chain of heap objects is traversed to the end. As each heap element is reached, the element is marked and the pointer is reversed. When the end of the chain is reached, the algorithm follows the reversed pointers. As a side chain is encountered, a new traversal is accomplished in a similar manner.

(c)   As a consequence of the variable size of heap objects, the free-list solution is not adequate, because of memory fragmentation. There might be no blocks of consecutive storage locations that can hold a new heap data object while the *total* amount of fragmented free space is larger than the requested amount. Free-storage compaction is thus necessary. The main difficulty is that pointers to active heap objects must be readjusted when heap objects are shifted to different locations.

The main problem with garbage collection is that "useful" processing time is lost every time the garbage collector is invoked. This can be particularly dangerous in real-time systems, because an urgent request for service might arrive from the environment just after the garbage collector has started its rather complex activity.

Garbage collection can be distributed more uniformly over processing time by using a *reference counting* scheme. In such a scheme, each allocated data object keeps track of how many other data objects reference it. When the count reaches zero, the storage area allocated for it can be relinquished. Unfortunately, this method does not work in the case of circularly linked heap objects. When there are no references from the stack to the circular structure, reference counts associated with each node of the list are not zero, but equal one. Solutions to this problem are cited in the Suggestions for Further Reading section at the end of the chapter.

Finally, we would like to mention that garbage collection can also be viewed as a process that is concurrently active with the program under execution. Parallel garbage-collection techniques might become of practical interest with the advent of new multiprocessor architectures. A multiprocessor dedicated to the execution of a high-level, heap-based programming language might reserve a processor to perform on-line garbage collection. The decreasing cost of processors will probably make this solution appealing in the future.

SUGGESTIONS FOR FURTHER READING
AND BIBLIOGRAPHIC NOTES

The systematic view of data aggregates and the classification of data-structuring methods presented in Section 4.2 are taken from C. A. R. Hoare in (Dahl et al. 1972). Hoare defines Cartesian products, finite mappings, sequences, discriminated unions, recursive data structures, and powersets. He also discusses implementation models for each data-structuring mechanism.

A critical comparison of ALGOL 68 and Pascal, with particular attention to their type structures, is presented by (Tanenbaum 1978) and D. M. Berry in (Wegner 1979).

Pascal and C are compared in (Feuer and Gehani 1982). (Habermann 1973), (Lecarme and Desjardins 1975), (Welsh et al. 1977), and (Tennent 1978) contain several comments on original Pascal and, in particular, show the insecurities of its type structure. (Fischer and LeBlanc 1980) discuss implementation issues of type checking for Pascal programs.

Abstract data types were introduced in (Liskov and Zilles 1974). Formal approaches to the specification of abstract data types are presented in (Liskov and Zilles 1975), (Wulf et al. 1976), (Guttag 1977), (Goguen et al. 1978), and (Guttag et al. 1978). (Gries and Gehani 1977) contains several insights into the concept of generic data type. The conference proceedings (ACM-SIGPLAN 1976) contains many papers on data types and data abstraction. An overview of programming language concepts related to data types can be found in the survey paper by P. Wegner in (Wegner 1979). Abstraction mechanisms and language design are studied in (Hilfinger 1983).

Besides CLU, Ada, Modula-2, and Smalltalk, other languages provide data abstraction facilities, for example, Euclid, Gypsy, Mesa, Alphard, and Russell. Alphard (Shaw et al. 1977), (Wulf et al. 1976), (Shaw 1981) and Russell (Demers and Donahue 1980a), (Demers and Donahue 1980b), (Demers and Donahue 1985) are particularly interesting from the data abstraction viewpoint. A class construct based on SIMULA 67 has been added to C recently; the resulting language is called C++ (Stroustrup 1984).

Implementation models for data objects are analyzed in the aforementioned paper by C. A. R. Hoare in (Dahl et al. 1972), in most compiler design textbooks—including (Gries 1971), (Aho et al. 1986), and (Barrett and Couch 1979)—and in other programming language textbooks, such as (Pratt 1984). Garbage collection is studied in (Schorr and Waite 1967), (Knuth 1973), and (Deutsch and Bobrow 1976). (Pratt 1984) contains a survey of garbage collection techniques for heap-based programming languages. The paper by U. Hill in (Bauer and Eickel 1976) presents a detailed discussion of special run-time techniques for ALGOL 68. Parallel garbage collection is discussed in (Steele 1975) and (Dijkstra et al. 1978).

EXERCISES

4.1 What are the differences between Pascal's (and ALGOL 68's) type-definition facilities and abstract data types?

4.2 What is strong typing, and what are its benefits?

4.3 Give simple examples that show that Pascal, as defined in the Report, is not strongly typed.

4.4 Design simple test programs to assess the type-compatibility rules adopted by your Pascal compiler.

4.5 Design simple test programs to verify the security of variant records in your Pascal implementation.

4.6 Design simple test programs to evaluate the security of pointers in your AL-GOL 68 implementation.

4.7 Design simple test programs to evaluate the security of pointers in your Pascal implementation.

4.8 Discuss the problematical issues of Pascal enumerations according to the criticisms raised in (Welsh et al. 1977) and (Tennent 1978). Give simple programs to illustrate your points.

4.9 Is the mode

union (int, ref int)

legal in ALGOL 68? Does a similar problem arise in Pascal?

4.10 The class *stack* declared in Section 4.5.1 has an attribute *first*, which is used to point to the first stack element, and the four attributes *pop, push, top*, and *empty*, which are used to operate on the stack instance. We discussed the problem that *first* is directly accessible from outside the class and thus unprotected. All variables and procedures declared in the outer block of a class are accessible from the outside. Why is it not possible to make *first* inaccessible by declaring it as a variable local to an inner block in the class? Can it be made local to one of the procedures?

4.11 Classes can be implemented by associating an activation record with each class. For each attribute, the activation record contains enough storage for its value if it is a variable, and a pointer to the code segment if it is a procedure. The code segment corresponding to the class implements the initialization code. The execution of a **new** statement causes the allocation of an activation record for the class and the execution of the initialization code.

(a) Can activation records for classes be allocated on a stack?

(b) Does each instance of a class require its own copy of the procedures that are attributes of the class?

4.12 How can discriminated unions be implemented in SIMULA 67? How can the INSPECT statement of SIMULA 67 be used to deal with discriminated unions in a safe way? What are the differences between this statement and the ALGOL 68 conformity clause?

4.13 What are the differences between SIMULA 67's classes and abstract data types?

4.14 What are the basic semantic differences between the CLU cluster and the Ada package?

4.15 Two CLU clusters with the following headings are given:

```
STACK= cluster is CREATE, PUSH, POP, TOP, EMPTY
QUEUE= cluster is CREATE, ENQUEUE, DEQUEUE, FIRST, EMPTY
```

Cluster STACK defines LIFO data structures. Cluster QUEUE defines FIFO data structures. Both abstract data types can store elements of the same type (say, integers).

(a) Design a function SAME that gives a true result if the sequence of items extracted from a stack (via operation TOP) and from a queue (via procedure FIRST) are the same.

(b) Function SAME would be more efficient if it had direct access to the data structures (e.g., arrays) used to represent stacks and queues. How can an Ada implementation solve this problem?

4.16 Let X be a n-dimensional Pascal array declared in procedure P, and let o be its offset within P's activation record. Let $lb_1, lb_2, \ldots lb_n$, and $ub_1, ub_2, \ldots, ub_n$ be the lower and upper bounds, respectively, of the n subscripts. How can the address of $X[i_1, i_2 \ldots i_n]$ be evaluated at run-time? (*Hint*: suppose that X is stored in row-major order).

4.17 How can mode **bits** of ALGOL 68 be used to implement powersets?

4.18 Assume that X is a subclass of Y, that is, X has been declared as Y **class** X **begin** . . . **end**. Given the two declarations

```
ref (X) a;
ref (Y) b;
```

Simula 67 allows both the following assignment statements.

```
a:- b;
b:- a;
```

One of these two assignment statements can be used to show that SIMULA 67 is not strongly typed. Which one? (*Hint*: consider accessing attributes of the class after each of the assignments.) Propose a rule that would prevent such assignments. Are there reasons not to use your rule?

4.19 ALGOL 68 and Euclid adopt structural type equivalence. As mentioned in Section 4.4.3, recursively defined types might cause the type-checking algorithm to loop forever. How do these languages solve this problem?

4.20 Discuss type compatibility as adopted by ISO Pascal.

4.21 Give arguments that show how Ada attributes support program portability.

4.22 What are the basic semantic differences between Ada packages and Smalltalk classes?

4.23 Compare the facilities provided by Ada and Modula-2 to define abstract data types.

4.24 Give a list of desirable properties of a language supporting abstract types and classify SIMULA 67, CLU, Ada, Smalltalk, and Modula-2, according to the list.

4.25 Using the principles underlying Smalltalk and choosing any self-explaining syntactic notation, give an object-oriented description of SIMPLESEM as described in Chapter 3.

Control Structures

This chapter is devoted to a detailed analysis of control structures—the mechanisms by which programmers can specify the flow of execution among the components of a program. In Section 2.3, we distinguished between unit-level control structures and statement-level control structures. For simplicity, we will start our analysis with the latter category. Unit-level control structures and their implementation models will be studied in Section 5.2.

5.1 STATEMENT-LEVEL CONTROL STRUCTURES

Statement-level control structures refer to language constructs that are used to order the sequence in which individual statements are executed. There are three kinds of statement-level control structures in traditional programming languages: sequencing, selection, and repetition. We analyze each of these separately in Sections 5.1.1 through 5.1.3.

We will see that statement-level control structures can have a great impact on the readability and maintainability of programs. In fact, programming is intellectually manageable only if we use control structures to relate program statements to one another in a sufficiently simple and regular scheme. Section 5.1.4 assesses the various statement-level control structures in this light.

5.1.1. Sequencing

Sequencing is the simplest structuring mechanism available in programming languages. It is used to indicate that the execution of a statement (B) must follow the execution of another statement (A):

A;B

where ";" (which can be read as "and then") denotes the sequencing control operator. Languages that adopt a line-oriented format (e.g., FORTRAN) use the end of the line implicitly to separate instructions and impose a sequencing mechanism among them. It is possible to group statements of a sequence together to form a unique *compound* statement. Several languages (e.g., ALGOL 60 and Pascal) use the bracketing keywords **begin**, **end** for this purpose, for example, **begin** A;B . . . **end**.

5.1.2. Selection

Selection control structures allow the programmer to specify that a choice is to be made among a certain number of possible alternative statements. The logical IF statement of FORTRAN is an example of a selection statement that specifies the execution of a statement according to a boolean expression. For example, the FORTRAN statement

```
IF (I.GT.O) I=I-1
```

decreases the value of I by one if I is positive.

More general and powerful is the **if** statement of ALGOL-like languages, which was later incorporated in the 1977 FORTRAN standard. Here a **then** and an **else** alternative allows the programmer to choose between two control paths as a consequence of a test, where an alternative may be any statement (e.g., a compound statement). For example, the program fragment

```
if i = 0
   then i:= j
   else begin i:= i + 1;
              j:= j - 1
        end
```

sets i to the value of j if $i = 0$; otherwise, it sets i to $i + 1$ and j to $j - 1$. If the keywords **begin**, **end** are omitted, $j: = j - 1$ is considered a statement following the selection, and thus also executed for $i = 0$.

The selection construct of ALGOL 60 raises a well-known ambiguity problem. In the example

if $x > 0$ **then if** $x < 10$ **then** $x:= 0$ **else** $x: = 1000$

it is not clear whether the **else** branch is part of the innermost conditional (**if** $x < 10$ . . .) or the outermost conditional (**if** $x > 0$ . . .). The execution of the above statement with $x = 15$ would assign 1000 to x under one interpretation, but leave it unchanged under the other. To eliminate ambiguity, the ALGOL 60 syntax requires an unconditional statement in the **then** branch of an **if** statement. Thus, the above fragment must be replaced either by

(i) **if** $x > 0$ **then begin if** $x < 10$ **then** $x: = 0$ **else** $x: = 1000$ **end**

or

(ii) **if** $x > 0$ **then begin if** $x < 10$ **then** $x := 0$ **end else** $x := 1000$ depending on the desired interpretation.

The same problem is solved in PL/I and Pascal by automatically matching an **else** branch to the closest conditional without an **else**. Thus, the brackets **begin**, **end** would be unnecessary in case (*i*). This disambiguation rule is explicitly stated in the language definition. Even though the rule removes the ambiguity, deeply nested conditional structures are difficult to read, especially if the program is written without careful indentation. The brackets **begin**, **end** thus should be used to make the desired interpretation explicit.

A syntactic variation that avoids this problem is adopted by ALGOL 68, which uses the keyword **fi** as an enclosing final bracket of the **if** statement. A sequence of statements is allowed between the keywords **then** and **else**, and **else** and **fi**. This makes it unnecessary to use the brackets **begin**, **end** to construct a compound statement. Thus, the above examples may be coded in ALGOL 68 as

```
if i= 0
   then i:= j
   else i:= i+1;
        j:= j-1
fi
```

and

```
if x>0 then if x<10 then x:= 0 else x:= 1000 fi fi
if x>0 then if x<10 then x:= 0 fi else x:= 1000 fi
```

depending on the desired interpretation. A similar solution was adopted by Ada, which uses the keyword **end if** to close a selection.

Both ALGOL 68 and Ada allow the programmer to use an abbreviation if more alternatives can be chosen, depending on different conditions. For example, the awkward program fragment

```
if a
   then S1
   else if b
           then S2
           else if c
                   then S3
                   else S4
                fi
        fi
fi
```

can be written in ALGOL 68 by using the contraction **elif** (Ada uses **elsif**) and eliminating the **fi** (**end if** in Ada) of the inner clauses

```
if a
   then S₁
elif b
   then S₂
elif c
   then S₃
   else S₄
fi
```

PL/I has adopted the special construct SELECT to specify selection among two or more branches. The above example can be coded in PL/I as

```
SELECT:
     WHEN (A) S₁;
     WHEN (B) S₂;
     WHEN (C) S₃;
     OTHERWISE S₄;
END;
```

Multiple-choice selection constructs are expressed in other languages, such as ALGOL 68, Pascal, C, and Ada, by the **case** statement, which specifies selection of a branch based on the value of an expression. For example, the following Pascal fragment evaluates *result* by manipulating *operand1* and *operand2* according to a boolean operator specified by a character-valued variable *operator*.

```
var operator: char;
    operand1, operand2, result: boolean;
    . . . . . . . . . . . . .
    case operator of
        '.': result:= operand1 and operand2;
        '+': result:= operand1 or operand2;
        '=': result:= operand1 = operand2
    end
```

In ALGOL 68, selection of a **case** branch can be based only on the value of an integer expression. The value of such an expression, say, i, selects the ith branch for execution. Pascal selection, on the other hand, can be based on the value of an expression of any ordinal type, and branches are explicitly labeled by one or more values that can be evaluated by the expression. Consequently, the order in which the branches appear in the text is immaterial.

Originally, Pascal did not specify the effect of a value of the selecting expression that is out of the range of values explicitly listed,* nor did it allow the programmer to specify in the construct which actions should be executed in this case. In ALGOL 68, an optional **out** clause can be specified; it is executed when the value of the selecting expression is not in the stated set of values. If the **out** clause is absent, it is equivalent to an **out** clause with a **skip** statement, which is equivalent to a null statement. Many Pascal implementations allow an **otherwise** alternative to cover this case.

The Ada multiple selection combines the positive aspects of ALGOL 68 and Pascal. First, branch selection uses expressions of both enumeration and integer types. Second, it is required that all possible values of the type of the discriminating expression be provided in the selections. Third, the abbreviation **others** can be used to represent values that are not explicitly listed. Therefore, the multiple selection of the previous example might be coded in Ada as follows.

```
case OPERATOR of
    when "."=>RESULT:= OPERAND1 and OPERAND2;
    when "+"=>RESULT:= OPERAND1 or OPERAND2;
    when "="=>RESULT:= OPERAND1 = OPERAND2;
    when others=> . . . produce error message . . .
end case;
```

A simple and powerful mechanism for specifying selection has been proposed by Dijkstra (1976). The general form of the construct is

```
if B1→S1
▯ B2→S2
▯ B2→S2
---
▯ BN→SN
fi
```

where B_i, $1 \le i \le N$, is a boolean expression called a *guard* and S_i, $1 \le i \le N$ is a statement list. $B_i \rightarrow S_i$, $1 \le i \le N$, is called a *guarded command*. The semantics of the **if** statement is that any S_i for which the guard B_i evaluates to true can be nondeterministically chosen for execution. If no guard evaluates to true, the program aborts; therefore, the programmer is forced to list all the possible choices.

The most interesting and novel feature of Dijkstra's construct is the abstraction that nondeterminism can provide. The programmer is not forced to overspecify programs when it is irrelevant which of a certain set of

---

*It is an error according to ISO Pascal.

choices is actually chosen. For example, the maximum of two numbers A and B can be evaluated elegantly as

```
if A ≤ B → MAX:= A
☐ A ≥ B → MAX:= B
fi
```

As we will see in Section 5.2.4.3, Ada contains a specialized form of the guarded **if** statement.

5.1.3. Repetition

Most useful computations involve repetition of a number of actions. Consequently, all high-level languages provide control structures that allow the programmer to specify looping over a certain set of instructions.

FORTRAN provides the DO statement, with which a fixed number of iterations can be specified by introducing a counter (the *loop control variable*) that assumes values over a finite integer set. For example

```
DO 7 I=1,10
 A(I)=0
 B(I)=0
7 CONTINUE
```

sets to zero the elements of index 1 through 10 of arrays A and B. Counter-driven iterative control structures are useful and have been adopted by most programming languages, including COBOL, ALGOL 60, C, and PL/I. Pascal allows counter-driven loops where the counting variable is of any ordinal type, as shown in the following example.

type *day*= (*sunday, monday, tuesday, wednesday, thursday, friday, saturday*);
var *week_day: day;*

    . . .
    for *week_day*:= *monday* **to** *friday* **do**
    . . .

Scanning days in reverse order can be written as

for *week_day*:= *friday* **downto** *monday* **do** . . .

Pascal also prescribes that the control variable and its lower and upper bounds must not be altered in the loop. The value of the loop control variable also is assumed to be undefined outside the loop. These restrictions, far from placing arbitrary constraints on the programmer, contribute to the readability and maintainability of the resulting programs by limiting the scope of the loop counter.

Repetition over a finite set of values can be used to model the frequent case in which the number of repetitions is known in advance, such as in the processing of arrays. Often, however, one does not know the number of repetitions in advance. For example, a program that processes all records in a file usually does not know the number of file elements. For this reason, most programming languages defined after FORTRAN provide condition-driven repetition structures, that is, repetition structures in which new iterations are executed until the value of a boolean expression is changed.

Pascal supports two condition-driven loop constructs. The first (**while** loop) describes any number of iterations, including zero. The second (**repeat until** loop) describes loops with at least one iteration. The file processing program mentioned can be written in Pascal as outlined here.

```
while not eof (f) do
  begin
    "read item from file f";
    "process item"
  end
```

The end-of-file condition *eof* is evaluated for file *f* before executing the body of the loop. The loop is exited if **not** *eof*(f) is false, that is, the end of file has been reached. Therefore, the program also works correctly in the case of an empty file.

The **repeat until** loop is similar, except that the exit condition is tested at the end of the body of the loop. In the example, if the file always contains at least one element we could write

```
repeat
  "read item from file f";
  "process item"
until eof (f)
```

In this fragment, the loop is repeated as long as the condition *eof*(f) is false.

The counter-driven and the condition-driven control structures of Pascal are combined by PL/I and ALGOL 68 into a single form that is composed of various optional parts. The general form of the ALGOL 68 loop can be written

for *i* **from** *j* **by** *k* **to** *m* **while** *b* **do** . . . **od**

where **do** and **od** enclose the loop body and the **for**, **from**, **by**, **to**, and **while** clauses are all optional. If the **for** clause is omitted, there is no explicit loop-control variable. If the **from** clause is omitted, 1 is implicitly assumed as the starting value of the control variable. If the **by** clause is omitted, the value that increases the counter after each iteration is 1.

For example

to 10 **do** a:= a+2 **od**

executes the loop 10 times, and therefore adds 20 to *a*.

Leaving out **for**, **from**, **by**, and **to** gives a condition-driven loop; leaving out the **while** also gives an endless loop that must be exited explicitly from within the loop.

The control variable of the loop in ALGOL 68 cannot be modified within the loop (as in Pascal), and its scope is defined to be the loop body. Thus, it is inaccessible outside the loop. The values of the expressions following **by** and **to** can be altered within the loop. As far as the loop is concerned, these expressions are evaluated only once, before the loop execution starts; any change to their operands within the loop does not affect the loop termination condition.

Ada has only one loop structure, with the following form.

```
iteration specification loop
       loop body
end loop
```

where *iteration specification* is either

while *condition*

or

for *counting_variable* **in** *discrete_range*

or

for *counting_variable* **in reverse** *discrete_range*.

In addition, the loop can be terminated by an unconditional exit statement

exit;

or a conditional **exit** statement

exit when *condition*;

If the loop is nested within other loops, it is possible to exit an inner loop and any number of enclosing loops.

```
MAIN_LOOP:
    loop

        loop . . .
```

```
        . . .
    exit MAIN_LOOP when A = 0;
        . . .
    end loop;
        . . . . . . . .
end loop MAIN_LOOP;
--after the exit statement, execution continues from here.
```

In the example, control is transferred to the statement following the end of MAIN_LOOP when A is found to be equal to zero in the inner loop. The exit statement is used to specify the premature termination of a loop. It has the same effect as the PL/I LEAVE statement.

Some languages also provide a mechanism to terminate the current iteration of a loop and go on to the next iteration. C's *continue* statement does exactly that. Although such constructs are not needed often, they are natural, for example, when we process a sequence of records and then in case of an error want to ignore the record being processed and proceed to the next record.

Using Dijkstra's guarded commands notation, loops are specified by bracketing the commands by the keywords **do**, **od**.

do B1 → S1
▯ B2 → S2
        . . .
▯ Bn → SN
od

The semantics of the statement is that at each iteration a statement S_i is executed, whose guard B_i is true, $1 \leq i \leq N$. If two or more guards are true, a choice is made nondeterministically. If none is true, the loop terminates. Selection and repetition statements based on guarded commands encourage the production of well-structured and elegant algorithms. Moreover, programs that use these constructs are amenable to the formal reasoning of program correctness.

5.1.4.   An Appraisal of Statement-Level Control Structures

Sequencing, selection, and repetition represent the programmer's basic control-structuring tools for organizing control flow among statements. Sequencing is an abstraction over the sequential fetch of instructions provided by the computer's program counter (SIMPLESEM's instruction pointer). Selection and repetition are abstractions of the very simple, but overly powerful control mechanism provided by the hardware to modify explicitly the value of the program counter, with conditional and unconditional jumps.

There are several reasons why abstract control structures are preferable to the lower-level mechanisms of explicit control transfer. First, they are more problem-oriented; thus, programmers can more easily express their intentions by using the general patterns of sequencing, selection, and repetition. Second, by using explicit jumps, programs can easily assume the well-known unreadable spaghetti-like structure shown in Figure 5.1.

As Dikjkstra observed in his famous letter on the effect of the **goto** statement (Dijkstra 1968a), programs that contain many jumps tend to contain many errors. Dijkstra's argument goes deeper than merely proposing the abolition of the **goto** statement. The **goto** statement is dangerous because it makes reasoning about programs difficult. It does so by breaking the sequential continuity of the program statements and violating the requirement that the solution structure should be reflected in the program structure.

Higher-level control structures ultimately will be translated into the conditional and unconditional jumps of the machine code of a traditional computer, but this should not concern the programmer. The burden of producing efficient machine code should rest entirely with the translator.

There is now widespread consensus that even in applications in which efficiency of programs is the primary goal, obscurity engendered by the use of machine-level control structures is too high a price to be paid. There have been proposals for adding higher-level control structures to existing machine-level languages; more recently, there has been a move toward higher-level languages for systems software applications (e.g., Bliss, C, Modula-2, Euclid, Ada).

As we have seen in Sections 5.1.2 and 5.1.3, a large variety of control structures have been proposed, and there is still no consensus as to which are the best for inclusion in a programming language. Even though sequencing, selection (**if then else**), and repetition (**do while**) theoretically provide a

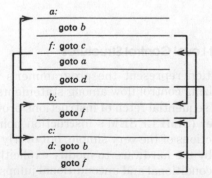

FIGURE 5.1 Spaghetti-like structure produced by explicit jumps.

sufficient set of control structures to code all the possible algorithms for a computer (Böhm and Jacopini 1966), using only these three control structures is often unnatural and results in awkward programs. Additional control structures, such as multiple selection (**case**), counter-driven loops (**for**), and condition-driven **repeat until** loops, although theoretically redundant, can enhance the writability and readability of programs.

A typical case of the practical inadequacy of the above restricted set of control structures arises when it is necessary to exit from the middle of a loop. As an example, suppose that a program processes a deck of cards, each card containing n integer values. The sum of the n values is zero for the last card of the deck. If the sum is not zero, the n values are "valid" and are further processed in an unspecified manner. The simplest solution to this problem can be abstractly written

```
do
   read the n values and evaluate the sum;
   if the sum is zero terminate the loop;
   process the n valid values
od
```

Expressing the program in terms of a **while** loop leads to an undesirable duplication of parts, as shown below.

```
read n values and evaluate the sum;
while sum = 0 do
   begin process the n values;
         read n values and evaluate the sum
   end
```

Similarly, expressing the program in terms of a **repeat until** loop leads to an unnecessary reevaluation of conditions.

```
repeat read n values and evaluate the sum;
   if the sum is not zero
      then process the n values
until the sum is zero
```

The initial solution, which uses an explicit control transfer to break the loop in the middle (using an Ada-like exit), is more natural to write, easier to understand, and more efficiently implementable.

Loops with exits in the middle can be easily coded with a **goto** statement. Because the unrestricted use of the **goto** statement can lead to badly structured programs but restricted uses of it are desirable in cases such as exit from a loop, several languages (e.g., Ada) provide a specific construct (**exit**) mirroring this case. The **exit** provides a restricted (and safe) form of forward **goto** that can be used only to terminate loops. A more general form of the **exit** statement, but one still more restricted than the **goto** statement, is given in Exercise 5.3.

There are cases where one would like to terminate the current iteration of a loop based on some condition that is discovered while executing the loop. This can be done in C with a *continue* statement. If a specialized construct is not available in the language, a programmer might decide to code a solution that uses the **goto** statement.

This phenomenon is quite general. The lack of specialized control structures to solve a problem may lead to unnatural and inefficient solutions, if the **goto** statement is not available. On the other hand, we do not know exactly which specialized control structures should be provided to cover all programming needs.

Most programming languages provide a rich set of disciplined control structures. Often, they also provide an unrestricted **goto** statement. Whether or not this is a good language-design choice is controversial. If programs are designed in a disciplined way, the need for the **goto** statement arises only occasionally. However, when the **goto** statement is available, there is no way to enforce a restricted use of it, and programmers can easily produce spaghetti-like programs. The only, partial, solution consists of adopting a programming standard that relies on **goto**s only for synthesizing "legitimate" control structures when the language does not provide them. Legitimacy can be defined based on the needs of the application.

To summarize, many factors influence the choice of the set of control structures to be included in a language; it is difficult to argue in absolute terms the merits of different solutions. For example, minimality of the set of control structures, which appears to be a reasonable goal as far as the ease of learning a language is concerned, conflicts with other goals, such as expressive power.

5.1.5 User-Defined Control Structures

An interesting property of the Pascal counter-based loop is that the control variable can be of any ordinal type, not just a subset of integers. Further abstraction is provided by languages such as CLU, Alphard, and Euclid, which allow the programmer to have control variables of any abstract data type and provide constructs for specifying how the sequence of values of such control variables should be produced. Even more general is the Smalltalk approach, where control structures are handled in the uniform world of objects, as we mentioned in Section 4.5.2.4.

Such languages can be viewed as *extensible*, because the user can augment the base language by defining new (abstract) data types, new operations (via procedures), and new control structures. Our presentation of user-defined control structures is based on the constructs provided by CLU.

In the CLU program fragment

```
for atom : node in list (x) do
    perform an action on atom
```

atom, the loop control variable, is of user-defined type *node,* and *list* is an *iterator,* which is a particular program unit yielding the sequence of values the **for** loop is to span. These instructions are meant to retrieve and manipulate all the nodes belonging to a list *x.*

The elements of the collection (a list, in the example) are provided by the iterator one at a time. The policy that selects the next element of the collection is hidden to the user of the iterator and implemented by the iterator. The iterator used above can be specified by a module that takes a parameter of abstract type *linked_list* and delivers a parameter of abstract type *node.*

```
list= iter (z : linked_list) yields (node)
        . . .
        yield (n)
        . . .
    end list
```

At each iteration of the loop (**for** *atom* . . .), module *list* is activated and a node yielded by it—by the operation **yield**—is assigned to *atom.* Remember that CLU uses assignment by sharing (Section 4.5.2.1) and, therefore, *atom* denotes the same object delivered by *list.* As a consequence of yielding, the iterator is suspended, its local environment is retained, and control flows back to the loop invocation. At each loop iteration, the iterator is resumed in the saved local environment. When the iterator indicates that the sequence of objects is exhausted, the **for** statement terminates.

The reader should notice that iterators are a special case of coroutines. They are units whose execution is always resumed from wherever they left off, because their local environment is retained from call to call. We explore iterators because they are explicitly restricted to implementing user-defined control structures. You will be asked to outline an implementation of iterators using coroutines in Exercise 5.4.

CLU iterators are called only by **for** statements, and each **for** statement invokes exactly one iterator. Thus, active invocations are always nested and can be implemented easily via a stack policy, as shown below.

5.1.6. Implementation Model for Iterators

We can distinguish among the following four actions associated with an iterator.

- *Calling an iterator,* corresponding to the first activation of an iterator caused by the initiation of a **for** loop.

- *Resuming an iterator,* corresponding to any activation of the iterator after the first iteration.
- *Yielding,* that is, the action of transferring control back from the iterator to the program executing the **for** statement.
- *Returning from an iterator,* when the end of the iterator is reached.

The iterator's activation record contains two return points and a dynamic link. The first return point (*normal return point*) is the address of the first instruction of the body of the **for** loop that calls the iterator. The second return point (*final return point*) is the address of the first instruction after the **for** loop, that is, the instruction to be executed on termination of the iterator. The dynamic link points to the activation record of the unit that executes the loop. The activation record of that unit contains an additional entry (the *resume link*) that is used to chain together in an *iterator chain* the information necessary to resume suspended iterators invoked by the current module (if any).

Calling an iterator resembles a conventional subprogram call: the activation record of the iterator is stacked, and the return points and the dynamic link (to the calling unit's activation record) are set.*

Yielding is different from the usual return from a procedure, because the activation record of the iterator remains on the stack. First, a *resume frame* is pushed onto the stack. The resume frame contains the information necessary to resume the iterator on the next iteration, that is, the address of the instruction where control will go after the iterator is resumed (*return point*) and a reference to the activation record of the iterator (*iterator link*). Second, resume frames for different, nested iterators are linked together via a resume link to form the iterator chain of the calling module, as explained later. Finally, the yielded value is assigned (by sharing) to the loop control variable of the invoking **for**, and control is transferred to the normal point specified in the iterator's activation record.

The iterator chain is a last-in/first-out data structure. After the body of a loop is executed, the resume frame of the iterator to be resumed is the one last inserted into the iterator chain for the current activation record. This resume frame is removed from the chain, and the information contained in it is used to resume the iterator.

Finally, returning from an iterator is identical to the normal return from a subprogram: the iterator's activation record is removed from the stack, and control transfers to the final return point specified therein.

The following example illustrates these mechanisms. Suppose that a module *M* contains the following nested loops.

---

*CLU modules are not statically nested and have no global variables. Therefore, there is no static link. Other languages with an ALGOL-like structure also can be accommodated in this scheme.

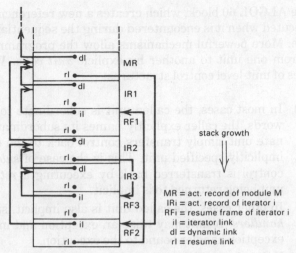

FIGURE 5.2 Configuration of the activation record stack in the presence of iterators.

```
for . . . in iter1 . . . do
  for . . . in iter2 . . . do
```

Also, suppose that module *iter2* contains the following loop

```
for . . . in iter3 . . . do
```

When *M* calls *iter1*, the activation record *IR1* is pushed on top of the stack. Yielding then pushes the resume *RF1*, and the resume link from *M*'s activation record (*MR*) is set to point to *RF1*. A call to *iter2* caused by the execution of *M*'s inner loop then pushes *IR2* on top of the stack. A subsequent call to *iter3* from *iter2*, followed by yielding from *iter3*, pushes *IR3* and *RF3* on top of the stack, and the resume link from *IR2* is set to point to *RF3*. Finally, yielding from *iter2* to *M* pushes *RF2* on top of the stack, and inserts *RF2* into the iterator chain originating in *MR*. After this action, the resume link from *MR* points to *RF2*, and the resume link from *RF2* points to *RF1*. Figure 5.2 sketches the cofiguration of the activation record stack at this point. Details of the structure of activation records are omitted for simplicity: only that information necessary to manage the activation record stack is shown explicitly.

5.2 UNIT-LEVEL CONTROL STRUCTURES

This section discusses the programming-language mechanism for specifying control flow among program units. The simplest mechanism is exemplified by the ALGOL 60 block, which creates a new referencing environment and is executed when it is encountered during the sequential progression of execution. More powerful mechanisms allow the programmer to transfer control from one unit to another by explicit *unit calls*. We will discuss four classes of unit-level control structures:

(i)   In most cases, the called unit is subordinate to the caller. In other words, the caller explicitly names its subordinate unit; the subordinate unit simply transfers control back to the caller, that is, to an implicitly specified unit. This is the case of *subprograms,* in which control is transferred back by executing a *return* operation. The unit being returned to is implicit.

(ii)   In other cases, the called unit is also implicit, such as for *exception handlers.* A unit may raise an exception and implicitly activate an exception handler bound to the exception.

(iii) Units also can be organized in a symmetrical scheme as a set of *coroutines,* in which case both units explicitly activate one another. The units proceed in an interleaved fashion (a special case of coroutines—iterators—was discussed in the last section.).

(iv)   Finally, units can be organized as a set of *concurrent* (or *parallel*) *units* (or *processes*). With concurrent processes, there is no notion of control being passed back and forth between units. Each is considered an autonomous unit.

The following sections contain a discussion of unit-level control structures according to the classification scheme we have just presented.

5.2.1   Explicitly Called Subordinate Units: Style Issues

This class covers subprograms, from FORTRAN subroutines and functions to Ada procedures. The basic run-time modeling issues of unit activation and return have been presented in Chapter 3. Chapter 3 also discussed parameter passing for both data and procedures. The case of type parameters (generic procedures) was studied in Section 4.5 in the context of abstract data types.

In this section we will discuss some problems related to subprograms that can have an impact on the quality of software. We will start from the syntactic notation of subprogram invocation and parameter passing; next, we will address the important concepts of side effects and aliasing in Sections 5.2.1.1 and 5.2.1.2.

In Section 3.7 we saw that the usual form of parameter correspondence in subprogram invocation is the so-called positional method, according to which formal parameters are bound to actual parameters based on their position in the call statement and the procedure header, respectively. The positional method has some disadvantages in terms of readability when the parameter list is long. An alternative form of parameter passing (optional, in Ada) is known as the *keyword method*. Procedure calls explicitly list the correspondence between actual and formal parameters. For example, a subprogram *INIT* with formal parameters *TABLE* and *VALUE*, intended to initialize all components of the integer array *TABLE* to the value of *VALUE*, can be called by writing (in Ada syntax).

```
INIT (TABLE =>X, VALUE =>V),
```

where X and V are the actual parameters corresponding to formal parameters *TABLE* and *VALUE*, respectively.

The keyword method is particularly valuable if the language allows default bindings to be specified for formal parameters. In such a case, a subprogram call can specify simply a subset of the actual parameters. In the example, if the subprogram heading specifies *0* as a default value for *V*, inserting all zeroes into array *B* can be written as

```
INIT (TABLE =>B);
```

As we saw in Section 3.7 parameters can be passed according to different conventions, but the most common ways are call by value and call by reference. The choice whether to pass a parameter by value or by reference can be dictated by several considerations, such as the desire to avoid unwanted side effects caused by inadvertent modification of formal parameters, or efficiency of implementation. In general, passing parameters by reference can be costly in terms of processing time if the formal parameters are used very often within the subprogram, because each access requires indirect addressing. However, if objects are large and/or are accessed only a few times, call by value can be costly both in terms of storage and processing time.

ALGOL 68 has a single parameter-passing mechanism, which is similar to call by value. However, a parameter can be of type **ref m**, that is, its value is a reference to a data object of type m. Therefore, it is also possible to achieve the effect of call by reference.

More precisely, the meaning of the call

```
p (i)
```

to procedure

proc *p*= (**int** a) **void**:
  (. . . *body* . . .)

is stated to be the same as

```
(int a = i;
( . . . body . . . ))
```

Therefore, a is set identically equal to i, that is, it acts as a constant integer within the scope of the call. So the parameter is almost like call by value, except that it cannot be changed.

Had the procedure been declared

proc p= (**ref int** a) **void**:
  (. . . *body* . . .)

then the call $p\,(i)$ would have been (conceptually) expanded to

(**ref int** a = i;
(. . . *body* . . .))

which enables the procedure to access the actual parameter i through the reference a. This is, exactly, call by reference. The rich type structure and the orthogonality of ALGOL 68 are thus exploited to obtain a uniform parameter-passing mechanism.

Call by result can model the so-called function subprograms provided by languages such as Pascal, where the name of the function subprogram acts as a local variable that will ultimately contain the value produced by the function subprogram itself.

Ada provides three parameter-passing conventions: **in**, **out**, and **in out**. By default, an unspecified convention is taken as **in**. An **in** formal parameter acts as a local constant whose value is provided by the corresponding actual parameter and cannot be modified by the subprogram. An **out** formal parameter acts as a local variable whose value is assigned to the corresponding actual parameter upon exit from the subprogram. An **in out** formal parameter acts as a local variable, and permits access and assignment to the corresponding actual parameter. The Ada definition does not say whether parameter passing must be implemented by sharing or by copy. The choice between the two implementations is left entirely to the translator, which may choose on the basis of efficiency. Ada programs that produce different results under the two implementations of parameter passing are called "erroneous." Unfortunately, the translator cannot catch erroneous programs, and therefore such programs may produce different results when compiled with a different compiler. The reason for the possible discrepancy between the two implementation is illustrated in Section 5.2.1.2.

Side effects and aliasing are two common causes of errors in subprograms. At the statement level, we saw that **goto**s can make reasoning about programs hard. A similar situation is caused by side effects and aliasing at the unit level, as we will see shortly.

5.2.1.1 Side Effects

Section 3.5 defined side effects as modifications of the nonlocal environment. Side effects are used principally to provide a method of communication among program units. Communication can be established through non-local variables. However, if the set of nonlocal variables used for this purpose is large and each unit has unrestricted access to the set of nonlocal variables, the program becomes difficult to read and understand. Each unit can potentially reference and modify every variable in the nonlocal environment, perhaps in ways other than those intended for the variable. The problem is that once a global variable is used for communication, it is difficult to distinguish between desired and undesired side effects. For example, if unit $u1$ calls $u2$ and $u2$ inadvertently modifies a nonlocal variable x used for communication between units $u3$ and $u4$, the invocation of $u2$ produces an undesired side effect. Such errors are difficult to find and remove, because the symptoms are not easily traced to the cause of the error. (Note that a simple typing error could lead to this problem.) Another difficulty is that examination of the call instruction alone does not reveal the variables that can be affected by the call. This reduces the readability of programs because, in general, the entire program must be scanned to understand the effect of a call.

Communication via unrestricted access to nonlocal variables is particularly dangerous when the program is large and composed of several units that have been developed independently by several programmers. One way to reduce these difficulties is to use parameters as the only means of communication among units. The overhead caused by parameter passing might make this solution unacceptable in time-critical applications. Alternatively, it must be possible to restrict the set of nonlocal variables held in common by two units to exactly those needed for the communication between the units. Also, it can be useful to specify that a unit can only read, but not modify some variable. These and other problems will be discussed in Chapter 6.

Side effects also are used in passing parameters by reference, where a side effect is used to modify the actual parameter. The programmer must be careful not to produce undesired side effects on actual parameters. The same problem arises with call by name. A more substantial source of obscurity in call by name is that each assignment to the same formal parameter can affect different locations in the environment of the calling unit. Such problems do not arise in call by copy.

Side effects are particularly disturbing for function subprograms. Function subprograms are invoked by writing the subprogram name within an expression, as in

$$w := x + f(x, \ y) + z$$

In the presence of side effects—in Pascal, for example—the call to f might produce a change to x or y (if they are passed by reference), or even z (if z is global to the function) as a side effect. This reduces the readability of the program. Also, one cannot rely on the commutativity of addition in general. In the example, if f modifies x as a side effect, the value produced for w is different if x is evaluated before or after calling f.

Besides affecting readability, side effects can prevent the compiler from generating optimized code for the evaluation of certain expressions. In the example

$$u := x + z + f(x, y) + f(x, y) + x + z$$

the compiler cannot evaluate function f and subexpression $x + z$ just once.

5.2.1.2 Aliasing

Two variables are *aliases* if they denote (*share*) the same data object during a unit activation (see Section 3.5). A modification of the data object under one variable name is automatically visible through all variables that share the object. An example is illustrated by the FORTRAN EQUIVALENCE statement. For instance, the statements

```
EQUIVALENCE (A, B)
A=5.4
```

bind the same data object to A and B and set its value to 5.4. Consequently, the statements

```
B=5.7
WRITE(6, 10)A
```

print 5.7, even though the value explicitly assigned to A was 5.4. The assignment to B affects both A and B.

Aliasing may arise during the execution of a procedure when parameters are passed by reference. Consider the following Pascal procedure, which is supposed to interchange the values of two integer variables without using any local variables.

```
procedure swap (var x, y: integer);
begin   x:= x+y;
        y:= x-y;
        x:= x-y
end
```

Before proceeding, examine the procedure and decide whether or not it works properly.

The answer is "generally yes"; in fact, the procedure works properly except when the two actual parameters are the same variable, as in the call

```
swap (a, a)
```

In this case, the procedure sets a to zero, because x and y become aliases and thus any assignments to x and y within the procedure affect the same location. The same problem may arise from the call

```
swap (b[i], b[j])
```

when the index variables i and j happen to be equal.

Pointers can cause the same problems. In fact, the call

```
swap (p↑, q↑)
```

does not interchange the values pointed at by p and q if p and q happen to point to the same data object.

The above aliases occur because of the following two conditions.

1. Formal and actual parameters share the same data objects; and
2. Procedure calls have overlapping actual parameters.

Aliasing also may occur when a formal (by reference) parameter and a global variable denote the same or overlapping data objects. For example, if procedure *swap* is rewritten as

procedure *swap* (**var** *x*: *integer*);
begin *x*:= *x*+ *a*;
      a:= *x*− *a*;
      x:= *x*− *a*
end

where *a* is a global variable, the call

```
swap (a)
```

generates an incorrect result, because of the aliasing between x and a. It is interesting to note that aliasing does not arise if parameters are passed by copy; such parameters act as local variables within the procedure and the corresponding actual parameters become affected only at procedure exit.

The disadvantages of aliasing affect programmers, readers, and language implementers. Subprograms are hard to understand because, occasionally, different names denote the same data object. This problem cannot be discovered by inspecting the subprogram: rather, discovery requires examining all the units that may invoke the subprogram. As a consequence of aliasing, a subprogram call may produce unexpected and incorrect results.

Aliasing also impairs the possibility of generating optimized code. For example, in the case

```
a:= (x− y * z) + w;
b:= (x− y * z) + u;
```

the subexpression $x - y*z$ cannot be evaluated just once and then used in the two assignments if a is an alias for $x, y,$ or z.

As the difficulties and insecurities of side effects and aliasing have been recognized, some languages have been designed to tame their use. Gypsy and Euclid are two notable examples. Like many languages of the late

1970s, Euclid and Gypsy are based on Pascal. Their major goal is to be used for writing verifiable systems programs. Side effects and aliasing (among others) were seen as features particularly troublesome for program verification, and even for reasoning about programs; they were therefore not included in either language. Euclid and Gypsy are the best-known languages to try such a whole-hearted approach. To simplify matters, we will restrict our discussion to Euclid.

We have defined aliasing as the ability to access the same data object with more than one name within the same unit instance. There are basically two ways to eliminate aliasing. One way is to do away completely with features that make aliasing possible, for example, pointers, reference parameters, global variables, and arrays. This would leave us with a very lean language indeed. The other approach, taken in Euclid, is to place restrictions on the use of such features to rule out the possibility of aliasing.

For reference parameters, the problems only arise if actual parameters are overlapping. If the actual parameters are simple variables, it is necessary to ensure that they are all distinct. Thus the procedure call

```
p (a, a)
```

is considered illegal by Euclid. Passing an array and one of its components also is prohibited. For example, the call

```
p (b[1], b)
```

to a procedure whose heading is

procedure p (**var** x: *integer*; **var** y: **array** [1:10] **of** *integer*)

is illegal because y [1] and x are aliases. These forms of illegal aliasing can be caught at translation time.
However, the call

```
swap (b[i], b[j])
```

to the procedure *swap* generates aliasing only if i is equal to j. Euclid specifies that in such a case the condition

```
i ≠ j
```

be generated by the translator as a *legality assertion*. In the testing phase, legality assertions can be compiled automatically into run-time checks by using a compiler option. If at run-time an assertion evaluates to false, execution is aborted and a suitable error message is produced. The main use of legality assertions, however, is in program verification. The Euclid system, in fact, includes a program verifier, and a Euclid program is considered correct only if the truth of all legality assertions is proven by the verifier.

Handling aliasing in the presence of pointers is more complex. Consider the following Pascal program fragment

var p, q: ↑T;
    . . .
    new (p);
    q:= p

The problem of aliasing between p↑ and q↑ is handled in the same way that arrays and array elements are handled, that is, p↑ and q↑ may be viewed as selectors that reference components of an implicitly defined collection of data—the set of all data objects of type T—the same way that b[i] and b[j] reference components of array b. An assignment to b[i] or b[j] is viewed as an assignment to the entire data object b, which happens to change the value stored in only one portion of b. Similarly, an assignment to p↑ or q↑ may be viewed as a modification of the set of components of type T.

This might appear to be an ingenious but tricky way of looking at the problem of aliasing for pointers. In fact, different data structures might be composed of dynamically generated components of the same type T. Viewing an assignment to p↑ as an assignment to the set of data objects of type T, that is, as a modification of any of such data structures, is not really helpful.

To allow an extra level of checking for nonoverlapping pointers, Euclid introduced the concept of a *collection* (see Section 4.4.4). The programmer is required to divide all dynamic objects into separate collections and indicate which pointers can point into which collections. Each pointer can be bound to only one collection. An assignment between two pointers is legal only if the two pointers point into the same collection.

Detecting illegal aliasing between pointers caused by procedure calls is now similar to the case of arrays. In fact, a collection C and a pointer bound to C are similar to an array and a variable used as an index. Dereferencing is exactly like indexing within an array. For example, if p and q point into the same collection, and p↑ and q↑ are both passed, the nonoverlapping rule requires the test

p ≠ q

to be produced as a legality assertion.

As we saw, aliasing also can occur between global variables and formal parameters of a procedure. In Euclid, detection of aliasing in such cases does not require any additional work. In fact, global variables must be explicitly *imported* by a subprogram if they are needed, and they must be accessible in every scope from which the subprogram is called. For each imported variable, it is also necessary to indicate whether it can be read or written or both. Thus, modifiable global variables can be treated by the aliasing detection algorithm as implicit additional parameters passed by reference.

The explicit importation of global variables allows the programmer to restrict the set of variables visible within a procedure to any subset of the (nonmasked) variables declared in the outer scopes. The translator thus can ensure that only visible variables are accessed in a unit and such accesses are legal, for example, that a read-only variable cannot be modified. This is an advantage over the pure ALGOL-like scope rules—especially for large programs, in which inner procedures automatically inherit all the (nonmasked) variables declared in the enclosing scopes and can modify them in an uncontrolled way.

Finally, Euclid functions—as opposed to procedures—are not allowed to have by-reference parameters and can import only read variables. Thus, their execution cannot cause side effects, and they behave like mathematical functions.

An important consequence of disallowing aliasing in procedures is that passing parameters by reference is equivalent to passing them by copy. Therefore, the choice of how to implement parameter passing can be made by the translator based exclusively on efficiency considerations. Remember that Ada does not specify whether parameter passing should be implemented by reference or by copy. Unlike Euclid, however, Ada does not require that programs with illegal aliasing be caught before execution time by a program verifier. Some illegal Ada programs might remain uncaught, and, consequently, a different implementation of parameter passing for the same program might produce different results.

The Euclid (and Gypsy) approach is certainly interesting, and the adopted solutions are clean. Some restrictions imposed by Euclid cannot be enforced by a traditional compiler and require a program development environment that includes a program verifier. In particular, all legality assertions need to be proven by the verifier. The success of the approach taken by Euclid and Gypsy is largely dependent on the level of success that program verification encounters among practitioners.

5.2.2   Implicitly Called Units

This section analyzes units that are called implicitly when an exception condition arises. The concept of "exceptional condition" cannot be stated in absolute terms. Programs are often required to behave "reasonably" under a wide range of circumstances, even in the presence of a failure of the underlying hardware/software, or events that happen so infrequently that they are considered anomalous, or invalid input data. However, what is considered a "normal" processing state is a design decision taken by the designer, and it depends on the nature of the application. Thus, an "anomalous" processing state (or *exception*) does not necessarily mean that we are in the presence of a "catastrophic" error, but that the unit executing is unable to proceed in a manner that leads to normal termination. The inability of the program to trap anomalous processing states and to handle them appropriately can produce software that works only under certain circumstances; it is not *fault-tolerant*.

Traditional programming languages (except PL/I) offer no special help in properly handling exceptional conditions. A number of recent languages attempt to provide systematic exception-handling features. With these features, the concern for anomalies may be moved out of the main line of program flow, so as not to obscure the basic algorithm.

The central issues raised by exception-handling schemes are

1. How is an exception declared, and what is its scope?
2. How is an exception raised (or signalled)?
3. How do we specify the units intended to be executed when exceptions are signalled (*exception handlers*)?
4. How is a raised exception bound to a handler?
5. Where does control flow after an exception is handled?

We examine question 5 first, because its solution has a strong impact on the power and the usability of the mechanism. The basic language design choice is whether, after execution of the appropriate exception handler, to allow control to return to the point where the exception was raised. In such a case the exception handler can perform some repairs and terminate, so that normal execution can continue. This point of view has been adopted by PL/I and Mesa. The resulting mechanism is very powerful and flexible, but it turns out to be difficult to master for inexperienced programmers. In fact, it can promote the unsafe programming practice of removing the symptom of an error without removing the cause. For example, the exception raised for an unacceptable value of an operand could be handled by arbitrarily generating an acceptable value.

The other solution consists of terminating the execution of the unit that raises the exception and then transferring control to the exception handler. Conceptually, this means that the action that raised the exception cannot be resumed. From an implementation point of view, this means that the activation record of the signaling unit can be deleted. Bliss, CLU, and Ada adopt this simpler scheme.

We will now review the exception-handling features offered by PL/I, CLU, and Ada.

5.2.2.1   *Exception Handling in PL/I*

Exceptions are called CONDITIONS in PL/I. Exception handlers are declared by ON statements:

```
ON CONDITION (exception_name) exception_handler
```

where *exception_handler* can be a simple statement or a block. An exception is explicitly raised by the statement.

```
SIGNAL CONDITION (exception_name);
```

The language also defines a number of built-in exceptions and provides system-defined handlers for them. Built-in exceptions are automatically raised by the execution of some statements (e.g., ZERODIVIDE is raised when a divide by zero is attempted). The action performed by a system-provided handler is specified by the language. This action can be redefined, however, as with user-defined exceptions:

```
ON ZERODIVIDE BEGIN;
              . . .
              END;
```

When an ON unit is encountered during execution, a new binding takes place between an exception and a handler. Once this association is established, it remains valid until it is overridden by the execution of another ON statement for the same exception, or until termination of the block in which the ON statement is executed. If more than one ON statement for the same exception appears in the same block, each new binding overrides the previous one. If a new ON statement for the same exception appears in an inner block, the new binding remains in force only until the inner block is terminated. When control exits a block, the bindings that existed prior to block entry are reestablished.

When an exception is raised (either automatically or by a SIGNAL statement), the handler currently bound to the exception is executed as if it were a subprogram invoked explicitly at that point. Therefore, unless otherwise specified by the handler, control subsequently will return to the point that issued the SIGNAL.

We see from the above discussion that the binding between an exception raised in a certain point of the program and the exception handler that is invoked is highly dynamic. Consequently, PL/I programs that use these constructs can be rather awkward—difficult to write and understand. Moreover, the language does not allow the programmer to pass parameters from the point raising the exception to the exception handler. Consequently, the necessary information flow can be established only by using global variables, which can be an unsafe programming practice. Furthermore, use of global variables is not always possible. For example, when a STRING-RANGE exception is raised, indicatig an attempt to access beyond a string's bounds, there is no practical way for the exception handler to know which string is involved if two or more strings are visible in the scope. Such situations often render the PL/I exception handling useless.

PL/I exception-handling mechanisms can be complicated further by explicitly *enabling* and *disabling* built-in exceptions; user-defined exceptions cannot be disabled, because they must be explicitly signaled anyway. Most built-in exceptions are enabled by default and bound to the standard system-provided error handler. Enabling a previously disabled exception (or an exception that is not enabled by default) can be specified by prefixing a statement, block, or procedure with the exception name, for example

```
(ZERODIVIDE) : BEGIN;
             ...
                END;
```

The scope of the prefix is static; it is the statement, block, or procedure to which it is attached. An enabled exception can be explicitly disabled by prefixing a statement, block, or procedure with NO *exception_name*. For example

```
(NOZERODIVIDE) : BEGIN;
               ...
                  END;
```

5.2.2.1.1 Implementation Model.

We will now outline an implementation of the PL/I exception-handling mechanism. When an ON unit is encountered during execution, the condition name and the reference to the handler's code are saved in an entry of the current unit's activation record. All entries of established ON units for a given unit activation U are made accessible through a fixed location in U's activation record. When a condition is raised, ON unit entries are searched, starting from the most recent, until an established ON unit for that condition is found. If none is found, the default action is taken.

The main disadvantage of this implementation is that the search may take a significant amount of time. That search only takes place, however, when an exception is raised. We can increase the efficiency of the search by adding to the cost of block exit and ON-unit processing. In particular, we can keep a table for all conditions that a program may raise. The entry for a condition C is a pointer to a stack of pointers to established ON-unit activation records for C. All stacks are empty initially. When an ON-unit is encountered during execution, a new entry is inserted on top of the appropriate stack. When a block activation terminates, all stacks pushed during that activation must be popped.

5.2.2.2 Exception Handling in CLU

CLU's exception-handling features are less powerful than those provided by PL/I, but they are easier to use and seem to provide effective ways of handling anomalous situations.

Exceptions can be raised only by procedures; that is, if a statement raises an exception, the procedure containing the statement returns with the exception. The exceptions that a procedure may signal are declared in the heading of the procedure. An exception is explicitly raised by means of a *signal* instruction. Built-in operations can raise a known set of exceptions; for example, a division can signal that the value of the denominator is zero.

When an exception is raised, the procedure returns to its immediate caller, which is responsible for providing a handler for the exception. Unlike PL/I, the procedure that raises the exception cannot be resumed, even after performing some recovery actions. Furthermore, the exception handler is statically bound to the point of call.

Exception handlers are bound to statements by **except** clauses in the syntactic form

⟨*statement*⟩ **except** ⟨*handler_list*⟩ **end**

where ⟨*statement*⟩ can be any (compound) statement of the language. If the execution of a procedure invocation within ⟨*statement*⟩ raises an exception, control transfers to ⟨*handler_list*⟩. A ⟨*handler_list*⟩ has the following form.

when ⟨*exception_list_1*⟩:⟨*statement_1*⟩

. . .

. . .

when ⟨*exception_list_n*⟩:⟨*statement_n*⟩

If the raised exception belongs to ⟨*exception_list_i*⟩, then ⟨*statement_i*⟩ (the handler body) is executed. When execution of the handler is completed, control passes to the statement following the one to which the handler is attached. If ⟨*statement_i*⟩ contains a call to a unit, another exception can be raised. In such a case, control flows to the **except** statement that encloses ⟨*statement*⟩. If the raised exception is not named in any exception list, then the process is repeated for the statically enclosing statements. If no handler is found within the procedure that issued the call, the procedure implicitly signals a language-defined exception **failure** and returns.

Another notable difference from PL/I is that exceptions can return parameters to their handlers, thus avoiding the use of global variables. A typical example is the **failure** exception whose return value is a string denoting the uncaught exception.

By design, CLU does not provide mechanisms for disabling exceptions. The argument is that unless an exception is proven not to occur, it would be unsafe to disable it. Also, disabling exceptions that can be proven not to occur can be done by an optimizing compiler, which would then save in both time spent in trying to detect impossible exceptions and space used for handlers.

5.2.2.2.1 Implementation Model. The implementation of CLU's exception handling is rather straightforward: when an exception is signaled, control returns to its caller as if it were a normal return—the only difference being that the return point is not the instruction that follows the call, but the closest exception handler.

The implementation of CLU associates each procedure with a (fixed-contents) *handler_table,* which stores information about all the handlers that appear in the procedure. Each entry of the table contains

(a) The list of exceptions handled by the handler.

(b) A pair of pointers to the portion of text of the procedure to which the handler is attached (the scope of the handler).

(c) A pointer to the handler body.

When an exception is raised within procedure P, the address of the instruction that issued the call is found in P's activation record. This value is used to find the appropriate return point by searching the caller's handler table.

5.2.2.3 Exception Handling in Ada

Ada's exception-handling features have similarities to the schemes used in Bliss and Gypsy. They also show resemblances to the CLU approach.

A program unit can explicitly raise an exception, as in

raise HELP;

Exception handlers can be attached to a subprogram body, a package body, or a block, after the keyword **exception**. For example

begin . . .
exception when HELP=> . . .
        when DESPERATE=> . . . .
end;

If the unit that raises the exception provides a handler for the exception, control is transferred immediately to that handler: the actions following the point at which the exception is raised are skipped, the handler is executed, and then the unit terminates. If the currently executing unit U does not provide a handler, the exception is propagated. If U is a block, its execution terminates and the exception is implicitly reraised in the enclosing unit. If U is a subprogram body, the subprogram returns and the exception is implicitly reraised at the point of call. If U is a package body, it acts like a procedure that is implicitly called when the package declaration is processed. If there is no handler associated with the package body, the exception is propagated to the unit that contains the package declaration.

Ada's exception-handling mechanism is multilevel, as opposed to the single-level mechanism of CLU. In other words, in Ada the exception raised by a unit also may be handled by units other than its immediate caller. The CLU restriction can be justified on the basis of methodical programming. In particular, CLU views a procedure as the implementation of an abstract action. The caller of a procedure wants the procedure to execute its abstract action, and need not know about its internal workings. The exceptions that a procedure may raise characterize the abstract behavior of the procedure, and thus must be known to the caller. However, the caller should not know about the exceptions raised by procedures that are (locally) used in the implementation of an abstract action. Obviously, a multilevel scheme can be explicitly programmed in CLU by having the caller signal the same exception as is raised by the invoked procedure. However, in such a case the exception would be explicitly part of the caller's abstraction. The same reasoning also explains why a CLU procedure must return upon an exception and cannot be resumed. To handle the exception in a way that allows the called unit to continue, requires the caller to know about the internal structure of the called unit.

Again, in contrast to Ada, CLU does not allow the unit that raises the exception to handle it. The justification for this is that by definition, exceptions are anomalous conditions that the signaling procedure is unable to handle. The Ada choice on this point, however, seems to be preferable, because it allows the programmer to specify easily some cleanup actions that the called unit might wish to execute before returning. CLU requires passing parameters back to the caller's handler to do the cleanup. This is probably one reason why Ada does not provide paramater passing to exception handlers.

5.2.2.3.1 *Implementation Model.*

Ada's exception-handling can be implemented using the handler table concept of the CLU implementation. The basic difference is that the exception handler is not necessarily provided by the immediate caller; therefore, it might be necessary to traverse the dynamic chain of procedure invocations to locate an entry for the required handler.

5.2.3 Symmetrical Units: Coroutines in SIMULA 67

Symmetrical units (coroutines) can be viewed as a group of program units that activate one another explicitly. As we saw in Section 2.3, when control is transferred to a unit, it resumes at the place where it last terminated. Consequently, units run in an interleaved fashion, according to a predefined pattern of behavior.

We have seen a special case of coroutines in Section 5.1.5 (iterators). We will treat the subject here in more general terms. In particular, we will provide a simplified view of the SIMULA 67 mechanism for instantiating symmetrical units and switching control from one coroutine to another.

A SIMULA 67 coroutine is an instance of a **class** whose general form is

```
class x (parameters);
    parameter declarations;
begin
    declarations;
    statement_list_1;
    detach;
    statement_list_2
end
```

If variables *y1* and *y2* are *references* to *x*, we can write

```
y1:- new x ( . . . ); y2:- new x ( . . . )
```

When **new** is encountered, a new instance of the class is created and the class body is executed. When **detach** is encountered, control is transferred back to the unit that issued the **new**. As a consequence of **detach**, the unit activation behaves as a coroutine that can be resumed and, in turn, can resume other coroutines.

For example, a four-player card game, in which all players use the same strategy, can be described as follows.

```
begin boolean gameover; integer winner;
    class player (n, hand); integer n;
                            integer array hand (1: 13);
    begin ref (player) next;
        detach;
        while not gameover do
        begin execute a move;
            if gameover then winner:= n
                            else resume (next)
        end
    end;
    ref (player) array p(1:4); integer i;
    integer array cards (1:13);
    for i:= 1 step 1 until 4 do
    begin generate the cards for the hand of player i in array
    cards; p(i):- new player (i, cards)
    end;
    for i:= 1 step 1 until 3 do
        p(i).next:- p(i+1);
    p(4).next:- p(1);
    resume p(1);
    print the winner's number
end
```

The first loop of the program (**for** $i := 1$ **step** 1 **until** 4 **do** . . .) creates the four players. They are subsequently linked together by the next loop (**for** $i := 1$ **step** 1 **until** 3 **do** . . .) and then player number 1 is resumed. From this point on, players **resume** each other according to the ordering established by the links. When the execution of the move (a procedure that is not detailed in the program) sets *gameover* to true, the identity of the winner is assigned to variable *winner,* the execution of the coroutine instance terminates, and control flows back to the program that activated the set of symmetrical units. The main program then prints the name of the winner and stops.

5.2.3.1   Implementation Model

The stack model of execution discussed in Chapter 3 is unable to support coroutines. When a coroutine A issues a resume to a coroutine $B,$ one must save (in A's activation record) the pointer to the instruction following the instruction **resume** (B). Moreover, A's activation record is not deallocated. Each coroutine requires an activation record stack that can grow and shrink independently of the other stacks. Thus, the creation of a set of coroutines can be viewed as the creation of a new execution stack, one for each coroutine. The run-time organization of the memory can be viewed as a *tree of stacks* (Figure 5.3).

5.2.4   Concurrent Units

As we saw in Section 2.4, there are cases in which the system we want to design can be characterized abstractly as a set of *processes* that proceed concurrently and interact only occasionally. A correct interaction can be guaranteed by the proper use of the *synchronization statements* (or *primitives*) provided by the programming language. This section reviews and evaluates three basic synchronization mechanisms: *semaphores, monitors,* and *ren-*

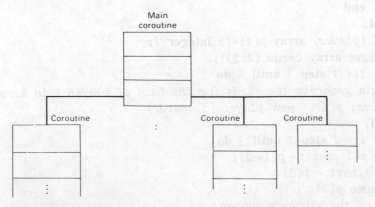

FIGURE 5.3 A tree of activation record stacks for coroutines.

dezvous. These three mechanisms are suited to a "shared-memory" model of concurrent processes, that is, concurrent processes that have access to a common memory. Other paradigms for concurrent programming have been developed that are perhaps more applicable to distributed systems. *Remote procedure call* extends the notion of a procedure call to the case where the caller and the callee units reside in different processes. Synchronization is achieved by the fact that the caller waits until the callee returns. The *message passing* paradigm is an extension of the Smalltalk-like messages to concurrent processes. Messages are used both for communication and synchronization. We must mention that, with appropriately disciplined usage, the Ada rendezvous also can be used for distributed processes. A detailed study of the various models and mechanisms is beyond the scope of this book and can be found in books on operating systems.

We have selected semaphores, monitors, and rendezvous from among the many proposals that have appeared in the literature because they represent the historical evolution of the concept of synchronization of concurrent units and have been incorporated into programming languages that are widely available.

5.2.4.1   Semaphores

Semaphores were invented by Djikstra and later introduced as synchronization primitives into ALGOL 68. A semaphore is a data object that can assume an integer value and can be operated on by the primitives P and V. ALGOL 68 uses the names **down** and **up**. The semaphore is initialized to a certain integer value when it is declared.

The definitions of P and V are

$P\ (s)$: **if** $s > 0$ **then** $s := s-1$
             else *suspend current process*

$V\ (s)$: **if** *there is a process suspended on the semaphore*
              then *wake up process*
              else $s := s+1$

The primitives P and V are assumed to be indivisible, atomic operations, that is, no two processes can be executing P and/or V operations on the same semaphore at the same time. This must be guaranteed by the underlying implementation, which should make P and V behave like elementary machine instructions.

The semaphore has (1) an associated data structure where the identity of processes suspended on the semaphore is recorded, and (2) a policy for selecting one process to be woken up when required by the primitive V. Usually, the data structure is a queue served on a first-in/first-out basis. However, we might want to assign priorities to processes and devise more complex policies based on such priorities.

The simple producer–consumer example of Section 2.3 can be solved by using semaphores as shown below (using an arbitrary, self-explanatory Pascal-like notation).

```
const n= 20;
shared var buffer of length n, with primitives append and remove
which update t, total number of buffered items;
semaphore mutex:= 1;  {to guarantee mutual exclusion}
          in:= 0;     {number of items in buffer}
          spaces:= n;{number of free spaces in buffer}
process producer;
       var i: integer;
       repeat
           produce (i);
           P (spaces);{wait for free spaces}
           P (mutex); {wait for buffer availability}
           append i to buffer;
           V (mutex); {finished accessing buffer}
           V (in)     {one more item in buffer}
       forever
end producer;
process consumer;
       var j: integer;
       repeat
           P (in);    {wait for item in buffer}
           P (mutex); {wait for buffer availability}
           remove item from buffer into j;
           V (mutex); {finished accessing buffer}
           V (spaces);{one more space in buffer}
           consume (j)
       forever
end consumer
```

The keywords **process** and **end** enclose the segments of code that can proceed concurrently, and **shared var** declares the variable(s) that can be accessed by the processes concurrently. Semaphores *spaces* and *in* are used to guarantee the logical correctness of the accesses to the buffer. In particular, *spaces* (number of available free positions in the buffer) suspends the producer when it tries to insert a new item into a full buffer. Similarly, *in* (number of items already in the buffer) suspends the consumer if it tries to remove an item from an empty buffer.

Semaphore *mutex* is used to enforce mutual exclusion of accesses to the buffer. This is necessary under the assumption that operations *append* and *remove* concurrently modify the value of t (total number of buffered items).

Variable t was introduced in Section 2.3.2.4 for the sole purpose of explaining the problem of mutual exclusion. Operations *append* and *remove* can be implemented easily in such a way that no need for mutual exclusion arises, provided (as happens in our case) the logical correctness of accessing the buffer is ensured (see Exercise 5.12).

Programming with semaphores requires the programmer to associate one semaphore with each synchronization condition. Our example shows that semaphores are a very simple but low-level mechanism, their use can be awkward in practice, and the resulting programs are often difficult to design and understand. Moreover, little checking can be done statically on programs that use semaphores. For example, a compiler would not be able to catch the incorrect use of a semaphore, such as the one resulting from a change of V (*mutex*) into P (*mutex*) in the *producer* process (see Exercise 5.9). Catching such an error is impossible because it requires the translator to know the semantics of the program, that is, that the operations on the buffer are to be executed in mutual exclusion, and *mutex* is used to guarantee such mutual exclusion. Therefore, semaphores require considerable self-discipline on the part of the programmer. For example, one should not forget to execute a P before accessing a shared resource, or neglect to execute a V to release it.

Using semaphores for synchronization purposes other than mutual exclusion is even more awkward. In the producer–consumer example, process *consumer* suspends itself by executing P (*spaces*) when the buffer is full. The programmer should not forget to write a V (*spaces*) after each consumption, as the producer may become blocked forever.

PL/I was the first language to allow concurrent units—called *tasks*. A procedure may be invoked as a task, in which case it executes concurrently with its caller. Tasks also can be assigned priorities. Synchronization is achieved by the use of *events*, which are similar to semaphores but only can assume one of two values: '0'B and '1'B.* A P operation on a semaphore is represented by a WAIT operation on the completion of an event E : WAIT (E). A V operation is represented by signaling the completion of the event: COMPLETION (E) = '1'B. PL/I extends the notion of semaphores by allowing the WAIT operation to name several events and an integer expression e. The process will be suspended until any e events have been completed. For example, WAIT ($E1$, $E2$, $E3$) (1) indicates the waiting for any one of the events: $E1$, $E2$, or $E3$.

ALGOL 68 allows one to describe concurrent processes in a parallel clause whose constituent statements are elaborated concurrently. Synchronization can be provided by semaphores, which are data objects of mode **sema**.

---

*'0'B and '1'B are boolean constants 0 and 1.

5.2.4.2 Monitors

Monitors describe abstract data types in a concurrent environment. Mutual exclusion in accessing the operations that manipulate the data structure is guaranteed automatically by the underlying implementation. Cooperation in accessing the shared data structure must be programmed explicitly by using the monitor primitives **delay** and **continue**.

Using the notation of Concurrent Pascal, the following program illustrates the use of monitors in the producer–consumer example.

```
type fifostorage=
monitor
    var contents: array [1 .. n] of integer; {buffer contents}
        tot: 0 .. n; {number of items in buffer}
        in, {position of item to be added next}
        out: 1 .. n; {position of item to be removed next}
        sender, receiver: queue;
    procedure entry append (item: integer);
    begin if tot = n then delay (sender);
        contents[in]:= item;
        in:= (in mod n)+1;
        tot:= tot+1;
        continue (receiver)
    end;
    procedure entry remove (var item: integer);
    begin if tot = 0 then delay (receiver);
        item:= contents[out];
        out:= (out mod n)+1;
        tot:= tot - 1;
        continue (sender)
    end;
begin
    tot:= 0; in:= 1; out:= 1
end
```

An instance of the monitor (i.e., a buffer) can be declared as

```
var buffer: fifostorage
```

and can be created by the statement **init** *buffer*.

The **init** statement allocates storage for the variables encapsulated within the monitor definition (i.e., *contents*—the contents of the buffer, *tot*—the total number of buffered items, and *in* and *out*—the positions at which the next items will be appended and removed, respectively) and executes the initialization statement (which sets *tot* to zero, and *in* and *out* to one).

The monitor defines the two procedures, *append* and *remove*. They are declared with the keyword **entry**, which means that they are the only exported procedures that can be used to manipulate monitor instances. Cooperation between the producer and the consumer is achieved by using the synchronization primitives **delay** and **continue**. The operation **delay** (*sender*) suspends the executing process (e.g., the *producer*) in the queue *sender*. The process loses its exclusive access to the monitor's data structure and is delayed until another process (e.g., the *consumer*) executes the operation **continue** (*sender*). Similarly, a *consumer* process is delayed in the queue *receiver* if the buffer is empty, until the *producer* resumes it by executing the instruction **continue** (*receiver*). The execution of the **continue** operation makes the calling process return from the monitor call. If there are processes waiting in the specified queue, one of them immediately will resume the execution of the monitor procedure that previously delayed it.

The structure of a Concurrent Pascal program that uses the above monitor to represent cooperation between a producer and a consumer is given below.

```
const n= 20;
type fifostorage= . . . as above . . .;
type producer=
process (storage: fifostorage);
var element: integer;
begin cycle
    . . .
    storage.append (element);
    . . .
    end
end;
type consumer= process (storage: fifostorage);
var datum: integer;
begin cycle
    . . .
    storage.remove (datum);
    . . .
    end
end;
var meproducer: producer;
    youconsumer: consumer;
     buffer: fifostorage;
```

```
begin
     init buffer, meproducer (buffer), youconsumer (buffer)
end
```

Processes are described here as nonterminating, cyclic activities (**cycle** . . . **end**). Two particular instances (*meproducer* and *youconsumer*) are declared as bound to an instance of the resource type *fifostage* and subsequently activated as concurrent processes by the **init** statement.

Monitors were proposed by Brinch Hansen and Hoare as a high-level synchronization mechanism. They have been implemented in Concurrent Pascal and Mesa.

5.2.4.3 Rendezvous

Rendezvous is the mechanism provided by Ada for describing synchronization of concurrent processes (*tasks*, in the Ada jargon). We will concentrate on the basic properties of the mechanisms; additional features and the interaction with other facilities provided by the language (such as scope rules and exception handling), will be ignored for the sake of simplicity.

An Ada task is a program unit that is executed concurrently with other tasks. Its structure is very similar in form to a package module. For example, the following task describes a process that handles the operations *append* and *remove* on a buffer.

```
task BUFFER_HANDLER is
     entry APPEND (ITEM: in INTEGER);
     entry REMOVE (ITEM: out INTEGER);
end;
task body BUFFER_HANDLER is
     N: constant INTEGER:= 20;
     CONTENTS: array (1 .. N) of INTEGER;
     IN, OUT: INTEGER range 1 .. N:= 1;
     TOT: INTEGER range 0 .. N:= 0;
begin loop
   select
     when TOT < N =>
        accept APPEND(ITEM: in INTEGER) do
                 CONTENTS(IN):= ITEM;
        end;
     IN:= (IN mod N) + 1;
     TOT:= TOT + 1;
   or
     when TOT > 0 =>
```

```
            accept REMOVE (ITEM: out INTEGER) do
                     ITEM:= CONTENTS(OUT);
            end;
            OUT:= (OUT mod N)+1;
            TOT:= TOT - 1;
        end select;
    end loop;
end BUFFER_HANDLER;
```

The visible part of task BUFFER_HANDLER specifies APPEND and RE-MOVE as *entries*. Entries can be called by other tasks in the same way as procedures. Unlike procedures, entry bodies are not executed immediately after the call, but only when the task owning the entry is ready to accept the call by executing a corresponding **accept** statement. At this point the calling and the called tasks can be viewed as meeting together in a *rendezvous*. If the calling task issues the call before the called task executes an **accept**, the calling task is suspended until the rendezvous occurs. Similarly, a suspension of the called task occurs if an **accept** statement is executed before the corresponding call. Note that a task can accept calls from more than one task; consequently, each entry potentially has a queue of tasks calling it.

The **accept** statement is similar to a procedure. After a repetition of the heading of the entry, the **do** . . . **end** part (**accept** body) specifies the statements to be executed at the rendezvous. Once a match between an entry call and the corresponding **accept** occurs, the caller is suspended until the **accept** body is executed by the called task. The accept body is the only place at which the parameters of the entry are accessible. Possible **out** parameters (as in the case of REMOVE) are passed back to the caller at the end of the rendezvous, that is, when the execution of the **accept** body is completed. Thereafter, the two tasks that met in the rendezvous can proceed in parallel.

The bodies of tasks PRODUCER and CONSUMER, which interact with BUFFER_HANDLER in the producer–consumer example, are sketched below.

PRODUCER
loop
```
        produce a new value V;
        BUFFER_HANDLER.APPEND(V);
        exit when V denotes the end of the stream;
end loop;
```

CONSUMER
loop
```
        BUFFER_HANDLER.REMOVE (V);
        consume V;
        exit when V denotes the end of the stream;
end loop
```

In the BUFFER_HANDLER example, **accept** statements are enclosed within a **select** statement. The select statement is similar to the guarded **if** statement of Dijkstra's language (Section 5.1.2) and specifies several alternatives separated by **or** that can be chosen in a nondeterministic fashion. The Ada selection is specified by an **accept** statement, possibly prefixed (as in our example) by a **when** *condition*. Execution of the **select** statement proceeds as follows.*

(a) The conditions of the **when** parts of all alternatives are evaluated. Alternatives with a true condition, or without a **when** part, are considered open; otherwise, they are considered closed. In the example, both alternatives are open if $0 < TOT < N$.

(b) An open alternative can be selected if a rendezvous is possible (i.e., an entry call already has been issued by another task). After the alternative is selected, the corresponding **accept** body is executed.

(c) If there are open alternatives but none can be selected immediately, the task waits until a rendezvous is possible.

(d) If there are no open alternatives, an error condition is signaled by the language-defined exception SELECT_ERROR.

5.2.4.4 A Comparison

Semaphores, monitors, and rendezvous are all primitives for modeling concurrent systems. We have already pointed out that semaphores are rather low-level mechanisms: programs are difficult to read and write, and no check on their correct use can be done automatically. Monitors, on the other hand, are a higher-level structuring mechanism. In a language such as Concurrent Pascal or Mesa, system structuring proceeds by identifying (1) shared resources as abstract objects with suitable access primitives, and (2) processes that cooperate through the use of resources. Resources are encapsulated within monitors. Mutual exclusion on the access to a shared resource is guaranteed automatically by the monitor implementation, but cooperation must be enforced by explicitly suspending and signaling processes via **delay** and **continue** statements. The distinction between active and passive multiprogramming entities (processes and monitors, respectively) disappears in Ada. Shared resources to be used cooperatively are represented by Ada tasks, that is, by active components representing resource managers. A request to use a resource is represented by an entry call, which must be accepted by the corresponding resource manager.

A system structured via monitors and processes can be easily structured via Ada tasks, and vice versa; the choice between the two schemes is largely dependent on personal taste. The Ada scheme probably mirrors more di-

---

*We are ignoring several of Ada's features that would complicate the implementation and our presentation.

rectly the behavior of a concurrent system in a distributed architecture, where remote resources are actually managed by processes that behave as guardians of the resource.

5.2.4.5 Implementation Issues

In a concurrent system, processes either are suspended on some synchronization condition or are potentially active, that is, there are no logical obstacles to their execution. In general, only a subset of potentially active processes can be running, unless there are as many processors as there are potentially active processes. In the common case of a uniprocessor, only one of such processes can be running at a time. It is thus customary to say that processes can be in one of the following states (see also Figure 5.4).

- Waiting
- Ready (i.e., potentially active, but presently not runnning)
- Running

In concurrent programming, the programmer has no direct control over the speed of execution of the processes. In particular, the user is not responsible for changing the state of a process from ready to running (operation of *selection* in Figure 5.4), which is done by the underlying implementation. Figure 5.4 shows that a process can leave the running state and enter the ready state as a consequence of the action of *preemption*.

Preemption is an action performed by the underlying implementation; it forces a process to abandon its running state even if, from a logical point of view, it could safely continue to be executed. A process can be preempted either after it performs a synchronizing statement that makes another suspended process enter the ready state (e.g., a V on a semaphore) or when some other condition occurs, such as the expiration of a specified amount of time (*time slice*). After the preemption of one process, one of the ready pro-

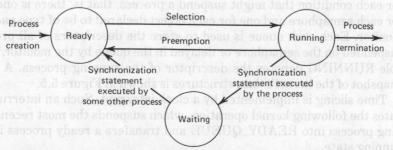

FIGURE 5.4 State diagram for a process.

cesses can enter the running state. This kind of implementation allows the programmer to view the system as a set of activities that proceed in parallel, even if they are all executed by the same processor. Only one process at a time can be executed by the processor, but each process runs only for a limited amount of time, after which control is given to another process. It is possible to have nonpreemptive implementation of concurrency. In this case, execution switches to another process only when the currently executing process deliberately suspends itself or requires the use of an unavailable resource.

The portion of run-time support of a concurrent language responsible for the implementation of the state transitions shown in Figure 5.4, is called the *kernel*. To illustrate the basic features of a kernel, consider the case of a single processor shared by a set of processes. For the sake of simplicity, we will ignore the problems of synchronizing processes with I/O devices and concentrate our attention on the interactions among internal processes. More complete discussions of these issues are traditionally (and more properly) addressed in textbooks on operating systems. Here we provide only a glimpse of the basic problems that are relevant to understanding concurrency features of programming languages.

The information about a process needed by the kernel is represented in a *process descriptor,* one for each process. The descriptor for a process is used to store all the information needed to restore the process from a waiting or blocked state to the running state. This information (called *process status*) includes the process priority (if priorities are used) and all information required to instruct the processor about the identity and point of execution of the process—notably, the contents of the machine registers (program counter, index registers, accumulator, and so on). Saving the status of the process when the process becomes suspended and restoring the status when the process becomes running is one of the kernel's jobs.

The kernel can be viewed as an abstract data type; it hides some private data structures and provides procedures that provide the only ways to use these data structures. The kernel's private data structures are organized as queues of process descriptors. The descriptors of ready processes are kept by the kernel in READY_QUEUE. There is also one CONDITION_QUEUE for each condition that might suspend a process, that is, there is one queue for each semaphore and one for each object declared to be of type *queue* in a monitor. Each such queue is used to store the descriptors of all processes suspended on the semaphore or delayed in the queue by the monitor. A variable RUNNING denotes the descriptor of the running process. A typical snapshot of the kernel's data structures is shown in Figure 5.5.

Time slicing is implemented by a clock interrupt. Such an interrupt activates the following kernel operation, which suspends the most recently running process into READY_QUEUE and transfers a ready process into the running state.

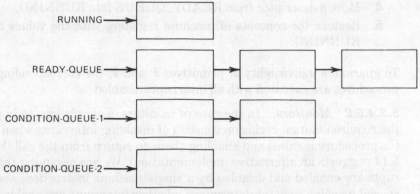

FIGURE 5.5 Data structures of the kernel.

Operation Suspend-and-Select

1. Save status of running process into RUNNING.
2. Enqueue RUNNING into READY_QUEUE.
3. Move a descriptor from READY_QUEUE into RUNNING.
4. Restore the contents of machine registers with the values found in RUNNING (this step is used to activate a new process).

5.2.4.5.1 Semaphores. If semaphores are provided by the language, primitives P and V can be implemented as calls to kernel procedures. A suspension on condition c caused by a P operation is implemented by the following private operation of the kernel.

Operation Suspend-on-Condition

1. Save status of running process into RUNNING.
2. Enqueue RUNNING into CONDITION_QUEUE_c.
3. Move a descriptor from READY_QUEUE into RUNNING.
4. Restore the contents of machine registers with the values found in RUNNING.

Awakening a process waiting on condition c, caused by a V operation, is implemented by the following private operation of the kernel.

Operation Awaken

1. Save status of running process into RUNNING.
2. Enqueue RUNNING into READY_QUEUE.
3. Move a descriptor from CONDITION_QUEUE_c into READY_QUEUE.

4. Move a descriptor from READY_QUEUE into RUNNING.

5. Restore the contents of machine registers with the values found in RUNNING.

To guarantee indivisibility of primitives P and V, the corresponding kernel procedures are executed with all interrupts disabled.

5.2.4.5.2 Monitors. In the case of monitors, a simple way to implement the required mutual exclusion consists of disabling interrupts when a monitor procedure is called and enabling them on return from the call (Exercise 5.14 suggests an alternative implementation). We are assuming that interrupts are enabled and disabled by a single machine instruction, and that a special machine register determines whether interrupts are enabled or disabled. This register is part of the process status and must be saved in the process descriptor when the process is suspended. For the sake of simplicity, we also are assuming that monitor procedures do not contain calls to other monitor procedures. When a process calls a monitor procedure, the value of the return point from the call is saved in an entry of the process descriptor. Operations **delay** and **continue** can be implemented by kernel procedures. In particular, **delay** is implemented by operation *suspend-on-condition,* and **continue** is implemented by the following operation.

Operation Continue

1. Save status of running process into RUNNING.

2. Set status of interrupts in RUNNING to *enabled.*

3. Set the image of the program counter in RUNNING to the return point from the monitor call.

4. Enqueue RUNNING into READY_QUEUE.

5. Let CONDITION_QUEUE_c be the queue mentioned by the **continue** statement. If CONDITION_QUEUE_c is not empty, then move a descriptor from CONDITION_QUEUE_c into RUNNING. Otherwise, move a descriptor from READY_QUEUE to RUNNING.

6. Restore the contents of machine registers with the values found in RUNNING.

Note that several steps of the kernel operations (e.g., step 3 of *suspend-and-select* and step 3 of *suspend-on-condition*) have been written deliberately to imply nondeterminism. These steps are exactly the points at which the implementation must select a suitable policy for making a deterministic choice. The part of the kernel responsible for this policy is called the *scheduler.* The scheduler can be very simple (e.g., all queues are handled as FIFO queues) or rather sophisticated (e.g., waiting times and priorities are taken into account).

5.2.4.5.3 Rendezvous.   In this section, we discuss some implementation issues of Ada's rendezvous mechanism. There is one queue of ready tasks (READY_QUEUE). Each entry has a descriptor that contains the following fields.

- A boolean value O describing whether the entry is open (O = true indicates that the task owning the entry is ready to accept a call to this entry).
- A reference W to a queue of descriptors of tasks whose calls to the entry are pending (*waiting queue*).
- A reference T to the descriptor of the task owning the entry.
- A reference I to the first instruction of the **accept** body (to simplify matters, we assume that no two **accept** statements for the same entry can appear in a **select** statement). This reference is significant only if the task owning the entry is ready to accept a call to the entry (that is, O = true).

We assume for simplicity's sake that the implementation of the synchronization statements is done by kernel operations that are noninterruptible, that is, interrupts are disabled and enabled by the kernel before and after executing such statements. The problem of passing parameters across tasks is ignored for the same reason.

The implementation of an entry call can be done by the kernel as follows.

1. Save status of running task into RUNNING.
2. Enqueue RUNNING into the queue associated with the entry.
3. If the entry is open, then close (i.e., set field O to false) all the open entries of the called task and move the descriptor of the called task into RUNNING; update the value of the program counter stored in RUNNING with the value stored in field I of the entry's descriptor. Otherwise, move descriptor from READY_QUEUE into RUNNING.
4. Restore the contents of machine registers with the values found in RUNNING.

When the **end** of the body of an **accept** statement is reached, the following kernel actions complete the rendezvous.

1. Save status of running task into RUNNING.
2. Move descriptor of caller referenced by field W of the entry's descriptor into READY_QUEUE.
3. Enqueue RUNNING into READY_QUEUE.

4. Move a descriptor from READY_QUEUE into RUNNING.

5. Restore the contents of machine registers with the values found in RUNNING.

The actions to be executed as a consequence of an **accept** statement (not embedded in a **select** statement) are

1. If the waiting queue of the entry is empty, then

1.1 Set field O of the entry's descriptor to true and save the address of the first instruction of the accept body into field I of the entry's descriptor.

1.2 Save the status of the running task into the task's descriptor and set field T of the entry's descriptor to reference the task's descriptor.

1.3 Move a descriptor from READY_QUEUE into RUNNING.

1.4 Restore the contents of machine registers with the values found in RUNNING.

2. If the waiting queue is not empty, then accept the rendezvous immediately, that is, continue the execution of the running task until the end of the **accept** body is reached.

To execute a **select** statement, a list of the open entries involved in the selection is first constructed. If this list is empty, then the exception SELECT_ERROR is raised. Otherwise, the following kernel actions are required.

1. If one or more entries of the list have a nonempty queue, then

1.1 Arbitrarily choose one.

1.2 Accept the rendezvous immediately: that is, continue to execute the **accept** body of the selected alternative.

2. If all entry queues are empty, then

2.1 Switch the status of all such entries to "open" and save the address of the first instruction of each open alternative's **accept** body into field I of the corresponding entry's descriptor.

2.2 Save the status of the running task into the task's descriptor and set field T of the entry's descriptor to reference the task's descriptor.

2.3 Move a descriptor from READY_QUEUE into RUNNING.

2.4 Restore the contents of machine registers with the values found in RUNNING.

SUGGESTIONS FOR FURTHER READING AND BIBLIOGRAPHIC NOTES

Statement-level control structures were the subject of active research in the early 1970s. Dijkstra (1968a) was first to stress the need for discipline in programming, and the influence of the **goto** statement on the production of obscure programs. Much of the subsequent research on "structured programming" was aimed at uncovering suitable control structures that could promote the writing of well-organized, readable programs. Böhm and Jacopini (1966) provide a formal justification to these works by showing that a limited subset of control structures (sequencing, **if then else, do while**) is sufficient to write any program. Knuth (1974) provides a comprehensive view of statement-level control structures and an in-depth comparison of many language proposals. Examples of extensions to machine-level languages to incorporate suitable high-level control structures are described in (Wirth 1968) and (Van der Poel and Maarsen 1974).

The user-defined statement-level control structures of CLU are described in (Liskov et al. 1977). An implementation model is presented in (Atkinson et al. 1978).

Programming-language constructs that make reasoning about programs hard are analyzed in several papers of (ACM-SIGPLAN 1977). Wulf and Shaw (1973) discuss the role of global variables. Popek et al. (1977) discuss side effects and aliasing. Reynolds (1979) categorizes most of such harmful features.

Exception handling is the linguistic feature that describes how programs can trap and handle undesired events to improve reliability. Randell (1975) and Parnas and Würges (1976) discuss program reliability and fault tolerance. Exception handling is studied in (Goodenough 1975) and (Levin 1977). MacLaren (1977) discusses exception handling in PL/I. Exception handling in CLU is presented in (Liskov and Snyder 1979), along with a comparison with other language proposals. CLU's implementation of exception handling is described in (Atkinson et al. 1978). Luckam and Polak (1980) give a formal description of exception handling in preliminary Ada.

The first description of coroutines comes from (Conway 1963). Knuth (1973) and Wegner (1968) provide an introductory view of coroutines. Marlin (1980) is a comprehensive text on coroutines that contains a survey of languages, a detailed semantic description, and a discussion of programming methodologies.

Concurrency in programming languages is traditionally studied as a branch of operating systems. The reader can refer to (Brinch Hansen 1973), (Brinch Hansen 1977), and (Peterson and Silbershatz 1985) for a study of operating system theory. The concept of semaphore was introduced in (Dijkstra 1968b) and (Dijkstra 1968c). Monitors were proposed by (Brinch Hansen 1973) and (Hoare 1974). Monitors were introduced in the programming languages Concurrent Pascal (Brinch Hansen 1975, Brinch Hansen 1977), and CSP/k (Holt et al. 1978a). The synchronization primitives presented by (Hoare 1978), (Hoare 1985) and (Brinch Hansen 1979) have strongly influenced the rendezvous concept of Ada (Welsh and Lister 1981). These proposals are aimed at providing synchronization primitives for processes in distributed systems. Distributed systems are composed of a number of largely autonomous processors connected by a communication medium. Distributed systems, such as local networks of small computers (e.g., microprocessors), are becoming increasingly popular. For a sampling of some research efforts in languages for distributed systems, see Argus (Liskov and Scheifler 1982) and NIL (Strom and Yemini 1983).

The language OCCAM (INMOS 1984) (May 1983) and an associated processor called the Transputer are based on (Hoare 1978). Transputers can be combined to build multicomputer systems easily. The resulting system is programmed in OCCAM.

Chill is a programming language for communications software that is not described here. The language provides a rich set of primitives for concurrency. Smedema et al. (1983) introduce Chill and compare it to Pascal, Modula-2, and Ada.

EXERCISES

5.1 You must design a program part that reads a sequence of integer values. The length of the sequence is unknown. The sequence is terminated by a "special value" (e.g., zero). All values read (except for the terminator) must be processed in an unspecified manner. The following Pascal-like program fragment provides a solution.

```
read item;
while item < > special value do
begin process item;
      read new item
end
```

Code this solution in C and briefly compare the two solutions in terms of readability and writability.

5.2 ALGOL 68 does not provide a **repeat** . . . **until** loop.

(a) Describe how you can simulate it. (**Hint**: you can write a loop with an empty loop body; the **while** clause can be a sequence of statements that delivers a boolean value!)

(b) Discuss this solution from readability and writability points of view.

5.3 Zahn (1974) proposes two new kinds of "event driven" control structures. Their general form is specified below, with some syntactic changes.

```
(A) begin quit on event1, event2, . . . , eventn;
          statement_list_0
```

```
      then event1: statement_list_1;
           event2: statement_list_2;
               . . .
           eventn: statement_list_n
      end
(B)do quit on event1, event2, . . . , eventn;
        statement_list_0
      then event1: statement_list_1;
           event2: statement_list_2;
               . . .
           eventn: statement_list_n
   od
```

Case A specifies the execution of the list of statements *statement_list_0*.

Case B specifies the repetition of *statement_list_0*. There is a new statement **raise** *eventname* that signals the occurrence of an event. Such a statement can occur within the part *statement_list_0* of cases A and B, provided that *eventname* is declared in the **quit on** clause of the statement. The effect of **raise** *eventname* is to transfer control to the statements that follow *eventname* in the **then** clause.

Evaluate Zahn's control structures. In particular, you should

a. Discuss the merits of Zahn's statement A.

b. Rewrite the program of Exercise 5.1 using Zahn's loop.

c. Translate the Pascal **do while** and **repeat until** into Zahn's loop.

In solving this exercise you should assume that sequences and **if then else** are the only control structures that can be used besides Zahn's statements A and B.

5.4 Show how the effects of CLU iterators could be implemented in a language that supports coroutines but not iterators.

5.5 Describe how history-sensitive FORTRAN subprograms (assuming they are supported by the implementation) can be used to simulate coroutines.

5.6 One way to handle exceptions raised in procedures in a programming language that does not provide specific exception handling features is to return a special code indicating the raised exception (Section 2.3.3.2). Another way is to transmit the recovery procedure as a parameter (Section 5.2.1.2). What are the differences between these two methods?

5.7 The implementers of CLU mention the following alternative implementation to the one described in Section 5.2.2.2.1. Instead of having a unique handler table for a procedure, a branch table is constructed for each invocation. Each entry of the branch table corresponds to an exception that can be raised by the called procedure.

a. Explain why the branch table (for each call) can be constructed at translation time. Could the same be done for a PL/I-like exception handling scheme?

b. Show how a **signal** can be implemented.

c. Compare the branch table method with the handler table method in terms of speed and space.

d. The implementation criteria for exception handling mechanisms stated by the CLU implementers are

- Normal-case execution efficiency should not be impaired at all
- Exceptions should be executed quickly, but not necessarily as fast as possible
- Use of space should be reasonably efficient.

According to these criteria, why is the handler table method to be preferred over the branch table method?

5.8 Consider an Ada subprogram that terminates abnormally after raising an exception. Why can an implementation of parameter passing by copy produce different results from an implementation that passes parameters by reference?

5.9 In the producer–consumer example implemented with semaphores in Section 5.2.4.1, suppose that V (*mutex*) is incorrectly written as P (*mutex*) in process *producer*. How does the system behave?

5.10 When semaphores are used to implement mutual exclusion, it is possible to associate a semaphore SR with each resource R. Each access to R can then be written as

```
P (SR);
access R;
V (SR)
```

What should the initial value of SR be?

5.11 In Modula-2, processes have been replaced by lower-level coroutines. Study the Modula-2 Report and discuss

- The rationale of this design decision.
- How higher-level concepts (processes, monitors) can be implemented.

5.12 The producer–consumer example of Section 5.2.4.1 uses a semaphore for enforcing mutual exclusion on access to the buffer. Can you write an implementation of operations *append* and *remove* such that no need for mutual exclusion arises? (**Hint**: Try to write a solution that does not use variable t.)

5.13 Some computers (e.g., the IBM 360) provide an indivisible machine-instruction test and set (*TS*) that can be used for synchronization purposes. Let X and Y be two boolean variables. The execution of the instruction TS (X, Y) copies the value of Y into X and sets Y to false. A set of concurrent processes that must execute some instructions in mutual exclusion can use a global boolean variable PERMIT, initialized to true, and a local boolean variable X in the following way.

```
repeat TS (X, PERMIT)
until X;
    instructions to be executed in mutual exclusion;
PERMIT:= true
```

1. In this case, processes do not suspend themselves; they are always executing (this is called *busy waiting*). Compare this solution to one based on semaphores in which P and V are implemented by the kernel.

2. Describe how to implement P and V on semaphores by using the test and set primitive in a busy wait scheme.

5.14 We implemented mutual exclusion of monitor procedures by disabling interrupts. An alternative solution uses a semaphore for each monitor and performs a P on the semaphore before entering a monitor procedure, and a corresponding V upon exit. Detail this implementation and compare the two solutions.

5.15 Show how an Ada task can be used to implement a semaphore.

Programming in the Large

"Human follibility—from grand to grandiose"

(Mills 1979)

The production of large programs—those consisting of more than several thousand lines—presents many challenging problems that do not arise when developing smaller programs. The same methods and techniques that work well with small programs do not necessarily apply to larger programs. As the lack of applicability of this "scaling up" has been recognized, approaches to the production of large programs have been pursued along three paths.

1. Management techniques to provide control over personnel assigned to a software project and monitor their progress.
2. Software design methodologies to attack the particular problems found in large programs. These methodologies have in turn led to the development of supporting language facilities.
3. Software development tools and environments to assist in the creative part and to automate as much as possible the noncreative parts of software development.

To stress the differences between small and large systems production, De-Remer and Kron invented the terms "programming in the small" and "programming in the large." Point 1 reflects the most striking difference between programming in the small and programming in the large. If only one person can produce the needed software, all problems boil down to the professional skill of one programmer and the availability of a suitable programming environment. The development of large software systems that require several programmers, on the other hand, is not merely a matter of "programming," but mainly a management problem. Successful management must be capable of estimating the resources necessary to accomplish a given task, assigning resources to the project at the appropriate times, breaking down the development effort into well-defined and clearly separated phases, monitoring each phase through periodic design reviews, and imposing a set of standards for each activity. Aron (1974) notes that the "emphasis on management rather than technology represents a major change in the nature of programming since the 1950s." Most of these issues, however, are beyond the scope of this book; the interested reader is referred to the literature referenced in the Further Reading section.

This chapter focuses on points 2 and 3. The two points are strongly related. For example, a program library can be viewed either as simply a tool or a necessary component of a methodology based on the incremental development and production of reusable software.

The chapter is organized as follows. Section 6.1 further motivates the distinction between programming in the small and programming in the large, with the aid of an example. Section 6.2 reviews software design methodologies and stresses the differences between design methodologies for small and large programs. Section 6.3 evaluates the features provided by current languages in support of programming in the large. Section 6.4 discusses the need for program development systems in which the language and a rich set of tools are integrated to provide a friendly programming environment, and reviews examples of contemporary environments.

6.1 WHAT IS A LARGE PROGRAM?

The concept of a large program is difficult to define. We certainly do not want to equate the size of a program (e.g., the number of source statements) with its complexity. Largeness relates more to the "size" and complexity of the problem being solved than to the final size of a program. Usually, however, the size of a program is a good indication of the complexity of the problem being solved.

Consider the task of building a reservation system for a particular airline. The system is expected to keep a database of flight information. Airline agents working at remote sites may access the database at arbitrary times and in any order. They may inquire about flight information, such as time and price; make or cancel a reservation on a particular flight; update existing information, such as local telephone number for a passenger. Certain authorized personnel can access the database to do special operations, such as adding or canceling a flight, or changing a plane type. Others may access the system to obtain statistical data about a particular flight or all flights.

A problem of this magnitude imposes severe restrictions on the solution strategy. The characteristics of such problems include

- The system has to function correctly. A seemingly small error, such as losing a reservation list or interchanging two different lists, could be extremely costly. To guarantee correctness of the system virtually any cost can be tolerated.

- The system is long-lived. The cost associated with producing such a system is so high that it is not practical to replace it with a totally new system. It is expected that the cost will be recouped only over a long period of time.

- During its lifetime, the system undergoes considerable modification. For our example, because of completely unforeseen new Federal regulations, changes might be required in price structure, a new type of airplane might be added, and so on. Other changes might be considered because experience with the system has uncovered some weaknesses. We might find it desirable to have the system find the best route automatically by trying different connections.

- Because of the magnitude of the problem, many people—tens or hundreds—are involved in the development of the system.

These characteristics impose severe requirements both on the system development process and the tools used, namely

- The work must be divided among different people. The work assigned to each person must be stated clearly and unambiguously. One person should not have to know the details of other persons' work, just how theirs interacts with his or hers.

- The system is built up from pieces developed independently by several people. We will call such pieces *modules*. These modules must be designed and certified independently. It would be beneficial if some of these pieces could be taken from already existing systems. Similarly, it would be beneficial if these pieces could be reused in future projects. Indeed, the application itself is so general that the entire system might be reused, with minor modifications, for different transportation systems.

- The system must be modifiable easily, that is, it should be possible to change the internals of one module without requiring changes to the entire system.

- It must be possible to show the correctness of the system based on the correctness of the constituent modules.

These characteristics illustrate the concept of a large program. These problems are less important with a one-person programming task; for example, there is less need for dividing the work and thus less emphasis on clear interface specifications. The possibility exists, at least in theory, of redoing the system from scratch, and so modifiability is less important. Correctness is involved only with one module and therefore is easier to assess. On the other hand, a large system is composed of a collection of interacting modules. If no systematic design methodologies are adopted, each module can interact with any other module in some subtle manner. Consequently, each module cannot be designed, understood, and proven correct apart from all the other modules. The complexity of such systems becomes unmanageable.

The boundaries between programming in the large and programming in the small cannot be stated rigorously. However, we can assume that programming in the large addresses the problem of modular system decomposition, but programming in the small refers to the production of individual modules. The methodologies useful for the two activities are discussed in Section 6.2. Section 6.3 evaluates programming languages in light of programming in the large.

6.2 PROGRAMMING IN THE SMALL VS. PROGRAMMING IN THE LARGE: DESIGN METHODOLOGIES

Research in software design methodologies has focused on top-down design as an effective way of mastering the difficulties of software production. In top-down design, a problem is iteratively decomposed into subproblems that can be solved independently.

When applied to small programs, the method is named *stepwise refinement*. Stepwise refinement has been illustrated in the literature as a process of writing and rewriting a program. At each step of development, the program consists of declarations and statements, some of them legal in the programming language, others abstract and to be refined at the next step. At each step of refinement, abstract declarations and statements can be left in the code as comments for documentation. The process continues until eventually the entire text is a legal program.

Although stepwise refinement is an effective methodology for programming in the small, it fails when applied to large programs. One reason is that it does not favor the recognition of commonalities between parts. Programmers are not encouraged to represent common parts by a unique abstraction, to be refined just once and invoked wherever necessary. Rather, each part is separately refined. Another reason is that the final program does not mirror the design process adequately, even if abstract statements are left as comments in the text. Moreover, abstract statements usually are written in informal English prose, and it may be necessary to read their refinement to understand precisely what they do.* Consequently, readability and modifiability of programs can be hampered for programs of substantial size.

Top-down design of large applications must support system decomposition into small-sized programs (modules). Following the principle of information hiding, the designer must distinguish clearly between what a module does—what the module exports for use by other modules—from how it does it—its internal details. A *module interface* should specify exactly the internally defined entities exported for use by other modules and the externally defined entities imported from other modules. Designing a module consists of designing its interface and, iteratively, any new subsidiary modules that will be used by the module.

As an example, consider the airline reservation problem of Section 6.1. We might have a *flight module,* which provides information about flights as they are scheduled. Given a flight number, the module provides the total number of seats, the time of departure, possible connecting flights and so on. The module also provides update operations, for example, to modify departure times. We might have a *reservation module* to handle reservation lists for all flights; given a flight number and date, it allows one to make or cancel reservations on a particular flight. A *statistics module* might provide operations that collect statistics on some or all flights. The reservation module must have a restricted access to the flight module. It can obtain information about flights (e.g., number of seats) but cannot perform any updates. For example, the design of the reservation module can be recorded as sketched below.

module *reservation*
    import function *number_of_seats* (*flight number*)
        return *integer* **from** *flight*;
    export procedure *make_reservation* (*flight_number, customer*);
        procedure *cancel_reservation* (*flight_number, customer*);

Function *number_of_seats* is imported from module *flight*; it receives a formal parameter of type *flight_number* and returns an *integer*. Procedures *make_reservation* and *cancel_reservation* have parameters of type *flight_number* and *customer*; they update the list of passengers for a certain flight.

Design is complete when all module interfaces have been specified. Only at this stage can we turn to the implementation of module bodies. The separation between the two phases of design and implementation distinguishes this approach from stepwise refinement. In stepwise refinement, design

---

*This last problem can be solved by stating the abstract statements in a formal notation.

and coding are developed hand in hand. Here we first decompose the system into modules, and then address the problem of implementing the module bodies (e.g., using stepwise refinements).

It can be argued that modular system decomposition can be driven by the recognition of two particular classes of abstractions: procedural abstractions and data abstractions. Procedural abstractions are operations that perform a mapping between input and output data objects. Data abstractions are a set of operations that manipulate a particular class of data objects. A module corresponds either to a procedural abstraction or a data abstraction. At each stage of top-down design, the problem to be solved is how to design an abstraction. Each abstraction is iteratively decomposed into subsidiary abstractions until the program is broken into pieces of moderate complexity.

6.3 LANGUAGE FEATURES FOR PROGRAMMING IN THE LARGE

This section discusses how programming languages support the needs of programming in the large and, in particular, the design methodology presented in Section 6.2. All programming languages provide features for decomposing programs into smaller and largely autonomous units. Such units are called *physical modules* in the sequel; we will use the term *logical module* to denote a module identified at the design stage. A logical module may be implemented by one or more physical modules.

Our discussion will be organized according to three criteria:

1. What is the notion of physical module supported by the language, and how well does it capture the logical properties specified at the design stage?

2. How can a program be built by combining physical modules? How does the program structure imposed by the language mirror the hierarchical modular decomposition found during design?

3. How independently can physical modules be implemented? In particular, how long-lived and reusable are physical modules?

The discussion will be centered around Pascal, SIMULA 67, and Ada. Pascal is viewed here as a representative of the class of ALGOL-like languages. Our conclusions about Pascal hold, with minor changes, for other members of the class, such as ALGOL 60 and ALGOL 68. A few comments on Modula-2, CLU, and Smalltalk also will be given after the section devoted to Ada.

6.3.1 Pascal

6.3.1.1 Modules

The only features provided by Pascal for physical modular decomposition
are procedures and functions. Procedures and functions, however, can only
implement procedural abstraction. To implement data abstractions, we
must separately describe type and procedure (function) declarations. In
fact, the language does not provide any mechanisms for data encapsulation.
As a result, there is no immediate one-to-one correspondence between the
logical modules identified during design and the physical modules of the
program.

6.3.1.2 Program Structure

Every program in Pascal has the following structure.

```
program programname (files);
    declarations of constants, types, variables,
            procedures and functions;
begin
    statements (no declarations)
end.
```

A program consists of declarations and operations. The operations are either the built-in ones provided by the language or those declared as functions and procedures. A procedure or function itself may contain the declaration of other procedures and/or functions. The organization of a Pascal
program is thus a tree structure of modules (static nesting tree—Section
3.6.2). The tree structure represents the textual nesting of lower-level modules. Nesting is used to control the scope of items declared within modules,
according to the static binding rule presented in Section 3.6.2.

To evaluate the structure of Pascal programs, consider the following example. Suppose that the top-down modular design of a module A identifies
two modules B and C providing subsidiary procedural abstractions. Similarly, module B invokes two private procedural abstractions provided by
modules D and E. Module C invokes a private procedural abstraction provided by F. Figure 6.1 shows a nesting structure for a program that satisfies the design constraints.

A basic problem with the solution of Figure 6.1 is that the structure does
not enforce the restrictions on procedure invocations found at the design
stage. Actually, the structure allows for the possibility of several other invocations. For example E can invoke D, B, and A; C can invoke B and A, and so
on. On the other hand, the structure of Figure 6.1 imposes some restrictions
that might become undesirable. For example, if we discover that module F

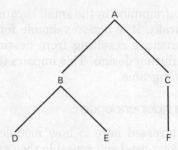

FIGURE 6.1   Static nesting tree.

needs the procedural abstraction provided by module E, the structure of Figure 6.1 is no longer adequate. Figure 6.2 shows a rearrangement of the program structure that is compatible with this new requirement.

The problem with the organization of Figure 6.2 is that the structure no longer displays the hierarchical decomposition of abstractions. Module E appears to be a subsidiary abstraction used by A, although the only reason for its placement at that level in the tree is that both modules B and F need to refer to it.

Similar problems occur for variables, constants and types. The tree structure does not forbid undesired access to variables declared in enclosing modules. In addition, if any two modules M_i and M_j must share a variable, this variable must be declared in a module M that statically encloses both M_i and M_j.

Further problems are caused by the textual layout of Pascal programs. The entire program is a single monolithic text. If the program is large, module boundaries are not immediately visible, even if the programmer uses careful conventions for indentation. A module heading can appear well before its body, because of intervening inner module declarations. Consequently, programs can be difficult to read and modify.

The problems with Pascal discussed in this section stem from block structure, and therefore hold for other ALGOL-like languages. Block structure is

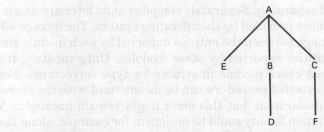

FIGURE 6.2   A rearrangement of the program structure of Figure 6.1.

adequate for programming in the small because it supports stepwise refinement quite naturally. It is not so valuable for structuring large programs. The program structure resulting from nesting interferes with the logical structure found during design. This impairs the writability, readability, and modifiability of programs.

6.3.1.3   Module Independence

The question addressed here is how modules can be developed independently, and how long-lived and reusable they are. These requisites are partly attained at the design stage by a clean definition of module interfaces and a systematic application of the principle of information hiding. In addition, it is desirable to support the separate implementation of modules. It should be possible to compile and certify modules separately. Separately compiled and certified modules should be kept in a library, ready for later reuse.

The original Pascal Report does not define a standard facility for separate compilation. Several implementations, however, do support it. In such a case, one might use Pascal to program each module as a separate compilation unit. Separately compiled modules would be combined to form a unique system in a logically distinct phase. This strategy for the implementation of large programs would overcome most of the problems discussed in Sections 6.3.1.1 and 6.3.1.2.

However, the lack of a Pascal standard for separate compilation leaves some important points unanswered:

1. What program entities can a separate compilation unit export?
2. How is a unit interface specified?
3. What amount of type checking across unit interfaces is prescribed to occur?

Different implementations can adopt different solutions to these points. As a result, Pascal programs developed at different installations may be incompatible.

In most current implementations, only outer-level procedures or functions can be compiled separately. Separately compiled units later are assembled via a standard linker provided by the operating system. The linkage editor resolves the bindings between the entities imported by each module and the corresponding entities exported by other modules. Unfortunately, the linkage editor does not check module interfaces for type correctness. For example, a call to an external procedure can be inconsistent with the corresponding procedure declaration, but this error might remain uncaught. A safer separate-compilation facility could be designed, for example, along the lines of the Ada scheme discussed in Section 6.3.3.

6.3.2 SIMULA 67

6.3.2.1 Modules

Logical modules can be represented in SIMULA 67 as procedures, functions, or classes. Although a class can collect a set of related data and subprogram declarations, it provides no means for hiding internal details from other modules. Information hiding can be achieved only by adoption of disciplined programming standards.

6.3.2.2 Program Structure

SIMULA 67 adopts a conventional ALGOL-like block structure. The unusual feature of the language is that blocks and classes may be prefixed by a class name. Prefixing a class defines a subclass (as discussed in Chapter 4). Prefixing a block can be illustrated by the following example. The following class—*list_processing*—defines a set of procedures that may be used in manipulating linked lists.

```
class list_processing;
    ref (element) first;
    boolean procedure empty;
            begin . . . check if list is empty . . . end;
    procedure insert (e);
            begin . . . insert element e in list . . . end;
    procedure remove (e);
            begin . . . remove element e from list . . . end;
begin
    first:- none
end
```

Prefixing a block with a class name makes the attributes of the class visible to the block. For example, a block that starts with the heading

```
list_processing begin . . .
```

has access to procedures *empty, insert, remove* and *first*. This idea has been used in an interesting way to supply a set of commonly used facilities to SIMULA 67 programmers. The two classes SIMSET and SIMULATION have been defined to contain, respectively, list-processing and simulation primitives. Any SIMULA 67 program may use these classes simply by using either name as a prefix. These classes may be viewed as providing two fixed libraries of reusable modules.

Prefixing supports top-down modular design. A top-level class may be written to contain only the most global design decisions. Successive subclasses of this class contain further design decisions based on earlier ones, that is, those at lower levels of abstractions. At the lowest level, the program is written prefixed by the most detailed class.

Most large programs—for example, operating systems—exist in many versions. We must be able to control the development of all the versions by exploiting their similarities and considering them all to be members of a *family of programs*. At each design level, certain decisions are made that exclude some family members. At the lowest level, one particular member remains. Because a change in a design decision at a certain level affects all design decisions at lower levels, a change in an earlier design decision affects the program more substantially than a change in a later design decision. The early design decisions thus should be the most general and the least likely to change. SIMULA 67's subclass mechanism can support this methodology. Different subclasses of a class represent different family members with the same ancestor. A class embodies—*inherits*—all the design decisions common to all its subclasses. A change in a subclass requires no modifications to the parent class, only to the lower-level subclasses.

The basic problem with SIMULA 67 is that prefixing is embedded within block structure. Consequently, the same criticisms raised for Pascal in Section 6.3.1.2 hold for SIMULA 67.

6.3.2.3   Module Independence

With disciplined use of classes, one can design programs through the composition of highly independent modules. As in the case of Pascal, the official definition of SIMULA 67 does not specify a standard for separate development of modules.

A separate compilation facility has been introduced in the DEC System-10 SIMULA 67 implementation. In this implementation, procedure and class declarations can be compiled as separate modules. Each separate module can declare a class or procedure as EXTERNAL, which indicates the use of a separately compiled module. Each separately compiled class or procedure must be compiled before any module that references it. This allows modules to be type-checked during compilation. This scheme forces a bottom-up system development: modules implementing subsidiary abstractions must be compiled before the module(s) using such abstractions.

6.3.3   Ada

6.3.3.1   Modules

An Ada module can be a (generic) subprogram, a (generic) package, or a task. Logical modules identified at the design stage can be mapped into Ada modules quite naturally. Moreover, the language-supported distinction between module specification and module body allows one to separate what is expected by the module from what is hidden within the module.

6.3.3.2   Program Structure

An Ada program is a linear collection of modules that can be either (generic) subprograms or (generic) packages. These modules are called units. One particular unit that implements a subprogram is the main program in the usual sense. Modules can enclose declarations of inner modules. Consequently, a unit can be organized as a tree structure of modules. Any abuse of nesting within a unit causes the same problems discussed for Pascal.

These problems can be mitigated by the use of the *subunit* facility offered by the language. This facility permits the body of a module embedded in the declarative part of a unit (or subunit) to be written separately from the enclosing unit (or subunit). Instead of the entire module, only a fictitious body (*stub*) need appear in the declarative part of the enclosing unit. The following example illustrates the concept of the subunit.

```
procedure X ( . . . . ) is      --unit specification
    W: INTEGER;
    package Y is                 --inner unit specification
        A: INTEGER;
        function B (C: INTEGER) return INTEGER;
    end Y;
    package body Y is separate; --this is a stub
begin --use package Y and variable W
        .
        .
        .
end X;
```

```
separate (X)
package body Y is
    procedure Z ( . . . ) is separate; --this is a stub
    function B (C: INTEGER) return INTEGER is
    begin --use procedure Z
        .
        .
        .
    end B;
end Y;
```

```
separate (X.Y)
procedure Z ( . . . ) is
begin .
        .
        .
end Z;
```

The prefix **separate** (X) specifies package body Y as a subunit of unit X. Similarly, **separate** (X.Y) specifies procedure Z as a subunit of package Y nested within X.

The subunit facility not only can improve the readability of programs, but supports a useful technique in top-down programming. When one is writing a program at a certain level of abstraction, it is best to leave some details to be decided at a lower level. Suppose you realize that a certain procedure is required to accomplish a given task. Although calls to that procedure can be immediately useful when you want to test the execution flow, the body of the procedure can be written at a later time.

The subunit facility, however, does not overcome all the problems·caused by the tree nesting structure. The textually separate subunit body is still considered to be logically located at the point at which the corresponding stub appears in the enclosing (sub)unit. It is exactly this point that determines the entities visible to the subunit. In the example, both subunits Y and Z can access variable W declared in unit X.

The last program structuring issue is how the interfaces (i.e., import/export relationships) among units are specified in Ada. A unit exports all the entities specified in its specification part. It can import entities from other units if and only if the names of such units are listed in a suitable statement (**with** statement) that prefixes the unit.

For example, the following unit lists unit X (a subprogram) in its **with** statement. Consequently, it is legal to use X within T's body.

```
with X;
package T is
        C: INTEGER;
        procedure D ( . . . );
end T;
package body T is
        .
        .
        .
end T;
```

Similarly, the following procedure U can legally call procedure T.D and access variable T.C. On the other hand, unit X is not visible by U.

with;
procedure U (. . . .) **is**

.

end U;

The interface of an Ada unit consists of the **with** statement, which lists the names of units from which entities are imported; and the unit specification, which lists the entities exported by the unit. Each logical module discovered at the design stage can be implemented as a unit. If the top-down design was done carefully, logical modules should be relatively simple. Consequently, the depth of nesting within units should be very small, or even null. Ada does not forbid an abuse of nesting within units. Actually, the entire program could be designed as a single unit with a deeply nested tree structure. More desirable program structures can be achieved only by adherence to certain program development standards, because the language does not provide any means to enforce them.

6.3.3.3 Module Independence

The set of units and subunits comprising a program can be compiled in one or more separate compilations. Each compilation translates one or more units and/or subunits. The order of compilation must satisfy the following constraints.

- A unit can be compiled only if all units mentioned in its **with** statement have been compiled previously.
- A subunit can be compiled only if the enclosing unit has been compiled previously.

In addition, unit specifications can be compiled separately from their bodies. A unit body must be compiled after its specification. The specification of a unit U mentioned in the **with** statement of a unit W must be compiled before W. On the other hand, U's body can be compiled either before or after W.

These constraints assure that a unit is submitted for compilation only after the compilation of unit specifications from which it can import entities. The compiler saves in a library file the descriptors of all entities exported by units. When a unit is submitted for compilation, the compiler has access to the library file. Consequently, it is able to perform the same amount of type checking on the unit whether the program is compiled in parts or as a whole.

If a package unit exports an encapsulated (private) data type, the type's representation is hidden to the programmer but known to the compiler, thanks to the **private** clause appearing in the package specification. Consequently, the compiler can generate code to allocate variables for such types declared in other units submitted for compilation prior to the package body (but after its specification).

When a unit is modified, it may be necessary to recompile several units. The change may potentially affect its subunits as well as all the units that name it in their **with** statements. In principle, all potentially affected units must be recompiled.

The separate compilation facility of Ada supports an incremental rather than a parallel development of programs, because units must be developed according to a partial ordering. This is not an arbitrary restriction, but a conscious design decision in support of methodical program development. A unit can be submitted for compilation only after the interfaces of all used units are frozen. Consequently, the programmer is forced to postpone the design of a unit body until these interfaces have been designed.

One of the goals of separate compilation is to support production of reusable software. Certified modules can be kept in a library and later combined to form different programs. The Ada solution is deficient on this point for package units exporting encapsulated (private) data types. The visible part (the specification) of such packages must include the type's operations and a **private** clause that specifies the type's internal representation. This representation is not usable outside the package body; it is there only for supporting separate compilation. Logically, this information belongs in the package body, together with the procedure bodies implementing the type's operations. Besides being aesthetically unpleasant, this feature has some unfortunate consequences:

- It violates the principle of top-down design. The representation must be determined at the same time as the specification of the data type, and both appear in the same textual unit.

- It limits the power of the language to support libraries of reusable modules, unless special care is taken in the implementation. For example, a module using FIFO queues is compiled and validated with respect to a FIFO queue package providing a specific representation for FIFO queues (e.g., arrays). The module must be recompiled if one wants to reuse it in a different program in which FIFO queues are implemented by a different data structure, even though the primitives for manipulating FIFO queues are the same in both cases.

6.3.4 Modula-2, CLU, and Smalltalk

The features for programming in the large provided by Modula-2 are very similar to those provided by Ada. Outer-level modules keep interfaces separate from their bodies, and both can be compiled separately. Opaque export allows types to be exported without the details of their representation. Because the instances of such types are constrained to be accessible via pointers (Section 4.5.2.3), there is no need to have the equivalent of Ada's **private** clause in the interface. In fact, the amount of storage to be allocated in client modules for such data objects is known *a priori*. This is a strong point of Modula-2. The restriction that abstract data types be accessible via pointers does not impose any unreasonable constraints—it implies just one indirection in accessing abstract objects—but, at the same time, supports strong intermodule decoupling. Changing the data structure for an abstract data type does not affect client modules either from a logical or from an implementation viewpoint.

CLU's separate compilation facility also is similar to Ada's, but allocates objects of an abstract type in the heap. Objects are created by a create procedure encapsulated within the cluster defining the abstract type. Created objects are accessed by other modules via pointers. Consequently, there is no need for such modules to know the representation of the abstract type. These modules need to know only the headings of the procedures that create and manipulate abstract objects. This is the only information that has to appear in the specification part of a module implementing an abstract type. To change the representation for abstract objects, the programmer does not need to recompile modules that use such abstract objects. As a result, CLU is more supportive of independent development than Ada.

Smalltalk provides features similar to those of CLU and SIMULA 67, but it abandons the static binding (and checking) principles on which these languages are based. Objects are created dynamically and accessed via pointer variables. The ability of an object to respond to messages depends on the object's class and its superclass(es), as we saw in Section 4.6.5. Because variables can be bound to objects of any type, type correctness of message sending can be checked only at run-time. As illustrated for SIMULA 67, the inheritance facility provided by the subclass mechanism supports hierarchical system decomposition.

As we shall see in Section 6.4.2, Smalltalk has been designed primarily as a language for powerful, interactive, personal computing. The language designers decided to trade extensive program checking for flexible interactive facilities for program manipulation. However, the same approach would not apply equally well when we move from a single-user environment to an environment where several programmers must cooperate in the implementation of a complex and large system.

6.3.5   An Ideal Scenario

The previous sections have stressed the conceptual differences between programming in the small and programming in the large. In particular, Sections 6.3.1 through 6.3.4 presented an evaluation of the features provided by existing programming languages in support of programming in the large. This section outlines an ideal scheme for the support of programming in the large. This scheme is somewhat similar to that found in Mesa.

The programming language should be composed of two sublanguages: the language for programming in the small (LPS) and the language for programming in the large (LPL). The more clearly distinguishable the two levels, the more readable the programs and the more suitable the language for programming large systems. Most current languages do not recognize LPS and LPL as two separate levels of system description and, therefore, merge them into the same notation. Mesa does, and provides a special LPL called Mesa Configuration Language (C/Mesa).

As an example of the distinction between LPL and LPS, consider a module that imports some external resources and exports some internal resources (data or procedures). The specification of imported and exported resources is indicated in the module interface written in LPS. For abstract types, only the allowed operations are specified—no representation details. The interface specification allows each LPS module to be compiled independently from other modules. In particular, each module can be type-checked completely with respect to its interface. LPS specifies imported resources without naming the module(s) that provides them. The LPL commands map resources imported by each module to resources exported by other modules.

For example, a module P, importing two procedures $P1$ and $P2$ and exporting a procedure $P3$, may have the following LPS interface specification.

```
import P1 (integer, boolean);
       P2 (integer, character);
export P3 (real, real);
```

A module Q with the interface specification

```
import . . . ;
export Q1 (integer, character);
```

and a module R with the interface specification

```
import . . . ;
export R1 (integer, boolean);
```

may be structured in a system by the following LPL commands.

```
bind P1 of P to R1 of R;
     P2 of P to Q1 of Q;
```

LPL is responsible for type checking the interface of each module with respect to the resources provided by other modules and specified in their own interfaces. It is also responsible for linking a set of validated LPS modules into a unique executable unit. LPL can be viewed as a glorified job control language that allows the programmer to specify the interconnections among the modules that constitute a software system. Besided facilities for specifying system configuration, an LPL should provide facilities for controlling versions and maintaining libraries of module descriptions. Such descriptions evolve as systems are developed, and LPL should support this evolution. This section basically concentrates on LPL as a language for system configuration.

LPL commands are executed by a translator that is somewhat similar to a linkage editor. This translator operates on object modules. To know whether an imported resource is provided by one module or another requires no recompilation of any module, but simply LPL processing. This approach favors the use of libraries of validated and reusable object modules.

This ideal scenario presents a problem for modules importing abstract data types. When these modules are compiled, the compiler ignores the representation of local variables of abstract type. In a heap-based language such as CLU, this lack of information is not a problem, because objects of an abstract type are allocated by the module implementing the abstract type, and other modules access them only via pointers (see also Section 7.3.3.4). In other languages, such as Ada, objects of an abstract type must be allocated at the activation of the modules where they are declared. But the run-time actions necessary to allocate variables of an imported abstract type become known only after LPL is processed. Consequently, the LPL processor must be capable of inserting such run-time actions into the object version of LPS modules.

The above discussion shows that the LPL processor is considerably more complex than the standard linkage editor. Besides binding imported resource names to the corresponding exported resources, it must perform intermodule type checking and, for some kinds of LPSs, generate code for storage allocation of abstract type variables.

The fact that this ideal scenario requires an entire extra piece of system software—the LPL processor—traditionally would be a reason to abandon the scheme. But as we have been stressing throughout, the ultimate goal is the attainment of an environment for reliable software development consisting of a language and other tools. The LPL processor should not be viewed as a tool that is necessitated by a language feature, but as one that supports a modular design methodology. Separating the linking function from the compiler corresponds to separating system structuring from module implementation.

The separation between the compiler and the linker that results from this scheme is somewhat reminiscent of the philosophy of older languages such as FORTRAN and PL/I. These languages, in fact, do have a separate compilation facility and separately compiled units are assembled by the linkage editor. However, the linkage editor is a low-level tool that does not type-check module interfaces. Using such a linkage editor instead of the LPL processor in the ideal scenario would mean abandoning the safety of strong typing at the system structuring level when errors are more costly.

6.4   SOFTWARE DEVELOPMENT ENVIRONMENTS

This chapter has emphasized the differences between programming in the large and programming in the small. We noted in Section 6.3 that most programming languages do not have specific facilities for supporting programming in the large. In Section 6.3.5, we noted that a type-checking linker is required for the language to help us distinguish between the two levels of activity. In theory, of course, such a facility is not necessary. Its utility lies in the help it can provide us in producing reliable software. This section reviews the kinds of tools used with programming languages for software production and shows the need for an integration of tools in a software development environment. Although most of these tools also are employed for programming in the small, their use becomes essential in a programming in the large environment.

The need for support tools was recognized very early in the programming era. In fact, assemblers were once viewed as helpful tools in programming the computer (in machine language). At present, a variety of development tools are often provided to establish friendly programming environments even on very small machines such as personal computers. When confronted with the task of programming large systems, one comes to appreciate the fact that the programming language by itself is not sufficient. In this framework, the computer is viewed by the individual programmer not as a personal computational resource, but as a warehouse of public and private tools. Some of the tools are provided by the system; others—the modules designed by other programmers—are developed for the particular project. The computer is also the medium through which all relevant information flows; it can be used for recording documentation, sending messages, and general management functions.

6.4.1   Basic Software Development Tools

Listed and described briefly below are the basic tools required for system development. These tools are basic in the sense that they are needed for any method of software development. Later, we will discuss some tools that support specific design methodologies.

1. Text Editor. That system component used to enter programs and other types of documents into the computer. The common method of program entry is by interactive text-editing, which makes it easier to make corrections to the program text.

There has been an evolution from basic line-oriented editors to screen-oriented editors to window-based editors. One now finds syntax-directed editors that know the syntax of the programming language and prevent the entry of any syntactically incorrect programs.

2. Macroprocessor. A simple translator that can replace specified strings in a source document with indicated target strings. More sophisticated macroprocessors allow the parameterization of the source string. This adds considerably to the tool's utility. A macroprocessor can be used

(a) *To overcome some language deficiencies,* such as the absence of symbolic constants. For example, one can use MAXSIZE in the program and just before compilation let the macroprocessor replace it with the specific value.

More generally, one can supplement a language with certain desired constructs. For example, RATFOR is a "structured" FORTRAN language based on this scheme. A number of control structures (e.g., **if, for, while**) have been defined as macros. A RATFOR program may contain these control structures. First, the RATFOR system replaces these macros by their defintion in terms of FORTRAN, and then the program is compiled by a standard FORTRAN compiler.

(b) *To increase the readability and writability of programs.* The use of a macroporocessor can lead to a reduction of clerical errors by giving a name to pieces of code that are repeated several times. One can then use this name instead of repeating the code. As the length of the named code segment increases, the advantages of this technique also increase. These writability advantages can be translated to readability advantages if one considers the input to the macroprocessor as the source program. The sequence of code that is repeated several times in the target program (i.e., the output of the macroprocessor) need only be read and understood once in the source program.

(c) *To replace subprogram calls with the body of the subprogram.* In this way, one can design the program such that every unit is regarded as a subprogram. The efficiency-related decision of whether to implement something as a subprogram or in-line code can be postponed and be based later on sample system runs. Ada supports this approach by providing a directive to the compiler (**pragma** INLINE *subprogram_name*) that can appear in the same declarative part as the named subprogram.

The C language depends explicitly on a macro preprocessor to provide symbolic constants, conditional compilation, and macro definition facilities.

3. Interpreter/Compiler. An interpreter is used to run a source program. It can usually produce better error diagnostics than a compiler and is therefore better suited for program debugging. On the other hand, an interpreter is less efficient in execution time. It would be desirable to have a compiler and an interpreter that accept the same language so that the interpreter can be used for debugging and the compiler for production. The INTERLISP system includes such a combination for LISP.

4. File System. A file system can be used to store data and/or programs either in source or object form. The programmer can thus keep libraries of program components on secondary storage. The system may provide help in administering such components by updating version numbers, creation dates, and so on. It also is possible to restrict access to the components to a specified set of users. Programmers working in a team thus can share their components, while the system prevents access to unauthorized users.

5. Linkage Editor or Linker. A linker takes several independently compiled modules and merges them into one. The availability of a linker has many advantages: it allows different programmers to work on different modules concurrently; and it allows one module to be compiled once and then used in building different systems. To carry the latter advantage further, one can create a library of reusable modules that at different times are combined in different ways. Finally, if a bug is found in one module, only that module need be recompiled. As we have seen, these are the advantages that *could* be attained in principle, depending on the rules of the language and the sophistication of the linker.

These are the basic tools required to make efficient use of a programming language. Even with these basic tools, the strong interdependence of language, methodology, and tools is apparent. A good example of this interdependence is the concept of separate compilation in a programming language, which requires the use of a linker and a library as tools and can support a methodology based on modular design and reusable software.

6.4.2 More Sophisticated Software Development Tools

The basic tools are used to aid the productivity of the coding phase of software development. Tools also have been developed for other phases and for the express purpose of supporting a specific design methodology.

There are a number of tools that support the requirements phase by helping in recording the various requirements and keeping them consistent. The other major use of these systems is in producing system documentation. PSL/PSA and SREM are two prominent examples of such systems. PSL/PSA provides a "language" (PSL) in which the requirements can be expressed and an analyzer (PSA) that examines the requirements for consistency and completeness. Because there is great variation in the requirements of systems in different application areas, these so-called *requirements systems* are suitable only for certain applications. For example, PSL/PSA is suited for business systems, but SREM is appropriate for real-time systems.

To support the certification phase there are *program verifiers,* which try automatically, or with the help of the user, to prove the correctness of a program with respect to a specification. Less ambitious than a program verifier is a *data flow analyzer,* which examines a program statically and tries to pinpoint potential sources of error, such as successive assignments to a variable without an intervening use of the variable, potential use of a variable before initialization, unreachable code segments, and so on. *Test data generators* help in producing data on which to test the program; test data should be saved for retesting the program after later enhancements. *Symbolic executors* can run the program on symbolic data and produce symbolic formulas that characterize the values of output variables and conditions for traversal of program paths. These formulas then are used by the programmer to reason about the program, for example, to synthesize test data that traverse a given program path.

The certification tools must have a knowledge of the semantics and syntax of the programming language built into them. They are heavily dependent on the semantics of the language. Those features that make reasoning about programs hard also make it hard for these tools to do their job.

A requirement shared by all program processing tools is that they need to operate on an internal representation of the program. If the tools are to be integrated and work well together, it is convenient for all to use the same representation. Although this requirement restricts some tools to using a representation that may not be ideal, the benefits of the compatibility of the tools outweighs this disadvantage. Such a uniform representation also would encourage the development of compatible programs—as evidenced in the UNIX system (Section 6.4.3), in which viewing files uniformly as sequences of characters allows the routing of output from one program to different destinations quite easily.

Another motivation for program development tools is to support certain program construction methodologies. One such methodology insists on developing a provably correct version of the program first, without particular concern for program efficiency. After a correct program has been achieved, the next task is to modify the program to make its efficiency acceptable. Necessary for that methodology are

- **Dynamic frequency analyzer**, which can run a program with typical data and determine which portions of the program are executed most often and therefore most in need of time optimization. It has been shown that programmers' intuition in pinpointing such areas of the code is not reliable.

- **Source program optimizer**, which can detect and transform inefficient code into a more efficient one.

- **Source program control**, which can maintain the different versions of a program and their relationships. These different versions are especially important during the maintenance phase, because the original version of the program, which was easier to program, is the one that is easier to modify as well.

Finally, a key component of a support environment is the *project database,* where all project artifacts (tools, documents, program modules in source and object form, test data, development plans, budgets, and so on) are kept and maintained. This is where the differences in the needs of programming in the small and programming in the large are more striking. If the application to be developed is large, complex, and requires the cooperation of several programmers, then the need for storing the above information and the relationships among the various pieces becomes vital for a successful management of its development and maintenance. The support system is particularly useful if it ensures that all data are up-to-date and consistent, guards against incompleteness and checks against unauthorized access, and if at any given time it provides facilities to package together all the elements that constitute a given version of the system being developed (or maintained). Maintaining multiple versions of the same module requires *version control* facilities. The building of multiple versions of a system from different versions of constituent modules is called *configuration management.*

The reader who is interested in the subject of software development environments can refer to the literature referenced in the Further Reading section at the end of this chapter. In what follows (Sections 6.4.3–6.4.5) we will restrict our discussion to three environments: the UNIX environment, the Ada environment, and the Smalltalk environment. In particular, we will concentrate on the relationship between the environment and the underlying programming language. Finally, in Section 6.4.6 we will draw some general conclusions and discuss the probable evolution of environments.

6.4.3   The UNIX Environment

The UNIX operating system was designed and implemented by D. M. Ritchie and K. Thompson of Bell Telephone Laboratories. Originally, it was designed to run on the DEC PDP-7 and then the PDP-11 computer family. Since then it has been implemented on a large variety of machines and has become a de-facto standard for small to mid-size computers. It is becoming available now on mainframes and supercomputers. This popularity is due largely to the ease and friendliness with which program development is supported. Also, the system is written almost entirely in the C programming language, and thus porting UNIX to new machines is an easily affordable task.

C is not a very high-level language, even though it features modern control and data-structuring mechanisms, and a large number of operators for the basic data types. On the other hand, C can be used as an implementation language even in critical systems software applications—such as operating systems—where execution efficiency is a major concern. Most of C's features can be implemented on today's computers in a straightforward manner, so that the experienced C programmer can easily guess how fast a C program will run by examining the source program.

The UNIX system provides a large number of tools to support programming in the C language. We will review some of these tools to show the integration of a programming language with a set of support tools.

C compiler. The compiler has a number of interesting and useful options. One is object code optimization, which usually is used only after the program has been debugged. Another option provides for the object code to be augmented with counters to keep track of how many times each routine is called. This, as we have seen, can guide the programmer to those parts of the program that are candidates for further optimization. It also can help the programmer to assess the thoroughness of testing by pinpointing which control paths have been traversed during execution. Another compiler option can be used to produce an object code that may be put in libraries or later may be combined with other object modules (possibly written in other languages).

C debugger. This tool allows a program to be run and debugged interactively. Under this system, the user can trace the execution of the program, stop the execution at different points, and examine and change the values of the program variables, all at source level, without any reference to the underlying machine structure. If the program terminates abnormally, a trace and an indication of the cause of failure can be produced.

Lint. The C compiler is not strong in detecting errors or producing good diagnostic messages. The task of program checking is left to *lint*, which searches a C-program for suspicious-looking coding. *Lint* can be used for different purposes. One is to enforce the type rules of C. The compiler does not do much type checking and applies many type conversions liberally; *lint*, on the other hand, is more strict and flags those code sequences that require automatic conversion. So *lint* can be used to make C appear to be almost a strongly typed language.

Lint also can do type-checking for intermodule references in a set of routines on different files. This way, large C programs can be divided into modules, and each module can be separately developed in any order. While compiling a module, the C compiler assumes the external references in each module are correct. Once some or all modules have been developed, *lint* can be used to check their type consistency. The division of labor between the compiler and *lint* simplifies the compiler, because it can concentrate on producing efficient object code quickly and not be sidetracked by error checking and producing diagnostic messages.

Lint also can help in producing portable programs. Under one of its options, *lint* flags those statements in the program that contain nonportable features, such as comparisons that depend on the machine's character representation.

The last class of properties that *lint* checks is that of error-prone constructions, which include unused variables and functions, functions that do not return values, variables used before they have been assigned, unreachable program segments, and boolean expressions whose values are compile-time constants (always true or always false). These conditions might originally exist in the program, or might appear after the program has gone through a number of modifications.

Linkage editor. The standard linker *ld* is used to combine several object modules into one.

cref. Cross-reference listings can be produced with *cref*. Both C programs and assembly language programs may be used as input to *cref*.

ctags. This tool produces a cross-reference for source programs written in different languages.

Error. This tool can be used to analyze the error messages produced by different language compilers.

Diff. This "difference" program finds the differences between two files. It is useful, for example, in quickly scanning the changes made to a file if an older version exists. It also can be used as a regression test tool by comparing two program output files.

Grep. This tool searches a text file for a given pattern. For example, one can search all files in a directory to see where a variable declaration is made or a variable is used. The *grep* program is one of the most frequently used UNIX commands.

Sed* and *awk*. These tools can be used to scan a file for particular patterns and replace these patterns with another pattern. For example, one might want to replace all occurrences of a variable name with another name, or a call to one procedure with another. Bentley (1985) shows how *awk* can be used to help in program testing.

Make. This tool is not designed for the exclusive use of C programmers, but can be used in any nontrivial system development in which (possibly) several languages are used. The motivation is that in building a large system consisting of several modules, the modules commonly are modified individually and therefore exist in several versions. The task of assembling the system into a running unit after one or more modules are changed, although in principle trivial, is rather time-consuming and error-prone. One has to remember which modules to recompile, relink, run through *lint*; which libraries to include and in what order; and so on. Using *make,* the user specifies in a file all the modules making up the system, their dependencies on one another, and what needs to be done to each module (e.g., compiled with C or FORTRAN). After the user makes some modifications to the system, *make* can be requested to reassemble the system by using the latest version of each module and running the user-specified sequence. It only recompiles, relinks, and so on the minimum number of required modules.

This tool is especially useful when several programmers are involved in the development of a system and update their modules independently.

SCCS (Source Code Control System). SCCS provides the ability to maintain multiple versions of text files (e.g., programs, data, documentation, and so on). SCCS saves the latest version of a text and all the incremental changes that allow previous versions to be recreated straightforwardly. The user can recall any version of a file, ask to see the differences between two versions of a file, or see the history of changes to a file. Such information is of vital importance during the maintenance phase.

yacc* and *lex. These are, respectively, a parser generator and a lexical scanner generator. Their use traditionally has been confined to compiler development, although they are being used increasingly in other applications. Any program that reads input and checks its validity requires at least a lexical scanner, which may be produced by *lex.* If, in addition, the program needs to read and interpret complicated input, it requires a parser, which may be generated with *yacc.* Finally, if the program takes different actions based on what input it has received—as is commonly the case with interactive programs—the full generality of *yacc* may be used by organizing the program as a syntax-directed translator: the semantic actions correspond to the actions the program needs to take for each input. In this case, *yacc* completely dictates the overall structure of the program and generates the parser and the scanner automatically. The programmer needs to define the input language—the lexical and syntactic structure of input—and the actions for each input.

These compiler generation tools may be viewed as a special case of *automatic software generators.* An automatic software generator is a system that generates a program from the program specification. The use of such a tool helps in the initial creation, validation, and maintenance of programs (because it is only necessary to modify the specification).

Shell. The *shell* is the command interpreter. It offers a programming language interface to the user. Its control structures and pattern-matching features can be used to write procedures or "scripts" that can be viewed as commands tailored for the user. In fact, many UNIX commands are implemented as *shell* scripts.

More important than the availability of these tools is their compatibility with one another and the operating system. For example, all files have a uniform format, and the different tools preserve this format. Therefore, the different text editors can be used on the same file. This is in sharp contrast to other systems in which each text editor requires a different file format; therefore, if a file is created with one editor, it is impossible to use another editor on it. Under UNIX, a different text editor may be used based on the requirements of the moment, regardless of the previous history of the file.

Another strong suit of UNIX is the ease with which these tools—and in general, any set of programs—may be combined. The operating system provides the ability to direct the output of one program to another through a *pipe* mechanism. For example, if A and B are two programs

$A \mid B$

says to run A, use its output as input to B, and run B (A and B are actually run concurrently in a true producer–consumer relationship, but this implementation issue need not concern us here). This facility is useful in the common case in which one program is needed to act on the output of another. For example, *lp* is a printer program that copies its input on the line printer. If we write a program, P, whose output we want to be printed, all we need say is

$P \mid lp$

In particular, we do not need to worry, when writing P, about the device on which the output is to be printed (as in FORTRAN); and we do not need to invoke a complicated job-control procedure to create an intermediate file for P to put its output on and then, in a separate step, print the results of this file (as in OS/360). In fact, all programs are written assuming that the input is from the standard input device (the terminal) and the output goes to the standard output device (the terminal). It is, however, quite easy to redirect the input and output.

For example,

$P < fi$

says that the input to P comes from the file *fi*;

$P > fo$

says that the output of P goes to the file *fo* (which will be created automatically if it does not exist already).

As another example of program composition under UNIX, consider the following sample work session [taken from (Kernighan 1984)]. The program associated to the command *who* lists all users currently logged in. For example

```
. . .          . . .
ghe      tty5      jul 27      17:44
jaz      tty4      jul 27      17:38
. . .
```

The program associated with the command *lc* counts the number of lines in a file. Thus, the following two commands

```
who> temp
  lc< temp
```

generate the list of logged-in users on file *temp* and count the lines of file *temp* (i.e., evaluates the number of logged-in users). The same could be done without a temporary file *temp* in the following way:

```
who | lc
```

The program associated with the command *grep* prints each line of its input file that matches the argument. Thus

```
who | grep ghe | lc
```

prints a value that represents the number of times user *ghe* is logged in.

These facilities combine to encourage the development of small, reusable programs, because every program being written is viewed as a potential component of a future system. According to Mitze (1980) "if one were to attempt to encapsulate the lifestyle used on most UNIX systems in a single phrase, a good candidate would be 'think small.'"

One creates complex programs not by writing them from scratch, but by interconnecting relatively small components. These components concentrate on single functions and therefore are easy to build, understand, describe, and maintain. The average length of a UNIX program written in C is rather small (about 240 lines long).

6.4.4 The Ada Programming Environment

The need for a complete environment supporting the development of Ada applications was realized by the U.S. Department of Defense when the language was still under design. After much debate, the requirements for an Ada programming support environment (APSE) were published in the STONEMAN document (DOD 1980). In this section we review the need for an APSE in the context of embedded computer applications (for which Ada was expressly designed), the basic functions of an APSE, and the STONEMAN approach to portability of APSEs.

Embedded applications are those applications where computers are embedded in a large system that dictates the required forms of interaction to which the software must conform. Very often, embedded applications have strict real-time requirements, must be tolerant of both hardware and software failures, and must provide secure access to classified information. Hardware and software often are developed jointly. Target machines are mostly special purpose, and provide little or no support for software development. These last two reasons motivate a host environment other than the target environment where the software development can take place.

Ada addresses an application area where assembly language programming has been (and still is) the dominant programming tool. Thus, the expected benefits in terms of realiability, maintainability, and portability of Ada programs will be ultimately measured against run-time efficiency.

An APSE is required to support program development, maintenance, and management for embedded applications written in Ada. The entire life cycle must be supported: from requirements and design specification to implementation, testing, and maintenance.

Tools of an APSE should have uniform interfaces and communicate via a central database, which is the heart of an APSE. Program modules, documentation, data, and any other kind of information used in the project are stored within the database. Access to the tool set and the database is accomplished by a software layer that provides a user interface and system interfaces to the databases and toolset. The STONEMAN document gives requirements for the database structure and the interfacing of all components in the APSE.

Portability is a key issue in Ada. It is important that programs be easily portable and programmers find a consistent environment when they move from one installation to another. The STONEMAN solution is to identify two lower levels within an APSE: the kernel (KAPSE) and the minimal environment (MAPSE). Figure 6.3, taken from (DOD 1980), illustrates this approach. The KAPSE provides a set of functions that can be viewed as the interface of a virtual machine supporting execution of Ada programs. Once these functions are available on a new machine, Ada programs can be immediately transferred and executed. The MAPSE provides the minimal set of tools needed to support Ada programming (editor, compiler, debugger, linker/loader, and so on). These tools are written in Ada and are supported by the KAPSE. Finally, APSEs are built on top of previous layers and realize full life cycle support according to state-of-the-art methodologies.

6.4.5 The Smalltalk Environment

We have discussed the principles of the Smalltalk language in Section 4.5.2.4. The Smalltalk language is almost inextricably intertwined with its environment: one cannot be completely appreciated without the other.

It is illuminating to go back to the motivations that inspired the Smalltalk project. Alan Kay, the principal designer of the Smalltalk environ-

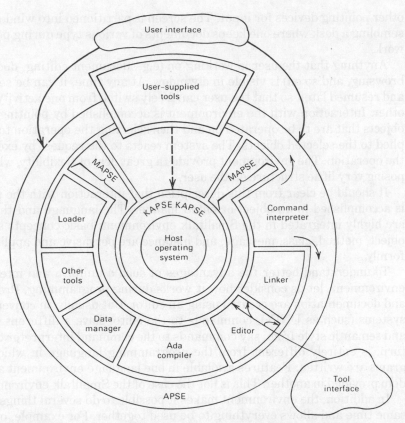

FIGURE 6.3 The Ada Programming Environment [taken from (DOD 1980)].

ment, conceived a research project that he called the Dynabook. The research has been conducted within Xerox Palo Alto Research Center (PARC) for more than 10 years. Intermediate results of the research were Smalltalk-72, Smalltalk-76, Smalltalk-78, and Smalltalk-80, which is the current Smalltalk licensed by Xerox. Early implementations of the environment have been available on the Alto computer, an experimental advanced workstation designed by Xerox Corporation.

The goal of the Dynabook project was to provide a flexible, powerful, easy-to-use environment for personal computing. Kay anticipated that in the 1980s it would be possible to put an enormous amount of computing power into a pocket-size computer. The real problem then would be how to take advantage of this opportunity: how to make computers useful for personal use, even for nonspecialists. The Smalltalk environment is the result of these ideas.

The Smalltalk environment integrates a high-level language with a bit-mapped graphical display for system output and a keyboard, a mouse, or other pointing devices for input. The screen is partitioned into windows, resembling a desk where one keeps documents of various type during personal work.

Anything that the user is working on (e.g., document editing, document browsing, and so on) is visible in a window. At any time, it can be set aside and resumed later, so that the user can freely switch from one activity to another. Interaction with the environment is accomplished by pointing to the objects that are to be operated on and then selecting the operation to be applied to the selected objects. The system reacts to the request by executing the operation. The environment provides a great deal of flexibility, while imposing very little structure on the user.

It should be clear from this description that interaction with the system is accomplished in an object-oriented manner. The language and the tools are highly integrated in the Smalltalk environment: basic concepts such as object, method, class, message, and instance are pervasive and applied uniformly.

To understand better the advantages of such a uniform and integrated environment, let us consider how it works during programming. Programs and documentation are created using an editor. But usually, in conventional systems (such as UNIX), commands to the editor have a different syntax and semantic style from, say commands to the command interpreter that, in turn, is entirely different from the programming language in which programs are written. Features available in one language environment are seldom provided in another. This is not the case of the Smalltalk environment.

In addition, the environment makes it possible to do several things at the same time and allows everything to be used together. For example, one can display the source code in a window, the related documentation in another, and examine the incoming mail in yet another. Moreover, one can copy a piece of mail message from one window into the documentation or program in another window.

The reader will note that much of the design of today's successful personal-computer software packages and even personal workstations, such as the Apple Macintosh, have their roots in the concepts behind the Smalltalk environment. In particular, the use of pointing devices and windows to support interaction were extensively explored first in the Smalltalk environment.

6.4.6 An Assessment of Programming Environments

How can we compare the Smalltalk and the UNIX environments? The basic difference is in the level of the integration and uniformity, which are much higher in the case of Smalltalk, and in the quality of the user interface, which is much more friendly in the case of Smalltalk. In UNIX, programs work together through pipes and the file system; not all programs can be connected to communicate with each other. In Smalltalk, everything is an object, and all objects can potentially communicate with each other. In UNIX, all subprograms must be linked to the program that uses them, and a change of any program unit implies relinkage. Also, if a subprogram is used in several programs, there are several copies of the same subprogram in the system. Again, there is nothing like that in Smalltalk.

The Smalltalk environment is intended to support one single user, whereas UNIX is a time-sharing operating system. Also, Smalltalk makes heavy use of computer resources in time and space, requires expensive bit-mapped graphics devices, and is not suitable for execution under conventional time-sharing operating systems.

Smalltalk is an example of a *monolingual, integrated* environment. A monolingual environment is an environment in which a single language is used to interact with all the tools. For example, the syntax and form of the command to list 10 lines in the editor or the debugger should be the same, or a debugger macro should be defined in the same way as an editor macro. Clearly, a monolingual environment is easier to learn and use.

In an integrated environment, the tools work well together. For example, when debugging a program, one can call the editor, fix the problem, recompile and relink all without exiting the debugger. Or, when debugging a program, one can invoke the mail system to read a message that reports a problem with the program being debugged and resume the debugger.

In the future, we can expect to see more powerful, more uniform, more integrated, and user-friendlier environments. One area that can offer a great increase in productivity is environments that can be tailored to—or adjust to—a particular user. A first step in this direction is tools, such as the EMACS editor (Stallman 1979), that allow the user to redefine the existing commands or define new ones. An example of a user-friendly feature is the DWIM facility of INTERLISP—which stands for Do What I Mean. It is a "spelling corrector" that has the ability to recover from user's typing errors and guess what the user intended.

Another area under investigation currently is the application of artificial intelligence to programming environments. Such tools as "programming assistants" currently are being investigated.

SUGGESTIONS FOR FURTHER READING AND BIBLIOGRAPHIC NOTES

The distinction between programming in the small and programming in the large was pointed out in (DeRemer and Kron 1976). The difficult and challenging problems arising in the production of large software systems are discussed in several books, such as (Metzger 1985), and (Brooks 1976). The papers by H. D. Mills, L. A. Belady and M. M. Lehman, C. L. McGowan and

R. C. McHenry in (Wegner 1979) address several aspects of programming in the large.

The methodology of stepwise refinement is described in (Wirth 1971b), (Wirth 1976a), and (Dijkstra 1972). Another methodology tries to develop a program and its correctness proof hand-in-hand. The methodology is based on the use of predicate transformers and invariants, and is illustrated in (Dijkstra 1976) and (Gries 1981). Both methodologies are adequate for designing small programs but are of little use for large programs. An interesting debate on this point is reported in (Wegner 1979). (See paper by D. Gries and the discussion by B. Liskov and D. Parnas.)

Methodologies supporting top-down modular design are described in (Parnas 1972a), (Parnas 1972b), (Myers 1975), (Myers 1978), and (Yourdon and Constantine 1978). The concept of "program families" is used in (Parnas 1975).

A critical evaluation of tree structure in structuring large systems is given in (Wulf and Shaw 1973). Clarke et al. (1980) offer further criticisms and advocate a nest-free structure for Ada.

Lauer and Satterthwaite (1979) describe the Mesa system and, in particular, how it supports the design of large systems.

Separate compilation facilities for Pascal are described in (Jensen and Wirth 1975), (Kieburtz et al. 1978), (LeBlanc and Fisher 1979), and (Celentano et al. 1980). Separate compilation facilities for SIMULA 67 are described in (Birtwistle et al. 1976) and (Schwartz 1978a). The use of SIMULA 67's prefix mechanism in top-down design is illustrated by several examples in (Birtwistle et al. 1973).

The need for sophisticated computer-aided software development systems is advocated by (Winograd 1979). Cheatham (1977) analyzes program development tools and the need for integrating them in a coherent system. PSL/PSA is discussed by Teichrow (1975); SREM is discussed by Alford (1977). PAISLey is an executable specification language (Zave and Schell 1986). Comprehensive views of contemporary software development environments are given in (Buxton 1980), (Hünke 1980), (Howden 1982), (Barstow et al. eds 1984), and (ACM SIGSOFT–SIGPLAN 1984). Among the papers appearing in (Hünke 1980), Cheatham (1980) proposes a common terminology and a number of axes along which to compare different environments; Buxton and Druffel (1980) discuss the requirements for Ada support environments [see also (DOD 1980)]; Standish (1980) outlines the Arcturus environment, which evolved to become an Ada environment [see (Standish and Taylor 1985)].

The UNIX system was originally described in (Ritchie and Thompson 1974). UNIX as a programming environment is discussed by (Kernighan and Mashey 1979), (Mitze 1980), (Kernighan and Pike 1984), and (Kernighan 1984). For references on the C language, see the Glossary at the end of the book. (Kernighan and Plauger 1976) describe a number of software tools available under UNIX. Bentley (1985) describes an interesting application of AWK for program testing.

Other interesting modern environments are Toolpack for FORTRAN (Osterweil 1984) and Gandalf for Ada (Habermann 1980), (Habermann and Perry 1980), (Tichy 1979), and (Medina-Mora and Feiler 1981). Ada environments and tools also are discussed in (IEEE-Software 1985).

INTERLISP (Teitelman and Masinter 1981) is a rich environment for LISP which pioneered many of the concepts of today's environments.

Many papers that discuss the relationship between the programming language and the environment are contained in (ACM SIGPLAN 1985). Also included are papers dealing with environments for PROLOG, Mesa, Smalltalk, and other languages. Heering and Klint (1985) classify the issues that arise in the design of integrated environments.

The application of artificial intelligence to programming environments and software engineering is discussed in (Barstow et al. 1984), (Balzer et al. 1983), and the special issue of the IEEE Transactions on Software Engineering (IEEE-TSE 1985).

EXERCISES

6.1 Discuss the effect of global variables on the writability and readability of large programs.

6.2 Present the main features of FORTRAN's separate compilation.

6.3 Why is the ALGOL-like program structure inadequate for programming in the large?

6.4 Design the interface of an Ada module that provides a symbol table for a translator (e.g., an assembler), and show how a separately compiled procedure can access the symbol table. The data structure representing the symbol table should be hidden to the procedure, and all accesses to the symbol table should be routed through abstract operations provided by the symbol table module. Can you compile the procedure before implementing a representation for the symbol table? Why? What is wrong if you cannot?

6.5 Suppose two Ada units $U1$ and $U2$ must use the same procedure P. Can P be embedded in a single subunit? Can P be embedded in a single unit? In the latter case, what are the constraints on the order of compilation?

6.6 Describe the tools that an ideal program-development system should provide to support independent development of modules, system structuring from independently developed modules, and complete intermodule type checking.

6.7 The following two sets of UNIX commands accomplish almost the same tasks. What is the difference between them?

(i) $x > file1$
   $y < file1 > file2$
   $z < file2$

(ii) $x \mid y \mid z$

The letters x, y, and z represent programs; *file*1 and *file*2 are files.

6.8 Using the *shell* and existing UNIX utilities, develop an application to manipulate examination results, with the following capabilities:

(a) To sort examination results according to either name or grade.

(b) To print the (sorted) list of students for each given grade.

(c) To print simple summaries, such as how many As, Bs, and so on.

6.9 An essential feature provided by the KAPSE is the ability to run a program taken from private files or as a system-provided tool written in Ada. As (Buxton and Druffel 1980) observe "inherently this is not representable in Ada language terms as essentially it enables a data structure produced by an Ada program (e.g., the compiler or linker) to be itself executed as a program." Explain why this is so. Are there any other languages where this would be possible?

7

Functional Programming

" . . . the next revolution in programming will take place only when both of the following requirements have been met: (a) a new kind of programming language, far more powerful than those of today, has been developed, and (b) a technique has been found for executing its programs at not much greater cost than that of today's programs." (Backus 1978b)

The majority of programming languages in existence today, including almost all the languages we have discussed so far, form a progression along the same lines of ideas. What characterizes this line of development and dictates its essential characteristics is the Von Neumann machine architecture. All the languages we have studied so far are abstractions built on this architecture.

In providing these abstractions, a language must strike a balance between usefulness of features and efficiency of execution. This concern for efficiency is evident in nearly all programming languages today. Efficiency of execution is measured by performance on a Von Neumann computer. Thus the Von Neumann computer architecture has formed the basis for the design of programming languages.

This chapter examines another basis for language design—mathematical functions. The contrast between these two bases for language design helps us appreciate the influence of the underlying model on a language. Some of the subtlest language features only can be explained in terms of this influence.

7.1 CHARACTERISTICS OF IMPERATIVE LANGUAGES

In the first six chapters, we have been primarily concerned with *imperative* or *statement-oriented* languages. This class of languages, which contains such different members as FORTRAN, COBOL, Pascal, Smalltalk, and Ada, draws its name from the dominant role played by imperative statements. The unit of work in a program written in these languages is a "statement." The effects of individual statements combine to achieve the desired results in a program. This section examines the close relationship between languages and the architecture of conventional computers. We will see that computer architecture has played a profound role in shaping imperative languages.

This influence can be seen in three pervasive characteristics of our languages:

1. **Variables** A major component of the architecture is the memory, which is comprised of a large number of *cells*. The memory is where the data are stored. The cells must be named, so that one can keep track of the location of the information.

   The need to name every cell is most apparent when programming in assembly languages. Values are stored in cells and can be accessed by naming such cells. In higher-level languages, the underlying notions of memory cell and name are represented by the concept of a variable—perhaps the most important concept in programming languages. A programming language variable is essentially a named memory cell in which values are stored. Thus, even though our purpose in programming is to produce values, we do not merely talk of values, but also of the cells in which the values of interest reside. The problems of side effects and aliasing arise from the existence of variables.

2. **Assignment Operation** Closely tied to the memory architecture is the notion that every value computed must be "stored", that is, assigned to a cell. This accounts for the eminence of the assignment statement in programming languages. The low-level notions of memory cell and assignment pervade all programming languages. They force on the programmer a style of thinking that is shaped by the details of the Von Neumann architecture.

3. **Repetition** A program in an imperative language usually accomplishes its task by executing a sequence of elementary steps repeatedly. This is a consequence of the Von Neumann architecture, in which the instructions are stored in the memory. The only way to accomplish anything complicated is to repeat a sequence of instructions.

7.1.1 An Imperative Program

To illustrate the interaction of these characteristics and their effects, let us consider the following Pascal program for producing prime numbers:

```
{print prime numbers in the range 2 .. n}
program primes (input,output);
    const n= 50;
    var i: 2 .. n;
        j: 2 .. 25;
        i_is_prime: boolean;
begin
    for i:= 2 to n do
    begin {is i prime?}
        j:= 2; i_is_prime:= true;
        while i_is_prime and (j <= i div 2) do
            if ((i mod j)<>0) then j:= j+1
                              else i_is_prime:= false;
        {if so, print its value}
        if i_is_prime then write (i)
    end
end.
```

The program is based on two loops, one nested within the other. The outer loops (**for** $i:=2$ **to** n . . .) sequences through the values in the range of interest (2 to n), and the inner loop checks each one of these numbers for "primeness." To understand each loop, we must mentally execute it for at least a few iterations, check its termination conditions, and then check the conditions under which it is executed correctly. In this case, the inner loop depends—in some not-so-simple ways—on the "index" of the outer loop (i). The outer loop also depends—in the **if** statement—on the assignment made in the inner loop.

In other words, the program is not hierarchical in the sense of each component being composed of several other (lower-level) components. Instead, each component uses the effect(s) of other ones. In our case, the inner loop builds on the outer loop's modifications to i, and the outer loop builds on the inner loop's modifications to i_is_prime. These components are intimately related. A component is used not to compute a value but to produce an effect—specifically, the effect of assigning values to variables. Control structures are used to order the statements such that the combined effects meet the desired end.

7.1.2 Problems with Imperative Languages

To summarize the preceding section, the essence of programming in imperative languages is the repeated and step-by-step computation of low-level values and the assignment of these values to memory locations. This is, of course, not the level of detail we want to deal with when programming a complicated application. Indeed, programming languages have been attempting more and more to hide this low-level nature of the machine.

A good example of this attempt is provided by expressions, which are a step removed from the cell-based memory because they allow the programmer to keep intermediate values anonymous. They hide the fact that all cells must be named. In the absence of side effects, component expressions of a complex expression are independent from one another. FORTRAN provided this advantage over assembly language—that was indeed one of FORTRAN's greatest achievements. ALGOL 60 extended FORTRAN's expressions further by providing conditional expressions. For example, instead of

if $x>y$ **then** *max*:= x
      else *max*:= y

we can use a conditional expression and write

max:= **if** $x>y$ **then** x **else** y.

The term *expression-oriented* (as opposed to *statement-oriented*) refers to languages in which expressions play a greater role than statements. Both are relative terms, and no language relies entirely on expressions or statements. We can say only that ALGOL 60 is more *expression-oriented* than FORTRAN.

ALGOL 68 is even more expression-oriented. It requires every construct to be an expression, that is, to have a value that can be used in other expressions. A block, for instance, can be used in expressions:

max:= **begin int** x,y;
          read $((x,y))$;
          if $x>y$ **then** x **else** y **fi**
      end

The value of the right-hand side is the value of x if $x>y$; otherwise, it is the value of y.

The usefulness of this generalization of ALGOL 68 is questionable. Expressions have been found useful mainly because they are simple and hierarchical. They can be combined uniformly to build more complex expressions. The component expressions of a complex expression are independent of one another. Expressions thus do not suffer from the influence of the Von Neumann architecture. An entire block in an expression, however, is quite different: it is capable of making the expressions as complicated as any other language construct, because an expression may be composed of any of these constructs. As a result, additional rules are needed to explain the semantics of expressions. In ALGOL 68 we must know that the last value computed in the block is the value of the block. If the value of the block is not used (e.g., assigned), coercion to **void** is applied automatically. Building upon a good idea—the expression—can go only so far. The generalization of ALGOL 68 makes the expressions also subject to the problems of naming, repetition, and assignment.

Actually, there are two somewhat disjoint domains in an imperative language: that of expressions, which is simple, regular, and hierarchical; and that of statements. It is the world of statements that is most influenced by machine characteristics. The world of expressions also loses its mathematical properties in the presence of such things as side effects or the construct given above.

Another example of the interference of the machine-level details with otherwise sound language constructs is offered by the procedure mechanism. Procedures localize much of the reasoning that must be done about the behavior of variables. They allow the building of independent components. But call by reference and global variables interfere with this high-level concept by enabling all memory locations to become addressable, thus revealing the cell-based memory.

Perhaps the most serious problem with imperative languages arises from the difficulty in reasoning about the correctness of programs. This difficulty is caused by the fact that the correctness of a program in general depends on the contents of each and every memory cell. The *state of the computation* is determined by the contents of memory cells. To understand loops, we must mentally execute them. To observe the progress of the computation through time, we must take "snapshots" of the memory at each step after every instruction, as we did with SIMPLESEM in Chapter 3. This is a tedious task when the program deals with large amounts of memory. We have seen that scope rules in languages limit this problem somewhat by reducing the number of accessible cells. We also have seen (in Chapters 5 and 6) that the use of global variables can make programs hard to analyze.

The problems with imperative languages discussed in this section can be summarized in terms of *referential transparency*. A system is said to be referentially transparent if the meaning of the whole can be determined solely from the meaning of its parts. Mathematical expressions—indeed, all mathematical concepts—are referentially transparent. For example, in the mathematical expression $f(x) + g(x)$, we can substitute another function f' for f, if we know that it produces the same values as f. If the same expression is an expression in Pascal (or any other conventional imperative language), we are not assured of this property. Indeed, if f or g change the value of their parameter (by-reference parameter) or modify some global variables, we are not even assured that $f(x) + g(x) = g(x) + f(x)$, or $f(x) + (x) = 2*f(x)$, that is, the meaning of the expression depends on the history of computation of the subexpressions. Assignment statements, parameters passed by reference, and global variables are the main reasons that imperative languages are not referentially transparent. Lack of referential transparency makes programs hard to read, modify, and prove correct. We have seen these problems in a similar perspective when we discussed side effects and aliasing in Section 5.2.1.

But we must remember that mechanisms such as global variables, call by reference parameters, and (in general) side effects, which appear to defeat the purposes of higher-level constructs, are introduced into languages to achieve execution efficiency. It is this efficiency that is based on the characteristics of the Von Neumann architecture. This explains the reasons behind Backus's belief quoted at the beginning of this chapter.

The next section will examine a style of programming based on functions and mathematics, rather than the Von Neumann memory, elementary actions, and repetition. The purpose is to see what alternatives exist if we disregard our reliance on the Von Neumann architecture.

7.2 THE ESSENCE OF FUNCTIONAL PROGRAMMING

Whereas the style of programming in a statement-oriented language consists of arranging for the execution and repetition of certain sequences of individual statements using appropriate control structures, the essence of functional programming is to combine functions to produce more powerful functions. Functional languages preserve the referential transparency of mathematics.

7.2.1 Functions

A *function* is a rule for mapping (or associating) members of one set (the *domain set*) to those of another (the *range set*). For example, the function "square" might map members from the set of integer numbers to the set of integer number. A *function definition* specifies the domain, the range, and the mapping rule for the function. Once a function has been defined, it can be *applied* to a particular element of the domain set: the application *yields* (or results in, or returns) the associated element in the range set.

For example, the function definition

```
square(x)  ≡  x*x , x is an integer number
```

defines the function named "square" as the mapping from integer numbers to integer numbers. We use the symbol "≡" for "is equivalent to." In this definition, x is a *parameter*. It stands for any member of the domain set.

At application time, a particular member of the domain set is specified. This member, called the *argument*, replaces the parameter in the definition. The replacement is purely textual. If the definition contains any applications, they are applied in the same way until we are left with an expression that can be evaluated to yield the result of the original application.

The application

```
square (2)
```

results in the value 4 according to the definition.

The parameter x is a mathematical variable, which is not the same as a programming variable. In the function definition, x stands for any member of the domain set. In the application, it is given a value—*one value*. Its value never changes thereafter. This is in contrast to a programming variable‧ which takes on different values during the course of program execution.

In the function definition, we bound the definition of the function $(x*x)$ to the name "square." It is sometimes convenient simply to use a function without giving it a name. We can do this by using *lambda expressions*. A lambda expression specifies the parameters and the mapping rule together. The symbol "." separates the specification of parameters from that of the mapping rule. For example

```
λx.x*x
```

is a function exactly the same as *square*, except that we have not assigned a name to it. It can be applied

```
(λx.x*x)2
```

just like "square."

The result of the application can be derived by replacing the parameter and evaluating the resulting expression.

```
(λx.x*x)2 ≡
    2*2 ≡
    4
```

We could in fact define *square* as

```
square ≡ λx.x*x
```

In other words, a lambda expression allows us to construct an expression whose value is a function. This is a useful property, as we will see shortly.

Lambda expressions can be used to define functions with more than one parameter, as in

```
sum ≡ λx,y.x+y
```

The parameters following the "λ" and before the "." are called *bound variables*. When the lambda expression is applied, the occurrences of these variables in the expression following the "." are replaced by the arguments. Variables in the definition that are not bound are called *free variables*. Bound variables are like local variables, and free variables are like nonlocal variables that will be bound at an outer level.

New functions may be created by combining other functions. The most common form of combining functions in mathematics is function composition. If a function F is defined as the composition of two functions G and H, written as

$$F \equiv G \circ H,$$

applying F is defined to be equivalent to applying H and then applying G to the result. For example, if we define

to_the_fourth $\equiv$ square $\circ$ square

then the value of *to_the_fourth (2)* is 16.

Function composition is an example of a *functional form,* also called a *combining form* or a *higher order function.* A functional form provides a method of combining functions; it is a function that takes other functions as parameters and yields a function as its result. Function composition is a functional form that takes two functions as parameters and yields the function that is equivalent to applying one and then the other as explained above.

7.2.2   Mathematical Functions vs. Programming Language Functions

Let us consider the differences between mathematical functions and those provided by conventional programming languages. The most important difference stems from the notion of a modifiable variable. The parameter of a mathematical function simply represents some value that is fixed at function application time; the function application results in another value. Data parameters in a programming language function, on the other hand, are names for memory cells; the function may use a name to change the contents in the cell. The function also may interact with the invoker of the function by changing other cells known to both of them. Because of these side effects, programming language functions, unlike mathematical functions, cannot always be combined hierarchically (like expressions). In other words, conventional programming language functions are not referentially transparent.

Another significant difference is the way functions are defined. In programming languages, a function is defined procedurally—the rule for mapping a value of the domain set to the range set is stated in terms of a number of steps that need to be "executed" in certain order specified by the control structure. Mathematical functions, on the other hand, are defined functionally—the mapping rule is defined in terms of applications of other functions. Mathematical functions are in this sense more hierarchical and nonprocedural.

Many mathematical functions are defined *recursively,* that is, the definition of the function contains an application of the function itself. For example, the standard mathematical definition of factorial is

$n! \equiv$ **if** $n = 0$ **then** 1 **else** $n * (n - 1)!$

The Fibonacci number sequence is defined as

$F(n) \equiv$ **if** $n = 0$ **or** $n = 1$ **then** 1 **else** $F(n - 1) + F(n - 2)$.

As another example, we can readily formulate a (recursive) solution for the prime numbers problem of Section 7.1.1. The following predicate function determines whether a number is a prime:

prime $(n) \equiv$ **if** $n = 2$ **then** true **else** $p(n, n$ **div** $2)$

where function p is:

$p(n, i) \equiv$ **if** $(n$ **mod** $i) = 0$ **then** false
                     else if $i = 2$ **then** true
                                 else $p(n, i - 1)$

Recursion is a powerful problem-solving technique. It is a natural and heavily used strategy, when programming with functions. However, as we have seen in Chapter 3, not all programming languages support recursive subprogram activations. When recursion is not permitted, the implementation of functions can become complicated and unnatural.

7.2.3 Functional (or Applicative) Languages

A functional programming language makes use of the mathematical properties of functions. In fact, the name "functional" (or "applicative") language is derived from the prominent role played by functions and function applications. A *functional* (or *applicative*) *language* has four components.

- A set of primitive functions.
- A set of functional forms.
- The *application* operation.
- A set of data objects.

The primitive functions are predefined by the language and may be applied. The functional forms are the mechanisms by which functions may be combined to create new functions. The application operation is the built-in mechanism for applying a function to its arguments and producing a value. The data objects are the allowed members of the domain and range sets. It is characteristic of functional languages to provide a very limited set of data objects with simple and regular structure (e.g., arrays in APL and lists in LISP). The essence of functional programming is to define new functions using the functional forms.

In addition to the four components, a functional language also provides a mechanism for binding a name to the new functions being defined. This is a convenience feature that affects the way we use the language. It avoids the repetition of the function definition each time the function is to be applied. For example, in Section 7.2.1 we defined a function and gave it the name *"to_the_fourth."* Had we not named the function, we would have had to use the definition

```
square∘square
```

whenever we needed to apply it.

The next section examines a purely functional language and illustrates its use.

7.3   A SIMPLE AND PURELY FUNCTIONAL LANGUAGE

John Backus, the originator of FORTRAN, has been working on a purely functional programming language since the early 1970s. This section presents a simplified view of Backus's work. In particular, we will define FP, a very simple language for functional programming.

The objects of the language are quite simple: an object may be an *atom* or a *sequence* (of objects); the empty sequence is known as **nil**. Atoms are sequences of characters such as *A, ABC, 26*.

There is a set of functions and a set of functional forms. There are no variables; all data must be used literally.

FP is actually a family of languages. Each member provides a choice of functions and functional forms. Backus maintains that the language should provide "widely useful and powerful primitive functions rather than weak ones that could then be used to define useful ones." The more functional forms a language has, the more "expressive" it is, because functional forms are the mechanisms for writing programs.

Following Backus's notation, we will show a sequence of n objects x_1, x_2, $\ldots x_n$ as

$$< x_1, \ x_2, \ \ldots \ x_n >$$

and application of function f to parameter x as

```
f : x
```

We will use the conditional expression **if_then_else** in the definitions. Remember that this language is not fully defined; we are just interested in the flavor of the language.

7.3.1 Primitive Functions

The language provides a number of primitive functions that roughly correspond to the built-in operations of imperative languages. Because sequences are the manipulable objects, the functions provide mechanisms for sequence manipultion. These functions can be broken into a number of different classes. Given below is a classification, along with some sample primitive functions. Of course, a particular language might include a different set of functions.

(a) *Selection operations*

Useful examples include functions FIRST, to extract the first element of a sequence; LAST, to extract the last element; TAIL, to extract everything but the first element. Thus,

$$\text{FIRST:} <x_1, x_2, \ldots \ldots x_n> \equiv x_1$$
$$\text{LAST:} <x_1, x_2, \ldots \ldots x_n> \equiv x_n$$
$$\text{TAIL:} <x_1, x_2, \ldots \ldots x_n> \equiv <x_2, \ldots \ldots x_n>$$

It would also be useful to be able to select an arbitrary element in a sequence simply by giving its position, that is,

$$i: <x_1, \ldots \ldots x_n> \equiv x_i, \quad 1 \le i \le n$$

(b) *Structuring operations*

These operations allow us to combine, dissect, or rearrange sequences.

(rotate right)	ROTR:	$<x_1, \ldots \ldots x_n> \equiv$ $<x_n, x_1, \ldots \ldots x_{n-1}>$
(rotate left)	ROTL:	$<x_1, x_2, \ldots \ldots x_n> \equiv$ $<x_2, x_3, \ldots \ldots x_n, x_1>$
(length)	LENGTH:	$<x_1, \ldots x_n> \equiv n$
(construct sequence)	CONS:	$<x, <x_1, x_2, \ldots x_n>> \equiv$ $<x, x_1 \ldots x_n>$

(c) *Arithmetic operations*

Arithmetic operations apply to sequences of two atoms and produce an atom as a result. We consider the usual operations "+", "−", "*", "/", "**div**" and the residue operation ("*mod*" in Pascal) "|", that is,

$$|: <x, y>$$

yields the remainder of the division "x **div** y." The unary minus will be denoted by NEGATE. Keeping the functional notation, we use the prefix form for all arithmetic operations (e.g., $+: <x, y>$) instead of the usual infix (e.g., $x+y$).

(d) *Predicate functions*

Predicate functions are functions whose results are truth values. We will represent true by the atom T and false by the atom F. A predicate function thus yields either T or F. In addition to the familiar predicates for comparing numbers (e.g., $<$, $>$, $=$), we also need predicates to inquire about sequences and atoms.

ATOM: $x \equiv$ **if** x is an atom **then** T **else** F
NULL: $x \equiv$ **if** x = **nil then** T **else** F

(e) *Logical operations*

Logical operations allow us to combine truth values. The usual operations are AND, OR, NOT.

(f) *Identity*

Function ID is the identity function, that is

ID: $x \equiv x$

7.3.2 Functional Forms

By far the most unusual feature of FP languages is the functional form. Because we are not used to functional forms in conventional languages, it is difficult to decide which functional forms are useful in an FP language. It is also difficult to get used to functional forms as programming constructs. Just as with conventional languages, it takes practice.

To introduce the reader to the power of functional form programming, we examine a few functional forms that Backus suggests are useful

(a) *Composition*

$(f \circ g): x \equiv f: (g:x)$

The functional form "$\circ$" is defined to take two functions as parameters; it results in a function that is equivalent to the application of the first parameter to the result of the application of the second parameter. In other words, this is the mathematical function composition. We have already seen an example of its use in the definition of the "*to_the_fourth*" function in Section 7.2.1.

To find the value of a function application that is a composition of other functions, we keep repeating the application steps as before, until no applications remain in the expression. In general, inner applications are performed first, then the next level out, and so on.

Example

ROTL$\circ$ CONS: $<x_1, <x_2, x_3>> \equiv$
ROTL: CONS: $<x_1, <x_2, x_3>> \equiv$
ROTL: $<x_1, x_2, x_3> \equiv$
$<x_2, x_3, x_1>$

It is truly surprising that in spite of the prevalence and importance of function composition in mathematics, no conventional programming language allows it as a primitive construct, explicitly or so succinctly.

(b) *Construction*

$$[f_1, f_2, \ldots f_n] : x \equiv <f_1:x, \ldots, f_n:x>$$

The functional form "[ ]" is defined to take as parameters n functions and to yield a function that is equivalent to applying each of the functions to the same parameter and forming a sequence of the results.

As an example of the use of construction, consider the task of producing the minimum, maximum, average, and median of a sequence of values. Having defined individual functions for each of the subtasks, the final task of combining them can be done with construction, for example

[MIN,MAX,AVG,MED]

is a function and can be applied or combined with other functions.

Example

```
[MIN,MAX,AVG,MED]:<0,1,2,3> ≡
<MIN:<0,1,2,3>, MAX:<0,1,2,3>, AVG:<0,1,2,3>, MED:
<0,1,2,3>> ≡
<0,3,1.5,2>
```

Notice the second step. We have a sequence consisting of four applications. Because of the absence of side effects, these applications can be evaluated in any order, or even simultaneously.

(c) *Insert*

$$/f:x \equiv \textbf{if } x \text{ is } <x_1> \textbf{ then } x_1$$
$$\textbf{else if } x \text{ is the sequence } <x_1, \ldots, x_n>$$
$$\textbf{and } n \geq 2 \textbf{ then } f:<x_1, /f:<x_2, \ldots, x_n>>$$

The functional form "/" takes one function as parameter and yields a function that is applicable only to sequences (i.e., not to atoms) and equivalent to applying the parameter functions to successive elements of the sequence. The most obvious use of "/" is in distributing a function defined for two parameters over a sequence of any number of elements. For example, assuming that the primitive function of addition ("+") has been defined to apply to two parameters, we can find the sum of a sequence of any length by the function "/+."

$$\begin{aligned}
/+ : <1,2,3,4> &\equiv +:<1,/+:<2,3,4>> \\
&\equiv +:<1,+:<2,/+:<3,4>>> \\
&\equiv +:<1,+:<2,+:<3,/+:<4>>>> \\
&\equiv +:<1,+:<2,+:<3,4>>> \\
&\equiv +:<1,+:<2,7>> \\
&\equiv +:<1,9> \\
&\equiv 10
\end{aligned}$$

This example shows the power of programming with functional forms. Consider the simple and succinct way in which we define the sum function "$/+$" and contrast it with how this function would have to be written in an imperative language.

(d) *Constant*

This functional form takes an object (x) as a parameter and produces a function.

$$\bar{x}:y \equiv x$$

For example

$$\bar{0}:y \equiv 0$$
$$\bar{T}:y \equiv T$$
$$\bar{1}:y \equiv 1$$

A sample use of this functional form is given in (g) below.

(e) *Apply to all*

$$\alpha\ f:x \equiv \textbf{if } x \text{ is } \textbf{nil then nil}$$
$$\textbf{else if } x \text{ is the sequence } <x_1,x_2,\ \ldots\ x_n>$$
$$\textbf{then } <f:x_1,\ \ldots\ f:x_n>$$

The functional form "α" takes a function as parameter and yields a function, applicable only to sequences, that is equivalent to applying the parameter function to each element of the sequence and forming a sequence of the results.

As an example of the use of "α," consider the following problem. We have a sequence of sequences. Each of the inner sequences contains two atoms. We want to produce a sequence each of whose elements is the sum of the corresponding two-element sequence in the argument. For example, applied to the argument $<<1,2>, <3,4>, <5,6>>$, our function should yield $<3,7,11>$.

The task can be simply done by the function

$$\alpha+$$

(See Exercise 7.1 for a generalization of this function, and Exercise 7.3 for an example of its use.)

Like the *insert* functional form, *apply to all* points to the contrast between imperative and functional programming. If the same operation is to be performed on each of the elements of a sequence, a programmer using an imperative language must design the operation, then design a "loop" to apply the operation to each element. Designing the loop entails dealing with such matters as the accessing of each element and detecting and handling end-of-sequence, empty sequence, and so on. In a functional programming language, however, designing the operation itself is all that is needed: *apply to all* takes care of the repetition implied by the "loop."

(f) *Condition*

$$(\text{IF } p \ f \ g):x \equiv \textbf{if } p:x = \text{T } \textbf{then } f:x \textbf{ else } g:x$$

The functional form IF takes three functions as parameters and yields either the second or the third function, depending on whether or not the result of the first function is the atom T.

This functional form can be used in tasks for which conditional statements are used in imperative languages; but because *p*, *f*, and *g* are all applied to the same parameter, its use requires a different approach. For example, the function

```
(IF ATOM NEGATE ROTR)
```

negates its argument, if it is an atom; or rotates it, if it is a sequence.

(g) *While*

$$(\text{WHILE } p \ f):x \equiv \textbf{if } p:x = \text{T } \textbf{then } (\text{WHILE } p \ f):(f:x) \textbf{ else } x$$

The WHILE functional form arranges for the repeated application of its second parameter as long as the application of its first parameter yields the atom T.

For example, let us write a function that produces the image of the argument sequence, except for leading zeroes. First we define the following function ISZERO, which determines whether or not an atom is zero.

```
= ∘ [ID,0̄]
```

Then we define the following function FIRSTZERO, which determines whether or not the first element of a sequence is zero:

```
(ISZERO∘FIRST)
```

Finally, we define the desired function as

```
(WHILE FIRSTZERO TAIL)
```

Following the first few steps of an application of this function helps us understand how much "execution" is involved in the application of such a simple-looking function.

```
(WHILE FIRSTZERO TAIL):<0,0,2> ≡
    if FIRSTZERO:<0,0,2> = T then (WHILE FIRSTZERO
    TAIL):(TAIL:<0,0,2>) else <0,0,2> ≡
(WHILE FIRSTZERO TAIL):<0,2> ≡
if FIRSTZERO: <0,2> = T then (WHILE FIRSTZERO TAIL):
(TAIL: <0,2>) else <0,2> ≡
(WHILE FIRSTZERO TAIL):<2> ≡
 . . . ≡
<2>
```

7.4 APPLICATIVE FEATURES IN EXISTING LANGUAGES

The previous section provided a glimpse of FP languages. These purely functional languages are being investigated as bases for a new generation of programming languages. They are not everyday programming languages, yet they provide us with a model for studying the potential benefits and drawbacks of functional programming. They also can help us evaluate the applicative and nonapplicative features of expressions. This section examines other important functional features in current languages.

7.4.1 LISP

Of all the existing programming languages, LISP (for List Processing) comes closest to being a functional language. In fact, the original LISP introduced by John McCarthy in 1960, known as pure LISP, is completely functional. To improve execution efficiency, however, current versions of LISP have introduced nonapplicative features into the language.

This section will show how close LISP comes to being a functional language. We do not intend to provide a complete discussion, or even an introduction, to LISP—simply to its functional characteristics. LISP is a good example of how a few simple primitives together with a few simple but powerful data-structuring facilities can yield an elegant and powerful language.

7.4.1.1 Objects

LISP objects are symbolic expressions that are either *atoms* or *lists*. An atom is a string of characters (letters, digits, and others). The following are atoms:

A
SYNAPSE
68000

A list is a series of atoms or lists, separated by space and bracketed by parentheses. The following are lists:

```
(FOOD VEGETABLES DRINKS)
((MEAT CHICKEN) (BROCCOLI POTATOES TOMATOES) (WATER))
(UNC TRW SYNAPSE RIDGE HP)
```

The empty list "( )", also called NIL, has special significance. Like the FP *sequence,* a *list* is the only data-structuring mechanism for encoding information in LISP.

A LISP program is itself a list. It is functional in that it is composed of applications of functions that produce results that may be used by other functions. Even the notation is functional, that is, prefix, as opposed to infix of other languages [e.g., (PLUS A B) instead of $A + B$].

7.4.1.2   Functions

There are very few primitive functions provided in pure LISP. Existing LISP systems have added to this list considerably. These new functions, however, can all be expressed in terms of the original primitive functions.

QUOTE is the identity function. It returns its (single) argument as its value. This function is needed because, in contrast to FP, the atom A does not represent itself but is the name of a value stored somewhere. The distinction between the name and value of objects, as we have seen, is a direct consequence of the memory architecture. The QUOTE function allows its argument to be treated as a constant. Thus, (QUOTE A) in LISP is analogous to "A" in conventional languages.

Examples

```
(QUOTE A) ≡ A
(QUOTE (A B C)) ≡ (A B C)
```

The most common functions are those that manipulate lists: CAR and CDR are selection operations, and CONS is a structuring operation. CAR returns the first element of a list; CDR returns all elements of a list except the first; CONS appends an element to a list. For example

```
(CAR (QUOTE (A B C)))  ≡  A
```

The argument needs to be "quoted," because the rule in LISP is that a function is applied to the *values* of its arguments. In our case the evaluation of the argument yields the list $(A\ B\ C)$, which is operated on by CAR. If QUOTE were missing, an attempt would be made to evaluate $(A\ B\ C)$, which would result in using A as a function operating on arguments B and C. If A is not a previously defined function, this would result in an error.

Other examples

```
(CDR (QUOTE (A B C))) ≡ (B C)
(CDR (QUOTE (A))) ≡ ( ) ≡ NIL
(CONS (QUOTE A) (QUOTE (B C))) ≡ (A B C)
(CONS (QUOTE (A B C)) (QUOTE (A B C))) ≡ ((A B C) A B C)
```

A few predicates are also available. A *true* value is denoted by the atom T and a *false* value by NIL.

ATOM tests its argument to see if it is an atom.

NULL tests its argument to see if it is NIL.

EQ compares its two arguments, which must be atoms, for equality.

Examples

```
(ATOM (QUOTE A)) ≡ T
(ATOM (QUOTE (A))) ≡ NIL
(EQ (QUOTE A) (QUOTE A)) ≡ T
(EQ (QUOTE A) (QUOTE B)) ≡ NIL
```

The function COND takes as arguments a number of (predicate, expression) pairs. The expression in the first pair (in left to right order) whose predicate is true is the value of COND.

Example

```
(COND ((ATOM (QUOTE (A))) (QUOTE B)) (T (QUOTE A))) ≡ A
```

The first condition is false because (A) is not an atom. The second condition is identically ture. The COND function, known as the McCarthy conditional, is the major building block for user-defined functions.

Function definition is based on lambda expressions. The function

$$\lambda x, y . x + y$$

is written in LISP as

```
(LAMBDA (X Y) (PLUS X Y))
```

Function application also follows lambda expressions.

```
((LAMBDA (X Y) (PLUS X Y)) 2 3)
```

binds X and Y to 2 and 3, respectively, and applies PLUS yielding 5.

The binding of a name to a function is done by the function DEFINE, which makes the function name known globally. Another function, LABEL, is used if we want to define the function to be known only locally.

```
(DEFINE (ADD (LAMBDA (X Y) (PLUS X Y))))
```

Now, the atom ADD can be used in place of the function above, that is, the atom ADD has a value that is a function.

The ability to name a function is especially useful in defining recursive functions. For example, we can define a function REVERSE to reverse the elements of a list:

```
(DEFINE (REVERSE (LAMBDA (L)
                 (REV NIL L))))
(DEFINE (REV (LAMBDA (OUT IN)
            (COND ((NULL IN) OUT)
                  (T (REV (CONS (CAR IN) OUT) (CDR IN)))))))
```

The REVERSE function calls a subsidiary function REV that works by picking the first element of a list and calling REV on the rest of the list.

The use of DEFINE is one of two ways in pure LISP that an atom can be bound to a value. The other is through function application, at which time the parameters are bound to the arguments. The conventional assignment is not present.

The variables in pure LISP are more like the variables in mathematics than those in other languages. In particular, variables may not be modified: they can be bound to a value and they retain that value throughout a given scope (i.e., function application); and at any moment, there is only at most one access path to each variable.

7.4.1.3   Functional Forms

Function composition was the only technique for combining functions provided by original LISP. For example, the *"to_the_fourth"* function of Section 7.2.1 can be defined in LISP as

```
(LAMBDA(X) (SQUARE (SQUARE X)))
```

(We assume SQUARE has been defined.) Most current LISP systems, however, offer a functional form, called MAPCAR, which is equivalent to "α" of FP. It allows the application of a function to every element of a list. For example

```
(MAPCAR TOTHEFOURTH L)
```

raises every element of the list L to the fourth power. Like α, this functional form reduces the need for repetition.

Using the above-cited functional features of LISP, we can write the prime-numbers program directly from the functions in Section 7.2.2. This is left as Exercise 7.10.

As a functional language, LISP is quite limited by the lack of a rich set of functional forms.

7.4.1.4   LISP Semantics

One of the most interesting aspects of LISP is that we can define its semantics quite simply—using LISP itself. We can define a LISP function, commonly called EVAL, that when given any LISP expression e will evaluate e.

We have already seen all the LISP primitives that are needed to define EVAL. One more concept, however, which is just a shorthand notation, will make the description of EVAL clearer. Because structural analysis of lists is a major part of most LISP programs, one often needs expressions with many combinations of CARs and CDRs such as (CAR (CAR(CAR X))) or (CAR (CDR (CAR (CDR X)))). The shorthand notation used in LISP is CxR where x stands for a sequence of the letters *A* or *D, A* representing CAR and *D* representing CDR. For example, (CAR (CAR (CAR X))) may be written as (CAAAR X) and (CAR (CDR (CAR (CDR X)))) may be written as (CADADR X). This notation, although not strictly necessary, makes programs much easier to read.

Figure 7.1 shows EVAL. EVAL has two parameters: E, the expression to be evaluated, and A, the referencing environment in which to evaluate E. A is initially NIL and gets updated with (*name, value*) pairs (called *associations*) through recursive calls to EVAL. EVAL works by looking for the different possible cases of LISP expressions and performing the needed action. The reader is invited to study the algorithm by applying it to some sample LISP expressions.

We can view EVAL in two ways:

1. EVAL is a definition of the semantics of the LISP language. Just as we saw with SIMPLESEM in Chapter 3, this definition assumes the existence of certain primitives, namely, the functions ATOM, COND, EQ, CAR, CDR, QUOTE, NULL, the atoms T and NIL, and the notion of a list.

2. EVAL is a LISP interpreter. In fact, this is how LISP was first implemented. In practice, EVAL either can be hand-translated into a language that is available on the machine or cross-compiled on a machine with a LISP compiler. Such a straightforward implementation, of course, cannot be expected to be efficient.

Examination of EVAL points out two important points about LISP:

- LISP programs are themselves lists. This means that programs and data can be used interchangeably. In particular, EVAL operates on lists that happen to be programs. The unification of the notions of data and programs gives LISP much of its power.
- The fact that LISP can be defined in itself so succinctly is proof of the power and elegance of LISP.

7.4.1.5 Nonapplicative Features in LISP

We have considered the applicative features of LISP. Even though it is possible to use LISP as a functional language, very few applications written in LISP are purely applicative. Efficiency considerations have forced the in-

```
(LABEL EVAL (LAMBDA (E A)
       (COND ((ATOM E)
              (COND ((EQ E NIL) NIL)
                    ((EQ E T) T)
                    (T (CDR ((LABEL
                              ASSOC
                              (LAMBDA (E A)
                                      (COND ((NULL A) NIL)
                                            ((EQ E (CAAR A)) (CAR A))
                                            (T (ASSOC E (CDR A))))))
                             E
                             A))))))
             ((ATOM (CAR E))
              (COND ((EQ (CAR E) (QUOTE QUOTE)) (CADR E))
                    ((EQ (CAR E) (QUOTE CAR))
                     (CAR (EVAL (CADR E) A)))
                    ((EQ (CAR E) (QUOTE CDR))
                     (CDR (EVAL (CADR E) A)))
                    ((EQ (CAR E) (QUOTE CADR))
                     (CADR (EVAL (CADR E) A)))
                    ((EQ (CAR E) (QUOTE CADDR))
                     (CADDR (EVAL (CADR E) A)))
                    ((EQ (CAR E) (QUOTE CAAR))
                     (CAAR (EVAL (CADR E) A)))
                    ((EQ (CAR E) (QUOTE CADAR))
                     (CADAR (EVAL (CADR E) A)))
                    ((EQ (CAR E) (QUOTE CADDAR))
                     (CADDAR (EVAL (CADR E) A)))
                    ((EQ (CAR E) (QUOTE ATOM))
                     (ATOM (EVAL (CADR E) A)))
                    ((EQ (CAR E) (QUOTE NULL))
                     (NULL (EVAL (CADR E) A)))
                    ((EQ (CAR E) (QUOTE CONS))
                     (CONS (EVAL (CADR E) A) (EVAL (CADDR E) A)))
                    ((EQ (CAR E) (QUOTE EQ))
                     (EQ (EVAL (CADR E) A) (EVAL (CADDR E) A)))
                    ((EQ (CAR E) (QUOTE COND))
                     ((LABEL EVCOND
                             (LAMBDA (U A) (COND ((EVAL (CAAR U) A)
                                                  (EVAL (CADAR U)
                                                        A))
                                                 (T (EVCOND (CDR U)
                                                            A)))))
                      (CDR E)
                      A))
                    (T (EVAL (CONS (CDR ((LABEL
                                          ASSOC
                                          (LAMBDA (E A)
                                                  (COND
                                                    ((NULL A) NIL)
                                                    ((EQ E (CAAR A))
                                                     (CAR A))
                                                    (T (ASSOC E
                                                              (CDR A))))))
                                         (CAR E)
                                         A))
                                   (CDR E))
                             A))))
             ((EQ (CAAR E) (QUOTE LAMBDA)
              (EVAL (CADDAR E)
                    ((LABEL FFAPPEND
                            (LAMBDA (U V)
                                    (COND ((NULL U) V)
                                          (T (CONS (CAR U)
                                                   (FFAPPEND (CDR U)
                                                             V))))))
                     ((LABEL
                       PAIRUP
                       (LAMBDA (U V)
                               (COND ((NULL U) NIL)
                                     (T (CONS (CONS (CAR U) (CAR V))
                                              (PAIRUP (CDR U)
                                                      (CDR V)))))))
                      (CADAR E)
                      ((LABEL
                        EVLIS
                        (LAMBDA (U A)
                                (COND ((NULL U) NIL)
                                      (T (CONS (EVAL (CAR U) A)
                                               (EVLIS (CDR U)
                                                      A))))))
                       (CDR E)
                       A))
                     A)))
             ((EQ (CAAR E) (QUOTE LABEL))
              (EVAL (CONS (CADDAR E) (CDR E))
                    (CONS (CONS (CADAR E) (CDR E)) A)))))))
```

FIGURE 7.1 LISP interpreter [Adapted from (McCarthy 1978)].

troduction of many nonapplicative features in LISP, and any realistic program makes heavy use of these features to achieve a reasonable level of efficiency.

The principal nonapplicative features added to LISP are SET and PROG. The SET function is simply the assignment statement. PROG is a function that takes a list of expressions as its argument. These expressions are executed 'n sequence, one after another. In other words, PROG allows expressions to be regarded as statements. Furthermore, within PROG one can use labels and **goto** statements for explicit control of the execution sequence.

Yet another way that LISP has been made less applicative is with the introduction of operations for modification of variables. For example, the operation RPLACA (for "Replace CAR") can be used to replace the first element of a list with another, that is, for efficiency reasons, operations are introduced that work by side effects rather than by producing values.

Even pure LISP shows the influence of machine architecture in its design. The most important effect of this influence occurs, as we have seen, in the distinction between names and values. Another occurs in the set of functions provided. The reason that the two selectors CAR and CDR are provided and, for example, selectors to get an arbitrary element of a list, or the last element, are not, is because of how lists are implemented. Because of the implementation, CAR and CDR can be performed with one memory reference, but the other ones cannot.

We have examined LISP only within a limited context. LISP is a powerful and interesting language with a wide following. It is the language of choice for developing experimental systems and a standard language in artificial intelligence. The references can be consulted for more information.

7.4.2   APL

APL was designed by Kenneth Iverson at Harvard University during the late 1950s and early 1960s. It is based on mathematics, with a few concessions to machine efficiency. The assignment operation is an integral part of the language. Yet APL can be viewed as an applicative language because of its heavy reliance on expressions.

Just as with LISP in the last section, we will examine the functional features of APL. It is not our purpose to cover APL fully.

7.4.2.1   Objects

The objects supported by APL are scalars, which can be numeric or character, and arrays of any dimension. Numeric 0 and 1 may be interpreted as boolean values. APL provides a rich set of functions and a few functional forms.

7.4.2.2 Functions

In contrast to LISP, APL provides a large number of primitive functions (called *operations* in APL terminology). An operation is either monadic (taking one parameter) or dyadic (taking two parameters).

All operations that are applicable to scalars also distribute over arrays. Thus, $A \times B$ results in multiplying A and B. If A and B are both scalars, then the result is a scalar. If they are both arrays and of the same size, it is element-by-element multiplication. If one is a scalar and the other an array, the result is the multiplication of every element of the array by the scalar. Anything else is undefined.

The usual arithmetic operations, $+$, $-$, $\times$, $\div$, $|$ (residue), and the usual boolean and relational operation, $\vee, \wedge, \not\vee, \not\wedge, \sim, <, \leqslant, =, \geqslant, >, \neq$, are provided. But there are also a number of unusual operations.

The operation "ι" is a "generator" and can be used to produce a vector of integers. For example, $\iota 5$ produces

```
1 2 3 4 5
```

The operation ";" concatenates two arrays. So $\iota 4; \iota 5$ results in

```
1 2 3 4 1 2 3 4 5
```

The operation "ρ" forms its right operand into an array of the desired dimensions (left operands). For example

$$2 \; 2 \; \rho \; 1 \; 2 \; 3 \; 4 \equiv \begin{array}{cc} 1 & 2 \\ 3 & 4 \end{array}$$

$$2 \; 3 \; \rho \; 1 \; 2 \; 3 \; 4 \; 5 \; 6 \equiv \begin{array}{ccc} 1 & 2 & 3 \\ 4 & 5 & 6 \end{array}$$

The compress operation "/" takes two arguments of the same dimensions and selects elements of its right-hand argument, depending on whether the corresponding left-hand argument is a (boolean) 1 or 0. For example

$$1 \; 0 \; 0 \; 1 \; / \; \iota 4 \equiv 1 \; 4$$

The left argument may consist of boolean expressions. For example

```
A<B B<C C<D / X
```

will pick certain values from X, depending on the comparisons on the left. X must be a three-element vector in this case.

The lines in a user-defined function are numbered consecutively starting with 1. A line may be labeled, in which case the label is equated to the line number. The only control structure in APL is the branch, shown as "$\rightarrow$"; it transfers control to the line whose number is specified as the argument. For example, $\rightarrow 3$ transfers control to line 3 of the function. If the operand is 0

or larger than the number of lines in the function, the branch is defined to be a function return; if the operand is a vector, the first element is used as the target; if the operand is null, no branch takes place at all.

The branch operation can be combined with the compress operation to build conditional and multiway branches. For example, $\rightarrow (A < B \ A = B \ A < B/case1 \ case2 \ case3)$ transfers to the appropriate label, depending on the relative values of A and B.

$$\rightarrow (A < B/case1)$$

transfers to *case1* if $A < B$; otherwise, the next statement is executed.

By now it must be clear to the reader that the branch is not an appropriate operation for a functional language. It does not allow the hierarchical building of expressions. This is one of the reasons that APL is a nonfunctional language. Another nonapplicative or imperative feature is the assignment ($\leftarrow$), which assigns the value of the right operand to the left-hand variable. The assignment operation does produce a value, and therefore it can be used in building expressions, for example

$$D \leftarrow C + B \times (A \leftarrow 2)$$

However, the introduction of assignment in an expression introduces the possibility of side effects.

There are many other primitive operations in APL. They can be regarded as mathematical functions because they operate on operands and produce values. User-defined functions are similar to the primitive functions in that they also are either monadic or dyadic (niladic functions correspond to subroutines). They are used in infix notation and thus can be used in expressions, just as built-in functions can.

7.4.2.3 Functional Forms

There are three functional forms (*operators* in the APL terminology) supplied by APL. They operate on APL's primitive operations to produce other operations. They are

(a) The **reduction** operator "/" (same symbol as compress), which is the same as the "insert" of FP (with the same symbol). For example, the sum of the elements of the vector A is given by

$$+/A$$

Again, compare this with summing the elements of a vector in an imperative programming language. The repetition and step-by-step computation are handled by the functional form.

If the right operand is a matrix, the reduction operation applies to successive rows, that is, if A is the matrix

1 2
3 4

then +/A is

3
7

which is represented as

3 7

In general, a reduction applied to an *n*-dimensional array results in an (*n – 1*) dimensional array.

(b) The **inner product** operator "." takes two primitive dyadic operations as arguments and produces a dyadic operations as result. The operands of an operation formed this way must be arrays that "conform" in size. For example, if they are matrices, the number of rows of the left operand must be the same as the number of columns of the right operand; the result will be a matrix with as many rows as the left operand and as many columns as the right operand. If *f* and *g* are two primitive dyadic functions, the effect of

A f.g B

is to apply *g*, element by element, to the corresponding rows of A and columns of B (i.e., first row of A with first column of B, and so on). This is followed by an *f* reduction (/*f*) on the resulting vector.

As an example of the power of inner product in building operations, matrix multiplication can be accomplished by:

+.×

Again, we can see the power of functional forms by comparing this solution with a matrix multiplication procedure in an ALGOL-like language.

(c) The **outer product** "°." takes one primitive operation as operand and has a dyadic operation as result. The operation °.*f* applied to arrays A and B (i.e., A°.*f* B) has the effect of applying *f* between each element of A and *every* element of B. For example, if A has the value (*1 2 3*) and B has the value (*5 6 7 8*), the result of A°.×B is the matrix

 5 6 7 8
10 12 14 16
15 18 21 24

The effect can be seen as forming a matrix with the rows labeled with elements of A and columns labeled with elements of B. The entries of the matrix are the result of applying the operation to the row and column labels. So the above matrix was derived from

×	5	6	7	8
1	5	6	7	8
2	10	12	14	16
3	15	18	21	24

The outer product finds many applications in data processing when producing tables of interest rates, taxes, and so on. It has other uses as well. As an example, to find which elements of A occur in B

$$A^\circ . = B$$

provides a map of boolean values, with a *1* in the position where an element of A equals an element of B.

In addition to these three functional forms, there are two operations in APL that can be used to modify the behavior of (certain) other operations. These are the *axis-specifier* and the *scan* operator. The axis specifier "[ ]" allows us to specify along which dimension of the operand the operation is to be applied (i.e., which index varies most rapidly). For example, if the matrix A has the value

$$1\ 2\ 3$$
$$4\ 5\ 6$$

then the plus reduction operation, $+/A$, has the result

$$6$$
$$15$$

that is, the elements added have indices *(1,1)*, *(1,2)*, *(1,3)* and *(2,1)*, *(2,2)*, *(2,3)*. The index varying most rapidly is the second one. Therefore, $+/A$ is equivalent to

$$+/[2]A$$

If, instead, we wanted to add the columns of A, we would write

$+/[1]A$

which would result in

$5\ 7\ 9$

The scan operator "$\setminus$" applies its argument operation to successively longer sequences of its other argument. It is useful for producing running totals and similar operations. For example

+ $\setminus$ 1 2 3 4

produces

1 3 6 10

Despite its many applicative features, APL does not go far enough in divorcing itself from the machine. The assignment operation is still quite present and side effects are a common means of accomplishing results. There are too few functional forms and they can be applied only to primitive functions. This is a serious weakness for an applicative language, because it means that the power of functional forms cannot be exploited fully.

7.4.2.4   An APL Program

Now let us return to the problem of producing the prime numbers in the range of 1 to N. The information about APL given in this section is rather limited but nevertheless sufficient to write this program. This section illustrates the APL style of programming contrasted to that of, say, Pascal.

We cannot use a solution directly based on the strategy derived in Section 7.2.2, because APL does not have the "apply to all" functional form. Even if it did, functional forms are not allowed to apply to user-defined functions.

Our emphasis should be on exploiting arrays and expressions rather than scalars, assignments, and repetition. Thinking in APL, we must produce a vector of prime numbers. We can start with a vector of numbers in the range 1 to N and compress it, using the compress operator, to be left with primes only. In other words, our task is to find the vector of boolean expressions in the following APL program:

vector of boolean expressions/ιN

We can start with the definition of a prime number: a number that is divisible only by 1 and itself. So, for each number in the range of interest, 1 to N, we can (a) divide it by all the numbers in the range and (b) identify those which are divisible only by two numbers.

Step (a) can be done with the residue operation and an outer product

$(\iota N)^{\circ} . | (\iota N)$

The result of this operation will be a vector of remainders. We are interested in whether the remainder is equal to 0.

$0 = (\iota N)^{\circ} . | (\iota N)$

Now the result is a boolean matrix indicating whether the numbers were divisible (1) or not (0).

In step (b), we want to see how many times the number was divisible, that is, the number of 1's in each row.

$$+/[2] \; 0 \; = \; (\iota N)^\circ.|(\iota N)$$

But we are only interested in those rows that have exactly two 1's.

$$2=(+/[2]0=(\iota N)^\circ.|(\iota N))$$

The result is a boolean vector indicating whether the index is a prime (1) or not (0). This is the desired vector of boolean expressions. To get the actual prime numbers, we apply compression.

$$(2=(+/[2]0=(\iota N)^\circ.|(\iota N)))/\iota N$$

The essence of this solution is that it builds successively more complicated expressions from simpler ones, and this is the only mechanism used for combining actions. This combining mechanism is simple and uniform regardless of the constituents being combined. It is mathematical in nature in that all operations and expressions are used in the way that they are used in mathematics.

Our program is a typical APL one-liner. It has been said that APL is flawed because its one-liners are not readable. But, to be fair, the readability of the above one-liner must be compared with the readability of the entire Pascal program that accomplishes the same task, rather than with one Pascal statement. It is likely that an APL programmer can understand the APL program with no more effort than is required by a Pascal programmer to understand the Pascal program. The important point is that the programmers must be fluent in the language *and* its style.

7.5 COMPARING APPLICATIVE AND IMPERATIVE LANGUAGES

Let us review the differences between applicative and imperative programming languages. Imperative languages are based on conventional computers, but applicative languages are based on mathematical functions. The characteristics of the two classes of languages are dictated by their two different foundations.

Imperative languages are more efficient in terms of execution time because they reflect the structure and operations of the machine. As a result, they require that the programmer pay attention to machine-level details. This influence can be seen in the style of programming promoted by these languages, which is based on naming of elementary cells, assignments to these cells, and repetition of elementary actions.

The functional programming style does not depend on these three actions. The simple and uniform data objects (e.g., sequences, lists, arrays) allow the design of data structures without concern for memory cells; rather than being assigned, values are produced by function application and passed on to other functions; and functional forms and operations that distribute over the data objects (as in APL) reduce the reliance on repetition. On the whole, functional programming appears to be at a higher level than imperative programming. It could thus make programming easier.

The cost of this ease of programming shows up in terms of execution efficiency. The inefficiency stems not only from all the function calls, but from the fact that many objects are created and discarded dynamically. The dynamic creation of objects such as lists and arrays cannot be efficiently supported (for LISP, garbage collection—see Section 4.6.4—was invented to deal with this problem).

We have seen that efficiency is so important that APL and LISP have opted for nonapplicative features to achieve it. But we must realize that efficiency considerations could be different with a different machine model.

For example, consider the prime-number program of Section 7.1.1. One technique for increasing the speed of our Pascal prime-number program is to use the history of what numbers have already been computed in the generation of future prime numbers. In particular, we only need to test if a number is divisible by prime numbers. In APL and LISP, however, the tendency is to repeat exactly the same operation for the entire set. If the program were executed on a multiprocessor, however, in which each prime number is computed on a separate processor, then the APL or LISP programs might indeed be more efficient.

An applicative programming language provides a natural way of exploiting a parallel machine architecture, because the inner applications can be applied in parallel.

These examples show the danger of designing our programming languages on the grounds of efficiency. Efficiency is dictated by the machine, and the machine should be there to support the language. We get trapped in a circle. Ideally, we should design a language based on what we know to be good problem-solving strategies. Then we can design a machine to support the language. Finding the right problem-solving strategy is the primary challenge. However, designing an architecture to support the language is also of decisive importance. If we must stay with out traditional machines, efficiency considerations will rule out functional languages. Different architectures supporting functional languages are presently being investigated, but it is premature to state whether they will become practically relevant.

Apart from efficiency problems, it is difficult to determine whether a purely functional language such as FP will be successful. The success of a language is not based on the mathematical elegance of its underlying principles as much as on a complex combination of its surface properties, the systems supporting it, and other tools available with it.

There is a long way to go before FPs yield a usable language. Do we need types? Input/output? What particular primitive functions and functional forms? The way these practical issues are decided will determine to a great extent whether the language will be accepted by the programming community. While we may reserve final judgment on functional languages, we must recognize that the functional programming *style* is definitely a strong candidate for at least some applications. We can adopt the style even in imperative languages. In particular, the use of abstract data types can lead to a more functional style of programming (see Exercise 7.12).

SUGGESTIONS FOR FURTHER READING AND BIBLIOGRAPHIC NOTES

The FP languages appear in (Backus 1978), which, together with (Backus 1973), is the major source for this chapter. These papers have sparked a great deal of interest in functional programming and its implications.

Pozefsky (1977) discusses programming in Backus's language. Berkling (1976) and Magó (1980) present machine architectures supporting efficient execution of functional programming languages.

Henderson (1980) is an excellent introduction to functional programming and covers the implementation of a functional language on a conventional computer. Henderson (1986) discusses the use of functional programming in rapid prototyping. Lambda calculus, which is one of the bases of functional programming, was invented by Church (1941).

Both APL and LISP are widely used and popular with their users. Both languages are supported by complete environments. The discussion of these languages in this chapter only has scratched the surface. The foundations of LISP are developed in McCarthy (1960). McCarthy et al. (1965), Siklóssy (1976), Allen (1978), and Winston (1984) provide good descriptions of LISP. Steele (1984) and Brooks (1985) describe the emerging Common LISP. Current work on LISP involves the addition of object-oriented features to the language; we mention Flavors (Weinreb and Moon 1980) and LOOPS (Bobrow and Stefik 1983), (Stefik et al. 1986). Sandewall (1978) and Teitelman and Masinter (1981) describe friendly and productive LISP systems. Steele and Sussman (1980) describe a microprocessor designed to execute LISP. Commercial LISP machines are now available.

APL was defined in the book *A Programming Language* (Iverson 1952), from which the name of the language derives. Iverson (1979) describes the usefulness of functional forms in APL. Tu and Perlis (1986) describe FAC, a functional APL language.

HOPE (Burstall et al. 1980), (Bailey 1985) is an example of a functional language that also offers strong typing.

Other bases for language design not mentioned in this chapter have been and are being tried. SNOBOL4 is based on Markov algorithms. SETL is based on set theory. PROLOG, which is based on logic, is discussed in the next chapter. The next chapter also contains a brief discussion of SNOBOL4 and SETL.

EXERCISES

7.1 The function $\alpha+$ of Section 8.3.2.**e** requires that each inner sequence of its argument sequence be of length 2. Modify this function to be able to work on inner sequences of any length.

7.2 Using FP, write the function "COMBINE," defined as

$$\text{COMBINE:} \langle \langle x_1, x_2, \ \ldots \ x_n \rangle,$$
$$\langle y_1, y_2, \ \ldots \ y_n \rangle \rangle \equiv$$
$$\langle \langle x_1, y_1 \rangle, \langle x_2, y_2 \rangle, \ \ldots \ \langle x_n, y_n \rangle \rangle$$

That is, "COMBINE" applies to two sequences of equal length and yields a sequence consisting of sequences of length 2. The ith inner sequence of the result is the ith element from the first argument and the ith element from the second argument.

Use any primitive functions from this chapter if needed.

7.3 Write a function to add two vectors represented as sequences:

$$\text{ADDV:} \ \langle \langle x_1, x_2, \ \ldots \ x_n \rangle, \ \langle y_1, \ \ldots \ y_n \rangle \rangle \equiv \langle x_1 + y_1, \ \ldots \ x_n + y_n \rangle$$

7.4 Write a function to add any number of vectors:

$$\text{ADDVS:} \ \langle \langle x_{11}, x_{12}, \ \ldots \ x_{1n} \rangle, \ \langle x_{21}, x_{22}, \ \ldots \ x_{2n} \rangle,$$
$$\ldots$$
$$\langle x_{m1}, \ x_{m2} \ \ldots \ x_{mn} \rangle \rangle \equiv$$
$$\langle x_{11} + x_{21} + \ \ldots \ x_{n1}, \ \ldots \ , x_{1m} + x_{2m} + x_{nm} \rangle$$

7.5 Write the prime number program of Section 7.2.2 in FP.

7.6 Define a "REPEAT" functional form.

7.7 Explain why LISP's COND is a function and not a functional form.

7.8 Design an FP language suitable for matrix operations such as addition and multiplication. What primitive functions and what functional forms are necessary and/or useful?

7.9 FPs, as defined by Backus, have an important attribute that was not discussed in the chapter. There is a special value "⊥" called "bottom" or "undefined," that is returned by functions for abnormal conditions. For example, if a function is applied to arguments it does not expect or if one of the arguments is "⊥," it returns "⊥." Why is this a useful property? How should the definitions of the primitive functions in Section 7.3.1 be modified to account for this feature?

7.10 Write the prime-number program using only functional features of LISP.

7.11 If you have a LISP system available, type in EVAL and try it.

7.12 This exercise is to show how abstract data types can be used to introduce a functional style into imperative languages. Define an abstract data type (in your favorite language) to represent "list" objects with the following allowable operations: CAR, CDR, NULL, ATOM. Now write a function to reverse lists.

7.13 Show that UNIX pipes can be viewed as a mechanism for function composition.

7.14 (Due to Jon Mauney) HOPE (Burstall et al. 1980) is an applicative language that is strongly typed. One of the most interesting aspects of the language is its polymorphic (generic) procedures. Compare HOPE's generic procedures with those of Ada. Is HOPE's type binding static or dynamic? Compare HOPE's approach to types with dynamic types of Smalltalk.

Logic Programming

In the previous chapter we discussed the basic concepts of functional programming and examples of programming languages that provide functional features. We stressed the basic departing lines from Von Neumann programming languages. In this chapter we discuss another unconventional approach—logic programming—and outline the basic structure of PROLOG, the best-known example of a logic programming language.

Although the idea of programming in logic has been around in a few groups within the research community for several years, wide interest in logic programming has grown only recently, mostly after the Japanese announced the central role that logic programming will play in their "Fifth Generation" project (Section 1.4).

8.1 THE "WHAT" VS. "HOW" DILEMMA: SPECIFICATION VS. IMPLEMENTATION

In Chapter 1 we presented the software development process as a sequence of phases through which system descriptions progressively become more and more detailed. We start from a declarative software requirements specification, in which we emphasize *what* the user needs and *what* the system is supposed to do, and progressively refine it into a procedural and executable description that algorithmically describes *how* the problem actually is solved mechanically. Languages like Ada, Modula-2, and Mesa attempt to deal with the what vs. how dilemma by allowing a module specification to be given separately from the module's implementation.

We have discussed at length that the level of programming languages is becoming higher and higher. For example, a language like Ada can be used in the design stage as a design specification language to describe the modular structure of software and module interfaces in a precise and unambiguous way. At present, however, design decomposition into modules and implementation of the internals of modules cannot be done automatically; it requires creativity by the programmer. This time-consuming, expensive, and error-prone activity is necessary because conventional computers cannot execute declarative descriptions. Thus, requirements must be detailed—translated—into a procedural description.

Logic programming tries to push the boundary of executable descriptions even higher, the ultimate goal being the possibility of executing specifications directly, with no need for refining them into lower-level procedural implementations.

In its simplest terms, we can describe logic programming in the following way: A programmer simply declares the facts and the properties that describe the problem for which the solution is sought. This information then is used by the system to solve the problem (*infer a solution*) without any need for more advice on how to handle the information. In logic programming, problem description is given in some logical formalism, such as predicate calculus. We will give examples of problem descriptions through *predicates* (also called *assertions*) of a hypothetical logic programming language. We will be rather "informal" in our use of logical "formalisms": we will basically rely on the intuitive concepts evoked by the formal notation. The reader who wishes to delve deeper into the issues of logic can refer to the Further Reading Section.

Example: Prime Numbers

We wish to specify the concept of a prime number. In words, a number is prime if it is an integer greater than one, and it is divisible only by itself and one. Assuming that our hypothetical logical language implicitly deals with integers, we can write the following predicate:

(1)   is_prime(x) **if**

$x > 1$

and

forall j such that $1 < j < x$, x **mod** $j < > 0$.

(x **mod** j is the remainder of the integer division between x and j)

This is a *declarative* description of what a prime number is which is an exact restatement of our previous description in natural language: it is only more formal. Many different implementations exist that are consistent with the specification. By using an imperative language, one can scan the interval 1 .. x in ascending order or descending order. Or, according to known properties of integers, one can scan the interval 1 .. x **div** 2, or even the interval 1 .. $sqrt(x)$. An example appears in the Pascal and APL programs that generate prime numbers in a given interval (see Sections 7.1.1 and 7.4.2.4).

This is another possible definition of a prime number: A positive integer is a prime number if no prime number less than it divides it. Also, two is the smallest prime number. The definition can be formalized as:

```
(2)    is_prime(2).
       is_prime(x) if
           x>2
           and
               forall y such that 2<y<x, is_prime(y) implies x mod
               y<>0.
```

According to this formalization, a number is prime if it satisfies either one or the other of the two assertions. Obviously, if the list of prime numbers not exceeding x is already available, this definition suggests a straightforward and efficient implementation. But, again, other implementations are possible.

Having specified a problem via some declarative logic-based description, we can submit a problem to be solved and ask the system to search for solutions that are consistent with the previously specified declarative body of knowledge. The problem to be solved is specified as a *goal* that must be proven as a consequence of the given declaration. In the examples, the goal to be proven might be whether a given integer, say, 54, is a prime number: *is_prime* (54)?

Thus, the whole notion of programming reduces to a formal specification followed by a request for proving goals. In response to such a request, the system tries to prove the goal by making inferences from its body of knowledge, and trying to cut the size of the search space to achieve reasonable efficiency. It is, of course, not surprising if efficiency of execution is not comparable to that of traditional procedural languages, at least in the present state of the art. This is the obvious price to pay for the savings in programming effort.

Example: Sorting

We wish to specify the concept of a sequence of integers sorted in ascending order. Assuming that the language provides the notion of an indexable sequence of integers (we use subscripts in the range $1 . . \text{length}(x)$ for this purpose), this can be done formally:

```
(3)    is_sorted(x) if
           forall j such that 1≤j<length (x), xⱼ≤xⱼ₊₁
```

Having done that, we can specify what it means when a sequence y is the sorted image of a sequence x:

```
(4)    sort(x,y) if
               is_permutation(x, y) and
               is_sorted (y)
```

Assertion (4) defines y as the sorted image of sequence x if y is a permutation of the values of x and y is sorted in ascending order. We assume that the concept of y being a permutation of x is specified elsewhere.

As we said before, logic programs are used by establishing a goal and then asking the system to prove it, starting from the known body of knowledge. In our case, the goal might be to prove that a certain given sequence is sorted, or that a given sequence is the sorted image of another given sequence, or even to produce a sequence that is the sorted image of a given sequence.

The previous discussion and examples allow us to draw these preliminary conclusions:

(a) Both imperative and functional programming languages are *procedural* in nature: they describe *how* a given sequence of statements or a given function computes the result of a given problem. Logic programming languages specify the problem in a *declarative* fashion: they describe *what* the goal is and let the underlying implementation search for a proof of the goal.

(b) With both imperative and logic languages, formulating the solution requires creativity. Just as there are different ways to program a sort routine procedurally, there are different ways of formulating it declaratively. The declarative approach allows us to concentrate more on the nature of the problem, but in the imperative approach we are more concerned with how to formulate the solution in terms of our primitive operations. We can restate this as: logic programming forces us to concentrate on the requirements phase more and apply creativity at that critical stage. In other words, declarative programming addresses the critical problems faced in software production at a much higher level than imperative languages.

(c) Logic programming provides a means for executable specifications. Even if the efficiency cannot be compared with conventional approaches, a logic language can be used in the requirements phase of software production to provide an early, rough implementation. This allows the user to experiment with the system and give the software designers early feedback on the adequacy of the requirements. The technique of building a rough implementation at a very early stage is known as *rapid prototyping*.

(d) As for functional languages, advances in computer architecture may make the whole issue of efficiency less and less relevant in the future, especially if we consider the overall savings in programming effort and the higher reliability we can achieve with logic languages.

Again, as for functional languages, efficiency gains will result basically from parallel execution, which will allow the implementation to follow several search paths concurrently when trying to prove a goal. For example, if one wishes to prove whether a given integer N is prime according to specification (2), the system might try to follow the two assertions at the same time. Obviously, in this case there would be little savings using concurrent searching, but in more complex cases the saving would be considerable.

8.2   EXAMPLES OF NONPROCEDURALITY IN LANGUAGES

In the next section we will discuss PROLOG at length. PROLOG is the best-known programming language that has been defined to support logic programming. In this section we show that nonprocedural—that is, declarative—aspects are present in several other existing languages, although such languages cannot be viewed as logic languages. In particular, we discuss database languages, SETL, and SNOBOL4.

The reader should notice that examples of nonprocedurality are present in other software systems. One of the earliest and most used examples that exploit nonprocedurality are parser–generators (e.g., *yacc*, as mentioned in Chapter 6). Instead of writing a parser for a language, one defines—*declares*—a language through its grammar and lets the parser generator produce the parser. The parser–generator can be viewed as translating the user's declarative description into an executable (procedural) program.

8.2.1   Database Languages

Database systems are becoming more and more popular. This is due to the widespread availability of such systems on low-cost personal computers, and their increasingly user-friendly interface via high-level query languages. One of the best-known database languages is SQL. A relational database can be viewed as a table of records called *tuples*. In SQL, retrieval of data from the relational database is accomplished by the SELECT statement. For example, if we have a relation CLASS containing tuples of the following kind:

FIRST_NAME	LAST_NAME	SEX	WHEN_BORN	WHERE_BORN
Marta	Ghezzi	F	1974	Italy
Darius	Jazayeri	M	1978	USA
Charlie	Brown	M	1981	USA
. . .	. . .			. . .

and a relation PARENTS containing tuples of the following kind:

F_LAST_NAME	FATHER	MOTHER	CHILD
Brown	Linus	Lucy	Charlie
Ghezzi	Carlo	Anny	Marta
Jazayeri	Mehdi	Mary	Darius
. . .	. . .	. . .	. . .

here are two sample SQL queries:

```
SELECT *
FROM CLASS
WHERE SEX = "M"
AND WHEN_BORN < 1980
```

This query selects all tuples in the relation CLASS such that the value of field SEX is M and the value of field WHEN_BORN is less than 1980, that is, all males born before 1980. The following—self-explanatory—query is slightly more complicated.

```
SELECT FATHER
FROM PARENTS
WHERE F_LAST_NAME =
      (SELECT LAST_NAME
       FROM CLASS
       WHERE WHEN_BORN > 1975
       AND WHERE_BORN = "Italy")
```

It is easy to see that the query language selects information stored in the database by specifying the logical (relational) properties that characterize such information. Nothing is said about how to access the information through suitable scanning of the database. It is interesting to note that earlier generations of database systems also were imperative, requiring the user to state how to find the desired tuples through pointers and other such mechanisms. The current declarative approach is definitely more suited towards the end-user who is not necessarily a computer programmer.

8.2.2 SETL

SETL is a very high-level, set-oriented language. It was designed and implemented at New York University in the early 1970s; it now is used as a software prototyping language. An example of the use of SETL for this purpose was the construction of the first validated Ada translator.

We do not intend to cover all the interesting features of SETL. We only are interested in the powerful declarative features embedded in the language.

SETL is an imperative, sequential programming language. *Sets, tuples,* and *maps* are SETL's most interesting data types. A set is like its mathematical counterpart: it is an unordered collection of objects of any type, without repetitions. A tuple is an ordered collection, where components are accessed through an index. A map is a collection of ordered pairs, where the first components constitute the domain of the map and the second components constitute the range. These set-theoretic elements of the language can be manipulated in a highly declarative fashion using predicate calculus formulas including the usual boolean operators and the quantifiers *for each* and *there exists*.

Examples of definitions that can be written in SETL (Krutchen et al. 1984) are:

(a)   {x in X | odd (x)}
Here we specify the subset of X where each element satisfies predicate *odd*.

(b)   exists x in X | Pred (x)
Here the result is true if there exists an element of X that satisfies predicate Pred.

(c)   [x : x in [2 . . 100] | not exists y in [2 . . x − 1] | x mod y = 0]
Here the result is the ordered collection (tuple) of all prime numbers less than 100.

The reader will notice these features promote a highly declarative programming style. The programmer can use very high-level, set-theoretic concepts without worrying about their implementation, which is done by the underlying SETL processor. Not surprisingly, the resulting programs can be quite inefficient. This is why a major use of an abstract language like SETL is the rapid development of prototypes.

8.2.3   SNOBOL4

The most used example of a declarative feature in current languages is the *pattern* of SNOBOL4. We already have seen SNOBOL4's unusual ARRAY and TABLE data structures in Chapter 4. The pattern is another one of SNOBOL4's data structures. In this section, we examine this data structure to illustrate the support it provides for a declarative approach to programming.

SNOBOL4 is a string-oriented language in that character strings are the most important primitive data type with many built-in operations. A *pattern* is a data structure that specifies *a set of strings*. A pattern is used in *pattern-matching statements* to examine a subject string for the presence of a pattern. For example, the statement

```
MESSAGE PAT
```

means "search the string MESSAGE for the occurrence of the pattern PAT." If, previous to this statement, we had executed these two assignment statements:

```
MESSAGE = 'THERE ARE NO ERRORS HERE.'
PAT     = 'ERROR'
```

then the above pattern-matching statement will *succeed*. The notion of success and failure of statements is used in SNOBOL4 to control the flow of execution in a program. Each statement can specify labels of target statements for *success, failure,* or *unconditionally*. For example

```
MESSAGE  PAT  :S(OK)F(NOTFOUND)
```

will transfer control to the statement labelled OK if the pattern-matching succeeds and to NOTFOUND otherwise.

The pattern PAT is the simplest kind of pattern we can have—simply one string. We may specify a pattern as a choice of patterns:

```
SUBJECT = 'I' | 'WE'
```

Now SUBJECT will match any string that contains either 'I' or 'WE' (or both). A pattern may be defined also as a concatenation of other patterns:

```
SENTENCE = SUBJECT VERB OBJECT '.'
```

The pattern SENTENCE will match any string that contains the patterns SUBJECT, VERB, OBJECT, followed by a period. The following program fragment defines the basics of a recognizer for the English language grammar of Section 3.1.1.1:

```
SUBJECT  = 'I' | 'WE'
VERB     = 'SEE' | 'HIT' | 'GRAB'
OBJECT   = 'HIM' | 'HER' | 'YOU'
SENTENCE = SUBJECT VERB OBJECT '.'
```

In fact, given the above statements, the statement

```
TEST SENTENCE
```

will succeed if a valid sentence (according to our grammar) occurs in the string TEST. This pattern will actually match a sentence anywhere in the string but SNOBOL4 provides facilities to constrain the pattern further, for example, to have one sentence and nothing more. We will not discuss these facilities here. What we want to do is to emphasize the declarative nature of this program. In this program, we describe the structure of a pattern and leave it to the underlying implementation—the SNOBOL4 interpreter—to find a way to search for the existence of the pattern. If we were solving the same problem in a Pascal-like language, we would spend most of our effort describing the procedures for the search.

What we have seen so far is actually only a small sample of SNOBOL4's pattern-matching power. One of the interesting features is the unevaluated expression that can be used to build *recursive* patterns. The unary operator * delays the evaluation of its operand. The expression *E is called an *unevaluated expression*. The unevaluated expression is evaluated when the interpreter encounters it as part of a pattern-matching operation. Consider the pattern PAT defined with assignment statement:

```
PAT = *PAT 'B' | 'A'
```

The value of PAT is stored as *PAT 'B' | 'A', postponing the evaluation of PAT (in *PAT) to pattern-matching time. At pattern-matching time, this pattern will match either 'A' or *PAT 'B', which at this time causes the pattern matcher to substitute a value for PAT. The current value of PAT is *PAT 'B' | 'A'. Therefore, PAT also will match 'AB' or *PAT 'BB'. Thus, we have a recursive definition for PAT, which causes it to match strings of the form

```
A
AB
ABB
ABB . . B
```

Now, recall from Section 3.1.1.1 that to specify the syntax of any interesting language, we need to use recursive productions. Suppose that we want to write a SNOBOL4 program to recognize arithmetic expressons as defined by the grammar in Section 3.1.1.1. The following two statements will do exactly what we want:

```
OPERATOR   = '+' | '-' | '/' | '*'
EXPRESSION = '(' *EXPRESSION ')' | *EXPRESSION OPERATOR
             *EXPRESSION | IDENTIFIER
```

Once again, note how closely this program mirrors our specification of the recognition problem for arithmetic expressions.

8.3   AN OVERVIEW OF PROLOG

PROLOG is the only logic language that has become known outside of research environments. Apart from its intrinsic virtues, this is partially due to the availability of implementations on a large variety of machines, including personal computers, and, most important, to the publicity of the Japanese "Fifth Generation" Project.

   In this section, we describe the basic features of the language and show how PROLOG comes close to being a logic language. Also, we show how and why it departs from being purely logical.

8.3.1 Facts, Rules, and Questions

Programming in PROLOG consists of:

(a) Modeling a situation (or a world) by specifying some *facts* about *objects* and *relationships* among these objects;

(b) Specifying some *rules* that govern the world that is being modeled;

(c) Asking the system to *infer* answers to *questions* by applying an inference procedure to its *knowledge base* of facts and rules.

Thus, a PROLOG program consists of a database of facts and rules; the program is executed in response to a query submitted to the system.

For example, the following facts describe the essential biographic data about famous music composers:

```
composer(monteverdi,1567,1643).
composer(bach,1685,1750).
composer(vivaldi,1678,1741).
composer(mozart,1756,1791).
composer(haydn,1732,1809).
composer(beethoven,1770,1827).
composer(schubert,1797,1828).
composer(schumann,1810,1856).
composer(brahms,1833,1897).
composer(verdi,1813,1901).
composer(debussy,1862,1918).
```

In what follows, we use the convention that the names of all objects and relationships start with a lowercase letter. The relation is given first, and the argument objects follow between parentheses, separated by commas. Each fact is terminated by a period. The ordering among objects within parentheses must be consistent, although which order is chosen is immaterial. We have chosen to follow the composer's name with the year he was born and the year he died.

Having specified some facts, we may ask the system questions such as:

?- composer(mozart, 1756,1791).

and the system would answer YES. Or we may ask:

?- composer(mozart,1902,1982).

and it would answer NO. The way to interpret YES and NO are "Yes, I can prove the question by using the information stored in the database," and

"No, I cannot prove the truth of the question by using the information stored in the database," respectively. Most interesting, we can ask:

$$?- \text{composer(mozart,X,Y)}.$$

and the system would answer:

```
X= 1756    Y= 1791;
NO
```

The meaning of this last question is "Are there values X and Y such that composer (mozart,X,Y) is in the database?" The answer should be interpreted as "The values $X = 1756$, $Y = 1791$ satisfy the question and there are no other solutions." In other words, X and Y act like *variables* (we assume that variable names start with uppercase letters).

To understand exactly the behavior of the system in response to questions, one should know that PROLOG treats the question as a goal to be proven by matching against the database. If the goal does not contain variables, a matching occurs as soon as a fact is found with the same name and the same arguments. If the goal contains variables, then variables are automatically bound to the arguments of the matching fact. We will come back to this match operation (called *unification*) in the next section.

After one answer is delivered, a ";" is interpreted by PROLOG as a command to resatisfy the same goal, but with different data (if any). In the case of the question "?-composer (mozart, X,Y)" a first match binds X to 1756 and Y to 1791; no other proofs of the goal are possible.

PROLOG variables are radically different from their Von Neumann counterparts. As for functional languages, they do not stand for modifiable repositories of values, but behave as variables in mathematics. We will come back to the binding policy for variables in the next section.

Now, let us turn to rules. Rules describe properties of the world being modeled. The form of such properties is of the type "p holds **if** p_1 holds **and** p_2 holds . . . **and** p_n holds." In terms of logic, these forms are special kinds of clauses, called *Horn clauses*. Horn clauses are interpreted by the PROLOG abstract processor as follows: to solve goal p, reduce it to the solution of goals p_1, p_2,. . . . Syntactically, Horn clauses are written in PROLOG as p:-p_1,p_2, . . . p_n; p is called the rule's *head*, p_1, p_2, . . ., p_n are called the rule's *subgoals*.

For example, we might wish to specify when two composers are contemporary (assuming that no two composers with the same name are in the database of facts). To do so, we add the following rules to our database of composers:

```
contemporary(X,Y):-composer(X,B1,D1), composer(Y, B2,D2),
        X\= Y, overlap(B1,D1,B2,D2).
    (predicate "\=" stands for "not equal")
```

```
overlap(B1,D1,B2,D2):-B2>=B1,B2=<D1.
overlap(B1,D1,B2,D2):-B1>=B2,B1=<D2.
```

The interpretation of the rule *contemporary* (X,Y) is: To prove that X is a contemporary of Y, prove that X is a composer, Y is a composer, X and Y are different, and the dates of birth and death overlap. It is obvious that the same information could be given by listing as facts all pairs of contemporary composers, but this solution would become impractical for a realistic database. Also, the addition of new composers to the database would require an update of the relation that states who is a contemporary of whom, to keep the database consistent. The rule allows us to state the meaning of "contemporary" compactly, and to rely on the system to infer the specific facts. This is analogous to specifying a grammar instead of all possible valid strings.

When a question is submitted to the system, it is matched against facts (as we saw above) and rule heads. If it matches a rule's head, all variables occurring in the rule become bound, as we saw before for facts. When a variable in a rule becomes bound, all its occurrences in the rule become bound in exactly the same way. Then, to prove the goal specified by the rule's head, the rule's subgoals must be proven, and during the proof of the subgoals other variables of the rule may become bound.

Here are some simple examples of interaction with the system that illustrate the concepts described above:

```
?-contemporary(monteverdi,verdi).
NO

?-contemporary(bach,vivaldi).
YES

?-contemporary(mozart,K).
     (here we wish to find
      all contemporaries of Mozart)
K=haydn;
K=beethoven;
NO

?-contemporary(X,Y).
     (here we wish to find all
      pairs of contemporaries)
X=bach     Y=vivaldi;
X=bach     Y=haydn;
X=vivaldi  Y=bach;
X=vivaldi  Y=haydn;
X=mozart   Y=haydn;
X=mozart   Y=beethoven;
```

```
X=haydn    Y=bach;
X=haydn    Y=vivaldi;
X=haydn    Y=mozart;
X=haydn    Y=beethoven;
X=haydn    Y=schubert.
```

(We stopped the search here deliberately; other contemporaries exist in the composers' database. If we did not have rules, we would have had to enter all these as facts ourselves if we wanted the system to be able to respond to queries about contemporary composers.)

```
?-contemporary(mozart,X),
    composer(X,A,B),
        overlap(A,B,1700,1750).
        (here we try to find a contemporary of
         Mozart who lived in the years 1700, 1750)
    NO
```

8.3.2 Unification and Backtracking

PROLOG is an interactive system: facts, rules, and questions are submitted interactively and answers are displayed on the terminal. A question is a goal that the system tries to prove. According to the given set of facts and rules, there may be several goal decompositions into subgoals that may be iteratively selected to conduct the proof. The underlying system must search this proof space to find solutions.

The machine support for execution of PROLOG programs can be described as goal-directed interpretation; more suggestively, the interpreter often is called an *inference engine.* This term makes it clear that problem-solving is achieved by inferring properties from the given facts and rules, until the goal is satisfied or the search procedure fails. This section illustrates how the PROLOG interpreter works in some detail.

When the interpreter tries to verify a goal, it searches the database (facts and rules) to find a matching fact or rule's head, as we sketched in the previous section. The fundamental operation performed by the PROLOG interpreter is *unification,* which is a blend of pattern matching and variable binding. Let us examine more closely how it is accomplished.

Unification selects a fact (or rule's head) if

(a) The name is the same as that of the goal to be proven;

(b) The number of arguments are the same;

(c) For all corresponding arguments (from left to right), one of the following conditions holds (This is a slightly simplified description of conditions):

- They are exactly the same constant;
- They are an unbound variable and a constant. In this case the variable becomes bound to the constant;
- They are both variables. In this case the variables *share,* that is, if one is already bound, then the other becomes bound to exactly the same object; if both are unbound, then both become bound to the same object as soon as one becomes bound.

If no matching fact (or rule's head) can be found by unification, the goal fails.

Another fundamental issue of the interpreter is how the search is organized; in particular, how the interpreter makes sure that all possible paths are eventually searched before failing and how it keeps track of the attempted paths. The PROLOG interpreter searches the database of facts and rules in a fixed order: *top to bottom* (the order in which the facts and rules are submitted to the system). Also, it proves the subgoals of a given rule from *left to right*. Each subgoal, in turn, is proven exactly as if it were a goal. Thus, the interpreter follows a rigid *depth-first* search. When a match between a goal and a fact (or rule's head) occurs, the interpreter keeps track of the position in the database of the matching fact (or rule). Thus, should the interpreter need to resatisfy the same goal (as we show next), it will proceed scanning the database from that point. This is the simplest way to ensure that the same search path is not followed twice.

Assume that the rule to be proven is $g: -g_1, g_2, \ldots g_n$. If g_1 fails ($i > 1$), the interpreter *backtracks*, that is, it returns to resatisfy g_{i-1}. If g_1 fails, then g fails. When backtracking returns to resatisfy a goal, all variables that were bound when that goal was satisfied return to an unbound state and the database is searched from the position of the previous match.

Example

Consider the database of composers we described in the previous section. If we ask the question:

```
?-contemporary(mozart,X)
```

This is the resulting trace of execution of the interpreter:

- *Goals to prove*: composer(mozart,B1,D1), composer(Y,B2,D2), mozart\ = Y, overlap(B1,D1,B2,D2).
- *Next Goal to prove*: composer(mozart,B1,D1).

- *Unification with fact*: composer (mozart,1756,1791). $B1$ becomes bound to 1756, $B2$ becomes bound to 1791.
- *Goals left to prove*: composer($Y,B2,D2$), mozart$\setminus = Y$, overlap(1756,1791,$B2,D2$).
- *Next goal to prove*: composer ($Y,B2,D2$).
- *Unification with fact*: composer (monteverdi,1567,1643). Y becomes bound to monteverdi, $B2$ becomes bound to 1567, $D2$ becomes bound to 1643.
- *Next goal to prove*: mozart$\setminus =$ monteverdi. It succeeds!
- *Next goal to prove*: overlap(1756,1791,1567,1643). It fails!
- *Backtrack to goal*: composer($Y,B2,D2$). Unification binds Y to bach, $B2$ to 1685, and $D2$ to 1750. Then goal *overlap*(1756,1791,1685,1750) fails again and this sequence of trials and failures continues until unification occurs with the fact *composer*(haydn,1732,1809). When this occurs, variable X becomes bound to haydn.

The reader is invited to check that if a semicolon is written at this point, after some trials, the interpreter will bind X to *beethoven*. Another semicolon will lead the interpreter to write NO.

After the previous description of how the PROLOG interpreter works, the reader might think that the issues presented are purely implementation-dependent; they should affect the efficiency of the search, but not the meaning of our programs. Unfortunately, this turns out to be false. Both the order in which facts and rules are listed (i.e., the order in which the database is searched) and the order in which subgoals are listed are significant. There are programs that behave correctly if facts and rules are listed in a certain order and subgoals are listed in a certain sequence, but enter an infinite loop or generate a run-time error if the order changes.

Example

Consider the following sequence of facts that define the tree data structure of Figure 8.1. The root of the tree is a. The fact *parent* (u,v) says that u is the parent node of v.

```
parent (a,b).
parent (a,d).
parent (a,k).
parent (k,l).
parent (k,m).
parent (b,e).
parent (b,f).
parent (f,g).
```

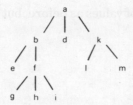

FIGURE 8.1 A tree structure.

```
parent (f,h).
parent (f,i).
```

The following rules describe the concept of an ancestor node of the tree:

```
ancestor (X,Y):-parent (X,Y).
ancestor (X,Y):-parent (Z,Y), ancestor (X,Z).    (i)
```

Suppose one wishes to find all ancestors of node h. You can easily verify that the following question

```
?- ancestor (U,h).
```

solves the problem. In the example, it provides the following sequence of answers:

```
U= f;
U= b;
U= a;
NO
```

As another example, the question

```
?-ancestor (b,U).
```

produces all nodes of the subtree rooted in b. You are invited to hand simulate the behavior of the abstract PROLOG processor in the following case:

```
?-ancestor (a,U).
```

You should verify that nodes are output in the following order: b, d, k, e, f, l, m, g, h, i.

As an experiment, let us change the order in which the two rules for *ancestor* were listed:

```
ancestor (X,Y):-parent (Z,Y), ancestor (X,Z).    (ii)
ancestor (X,Y):-parent (X,Y).
```

In this case, you can easily prove that the question

```
?-ancestor (U,h).
```

provides the same set of values as before, but in a different order:

```
U=a;
U=b;
U=f;
NO
```

As another experiment, let us reverse the order of the two subgoals in the first rule for *ancestor*:

```
ancestor (X,Y):-ancestor (X,Z), parent (Z,Y).    (iii)
ancestor (X,Y):-parent (X,Y).
```

In this case, the question

```
?-ancestor (U,h)
```

makes the system enter an infinite loop. In fact, the goal

```
ancestor (U,h)
```

generates the subgoal

```
ancestor (U,Z)
```

which, in turn, generates the subgoal

```
ancestor (U,Z')
```

and so on. You can easily verify that an infinite loop is generated also by the following question

```
?-ancestor (a,U)
```

In conclusion, the three sample set of rules (*i*), (*ii*), and (*iii*) show that both the order in which the rules are given and the order in which the subgoals are listed in rules are important. Thus, we may say that PROLOG is not purely declarative. The underlying, hidden control flow followed by the interpreter affects the semantics of programs and thus the programmer must be aware of the implementation strategy adopted by the interpreter. As case (*iii*) illustrates, the programmer must be careful not to interchange subgoals of a rule; otherwise the built-in left-to-right strategy followed by the interpreter in solving subgoals may generate unexpected errors. Similarly, case (*ii*) shows that care must be taken in changing the order of facts and rules. Facts and rules are not merely a set of assertions on the world being modelled; the sequential order in which they are given may influence the program's behavior.

8.3.3 General Data Structures

PROLOG built-in types are atoms and numbers. Atoms are uninterpreted strings of symbols, like the composers' names in the example of Section 8.3.1 or node names in the case of the tree discussed in the example of the previous section. Numbers can be used in comparisons (as for the overlap rule of Section 8.3.1) and arithmetic computations.

Two aggregate constructors also are provided by PROLOG to define complex data: the *record-like structure* and the *list constructor*. Structures are exactly like facts, that is, they are a *functor* followed by a list of *components* enclosed within parentheses. For example, one can write the following facts:

```
birth_place(wien,composer(schubert,1797,1828)).
birth_place(hamburg,composer(brahms,1833,1897)).
```

where the second components (i.e., composer) are structures. One also can write questions such as

```
?-birth_place(X,composer(brahms,Y,Z)).
```

which will bind *X* to *hamburg,* *Y* to 1833, and *Z* to 1897; or

```
?-birth_place(hamburg,composer(A,1833,1897)).
```

which will bind *A* to *brahms.*

This example shows another interesting property of PROLOG: The language does not make a fixed and explicit distinction between input and output parameters, as do procedural languages. Rather, what is input and what is output is determined dynamically, as questions are posed.

The property that program components, like facts and subgoals, are exactly like structures, that is, programs and data are indistinguishable, gives PROLOG the same flexibility and power as we saw for LISP.

The other important PROLOG data structure is the *list*. For example, the LISP list

```
(CARLO(MARTA SILVIA GIACOMO) MEHDI(DARIUS RYAN))
```

can be represented in PROLOG as

```
[carlo,[marta,silvia,giacomo], mehdi,[darius,ryan]]
```

The empty list NIL of LISP is represented by [ ]. The notation [*X* | *Y*] stands for the list whose CAR is *X* and whose CDR is *Y*. As a simple example of lists, here is a PROLOG fragment that checks whether an element is in a list:

```
belongs_to (A,[A|B]).
belongs_to (A,[C|B]):-belongs_to (A,B).
```

According to the first rule, A is in a list if it is the first element of the list. The other rule says that A is in the list if it is in the tail.

Suppose that the fragment is used to check set membership, where a set is represented as a list and there are no repeated elements. If the goal *belongs_to* succeeds, then we would like to state that possible failures of other goals should not imply a backtracking trying to match with the second rule for *belongs_to,* because this is guaranteed to fail *a priori.* PROLOG allows this via an operator (the "cut", represented as "!"), having the following properties:

- It is a goal that never fails;
- It cannot be resatisfied; i.e., if during backtracking one tries to resatisfy it, the goal that was unified with the left-hand side of the rule fails.

Thus, if we have a rule like

```
a:-b, c, !, d, e
```

the cut will forbid any attempt to resatisfy goals c and b.

Using the cut, the previous description of *belongs_to* may be restated as:

```
belongs_to (A,[A|B]):-!.
belongs_to (A,[C|B]):-belongs_to ([A,B]).
```

Another typical use of the cut operator is in the PROLOG description of assertions like **if** A **then** $X(Y)$ **else** $X(Z)$, which can be written as

```
X(Y):-A!.
X(Z):-.
```

After matching with the first assertion, the cut prevents backtracking from proceeding to the second assertion.

The cut operator is yet another example of how PROLOG diverges from being purely declarative. It is a low-level operator that is used to affect the flow of control that the interpreter would otherwise follow and, obviously, requires knowledge of the built-in strategy followed by the interpreter. In most cases, the use of cut is due to poor programming practice: very often, it is used to simulate an imperative programming style in logic. However, there also are cases where the use of cut is mandatory. As indicated by VanEmden (1980), cut can be viewed as the logic counterpart of the GOTO of imperative languages. Because it can make programs awkward, its use should be consciously restricted to specific cases.

8.3.4 Applications

Logic programming languages are becoming increasingly popular, particularly in artificial intelligence applications such as knowledge-based expert systems. Knowledge about the particular application domain is represented as a set of facts and rules, and the underlying interpreter behaves as a built-in inferential engine that can make deductions and match them against the goals the system is asked to prove. Presently there are PROLOG applications that understand typewritten natural language, solve simple mechanics problems, perform drug analysis, and so on.

Natural language interfaces are typical PROLOG applications. In fact, derivation of a language recognizer or translator is quite an easy job in PROLOG. For example, if one takes the simple grammar fragment introduced in Section 3.1.2:

```
<sentence>  → <subject> <verb> <object>
<verb>  →see | hit | grab
<subject>  →I | we
<object>  →him | her | you
```

here is the corresponding PROLOG implementation that checks whether a certain string is correct according to the grammar. The PROLOG implementation can be obtained from the BNF notation in a straightforward fashion:

```
sentence (X,Y):-subject (X,Z), verb (Z,U), object (U,Y).
subject ([i|X],X).
subject ([we|X],X).
verb ([see|X],X).
verb ([hit|X],X).
verb ([grab|X],X).
object ([him|X],X).
object ([her|X],X).
object ([you|X],X).
```

The hypothesis is that the string to be recognized is represented as a list, such as [*i,see,you*]. All goals are represented as having two arguments: the first argument is the string where we wish to recognize a prefix belonging to the nonterminal that names the goal. The second is the list we are left to recognize after the prefix has been recognized. For example, the fact *subject* ([*i* | *X*],*X*) says that *i* is a *subject* followed by an *X*. Recognition is invoked as in this example:

```
?-sentence ([i,see,you],[ ]).
```

and the system answers:

YES

which means that after recognition of the string we are left with an empty string.

Another natural application of PROLOG is in *intelligent* (or *deductive*) databases. PROLOG facts are exactly like tuples in a relational database, and rules are a powerful extension to conventional relational databases, in that they allow deductions to be made starting from the data represented as facts. The composers' example given in Section 8.3.1 illustrates this point.

8.4   PROLOG AND SNOBOL4: UNIFYING CONCEPTS

The PROLOG goal searching and SNOBOL4's pattern-matching share many similarities that may not be obvious at first. These similarities are the result of the basic decision in both languages to allow the programmer to express his or her intent declaratively and let the implementation find a procedural solution. In both cases, we can view the task of the interpreter to be a search in a *search space* according to a *search criterion*. In PROLOG, the database of facts and rules provides the search space. The search criterion is provided by the goal as given in the user input. In SNOBOL4, the pattern provides the search space; the string that is being matched against the pattern can be viewed as the goal, or the search criterion. In both cases, it is possible to produce very large spaces and, for efficiency reasons, it is important for the programmer to be able to control the search.

In both languages, to provide correct and efficient search criteria, the programmer needs to know the interpreter's search procedure. We have seen that in PROLOG, the order in which rules and subgoals are stated can affect the correctness and termination of the program. The same idea applies to the order in which we specify the components of a pattern in SNOBOL4. Just as we need to know that the PROLOG interpreter searches left to right, top to bottom, we also need to know that the SNOBOL4 pattern matcher works left to right, top to bottom. In this case, the alternatives are considered to go top to bottom and concatenations are considered to go left to right. In both languages, the interpreter may make a wrong choice during the search and therefore requires the capability to backtrack. Both languages offer the programmer a mechanism to control this backtracking. The SNOBOL4 FENCE is analogous to PROLOG's cut: it is a pattern that will cause a failure of the match if the interpreter tries to backtrack past it.

The similarities between these two languages are quite interesting because SNOBOL4 and PROLOG are in many ways very different languages. The similarities illustrate how the same concepts can be applied in seemingly different settings.

8.5 CONCLUSIONS: THE FUTURE OF LOGIC PROGRAMMING

So far, we have seen what the potential of logic programming is and how PROLOG can be viewed as a good approximation of what a logic programming language should be like. Programming in PROLOG is based on a particular way of expressing predicates: Horn clauses. The programmer uses a declarative, nonprocedural language to specify a system, and lets the underlying implementation interpret clauses in a procedural fashion. Unfortunately, for implementation efficiency reasons, the logical programming paradigm is not strictly followed. Several procedural aspects are present in the language that make it diverge from being purely declarative. Also, the sequential, top-down and left-to-right search strategy that is built into the behavior of the PROLOG interpreter, and the availability of extra-logical operators like cut to affect backtracking hinder the possibility of parallel execution of PROLOG programs.

Efficiency of execution is a major problem in logic programming, at least on present-day machines. Thus, even if a logic programming language might be most suitable for a certain application, efficiency reasons may restrict its use primarily to a rapid prototyping tool. One of the main goals of the Japanese Fifth Generation Project is to build machines that support efficient execution of logic-based languages: to make the purpose of these machines clear, their power is usually measured in terms of logical inferences per second (LIPS). The goal is to obtain performances around millions of LIPS. The best present-day PROLOG implementations achieve a few tens of thousands of LIPS.

The Fifth Generation Project envisions that these machines will play an essential role in future society, which will be strongly based on knowledge processing. Future machines will be able to interact with humans through spoken and written natural language, they will be able to translate from one language to another, and they will be able to understand pictures. As McCorduck says (1983), the project has been inspired by a "noble vision of the future. Here is a future where knowledge—not mere information, but knowledge of the highest quality, pared, shaped and tailored to individual needs—will be accessible to anyone, anywhere, any time, in fast, powerful, and useful ways."

A widespread consensus has resulted from the project both within the international research community and agencies and industries; there is much debate, however, on whether logic programming languages are the best tools to implement the future systems.

Having seen different programming language concepts, the different programming paradigms they support, their merits and their drawbacks, one wonders whether it is the right time to make such a whole-hearted choice of one programming style. Also, one wonders whether it really makes sense to choose just one style, independent of the application. Bobrow (1984) argues very convincingly that logic programming should be combined with other styles, such as object-oriented and functional and, most important, that integration should take place within a flexible and friendly computing environment. We end this chapter with a quote from Bobrow (1984).

A programming paradigm or style of programming supports the expression of a programmer's intent. Some common programming paradigms are the function-oriented paradigm of LISP, the object-oriented paradigm of Smalltalk, and the logic-oriented paradigm of PROLOG. A language supports a paradigm if it provides the primitives of that paradigm, composition methods, and an appropriate user language to make programs written in the paradigm clear. A language must also allow effective execution of programs written in that style, for quantitative changes in running time make for qualitative changes in a system.

In the Turing machine sense, all common programming languages are universal. However, different techniques for expressing the knowledge may be more "natural", depending on the form of the problem, and the person's view of the problem. The costs to be considered include the cost of learning, the cost of debugging, the costs of change, and the cost of running the application. Because the different paradigms organize and factor programs in different ways, for a particular part of an application, the various costs of using a particular paradigm can vary across parts of a single application. By allowing the user to have a choice, the total cost can be lowered.

SUGGESTIONS FOR FURTHER READING AND BIBLIOGRAPHIC NOTES

The reader interested in understanding the principles of logic can refer to (Mendelson 1964). The logic-programming paradigm has been pioneered by Kowalski; see, for example, Kowalski (1979a) and Kowalski (1979b). Robinson (1983), Genesereth and Ginsberg (1985), and Hogger (1984) are good introductions to logic programming.

Database languages are described in the literature on database systems, for example, (Ullman 1982). SETL is described in (Schwartz 1974), (Kennedy and Schwartz 1975), and (Krutchen et al. 1984). For SNOBOL4, refer to the language glossary at the end of the book. ICON (Griswold and Griswold 1983) is a recent language that combines the interesting features of SNOBOL4 with a more traditional syntax and introduces some new concepts of its own.

PROLOG was defined and implemented by a group in Marseilles (France) led by A. Colmerauer (Roussel 1975). Colmerauer et al. (1983) is probably the most complete description of the principles behind the language and its current trends. Colmerauer (1985) is a short introduction to the language. Clocksin and Mellish (1985) is an excellent textbook of PROLOG; the PROLOG syntax used there has been adopted in our examples. Cohen (1985) provides an introduction to the processing of PROLOG programs. Campbell (1984) describes the issues involved in PROLOG implementations.

Other examples of logic-based languages are PLANNER (Hewitt 1969), a simple version of which—MICROPLANNER—is described in (Sussman et al. 1970), and CONNIVER (McDermott and Sussman 1974). These languages were defined as research tools for automatic theorem-proving. Lucid is another example of a declarative language that is oriented towards supporting proofs of program correctness (Ashcroft and Wadge 1977). OPS5 (Brownston et al. 1985) is a *rule-based* language that is closely related to logic languages. Other development tools for expert systems presently are being developed; we do not address the issue here.

The unification procedure upon which the PROLOG interpreter is based is derived from Robinson's resolution principle, which was invented to support mechanical theorem-proving (Robinson 1965). An efficient implementation is described by (Martelli and Montanari 1982).

The relation between PROLOG and logic programming is discussed in (McDermott 1980), (VanEmden 1980), (Kowalski 1981), and (Robinson 1983). Bobrow (1984) presents a critical view of logic programming, particularly of PROLOG, and advocates that no one of the known paradigms—imperative, functional, and logical—is entirely satisfactory if taken alone. His viewpoint is that we should search for an integration of the different paradigms. IEEE-Software (1986) contains several papers on languages that attempt to combine several paradigms.

The Japanese Fifth Generation Project has been one of the major events in the computing world since it was announced in 1981. Since then, the project has been described in many papers, books, and conference proceedings. We simply mention here (Feigenbaum and McCorduck 1983) and the special section on the topic in *Communication of the ACM*—September 1983 [in particular, (McCorduck 1983) and (Shapiro 1983)]. "Strategic computing" is a somewhat similar project which has been launched in the U.S. by DARPA (Stefik 1985). Its goals span the fields of artificial intelligence, computer science, and microelectronics. It does not emphasize logic programming exclusively.

EXERCISES

8.1 Give a logic specification of predicate *is_permutation* introduced in Section 8.1.

8.2 What are the strings matched by the following SNOBOL4 pattern

```
EXPRESSION = '(' EXPRESSION ')' | EXPRESSION OPERATOR
EXPRESSION | IDENTIFIER
```

where

```
OPERATOR = '+' | '-' | '/' | '*'
```

8.3 What are the strings matched by the following SNOBOL4 pattern

```
EXPRESSION = *EXPRESSION OPERATOR *EXPRESSION |
'(' *EXPRESSION ')' | IDENTIFIER
```

where

```
OPERATOR = '+' | '-' | '/' | '*'
```

8.4 Write the specification of a Fibonacci number. Remember that the first two Fibonacci numbers are 0 and 1, and any other Fibonacci number is the sum of the two Fibonacci numbers that precede it.

8.5 Take the list of courses offered by the Computer Science Department and the recommended prerequisites. Write a PROLOG database that can answer questions on curricula; in particular, it should be able to check whether a certain course sequence conforms to the recommendations.

8.6 Suppose you are given the description of a castle in terms of tuples of relation "from_to" that specifies which room is reachable from a given room. For example

```
from_to (a,b).
from_to (a,c).
from_to (c,d).

. . . . . .
```

Assume that the relation is unidirectional (i.e., if one can go from x to y, that does not necessarily mean that one also can go from y to x; if this is the case, then it must be explicitly stated as a fact). Write a PROLOG program to test whether it is possible to exit from the castle starting from a certain room (assume "z" denotes exit.)

8.7 Suppose that relation *from_to* of Exercise 8.6 is made symmetrical by adding the rule

```
from_to (X,Y):- from_to (Y,X).
```

Discuss the problems that arise in this case.

8.8 Suppose that we interchange the rules in the PROLOG program for *belongs_to* shown in Section 8.3.3 (version without cut). Describe the behavior of the PROLOG interpreter when a goal such as *belongs_to* $(a,[a,b,c])$ is submitted for evaluation.

8.9 PROLOG provides primitives to add new facts and rules to the database. Explain how you can use this facility to create programs with a state, by simulating Von Neumann variables. Present a criticism of this programming practice.

8.10 McDermott (1980) states that in PROLOG "a program used to generate a result can be used to check one as well." Give an example of a PROLOG program that illustrates this statement.

8.11 (McDermott 1980) Write a PROLOG program that appends two lists. Write the program in such a way that:

- It can be used to append two lists, for example, ?-append ([a,b],[x,y],X).
- It can be used to check if a list is the result of appending two lists, for example, ?-append ([a,b],[x,y],[a,b,x,y]).
- It can be used to produce the different pairs of sublists of a given list, for example, ?-append ($X,Y,[a,b,x,y]$).

8.12 Write a PROLOG program that recognizes the language of arithmetic expressions described in Section 3.1.1.1. Describe why direct translation of the grammar into a PROLOG program is not feasible in this case. More generally, discuss the problems caused by left-recursive grammar rules, that is, rules of the type $<N> \rightarrow <N>x$, where x is any sequence of terminal and nonterminal symbols.

8.13 Another search strategy that an interpreter for a logic language might follow is "breadth-first" search. If one describes the search space as a tree, where each node is a goal and the descendants of a node are the subgoals, "breadth-first" implies a visit of the tree level by level. Describe all the differences you see in this approach versus the conventional approach. Show the advantages and the disadvantages of the method.

8.14 Consider the tree example discussed in Section 8.3.2. Compare the efficiency of solving the goal

?-ancestor (U,p).

in the cases of the two sets of rules (*i*) and (*ii*).

8.15 Write a SNOBOL4 pattern that will cause an endless loop during pattern matching.

An Introduction to Formal Semantics

According to the definition given in Chapter 3, the semantics of a language describes "the meaning" of any syntactically correct program in that language. In Chapter 3 we described the meaning of basic language concepts, such as variables, bindings, and run-time structures, in terms of a virtual machine. That approach is, what we have called *operational semantics*.

In this chapter we introduce two formal—that is, mathematical—ways of defining the semantics of a programming language: *axiomatic semantics* and *denotational semantics*. Our purpose is to illustrate the spirit of how language semantics can be defined formally, and how the two styles differ in flavor from one another and from operational semantics. We do not intend to cover the details of the definition of complete and realistic programming languages. We also warn the reader that treating additional constructs and details of real programming languages is not simply a matter of adding more details to the formal description. Depending on the nature of the construct or detail, new problems may arise that may require new and perhaps as yet unknown mathematical solutions.

Also, we restrict our attention to the formal semantics of imperative languages, which constitute the main body of this text. Dealing with nontraditional languages would require the development of additional mathematical background, which is out of the scope of this text.

9.1 THE NEED FOR FORMAL SEMANTICS

Why is formal semantics useful? Why is a natural language description, such as the Pascal Report, or the Ada Reference Manual, or an operational view such as that presented in Chapter 3, inadequate? Informal natural language descriptions, even if they refer to well-understood abstract concepts, such as the SIMPLESEM virtual machine of Chapter 3, lack precision; very often they are ambiguous, incomplete, and inconsistent. Worse yet, determining that such a definition is unambiguous, complete, and consistent is a nontrivial and certainly not a mechanical task.

These are the most important benefits of formal semantics:

1. Rigorous and unambiguous definition. The language that is used to formally specify semantics, called *metalanguage,* is based on well-understood and simple mathematical concepts. This is similar to what we have seen for formal descriptions of the syntax of programming languages. BNF or syntax diagrams are the metalanguages used to specify the syntax of programming languages. In our case, giving semantics to language L by using metalanguage M can be viewed as translating from L to M. If M is a complex, nonmathematical language, we would have a circular problem, because M itself would require a formal specification of its semantics. Instead, no such need arises when M is simple and based on mathematical concepts. The resulting description is rigorous and unambiguous.

2. Basis for language comparison. The ability to compare different features, perhaps in different languages, to choose a language or evaluate alternative design decisions is often an elusive goal. The operational model developed in Chapter 3 is certainly of great help, but one hopes that formal semantics provides an even more detailed and precise basis for comparisons.

3. Independence from implementation. When a concept is described in terms of an implementation—be it abstract or concrete—one uses a number of exogenous, ancillary, implementation-dependent concepts. These do not deal with the essence of the concept, which is independent of any implementation. To circumvent this problem, one might say that a given implementation represents the equivalence class of all correct implementations (i.e., implementations that give the same results for any program and any given input). For example, our SIMPLESEM machine described in Chapter 3 uses static links to access nonlocal environments, and details have been given to show how static links are installed and used at run-time. Exercise 3.21 shows another implementation in terms of a "display." The two implementations belong to the same equivalence class of correct implementations of nonlocal environments. The essence of the concept they implement is the same, but numerous (and different) implementation-dependent details must be given in the specification. In conclusion, implementation-based semantic definitions, such as the operational definition of Chapter 3, cannot distinguish between what is the pure essence of a language concept and a specific implementation: they lack abstraction and easily can become cluttered with details.

4. Basis for correctness proof of implementation. A language implementation is defined correct if it conforms to the formal semantic specification. The formal description is *the* reference for solving any controversial issue. Implementations may differ from one another as far as efficiency is concerned, but the meaning of syntactically correct programs remains the same.

5. Basis for program correctness proofs. To prove that a given program is correct with respect to a given specification, the effect of the program must be clearly understood, that is, the language semantics should be specified rigorously. For example, as we have seen in Chapter 4, the original Pascal Report does not define variant records precisely. As a result, one may be unable to understand precisely the meaning of a given program that uses variant records, and thus to prove whether the program meets its specification.

Points 4 and 5 also show that formal semantics have the potential of providing mechanical support to correctness proofs. The only way for a computer to aid in the verification of a language implementation or the correctness of a program is to start from a precise, formal language definition.

Having seen the advantages of formal semantics, one wonders whether there is a need for informal semantic descriptions, such as those of traditional language standards. In practice, both formal and informal descriptions are needed. The interplay between formal and informal semantics is as follows: When a language is being designed, one usually starts from an informal definition. The informal description then is converted into a formal description, and this may uncover inconsistencies, ambiguities, and incompletenesses in the informal description. The process is iterated until the design is satisfactory. The final formal semantics description then is used as a basis for deriving more informal reports on the language. These definitely are needed in practice. Because they are more readable then their formal counterparts, the reader only needs to refer to the formal definition when the informal documents do not provide a satisfactory answer. Also, the practical use of the language should not require as a prerequisite the mathematical skills needed to manage formal semantics.

9.2   STYLES OF FORMAL SEMANTICS

As we have seen in the previous section, formal semantics of a programming language maps every syntactically correct language construct into a metalanguage that is based on a well-understood mathematical notation. Consequently, formal semantics can be specified as a set of translation rules from the domain of language constructs to the range of well-formed formulas of the formalism.

We distinguish between two kinds of formal semantics: axiomatic semantics and denotational semantics. *Axiomatic semantics* describes the meaning of each syntactically correct program by associating to it properties of variables (in terms of predicate calculus) that hold before execution starts and after the program halts. Thus the metalanguage of axiomatic semantics is a logic language, such as predicate calculus. *Denotational semantics* describes the meaning of a program by associating to it a function from the input domain to the output domain. In this case the metalanguage is that of functional calculus.

The fundamental concepts needed to model the semantics of a programming language are the *state of computation*, and how this state is *transformed* by various language constructs. In the informal operational semantics of Chapter 3, the state was described in terms of data structures of the abstract SIMPLESEM processor, and state transformations were described in terms of changes to the processor's data structures. In Sections 9.3 and 9.4 we will see how this can be done formally.

The rest of this chapter is organized as follows: Our discussion of formal semantics starts in Section 9.3 with axiomatic semantics, which is highly intuitive and does not require deep mathematical knowledge to be appreciated in practice. In Section 9.3.1 we also will give a glimpse of how axiomatic semantics support formal proofs of program correctness. Section 9.4 will outline the basics of denotational semantics. Finally, in Section 9.5 we will contrast the two styles and draw some conclusions.

9.3   AN INTRODUCTION TO AXIOMATIC SEMANTICS

Axiomatic semantics is based on mathematical logic. The state of computation is described by a logical expression (called a *predicate* or *assertion*) on program variables that must be true in that state. Intuitively, whereas in operational semantics the state of computation for a program is determined by the data structures of the modeling machine, in axiomatic semantics it is determined by a predicate on the values of the program variables.

Because in this chapter we are only interested in the flavor of formal semantics, our use of the concepts of logic will be rather informal and intuitive. To go deeper into the subject, the reader needs a background of mathematical logic, which is not required to understand the spirit of the method and its use. The Further Reading Section at the end of the chapter provides references to the literature on this subject.

A predicate P that is required to hold after a statement S is called a *postcondition* for S. A predicate Q such that the execution of S terminates and postcondition P holds upon termination is called a *precondition* for S and P. For example, $y = 3$ is one possible precondition for statement $x := y + 1$, that leads to postcondition $x > 0$. The predicate $y \geq 0$ is also a precondition for statement $x := y+1$ and postcondition $x > 0$. Actually, $y \geq 0$ is the *weakest precondition*, that is, the *necessary and sufficient* precondition for statement $x := y+1$ that leads to postcondition $x > 0$. A predicate W is called the weakest precondition for a statement S and a postcondition P, if any precondition Q for S and P implies W, that is, W holds for any precondition Q. Among all possible preconditions for statement S and postcondition P, W is the weakest: it specifies the fewest constraints. If we write implication as " $\Rightarrow$ ", for our example we have

$$y = 3 \Rightarrow y \geq 0$$

In general, given an assignment statement $x := E$ and a postcondition P, the weakest precondition is obtained by replacing each occurrence of x in P with expression E. We express this weakest precondition with the notation $P_{x \to E}$. In the example, $P_{x \to y+1}$ is $y+1 > 0$, that is, $y \geq 0$.

To characterize the semantics of a programming language, we would like to describe the effect of each language construct in terms of the transformation of predicates it implies. To this end, we will define a function *asem* (for *axiomatic semantics*, also called a *predicate transformer*) that for any statement S and any postcondition P, has as its value the weakest precondition W. It is written as

$$asem\ (S, P) = W$$

In the case of an assignment statement $x := E$, we have

$$asem\ (x := E, P) = P_{x \to E}$$

This characterization of assignments is correct under the assumption that the evaluation of the right-hand side of the statement does not have any side-effects. Moreover, the variable being assigned cannot be an alias of other program variables. In such cases the execution of the assignment also may affect variables not appearing at the left-hand side of the statement, and the given semantics would be incorrect. This is an example of how side-effects and aliasing can complicate formal as well as informal reasoning about programs.

Let us give an intuitive explanation of how *asem* (S,P) can be described as giving the semantics of S. Consider how we can use the function we have just given for assignment statements. Suppose we want to know whether the statement $x := x+1$ will produce the result $x > 5$. The function *asem* can be used to tell us that $asem(x := x+1, x > 5) = x > 4$, that is, as long as we start with a computation state that ensures the truth of $x > 4$, then the given assignment statement will achieve the desired effect. In other words, we can predict the exact effect or meaning of statements if we have the *asem* function.

Simple statements, such as assignment statements, can be combined into more complex actions by statement-level control structures. Therefore, *composition rules* are needed to characterize the semantic effect of combining individual statements into a program segment. For example, for sequencing, if we know that

$$asem\,(S1,P)=Q$$

and

$$asem\,(S2,Q)=R$$

then

$$asem\,(S2;S1,P)=R$$

The cases of selection and iteration are more complex. If B is a boolean expression and $L1$, $L2$ are two statement lists, then let **if**-stat be the following statement:

if B **then** $L1$ **else** $L2$ **fi**

If P is the postcondition that must be established by **if**-stat, then the weakest precondition is given by

$$asem(\textbf{if}\text{-stat}, P)=B \Rightarrow asem(L1, P)\ \textbf{and not}\ B \Rightarrow asem\,(L2, P)$$

For example, given the following program fragment (x, y, and *max* are integers)

if $x>=y$ **then** $max:=x$ **else** $max:=y$ **fi**

and the postcondition

$$(max=x\ \textbf{and}\ x \geq y)\ \textbf{or}\ (max=y\ \textbf{and}\ y>x)$$

the weakest precondition is easily proven to be *true,* that is, the statement satisfies the postcondition without any constraints on variables.

Suppose now that P is the postcondition that must be established by the following loop

while B **do** L **od**

where B is a boolean expression and L is a statement list. The problem is that we do not know how many times the body of the loop is iterated. Indeed, if we knew, for example, that the number of iterations were n, the construct would be equivalent to the sequential composition

$L;L; \ldots ; L$

of length n. Thus the semantics of the statement would be straightforward.

To overcome this difficulty, let us first reconsider why we have chosen to refer to weakest preconditions in our formalization of semantics. The reason is that weakest preconditions give an *exact* characterization of semantics. If we choose to refer to any other preconditions, they provide only an *approximate* characterization of semantics: they are only a *sufficient* precondition that can be derived for a given statement and a given postcondition. In fact, if any precondition for a given statement and a given postcondition holds, then the weakest precondition also holds. In other words, the constraints on the state specified by a nonweakest precondition are stronger than what is needed to ensure that a certain postcondition holds after execution of a statement. If we relax our requirement and accept nonweakest preconditions as an (approximate) specification of semantics, here is how **while** statements can be handled.

Given the **while** statement and a postcondition P, we wish to determine a precondition Q for the **while** statement and predicate P. Q must be such that

(a) The loop terminates.

(b) At loop exit, P holds.

Thus predicate Q can be written as $Q = T$ **and** R, where T implies termination of the loop and R implies the truth of P at loop exit. Determining two predicates T and R that satisfy these properties is not straightforward and requires ingenuity. For simplicity's sake, we ignore the problem of termination and focus our attention on inventing R. Suppose we are able to identify a predicate I that holds both before and after each loop iteration and, when the loop terminates (i.e., when the boolean expression B is false), I implies P. I is called an *invariant predicate* for the loop. Formally, I satisfies the following conditions.

(i) I **and** $B \Rightarrow$ asem (L, I)

(ii) I **and not** $B \Rightarrow P$

If we are able to identify a predicate I that satisfies both i) and ii), then we can take I as the desired predicate R, because P holds upon termination if $R = I$ holds before executing the loop.

In conclusion, the method of loop invariants allows us to approximate the evaluation of semantics of a **while** statement; the precondition is one possible valid precondition, not necessarily the weakest. Because the major use of axiomatic semantics is in providing programs correct (or deriving correct programs), as we will see in the next section this inconvenience does not cause us much trouble.

9.3.1 Axiomatic Semantics and Program Correctness

An in-depth study of the issues involved in the study of program correctness is beyond the scope of this book. However, we are now in a position to state precisely what we mean by *a correct program*, and to give a glimpse of how programs can be proven correct. We also will mention an interesting methodical approach that uses axiomatic semantics to guide in the derivation of programs that are correct in the first place.

First of all, the correctness requirements of the program must be specified formally by giving two predicates: a precondition IN (or *input assertion*) on input variables and a postcondition OUT (or *output assertion*) on input and output variables. The job of verification is to show that if IN holds before executing the program, execution terminates in a state where OUT holds. This proof requires the use of the semantic characterization of statements such as the one described in the previous section.

Program verification is illustrated here with the aid of a simple example. Consider the following program fragment, in which all variables are assumed to be integers.

```
i:= k; sum:= k;
while i>1 do
      i:= i-1;
      sum:= sum+ i
od
```

Let the input assertion be

$$IN: k>0$$

and let the output assertion be

$$OUT: sum= \sum_1^k j$$

We want to prove the fragment correct with respect to IN and OUT.

The termination of the loop is obviously assured, because variable i is altered only by instruction $i:=i-1$ and, thus, assumes a decreasing sequence of values, which would eventually make "$i>1$" false. For the invariant, the predicate

$$I: sum= \sum_1^k j \text{ and } 0<i\leq k$$

can be proven easily to satisfy conditions **i)** and **ii)** of the previous section (we leave this proof to the reader). Thus, starting the execution of the loop with variables satisfying I assures termination in a state satisfying OUT. Finally, it is also easy to prove that I holds after the instructions

```
i:= k; sum:= k;
```

if the precondition $k>0$ holds before the two instructions. In conclusion, if IN holds before executing the fragment, execution terminates in a state where OUT holds, that is, the program is correct with respect to IN and OUT.

Given the input and output assertions, program verification proceeds by deriving *intermediate assertions* that must be proven to hold at various points in the program. In particular, as we have seen, intermediate assertions must be supplied by the verifier (human or machine) in the form of loop invariants. Other examples of intermediate assertions are the legality assertions generated by the Euclid compiler, which we mentioned in Chapter 5. In addition, Euclid allows the programmer to specify **assert** statements in the program. The Euclid's **assert** statement is used to supply intermediate assertions to be proven by the verifier as an integral part of the program. In this way, assertions become part of the documentation of the program. Moreover, compiler options allow the programmer to transform **assert** statements into run-time checks during the testing phase or, alternatively, to suppress their evaluation. Finally, if a verifier is part of the set of tools provided by the programming environment, assertions can be proven by the verifier and the program is fully certified statically.

The mechanical verifier cannot proceed in a purely automatic fashion, but must interact with the user. In particular, the user must use ingenuity to invent loop invariants that are needed in the derivation of a precondition for a given program containing loops and a given output assertion.

The influence of programming language features on the process of reasoning about programs is felt both by human readers and mechanical program verifiers. Many features that make reasoning about programs difficult for humans also are hard to deal with for a program verifier. For example, side-effects in functions complicate the evaluation of the weakest precondition for assignments, as the following example shows. Let $y := f(x) + z$ be an assignment statement and $P(z)$ be a predicate on variable z that must hold as a postcondition for the assignment. The absence of side-effects guarantees that $P(z)$ also is the weakest precondition. The possibility of side-effects, however, requires examining the function f, which might modify z. Moreover, the verifier—be it human or automatic—must be careful if aliasing is permitted by the language. In the example, $P(z)$ would not be the weakest precondition if z and y are aliases.

What is the practical influence of program verification on the programming activity? Unlike what many computer scientists foresaw in the past, program verification has not become common practice in everyday programming and probably never will. Nevertheless, program verification issues have a deep influence on programming and programming languages. They stimulate a rigorous approach to programming and provide a formal definition of programming languages. Even in the absence of a mechanical program verifier, rigorous reasoning about program correctness can help the programmer in discovering possible errors. Intermediate assertions that should be proven by the verifier (e.g., loop invariants) can be expressed as run-time checks; this is a useful way of certifying programs via systematic testing.

Another important use of axiomatic semantics is in the methodologies that try to derive programs that are correct in the first place. This approach has been exemplified by Dijkstra, who illustrated a calculus that, given input and output predicates, can be used to synthesize correct programs. This is a *constructive approach*: programs are not proven correct *a posteriori*, after being written, but are derived correct by the calculus. The approach has been demonstrated to work on examples of low-to-moderate complexity, but it is not clear if (and how) it can be used in more complex and larger applications. Further discussion of this topic is beyond the scope of this text, and belongs in the area of programming methodology. The reader interested in the subject will find references to the literature in the Further Reading section.

9.4   AN INTRODUCTION TO DENOTATIONAL SEMANTICS

As we said in Section 9.2, denotational semantics associates to each program a function from the input domain to the output domain. To do so, as we did for axiomatic semantics, it is necessary to formalize the notion of *state*, that is, the concepts of *memory* (that binds identifiers to values), *input,* and *output*. Instructions of our programming language will be modeled through the state transformation they imply. For simplicity, we assume that our programs deal only with simple integer values and booleans, which may result from relational expressions. Symbol Z stands for the set of integers; symbol "*undef*" stands for the undefined value.

For any given program P, P's state s_P is formalized by a triple

$$< \text{mem}_P, i_P, o_P >$$

where:

- mem_P is a function that gives the value of each identifier. If Id_P is the set of P's identifiers, we can write:

$$\text{mem}_P: Id_P \rightarrow Z \cup \{\text{undef}\}$$

- i_P and o_P are the input and output streams, respectively. Both are strings of integers, that is, i_P and o_P are elements of Z^* (symbol $*$ denotes the reflexive and transitive closure of a set. Thus Z^* is the set of all sequences of integers, including the null sequence.)

Each language instruction will be specified now in terms of a state transformation. To this end, we define a function *dsem* (for denotational *semantics*) for each construct of the language and we define how *dsem* can be constructed for each program in terms of function *dsem* for individual statements. To make the notation more readable, an abbreviation for the name of the construct will be used as a subscript of *dsem* in our formal definitions; S will denote the set of states.

Let us start our analysis with *arithmetic expressions*. Assuming that expression evaluation does not produce any side-effects, arithmetic expressions do not cause any state change; thus semantics of arithmetic expressions simply describe how a value is produced by expression evaluation. If EX is the set of all legal arithmetic expressions, we can write:

$$dsem_{EX}: EX \times S \rightarrow Z \cup \{error\}$$

where

$dsem_{EX}(E, s) = error$ if $s = <mem, i, o>$ and $mem(v) = undef$ for some
    variable v occurring in E; otherwise
$dsem_{EX}(E, s) = e$ if $s = <mem, i, o>$ and e is the result of evaluating E
    after replacing each variable v occurring in E with
    $mem(v)$.

According to this definition, an error can arise only because of undefined operands. For simplicity, we ignore the possibility of overflows and underflows during execution. Also, we implicitly assume here—and in what follows—that programs are statically correct; thus, for example, type errors can be ignored.

Let AS be the set of all legal *assignment statements*. Semantics of assignment statements can be defined as a state-transformation function.

$$dsem_{AS}: AS \times S \rightarrow S \cup \{error\}$$

where

$dsem_{AS}(x: = E, s) = error$ if $dsem_{EX}(E, s) = error$; otherwise
$dsem_{AS}(x: = E, s) = s'$ where $s' = <mem', i', o'>$, $s = <mem, i, o>$,
    $i' = i, o' = o, mem'(y) = mem(y)$ for all $y \neq x$,
    $mem'(x) = dsem_{EX}(E, s)$

Suppose that *input statements* are written in our language as $x: = $**read** ( ), which means that the next input value read is assigned to x. Intuitively, the effect of such a statement is a state modification that affects both the memory and the input stream. Formally, let RD be the set of all legal **read** statements. Then

$$dsem_{RD}: RD \times S \rightarrow S \cup \{error\}$$

where

$dsem_{RD}(x: = $**read( )**$, s) = error$ if $s = <mem, i, o>$ and i is empty; otherwise
$dsem_{RD}(x: = $**read( )**$, s) = s'$ where $s = <mem, i, o>$, $s' = <mem', i', o'>$,
    $o = o', i = li'$ for some l in Z and some i' in Z^*,
    $mem(y) = mem'(y)$ for all $y \neq x$, and $mem(x) = l$

Similarly, if WR is the set of all *write statements,* we define

$$\text{dsem}_{WR}: WR \times S \rightarrow S \cup \{error\}$$

where

$\text{dsem}_{WR}(\textbf{write}(x), s) = error$ if $s = <mem, i, o>$ and $mem(x) = undef$, otherwise
$\text{dsem}_{WR}(\textbf{write}(x), s) = s'$ where $s = <mem, i, o>$, $s' = <mem', i', o'>$,
$\qquad mem = mem', i = i', o' = oO$, where $O = mem(x)$

Now, let us turn to compound statements. First, let SL be the set of all *statement lists.* Semantics can be specified by the function

$$\text{dsem}_{SL}: SL \times S \rightarrow S \cup \{error\}$$

We define *dsem*$_{SL}$ recursively as follows. First, if the statement list is the empty list, the state does not change:

$$\text{dsem}_{SL} (\text{empty\_list}, s) = s$$

Second, if the statement list is a statement T followed by a statement list L and *dsem* describes T's semantics:

$$\text{dsem}_{SL} (T; L, s) = error \text{ if dsem } (T, s) = error; \text{ otherwise}$$
$$\text{dsem}_{SL} (T; L, s) = \text{dsem}_{SL} (L, \text{dsem } (T, s))$$

As far as *selection* is concerned, let us refer to a Pascal-like **if . . . then . . . else . . . fi** statement. If the statement list in the **else** branch is empty, then our selection statement can be abbreviated as **if . . . then . . . fi.** If IF is the set of all correct selections we can write in our language, we define

$$\text{dsem}_{IF}: IF \times S \rightarrow S \cup \{error\}$$

If B is a boolean valued relational expression, $L1$ and $L2$ are two statement lists; we have:

$\text{dsem}_{IF}(\textbf{if } B \textbf{ then } L1 \textbf{ else } L2 \textbf{ fi}, s) = error$ if $\text{dsem}_{BOOL} (B, s) = undef$; otherwise
$\text{dsem}_{IF}(\textbf{if } B \textbf{ then } L1 \textbf{ else } L2 \textbf{ fi}, s) = U$ where if $\text{dsem } (B, s) = true$, then
$\qquad U = \text{dsem}_{SL}(L1, s)$, else
$\qquad U = \text{dsem}_{SL}(L2, s)$

Semantic function *dsem*$_{BOOL}$ describes the boolean result of a relational expression. It can be defined exactly like *dsem*$_{EX}$ and its definition is left to the reader.

Finally, we define the semantics of a Pascal-like **while . . . do . . . od** statement. If DO is the set of all syntactically correct loops, we define

$$\text{dsem}_{DO}: DO \times S \rightarrow S \cup \{error\}$$

If B is a boolean expression and L is a statement list, we can define *dsem*$_{DO}$ as a *recursive function*

$\text{dsem}_{DO}(\textbf{while } B \textbf{ do } L \textbf{ od}, s) = error$ if $\text{dsem}_{BOOL} (B, s) = undef$; otherwise
$\text{dsem}_{DO}(\textbf{while } B \textbf{ do } L \textbf{ od}, s) = s$ if $\text{dsem}_{BOOL} (B, s) = false$; otherwise

$$\text{dsem}_{DO}(\textbf{while } B \textbf{ do } L \textbf{ od}, s) = error \text{ if dsem}_{SL} (L, s) = error; \text{ otherwise}$$
$$\text{dsem}_{DO}(\textbf{while } B \textbf{ do } L \textbf{ od}, s) = \text{dsem}_{DO}(\textbf{while } B \textbf{ do } L \textbf{ od}, \text{dsem}_{SL}(L, s))$$

Finally, if PROG is the set of all statically correct programs in our language, the *language semantics* is defined by the following function:

$$\text{dsem}_{PROG}: \text{PROG} \times Z^* \to Z^* \cup \{error\}$$

(Z^* represents both the input—when it appears to the left of '$\to$'—and the output domain). If L is the statement list that constitutes a program, function $dsem_{PROG}$ is defined as:

$$\text{dsem}_{PROG}(L, i) = \text{out} (\text{dsem}_{SL} (L, \text{init} (i)),$$

where

- init $(i) = \,<mem0, i, o>, mem0(x) = undef$ for all identifiers x, o = empty
- out $(error) = error$
- out $(<mem, i, o>) = o$

If we wish to formalize additional constructs of the language, we may run into unexpected problems that cannot be handled within the current theoretical framework. For example, the current model does not allow us to deal with aliasing. Because in our model *mem* maps identifier names directly to values, there is no way to specify that two identifiers share the same object. Also, in our model the result of the function *dsem* associated with some construct is passed to the function associated to the construct that follows it in the program. This does not model the case where a jump or a procedure call causes a break in the sequential control flow. A denotational specification can be given to cover these cases too, but this requires additional mathematical sophistication.

Before closing this section, let us consider an example.

Example

Consider the following program P

```
read (n); fact:= 1; i:= 1;
while i <= n do
     fact:= fact * i;
     i:= i+1
od;
write (fact);
```

We wish to evaluate P's denotational semantics. Obviously, if the input stream is empty we have

$$\text{dsem}_{PROG}(P, \text{empty}) = error$$

(The formal proof of this is left to the reader.) Let us consider now an input string consisting of one integer value z. We have

(a) $dsem_{PROG}(P, z) = out\ (dsem_{SL}\ (\textbf{read}\ (n);\ \ldots;\ \textbf{write}(fact),\ <mem0,$
$$z, empty>))$$
$$= out\ (dsem_{SL}\ (fact: = 1;\ \ldots,\ \textbf{write}(fact),\ <mem1,$$
$$empty, empty>)),$$

where $mem0\ (x) = undef$ for all identifiers x, $mem1\ (x) = undef$ for all identifiers $x \neq n$, $mem1\ (n) = z$.

Skipping a few trivial steps, we get

(b) $dsem_{PROG}(P, z) = out\ (dsem_{SL}\ (\textbf{while}\ \ldots;\ \textbf{write}\ (fact),\ <mem2,$
$$empty, empty>))$$

where $mem2(n) = z$, $mem2(fact) = 1$, $mem2(i) = 1$, $mem2(x) = undef$ for any other identifier x.

Let us examine the **while** loop.

(c) $dsem_{DO}(\textbf{while}\ \ldots\ \textbf{od},\ <mem2, empty, empty>) =$
if $dsem_{BOOL}\ (i < = n,\ <mem2, empty, empty>) = false$
then $<mem2, empty, empty>$
else $dsem_{DO}(\textbf{while}\ \ldots\ \textbf{od},\ dsem_{SL}(fact: = fact*i;\ i: =$
$i + 1,\ <mem2, empty, empty>)) =$
if $dsem_{BOOL}\ (i < = n,\ <mem2, empty, empty>) = false$
then $<mem2, empty, empty>$
else $dsem_{DO}(\textbf{while}\ \ldots\ \textbf{od},\ <mem3, empty, empty>)$
where $mem3(n) = mem2(n)$, $mem3\ (fact) = mem2\ (fact)*mem2$
(i), $mem3(i) = mem2(i) + 1$, $mem3(x) = undef$ for any other identifier x

Equation (c) defines recursively a function $dsem_{DO}$ from S to $S \cup \{error\}$. To solve it, we must rely upon the theory of recursive functions that underlies denotational semantics. Without entering into the details of the theory, we give the resulting function:

$$dsem_{DO}(\textbf{while}\ \ldots\ \textbf{do},\ <mem2, empty, empty>) = <mem2', empty,$$
$$empty>$$

where $mem2'(fact) = mem2(n)! = z!$ From **b** and the above $dsem_{DO}$ we obtain

(d) $dsem_{PROG}(P, z) = out\ (<mem2', empty, z!>) = z!$

This example has given a denotational semantics to a very simple iterative Pascal-like program. In particular, it has shown that denotational semantics is founded on the theory of recursive functions; functions that define the semantics of a program are described through recursive equations and one must be able to solve them. For more information, the interested reader is referred to the literature in the Further Readings section of this chapter.

9.5 CONCLUSIONS

This chapter introduced the concept of formal semantics and illustrated the spirit of two different approaches: axiomatic semantics and denotational semantics. The mathematical prerequisites needed to develop the subject in more depth prevented us from discussing more details, particularly in the case of denotational semantics.

Although, in practice, languages are seldom described formally, formal definitions can be useful and will be used more in the future. As we anticipated in Section 9.2, we envisage an interplay between formal and informal specification techniques in the definition of semantics. In particular, we suggested that the informal reports on the use of the language should be derived systematically from the formal definition. The official definition of the language should be formal, and we should refer to it every time a conflict arises in the interpretation of the informal reports.

Besides providing a notation for describing languages, formal semantics supports rigorous reasoning about programs. In particular, it supports (mechanical) program verification. We have seen this for axiomatic semantics, which is more intuitive, but there also are proof techniques that derive from denotational semantics (see the Further Readings section). Verification issues, in turn, have influenced the design of programming languages (this is yet another reason why we have presented the topic here). Another area where formal semantics can be useful is the automatic production of language translators from the language's semantic description. Both axiomatic and denotational semantics have been used for this purpose.

Denotational and axiomatic semantics are based on different mathematical foundations. Denotational semantics is based on functions, in particular, recursively defined functions. Axiomatic semantics is based on logic, in particular, predicate calculus. Both are formal and can support correctness proofs; the choice of one or the other is mostly a matter of individual taste and mathematical background. Axiomatic semantics is more easily readable; its style is more closely related to a declarative specification style where one states the properties of the mechanism that is being defined without saying anything about the implementation. The style of denotational specifications, on the other hand, is more in terms of a highly stylized and very abstract implementation.

SUGGESTIONS FOR FURTHER READING AND BIBLIOGRAPHIC NOTES

Formal semantics of programming languages usually is treated in specialized texts and taught in specialized courses. We have only introduced the subject here because a more complete treatment cannot be done in a single chapter of a book.

Mandrioli and Ghezzi (1986) present the mathematical background needed to develop the formal description of semantics of programming languages and provide a discussion of axiomatic and denotational semantics. Tennent (1976) and Gordon (1979) are excellent introductions to denotational semantics. A denotational technique is described by Bjørner and Jones (1978).

Dijkstra (1976) defines programming language semantics in terms of weakest preconditions and illustrates the use of the concept in a methodology for developing correct programs. Given the input and output predicates, Dijkstra illustrates a calculus that allows one to derive a program that is correct with respect to the predicates. The approach is further developed by Gries (1981).

Hoare and Wirth (1973) and Alagić and Arbib (1978) present an axiomatic description of Pascal semantics. Tennent (1973) presents a formal definition of SNOBOL4. Kahn et al. (1980) give a preliminary report on the formal definition of Ada; a complete formal definition of semantics is presently under development. ALGOL 68 has been among the first languages for which a formal definition has been given (van Wijngaarden et al. 1976). The formalism used there is based on so-called two-level grammars. An axiomatic definition of ALGOL 68 has also been given (Schwartz 1978b).

The mathematical foundations of axiomatic semantics and program verification were laid by Floyd (1967) and Hoare (1969). A presentation of the Floyd–Hoare theory is contained in (Manna 1973). Manna (1973) discusses the method of computational induction for proving functional programs correct using denotational semantics. The theory of program correctness also is studied in (DeBakker 1980).

The evolving state-of-the-art of the field of automatic program verification is surveyed in (Yeh 1977b), by London's paper in (Wegner 1979), and by Good (1985). DeMillo et al. (1979) argue that program verification cannot be used in practice to guarantee software reliability, because of the nature of proofs. It reports examples from mathematics in which proofs of theorems are shown to contain errors years after their truth were accepted.

EXERCISES

9.1 Describe the axiomatic semantics of the following Pascal statements:

- **repeat . . . until.**
- **for.**
- **case.**

9.2 Describe the axiomatic semantics of Dijkstra's guarded **if** and **do** statements.

9.3 Give an example of an assignment statement with a side-effect that invalidates the rule given in Section 9.3 to evaluate the weakest precondition.

9.4 Consider the Pascal-like program of the example given in Section 9.4. Using axiomatic semantics, prove it correct with respect to the following input and output assertions:

$$\text{IN: } n>0$$
$$\text{OUT: } fact=n*(n\text{-}1)*(n\text{-}2)*\dots*1$$

9.5 Write an iterative Pascal program that evaluates the product of two positive integers m and n by repeated additions. Prove the program correct with respect to the following assertions:

$$\text{IN: } m>0, n>0$$
$$\text{OUT: } prod=m*n.$$

Does the program work properly, with exactly the same postcondition, if either $m \geq 0$ or $n \geq 0$? If the answer is yes in one such case, why can we say that IN is not the weakest precondition?

9.6 What is the weakest precondition for some postcondition P and a program that contains a loop that never terminates? For example

```
i:= 0;
while i >= 0 do
    i:= i + 1
od
```

9.7 Give a denotational description of the Pascal **case** statement.

9.8 Give a formal definition of $dsem_{\text{BOOL}}$, which was introduced but not defined in Section 9.4.

9.9 Give a denotational description of the Pascal **repeat** statement.

9.10 Suppose that two concurrent processes $P1$ and $P2$ are executing the statement lists $L1$ and $L2$, respectively. Suppose that these processes also access some shared variables in mutual exclusion. Does $dsem_{\text{SL}}$ defined in Section 9.4 describe the semantics of $L1$ and $L2$ correctly? Why? Why not?

Language Design

". . . consolidation, not innovation . . ."   *(Hoare 1973)*

The leitmotiv of this book is that programming languages are tools for software production. The previous chapters have expounded this viewpoint in depth by discussing programming language concepts, and comparing and evaluating the many solutions adopted by existing programming languages. We have suggested a number of criteria for evaluating programming languages, centered around the concepts of data types, control structures, program correctness, and programming in the large. Viewed slightly differently, however, these criteria also suggest a number of guidelines for programming language design. As we examine language design issues in this chapter, therefore, we will encounter many considerations that we have seen in previous chapters. This chapter, then, is mainly recapitulatory; we will try to put together the many facets of the problem and, in several cases, show how different language features, each desirable in itself, can interfere with one another when combined.

According to C. A. R. Hoare (Hoare 1973),

> The language designer should be familiar with many alternative features designed by others, and should have excellent judgment in choosing the best and rejecting any that are mutually inconsistent. He must be capable of reconciling, by good engineering design, any remaining minor inconsistencies or overlaps between separately designed features. He must have a clear idea of the scope and purpose and range of application of his new language, and how far it should go in size and complexity. . . . One thing he should not do is to include untried ideas of his own. His task is consolidation, not innovation.

Having designed a language, it is also necessary to design an implementation for it. According to Wirth (1975a), "In practice, a programming language is as good as its compiler(s)." In fact, much of the popularity of older languages such as FORTRAN probably stems from the availability of efficient, reliable compilers, that produce efficient code and have good diagnostic systems. Wirth further states that "a successful language must grow out of clear ideas of design goals and *simultaneous* attempts to define it on a computer, or preferably even on several computers."

Finally, one should not forget that the user of a language often interacts with other tools provided by the programming environment. In most existing solutions, as we have seen, such interactions are not carried out within a unified environment. Instead, they use independent support tools such as text editors, linkers, and compilers. This often allows the programmer to circumvent the features of the language designed to enhance program reliability. For example, job-control language commands can be used to combine several separately compiled units into a unique executable program. However, the invoked linkage editor provided by the system does not (usually) type-check the components' interfaces. Similarly, the standard text editor provided by the system does not guarantee that a correct program is left in a syntactically correct state after modification. Integrating the language with the tools into a coherent programming environment should be a prominent design goal; in fact, there is a definite trend in this direction.

10.1 DESIGN CRITERIA

Programming languages must assist the programmer in designing, documenting, and validating programs. As such, language design criteria can be classified according to the following principles: program writability, readability, and reliability. Each of these principles will be discussed separately, in Sections 10.1.1, 10.1.2, and 10.1.3, respectively.

We also should remember that programming languages ultimately are executed by computers. *Efficient translation* and *efficient execution* are thus two additional goals of language design. In most practical cases, efficient execution of compiled code is more important than efficient translation, because programs, once delivered, are executed many times or even continuously (for monitoring programs) without being recompiled. However, in certain environments (e.g., educational, research, or software development organization), programs are translated more often than they are run.

The requirements of the translator sometimes have influenced language design, but only in minor aspects. The usual rule (e.g., in Pascal) that each name be declared before being used, which allows programs to be translated in a single pass, is such an example. (The rule does constrain the Algol-like scope rules given in Chapter 3, but is justified from a readability point of view.)

The requirement of efficient execution is difficult to state without reference to a particular machine architecture. It is assumed as a design goal in this chapter, but implicitly and informally. However, it is worth mentioning that in some instances, efficient execution becomes such a prominent design goal that the programming language directly reflects aspects of the underlying architecture. This is especially true of languages for systems programming applications. Discussed below are language design criteria for machine-independent languages, that is, languages intended to run on any machine. References to machine-dependent high-level languages are given in the Further Reading section.

Machine independence itself is a language design goal whose attainment requires special attention. Many supposedly machine-independent languages turn out to contain machine-dependent features. One example is the restriction of the cardinality of Pascal sets imposed by implementations to make sets representable by a single word.

10.1.1 Writability

Programming languages assist in program design by providing constructs that make the adopted design methodology easily expressible. This means that a programmer can concentrate on understanding and solving the problem rather than the tools used for expressing solutions. The basic properties that contribute to writability can be classified as simplicity, expressiveness, orthogonality, and definiteness. These properties can hardly be defined formally, and often complement one another.

10.1.1.1 Simplicity

A language should be easy to master. All different features should be easy to learn and remember, and the effect of any combination of features should be predictable and easily understood. A typical example of a language that does not satisfy this requirement is PL/I. The number of different features that are present in the language make it difficult to master in its entirety; even a look at the size of the reference manual can be discouraging and frustrating.

It is often claimed that the programmer who cannot (and does not need to) understand the entire language can live happily with a subset. As Hoare (1973) points out, this claim is not justified. Knowledge of a subset may be sufficient for programs that work as the programmer intended; but if the program does not work properly and accidentally invokes some unknown feature of the language, then serious troubles arise for the programmer.

Simplicity is impaired if the language provides several alternative ways of specifying the same concept. Providing more than one form to denote a concept increases the size of a language and favors the development of "dialects" that use only subsets of such forms. A user expert in one dialect can have difficulties in understanding programs written in a different dialect. An example of this problem can be found in COBOL, in which both a concise, mathematical notation and an English-like notation are supported. For example, one can write either.

```
MULTIPLY WORK_HOURS BY HOURLY_PAY GIVING DAILY_PAY
```

or

```
DAILY_PAY = WORK_HOURS * HOURLY_PAY
```

PL/I provides many features that cause the same problem. For example, access to record components can be done either by full qualification (i.e., specifying all field selectors) or partial qualification (when no ambiguity arises). Declarations have default values for unspecified attributes.

C offers many examples of this problem. Adding 1 to the integer variable a can be done by any one of the following four statements.

1. $a++;$
2. $a = a + 1;$
3. $a += 1;$
4. $++a;$

Element i of array a may be accessed as $a[i]$, or as

```
*(a+i)
```

A component x of a structure S pointed at by pointer p can be retrieved by either p→x or (*p).x.

Ada suffers from similar problems. For example, parameters can be transmitted to subprograms with the keyword method, the positional method, or a mixture of the two (Section 5.2.1). Record values can be specified in a similar way. For example, a variable X of the following type T

type T **is**
  record
    A : CHARACTER;
    B : INTEGER;
  end record;

can be assigned a value by

```
X:= (B⇒3, A⇒'F');
```

or

```
X:= ('F', 3);
```

Simplicity also is impaired if the language allows different semantic concepts to be expressed by the same syntactic notation. An example is offered by the following statement in FORTRAN:

```
SUM(I,J) = I + J
```

On the one hand, this can be an assignment to an element of the array SUM if SUM has been declared as an array. On the other hand, this could be a "statement function," which defines SUM as a function that takes two parameters (I and J) and returns their sum. Thus, the meaning of this statement can change radically if the user makes the common error of forgetting to declare the array SUM. Such an error is especially possible in FORTRAN because variables are not required to be declared.

Overloading is another example. We have stated that a judicious use of overloading can be useful (Section 4.1). Arithmetic operators are usually overloaded; this reduces the number of operators and makes the language simpler.

Some languages (e.g., ALGOL 68, C^{++}, and Ada) generalize the concept of overloading to user-defined operators and subprograms. A call to an overloaded subprogram is ambiguous (and illegal) if the types and the order of actual parameters (or the names of formal parameters in the Ada keyword method) are not sufficient to identify exactly one subprogram declaration. Overloading combined with the scope rules of the language can easily make programs difficult to read.

Finally, there are cases in which different, seemingly simple language features interact to produce programs whose behavior is hard to predict. For example, consider the interaction between subprogram parameter-passing and exception handling in Ada. A subprogram raising an exception can produce different results if parameter passing is implemented by sharing or by copy. An example of combination of features that generate a behavior that is difficult to predict is illustrated by multitasking and exception handling in Ada. (We urge the reader to refer to the language manual on this point.)

Simplicity alone, however, can be a deceptive goal. For example, machine languages are usually simple, in the sense that the number of machine instructions is often rather small and each machine instruction has a definite, easily understood effect. The difficulty with machine language programming arises not strictly from the use of the language, but from its low level. The complexity in this case is not in the language, but in the difficult process of mapping a solution into elementary actions performed by the machine on unstructured data.

10.1.1.2 Expressiveness

The aboved discussion criticizes machine languages on the grounds of their low expressive power. Expressiveness of a language is a measure of how naturally a problem-solving strategy can be mapped into a program structure. One central point expounded in this book is that abstraction on data and control, along with modularization mechanisms, are the basic structuring tools used in program design. They can be used by the programmer at various levels, from the overall strategy—in the decomposition of a complex task into simpler subtasks and the design of the subtask interfaces—to the details of coding and data representation.

It is important to recognize that expressivity is a function of what is being expressed. For example, different expressive powers are needed for implementing operating systems or banking applications. If a language attempts to satisfy the needs of these different levels, it must allow the separation of these levels in the program. C is an example of a language that allows the programmer very low-level access to machine resources. It has adequate expressive power for applications that need to deal with the computer at a very low level, but provides no facilities for separating the parts of the program that work at different levels. C^{++} attempts to remedy this problem by adding a class construct to C. Pascal has no facilities for dealing with machine-level details. Modula-2 and Ada, on the other hand, not only provide expressive power at a low level, but provide facilities for hiding the low-level processing from other parts of the program that can operate at higher levels of abstraction.

Pascal is perhaps the best-known example of a simple language with a high expressive power at its chosen level of abstraction, even though it fails to provide adequate modularization mechanisms. Its rich set of control and type structures is responsible for much of its success.

10.1.1.3 Orthogonality

The appealing simplicity and expressiveness of Pascal is often impaired by its lack of orthogonality. Orthogonality means that any composition of the basic primitives should be allowed. This would achieve the greatest degree of generality, without any restrictions or special cases. An example of Pascal's lack of orthogonality is given by procedures (functions) and procedure (function) calls, which are subject to the following restrictions.

- Files cannot be passed by value.
- Components of a packed data structure cannot be passed by reference.
- Procedures and functions passed as parameters can only have by-value parameters.*
- The type of formal parameters must be stated in the procedure (or function) heading, except for procedure (or function) parameters.
- Functions only can return values of a restricted set of types; they cannot return arrays, records, sets, and files.

Another example is given by Pascal's constant declarations, such as **const** $null = 0$, that allows constants to be given a symbolic name. Pascal

---

*This problem has been removed by the ISO Standard.

does not allow pointers or structured objects (such as arrays and records) to be given a constant value. Finally, variables of an enumerated type can be initialized only by assignments and not by input values. In fact, such variables cannot be read (nor written). This often makes Pascal programs awkward. The programmer is forced to code input values of an enumerated type into, say, integers, and then to convert them to the desired enumerated type explicitly in the program.

The lack of orthogonality can be disturbing. The programmer cannot apply uniform generalizations, which might be illegal, and must often refer to the language manual to confirm the legality and correctness of what is being written.

ALGOL 68 is perhaps the best-known example of an orthogonal programming language. For example, objects of any type are permitted as parameters and results of subprograms. Identity declarations—the ALGOL 68 mechanisms for defining constants—have the form

m *id* = *e*

where **m** is a mode, *id* is an identifier, and *e* is an expression. Here **m** can be *any* (nonvoid) mode and *e* can be *any* expression whose value is assigned nonmodifiably to *id*. Even more generally, identity declarations are used to declare procedures and functions in the conventional way, as in

proc *sum* = (**real** *a, b*) **real:** *a* + *b*;

As a design goal, orthogonality should not be considered a replacement for simplicity. However, the tradeoff between the two goals is hard to quantify and appears to be a central decision in language design. It is not always clear whether it is better to have a few simple concepts with general, restriction-free composability or a larger collection of less simple concepts with several minor restrictions. In fact, the composition of orthogonal features in ALGOL 68 can lead to exceedingly hard-to-understand programs (and hard-to-implement compilers). For example, almost every ALGOL 68 construct, including those that look like conventional statements, can in principle yield a value, as the following fragment illustrates:

```
(real x, y; read ((x, y)); if x< y then a else b fi):=
b + if a:= a+1; a> b then c:= c + 1; + b
                    else c:= c - 1; a
   fi
```

The left-hand side of this assignment statement is a unit that declares local variables *x* and *y*, and yields variable *a* or *b* as its value, depending on the values read for *x* and *y* (*a, b,* and *c* are assumed to be **real** global variables). The second operand of the right-hand side expression is expressed as a conditional. The value of

```
a:= a+1; a> b
```

is the value of the final component, that is, a boolean. Similarly, the value of

```
c:= c+1; + b
```

is the real value $+b$, which can be used as a component of an expression. Orthogonality is also a distinctive feature of Smalltalk. The language is built around a limited number of concepts—classes, objects, messages—that are applied consistently and permeate the whole of the language.

According to Wirth (1975**a**), "If we try to achieve simplicity through generality of language we may end up with programs that through their very conciseness and lack of redundancy elude our limited intellectual grasp. . . . The key, then, lies not so much in minimizing the number of basic features of a language, but rather in keeping the included facilities easy to understand in all their consequences of usage and free from unexpected interactions when they are combined." The balance between orthogonality and simplicity that we need to achieve perhaps can be called "predictability." The combination of language features should not provide unexpected results; based on the knowledge of the language primitives, it should be possible to predict the effect of their various combinations.

We may say—in rather simplistic terms—that Pascal is simple and rather expressive, but not orthogonal. ALGOL 68 and Smalltalk are orthogonal and rather expressive, but not simple. Ada is expressive, but neither simple nor orthogonal. Mathematically based languages, such as functional and declarative languages, have the potential of achieving both simplicity and orthogonality because of the property of referential transparency that results in a restricted amount of interaction among language elements and the simplicity of the combining forms.

10.1.1.4 Definiteness

An important issue in the usability of a programming language is the accuracy of the description of its syntax and semantics. Vagueness is an enemy of the programmer in two important aspects. First, the programmer cannot rely completely on the language, and any attempt to find a definite response by referring to the definition results in mere frustration. Second, different implementations can choose to resolve ambiguously stated features differently, with unfortunate consequences for program portability.

Pascal was defined by a rather informal report that is attractively simple and easily readable, but leaves a considerable number of subtle questions unresolved. The syntax of the language is defined by a simple context-free BNF grammar that does not rule out an infinite number of incorrect programs. For example, the grammar does not specify that an arithmetic expression, such as $x + 3.75$, cannot be assigned to a boolean variable. Thus, syntactically correct programs are legal Pascal programs only if they satisfy an additional set of conditions described by the Report in English prose, with all the ambiguities (and omissions) that that entails. A formal axiomatic definition of Pascal has been given also. This definition, however, does not deal with procedures in their full generality and fails to answer questions about type compatibility that also are left unanswered by the Report. As a result of the standardization process, a more rigorous definition has been produced that attempts to solve these problems.

C is another example of a language whose original definition left many subtle questions unanswered. As long as there was only one compiler available for the language, the compiler could be used to resolve any ambiguities in the definition—whatever the compiler did was taken to *be* the definition. With each new C compiler, however, each implementor interpreted the semantics in a different way and thus the C compilers all behave slightly differently for some of the language constructs. There is currently an effort under way to establish an ANSI standard for C and to define its semantics precisely in the process.

ALGOL 68 is defined by an extremely precise document: the Revised Report. The syntax of the language is described by a W grammar that takes all context-sensitive aspects of the language into account. The semantic description is given in a stylized version of English that is seldom ambiguous. The ALGOL 68 definition is complete. The Report explicitly defines all checking and processing that is to be done at compile-time (including mode compatibility) and all actions to be executed at run-time (including signaling run-time errors).

The ALGOL 68 Report is generally considered to be very hard to read; in fact, the need for a more palatable language description was soon recognized and led to an official informal introduction to the language (Lindsey and Van der Meulen 1977). Unreadability, however, is perhaps more a property of formal definitions in general than of the language itself. In fact, the question of how to provide clear and simple formal descriptions of programming languages is still a matter for investigation.

As we discussed at length in Chapter 9, formal semantics will play an important role in the future. A possible scenario is that formal semantics will be used for official language definitions and more readable, informal natural language descriptions will be derived from them systematically.

10.1.2 Readability

Readability is the main factor influencing program modifiability and maintainability. Consequently, it has a considerable impact on the overall cost of software production. Readability is strictly related to writability: language features that favor program writability usually favor readability also. This is not surprising, because when writing a program, the programmer must often reread parts of it. Simplicity and expressiveness greatly encourage and assist the programmer to write self-documenting code, and even to develop a clear writing style. In particular, abstractions on data and control and program modularization give the greatest assistance in understanding the program gradually through levels of increasing detail. Thus, the distinction between readability and writability is often somewhat arbitrary.

An important aspect of readability is program documentation. The documentation explains to a human reader how a program works, so that subsequent modifications to meet changing requirements or to maintain the program, can be done successfully. There is widespread consensus that "the view that documentation is something that is added to the program after it has been commissioned seems to be wrong in principle and counter-productive in practice. Instead, documentation must be regarded as an integral part of the process of design and coding" (Hoare 1973).

Comment conventions of the programming language play an important role in program documentation. In line-oriented languages (i.e., languages in which each statement occupies a line), a comment starts either in a fixed-line position or with a special marker reserved for this purpose. On the other hand, stream-oriented languages (i.e., languages in which the text is viewed as a continuous stream of characters) introduce special delimiters, such as "{" and "}" in Pascal, to enclose comments, which can appear anywhere in the program.

This has an unfortunate and frequently occurring consequence. When the closing delimiter is forgotten by the programmer, entire pieces of program are taken as further comments and thus ignored by the translator. Even worse is the case of ALGOL 68, which uses the same symbol (**comment, co**, ¢, or #) as both opening and closing delimiters. Forgetting one of them can cause a comment to be treated as program text, and *vice-versa*. Line-oriented languages do not suffer from this problem because the end of the line is interpreted as an implicit closing delimiter. The Ada convention that a comment is implicitly terminated at the end of the line is a good solution. This approach, however, makes it less convenient to comment out blocks of text that are more than one line long.

The lexical conventions of the language have an influence on program readability. Strict restrictions on the length of identifiers, as in FORTRAN and C, can force the programmer to give cryptic names to variables and procedures. Readability is further enhanced if the underscore character '_' or a space can be used in identifiers. For example, record field identifier *spouse_name* or *spouse name* is preferable to *spousename*. Pascal forbids underscore characters and spaces inside identifiers. For readability purposes, we have largely ignored this annoying restriction in our examples. A good compromise, if the language allows upper and lower case letters, is to start each part of the name with an upper case letter, for example, *SpouseName*.

The symbols used by a language to separate lexical units in a program can have a surprising effect on readability. In most cases, blanks and line terminators are used as separators. This is not the case in FORTRAN, where blanks are insignificant and ignored by the compiler. The following example shows that the interaction of this feature with the implicit declaration rules of the language can produce uncheckable incorrect programs.

```
DO 7 I = 1.15
. . .
7 CONTINUE
```

This fragment is intended to be a loop that is iterated for variable I taking on all values in the range 1 . . 15. Unfortunately, the program contains a trivial typing error: a period is used to separate the lower and upper bounds of the loop index, instead of a comma. This seemingly innocuous error cannot be trapped statically. In fact, the compiler interprets 1.15 as a real constant and DO7I as a perfectly legal, implicitly declared real variable. The presence of a blank to separate DO, 7,and I is ignored.

Another key factor influencing program readability is the *syntax* of the language. Explicit delimiters (**if** . . . **fi**, **do** . . . **od**, **case** . . . **esac**, and so on) are preferable to the **begin** . . . **end** pairs required by Pascal for grouping statements, because they clearly indicate the purpose of the group of statements. In stream-oriented languages the syntactic structure of the program can be made evident by adopting suitable conventions for indentation. Although this is an effective method of self-documentation, it is difficult to achieve in practice. The programmer often starts writing a program with good intentions, but, as soon as the program undergoes some modifications, the initial careful indentations are lost, and the program assumes a sloppy and confused structure. Reindenting the entire program can be costly and error-prone if done manually. Some programming environments, however, contain a specialized tool (called a *pretty-printer*) that can automatically reindent the program by means of a text processing procedure.

The problem is completely avoided by so-called syntax-directed editors (SDEs). SDEs are used to create programs that are guaranteed to be correct syntactically. Programs are not created and manipulated as text. Rather, commands are given to the SDE to expand the program according to the syntax rules of the language and the resulting textual representation is displayed with appropriate indentation provided automatically.

Program readability is affected by the semantics of the language also. Throughout this text we have discussed at length language features that make programs hard to analyze, and we also have discussed language proposals that tend to minimize (or eliminate altogether) some undesirable effects. For example, procedures with parameters passed by reference and global variables can produce aliasing. Euclid imposes semantic restrictions that make aliasing illegal (and detectable).

As already mentioned, semantic restrictions make programs more readable, at the price of reduced generality. For example, a database system is intrinsically based on the fact that a recorded set of data is concurrently viewed as a set of different logical entities by different classes of users. A particular database might be viewed by a payroll program as a set of data about individual employees, but it might be viewed as a set of hierarchically organized working groups for managerial purposes. In other words, database systems are intrinsically based on side-effects and aliasing, and it is hopeless to design such systems with a language that gets rid of these features.

It is important to note that in all of the foregoing discussions of readability, the term means "readability by a person familiar with the language." Thus, the fact that the Pascal statement

$A := B + C$

may be written in COBOL as

```
ADD B TO C GIVING A
```

does not make COBOL more readable. The COBOL statement has more of an English-like syntax, which may give a nonprogrammer the false feeling of understanding the program. If we could indeed describe the entire program in pseudo-English, then that language would be more readable by all people familiar with English. There are some practical examples of this at present, but generalized solutions are still beyond the state-of-the-art. Thus the COBOL solution merely leads to verbosity and is, in fact, dangerous because it might give rise to a false sense of understanding.

Finally, readability is even more important when a team of programmers is involved, rather than one programmer alone. In a team, it is important to be able to institute conventions and reduce the amount of individual variations so that programs written by one team member can be read by another team member. As mentioned in Section 10.1.1.1, a language that allows the expression of the same concept in several ways encourages the development of local "dialects." It is inevitable that some programmers will become comfortable with one form and others with another. The two groups will have difficulty reading one another's programs. The variations, rather than encouraging creativity, hamper readability and cooperation.

10.1.3　Reliability

Needless to say, program reliability is strictly related both to writability—the easier we can write programs the more confident we are of the correctness of what we are writing—and to readability—the easier we can read programs the better we can reason about their correctness.

Reliability can be enhanced if the language makes a rigorous distinction between static and dynamic checks that must be performed on programs.

Such a distinction makes programmers fully aware of the degree of validation of the program at each step of its processing. ALGOL 68 and Ada are two examples of languages that make this distinction.

Because of the intrinsic unreliability, languages should not support features that are either impossible or too hard to check. An example of the former is provided by the parameter-passing conventions of Ada, which can give different results in the presence of aliasing. An example of the latter is given by Pascal variant records.

An attractive language design goal is to make programs statically checkable as far as possible, because run-time checks alone not only cannot certify program correctness, but also lead to slow execution speed. Some languages allow run-time checks to be turned off on request, to make programs efficiently executable after they have been thoroughly certified. This solution has its own risks, as is sharply pointed out by Hoare (1973): "It is absurd to make elaborate security checks on debugging runs, when no trust is put in the results, and then remove them in production runs, when an erroneous result could be expensive or disastrous. What would we think of a sailing enthusiast who wears his life-jacket when training on dry land but takes it off as soon as he goes to the sea?"

Reliability can be enhanced by a language that allows programs to be developed and certified one module at a time. Thoroughly certified program modules can be kept in a library and combined at any time to build new programs. The Ada separate compilation scheme, as we saw in Chapter 6, is a step in this direction.

Modifiability also contributes to reliability, because during maintenance we must be able to modify the program while retaining its reliability. The syntax of the language largely determines the ease of program modifiability. Again, the ALGOL 68 and Ada explicit delimiters have advantages over the **begin . . . end** pair required by Pascal for grouping statements. Adding a new statement to a single-statement **else**-branch or loop-body in Pascal requires adding a bracketing pair of keywords **begin** and **end**. These words are easy to forget, and their absence will produce incorrect programs. This is especially troublesome because the program will in all probability be syntactically valid.

There is a strong relationship between program reliability and rigorous definition of the language semantics. Besides affecting definiteness (Section 10.1.1.4), formal semantics provides the basis for program verification, as we saw in Chapter 9. A program verifier for the language can become a major component of the programming environment.

Finally, reliability of a language depends on the reliabilty of its implementation. The larger and more complex the language, the more difficult it is to produce reliable implementations. It is certainly easier to produce a reliable Pascal compiler than an equally reliable PL/I or Ada compiler.

10.2 A PERSPECTIVE ON LANGUAGE DESIGN

In this book, we have studied many language concepts that are instrumental in the development of programming languages. In this last chapter, we have studied some criteria that can be used to judge programming language designs. How can one use this knowledge? The following are some practical applications of what we have studied:

(a) Language Selection. One of the most important decisions to make at the start of a programming project is to select an implementation language. Knowing about existing languages and the ability to critically evaluate a language enables one to make an educated choice.

(b) Language Design. The most obvious application of what we have studied is in the actual practice of language design. Although one is seldom in a position to design a new programming language, the design of the user interface to most software systems (e.g., database systems, operating systems) usually can be viewed as a language design activity. Such a language needs to be designed according to exactly the same criteria that programming languages are designed.

(c) Language Use. In practice, we almost always have to program in a language that has many imperfections. Knowing the strengths and weaknesses of languages and the ability to spot them in a new language makes one a better user of the language. It enables one to stay away from insecure or expensive features, and to use them carefully if avoidance is not possible.

(d) Language Extension. In many practical situations, one is forced to use a language that is not suited well to the application. A common practice in these situations is to extend the language by adding new features. Knowledge of existing languages and different programming paradigms helps one in selecting the "right" extensions, and knowledge of design principles enables one to make the extensions without compromising the integrity of the base language.

SUGGESTIONS FOR FURTHER READING AND BIBLIOGRAPHIC NOTES

Much of the material presented in this chapter has been inspired by Hoare (1973) and Wirth (1975a). Language design also is studied in (Richard and Ledgard 1977). The ALGOL 68 and Pascal designs are compared by Tanenbaum (1978). Hoare and Wirth (1973) give a formal definition of Pascal. The ALGOL 68 Revised Report provides a formal definition of the language. The development of Ada illustrates quite well the relation between programming language requirements and programming language design (Fisher 1978). The U.S. Department of Defense set down the requirements in a series of documents that were reviewed extensively by the Armed Forces, industrial organizations, universities, and foreign military departments. The culmination of this process was the Steelman Report (DOD 1978). Ada was chosen among a set of languages designed to meet such requirements. The Ada preliminary design (ACM-SIGPLAN 1979) subsequently was reviewed, and the present standard appears in (ANSI-MIL 1983). (Kahn et al. 1980) is a preliminary report on the formal definition of the language. Work on a complete formal definition of Ada is presently in progress within the Multi-Annual Programme sponsored by the Commission of the European Communities. Hoare (1981) discusses the author's experience in the design and implementation of programming languages and presents an initial, critical evaluation of many features of Ada. Wichman (1984a), Parnas (1984), and Wichman (1984b) also assess the Ada language.

This chapter has studied the design of machine-independent high-level programming languages. In several system software applications, absolute independence from the machine cannot be achieved with acceptable efficiency. One solution to this problem consists of augmenting assembly languages with a few high-level constructs (e.g., control structures). This solution is well illustrated by PL360 (Wirth 1968) and several languages described in (van der Poel and Maarsen 1974). More recent solutions provide truly high-level languages for systems software applications. However, such languages provide limited escapes from the high-level language into a machine-dependent domain. Bliss, C, Mesa, Euclid, and Modula-2 follow this general philosophy.

Brinch Hansen (1980a and b) argues that even Pascal is not simple enough and many features have been either eliminated or greatly simplified in order to design Edison. Brinch Hansen (1980c) gives examples of Edison programs.

EXERCISES

10.1 Some programming languages permit the use of overloading. Give examples of overloading in Pascal, ALGOL 68, and Ada (Ada is particularly supportive of overloading). Discuss the effects of overloading on both readability and writability.

10.2 Give examples of nonorthogonal Ada features.

10.3 Give examples of automatic type conversions in programming languages. What is the effect of these conversions on readability and writability?

10.4 Read and criticize Hoare (1981).

10.5 Read and criticize Wichman (1984a), Parnas (1984), and Wichman (1984b).

A Glossary of Selected Programming Languages

ADA

Overview

Ada has been designed mainly to support embedded computer applications with real-time and concurrent requirements, numerical applications, and systems programming.

Data Types

Ada provides built-in types and constructors. The precision of numeric data can be controlled by the programmer. Ada distinguishes carefully between static and dynamic properties of types. Several insecurities of Pascal types have been eliminated. The package construct (see below under "Programming in the Large") can be used to define (generic) abstract data types.

Control Structures

Ada provides Pascal-like control structures. It provides a specialized **exit** statement to exit from loops as well as the **goto** statement. The language also provides a rich set of unit-level control structures: namely, procedure and function calls, exceptions, and concurrent activations.

Program Correctness

Ada retains several harmful features (such as **goto** and side-effects). Aliasing is termed illegal, but erroneous Ada programs can remain undetected. A preliminary formal definition of Ada is described in (Kahn et al. 1980). Other efforts in this area are in progress.

Programming in the Large

Besides subprograms and functions, packages are the major program structuring units in Ada. Packages collect related declarations and provide initialization. Several procedures also may be packaged together. Units can be nested, à la ALGOL. They also can be separately compiled according to a partial ordering rule.

Official Definition

(ANSI/MIL 1983), which supersedes previous definitions, such as (ACM-SIGPLAN 1979).

Important Papers

(Fisher 1978), (DOD 1978), (ACM-SIGPLAN 1979), (DOD 1980), (ACM-SIGPLAN 1980), (Kahn et al. 1980), (Computer 1981), (IEEE-Software 1985), (ACM-Ada 1985). ACM publishes the periodical Ada Letters, which contains most current information about the language and its developments.

Textbooks

(Barnes 1982), (Gehani 1983),(Habermann and Perry 1983).

ALGOL 60

Overview

ALGOL 60 (**Algo**rithmic **L**anguage 19**60**) is an algebraic language for scientific computations. It has influenced the design of almost every language since 1960.

Data Types

The type of all data must be explicitly declared. Besides the built-in types, **integer**, **real** and **boolean**, the language provides dynamic arrays. User-defined types are not supported. ALGOL 60 provides semistatic and semi-dynamic variables.

Control Structures

ALGOL 60 provides **if-then-else** and counting and condition-driven loops. **Goto** and multiway branching are also provided. Procedure calls comprise the only unit-level control structure. Recursive calls are permitted.

Program Correctness

The language provides several harmful features. The **goto** is available. Procedure and function calls may generate side-effects, thanks to call by name (which is the default) and access to global variables. The syntax of the language has been defined formally, but its semantics is described only in informal English prose.

Programming in the Large

Procedures (and blocks) are the only abstraction mechanisms provided by ALGOL 60. Programs are tree-structured, and inner units automatically inherit outer declarations. The nested scope structure was introduced by ALGOL 60.

Official Definition

(Naur 1963).

Important Papers

(Knuth 1967), (Perlis 1978), (Nauer 1978).

Textbooks

(Dijkstra 1962); see also (Sammet 1969).

Implementation Issues

(Randell and Russell 1964), (Gries 1971), (Wichmann 1973).

ALGOL 68

Overview

ALGOL 68 was designed to communicate algorithms, to execute them efficiently on a variety of computers, and to aid in teaching them to students.

Data Types

ALGOL 68 provides built-in types and constructors to build new types. The language does not provide abstract data types. Type compatibility is defined by structural equivalence. The language provides for extensive automatic type conversions (coercions). The language is strongly typed.

Control Structures

ALGOL 68 provides **if-then-else**, **case**, generalized loop, and **goto**. Procedure calls govern the flow of control units; procedures may be passed as parameters. The language supports concurrent execution and provides semaphores for synchronization.

Program Correctness

The language provides the **goto** statement and permits (controlled and limited) side-effects. In the official language definition, the semantics is defined partly formally, partly in seminformal English (van Wijngaarden et al. 1976). The semantics of ALGOL 68 also has been defined axiomatically in Schwartz (1978**b**), in an attempt to aid program verification.

Programming in the Large

The only abstraction capabilities are blocks, procedures, and user-defined operators. Programs are tree-structured and inner modules automatically inherit outer declarations. The official language definition does not specify a standard separate compilation facility.

Important Papers

(Branquart et al. 1971), (Lindsay 1972), (Tanenbaum 1976), (Valentine 1974), (Tanenbaum 1978).

Textbooks

(Lindsay and van der Meulen 1977), (Pagan 1976).

Implementation Issues

(Peck 1970), (Hill 1976), (Branquart et al. 1976).

APL

Overview

APL (**A Programming Language**) has been designed as a notation for expressing mathematical algorithms concisely. APL is supported by an interactive programming system that has contributed to its popularity among scientific programmers who use the computer as a powerful desk calculator, and among other classes of users.

Data Types

APL is a dynamically typed language. Built-in types are numeric, character, and boolean. It provides a rich set of operations on arrays, which eliminate the need for element-by-element manipulation for most array operations. Arrays are the only aggregate-structuring method.

Control Structures

APL provides very powerful composition rules for operations, and APL programs often take the form of one-liners. The language provides only rudimentary control structures, including the jump.

Program Correctness

Program readability suffers from dynamic binding. Interactive execution provides a flexible testing support, which is particularly valuable for programs that are not too large.

Programming in the Large

APL programs can be decomposed into subprograms. Nonlocal referencing is based on dynamic scope binding, which can hamper readability and modifiability of large programs. APL is supported by a complete programming system.

Official Definition

(Iverson 1962).

Important Papers

(Falkoff and Iverson 1978), (Iverson 1979), (Iverson 1980).

Textbooks

(Polivka and Pakin 1975).

Implementation Issues

(Breed and Lathwell 1968).

BASIC

Overview

BASIC (**B**eginner's **A**ll-purpose **S**ymbolic **I**nstruction **C**ode) was invented by J. G. Kemeny and T. E. Kurtz in the mid-1960s as an educational tool. It has a simple algebraic structure and is supported by a simple interpretive implementation. The language became extremely popular with the advent of personal and home computers.

Data structures, control structures, and programming in the large

BASIC provides limited control and data structures, and is mainly intended for development of small-size individual applications. The language is presently not standardized, except for a minimal subset (ANSI 1978a). Other standardization efforts are underway. At present, however, the language exists in many dialects.

Textbooks

(Albrecht et al. 1978). Kemeny and Kurtz (1985) discuss the principles underlying the design of BASIC.

BLISS

Overview

Bliss is a high-level, expression-oriented language for writing systems software. It is presently used for this purpose on DEC machines.

Data Types

Data have no types. Data structures are defined not by their storage layout, but in terms of the algorithm used to access an element of the structure.

Control Structures

Bliss is a block-structured, **goto**less, expression-oriented language. Every executable construct is an expression and computes a value. Expressions may be concatenated with semicolons to form sequences. Bliss also provides conditional statements, loop statements, **leave** statements (for exit from loops), and subprograms (called **routines**). It also provides features for exception handling.

Program Correctness

Bliss provides advantages over assembly languages, which would otherwise be used for the same applications. Formal program correctness, however, was not a design goal.

Programming in the Large

Bliss has a conventional ALGOL-like structure. It has both blocks and routines. Routines can be external.

Official Definition

(Wulf et al. 1972).

Important Papers

(Wulf et al. 1971).

Implementation Issues

(Wulf et al. 1975).

C

Overview

C was developed for writing systems programs for the PDP-11. It has been generalized and implemented on many computers, large and small. It is supported by a full set of tools in the UNIX operating system. A portable subset has been defined. C has become an extremely popular language for systems programming, especially under UNIX. A superset of C, called C^{++}, has been developed at AT&T (Stroustrup 1984).

Data Types

The primitive data types can be combined to form arrays, structures, and unions (similar to ALGOL 68 **union**). The precision of integers and reals can be specified. Type conversions are applied freely and automatically. Pointers are qualified, although type checking in general is quite lax.

Control Structures

Repeat, while, and for loops are provided, with possibility of exit from loop (break) or skipping the rest of the current loop iteration (continue). A limited form of the case statement and the general goto are also available. Function and procedure calls are the only unit-level control structures.

Program Correctness

No special attention has been paid to this issue. The goto, pointer, side-effects, and automatic type conversion are all present. Readability can be a problem because of the existence of many different ways of stating the same concept and the possibility of producing extremely terse code. The syntax of the type declarations is rather cryptic. The definition is informal and leaves many questions unanswered.

Programming in the Large

Functions and procedures are the only program-structuring mechanisms. They may not be nested but may include nested blocks. Procedures and functions may be compiled separately, but type checking across modules is not done by the compiler.

Official Definition

(Kernighan and Ritchie 1978). An ANSI Standard is under development.

Important Papers

(Feuer and Gehani 1982).

Textbooks

(Kernighan and Ritchie 1978), (Zahn 1979), (Plum 1983), (Gehani 1985).

Implementation Issues

(Johnson 1978).

CLU

Overview

CLU was designed to support a programming methodology based on the recognition of abstractions.

Data Types

CLU provides built-in types and constructors. The **cluster** construct allows the programmer to define abstract data types. Data objects are uniformly accessed via pointers. An assignment changes the reference bound to a name, rather than changing the value in the cell referenced.

Control Structures

CLU provides conventional predefined statement-level control structures. There is no **goto**, only a **break** statement to exit from loops. In addition, the programmer can define new looping control structures via iterators. CLU provides exception handling facilities.

Program Correctness

Several harmful features, such as **goto** and global variables, are absent from CLU. However, assignment by sharing encourages heavy use of side-effects. The semantics of CLU is defined in informal English prose. Verification is not explicitly addressed, although it is claimed that CLU supports it.

Programming in the Large

Iterators, procedures, and clusters provide a suitable basis for modular system decomposition. Procedures and iterators can be declared within clusters, but there is no other nesting. Iterators, procedures, and clusters can be compiled separately, in any order. When a module is compiled, only the interfaces of used modules need to have been compiled already.

Official Definition

(Liskov et al. 1978), (Liskov et al. 1981).

Important Papers

(Liskov and Zilles 1974), (Liskov 1974), (Liskov and Zilles 1975), (Liskov et al. 1977), (Liskov and Snyder 1979).

Implementation Issues

(Atkinson, et al. 1978).

COBOL

Overview

COBOL (**CO**mmon **B**usiness **O**riented **L**anguage) is a language for business applications. COBOL programs usually perform very simple computations on large amounts of data. It is perhaps the most widely used language today, but it did not have a significant influence on later language designs. Very often, COBOL applications interact with a database.

Data Types

Data are described in a DATA DIVISION. Most data are grouped as components of records, which are stored in a file. COBOL provides instructions for handling records and files. The types of individual record components and simple variables must be declard. Numbers and character strings of programmer-specified precision are the basic types.

Control Structures

COBOL provides a restricted form of IF-THEN-ELSE, the GOTO statement, and a PERFORM statement that serves both as a loop statement and a unit call. The PERFORM provides control transfer to the unit and return from the unit without changing environment. The early versions of COBOL did not provide true subprograms. This is also true for many present implementations of COBOL subsets.

Program Correctness

This was not an issue in the design of COBOL. To facilitate the use of the language, COBOL introduces a natural-language-style programming. Programs easily become verbose and errors are difficult to spot. The syntax of COBOL is defined formally; its semantics is not.

Programming in the Large

A COBOL program consists of an IDENTIFICATION DIVISION, which identifies the programmer and the program; and ENVIRONMENT DIVISION, which specifies the hardware configuration and the relation between logical and physical files; a DATA DIVISION, which specifies the structure of data; and a PROCEDURE DIVISION, which specifies the algorithms that operate on data. No real modularity can be achieved within the PROCEDURE DIVISION.

Official Definition

(ANSI 1968), (ANSI 1974).

Important Papers

(Sammet 1978).

Textbooks

(Brown 1977). The essentials of COBOL can be found in (Rosen 1967) and (Sammet 1969).

CONCURRENT PASCAL

Overview

Concurrent Pascal is a language for writing structured concurrent programs—in particular, operating systems. It is an extension of Pascal.

Data Types

The language provides the types of Pascal and **class** types to define abstract data types. **Process** types and **monitor** types are the basic tools for describing concurrency. **Class** types, **process** types, and **monitor** types are collectively called system types.

Control Structures

The language provides the statement-level control structures of Pascal. In addition, a **process** type can repeat the execution of a set of statements forever by a **cycle** statement. Unit-level control structures are procedure and function calls, as well as concurrent activation of processes (by an **init** statement).

Program Correctness

The language supports the writing of well-structured, readable concurrent programs. The language supports extensive static checks. In particular, it guarantees statically that no deadlock (processes blocking each other) ever occurs. The language is amenable to program verification (Hoare 1974), (Howard 1976a), (Howard 1976b).

Programming in the Large

A program consists of nested definitions of system types. The outermost system type is an anonymous process (initial process). The initial process is instantiated after the program is loaded; in turn, it initializes the other components. The language supports modular system decomposition but relies on an ALGOL-like tree structure.

Official Definition

(Brinch Hansen 1975).

Important Papers

(Hoare 1974), (Howard 1976a), (Howard 1976b).

Textbooks

(Brinch Hansen 1977).

Implementation Issues

(Hartmann 1977).

EUCLID

Overview

Euclid is a language designed for writing verifiable system programs.

Data Types

Euclid's type structure is based on Pascal, but several unsafe features of Pascal are absent. Type compatibility is rigorously defined. The tag field of variant records cannot be assigned by itself. Pointers are bound to collections. The language is strongly typed, but the programmer can explicitly override type checking at compile-time, if need be. Abstract data types can be implemented by modules (see below under "Programming in the Large").

Control Structures

Euclid provides Pascal-like control structures. There is no **goto**, but an **exit** statement is provided to exit from loops. The **module** construct can be used to define new looping control structures (similar to CLU's iterators). Unit-level control structures are procedure and function calls.

Program Correctness

Euclid does not provide **goto**. Functions cannot produce side-effects. Syntactically correct programs allow potential aliasing, and the compiler generates legality assertions that must be proven to certify program correctness. The Euclid system includes a verifier. Both user-supplied assertions and compiler-generated legality assertions must be proven by the verifier.

Programming in the Large

Besides procedures and functions, Euclid provides a **module** construct that can be used to define both control and data abstractions. Modules are similar to Ada **packages**. They can be nested, but there is control over imported global entities. External modules can be compiled separately.

Official Language Definition

(Lampson et al. 1977).

Important Papers

(Popek et al. 1977), (Elliott and Barnard 1978), (London et al. 1978), (Wortman 1979).

Implementation Issues

(Holt et al. 1978**b**).

FORTRAN

Overview

FORTRAN (**For**mula **Tran**slator) is a language for scientific and numeric applications. The language has been designed with the primary goal of execution efficiency. FORTRAN 66 (ANSI 1966) has been superseded by FORTRAN 77 (ANSI 1978b) as a standard. Work is underway on FORTRAN 8X.

Data Types

FORTRAN provides booleans, integer, real (both single and double precision), and complex numbers. Fixed-sized array is the only aggregate constructor. Data may be either explicitly or implicitly declared. User-defined types are not supported. FORTRAN 77 supports strings; FORTRAN 66 does not.

Control Structures

FORTRAN provides logical IF statements (with a single-statement THEN branch in the case of FORTRAN 66.), three-way branch, counting loops, and GOTOs. Subprogram calls are the only allowed unit-level control structures. Recursive calls are not allowed.

Program Correctness

FORTRAN provides several harmful features. The GOTO must be used often, because of the lack of suitable control structures. It can be misused easily. Aliasing is possible (via EQUIVALENCE). Subprograms may generate side-effects by manipulating actual parameters (transmitted by reference) or global variables (specified by COMMON). The language is defined in informal English prose.

Programming in the Large

FORTRAN supports flat program structures (i.e., no nested units). A program is a collection of external subprograms that may share COMMON data. Subprograms may be compiled independently and assembled to construct a system. Intermodule type checking is usually not provided.

Official Definition

(ANSI 1966), (ANSI 1971), (ANSI 1978b).

Important Papers

(Backus 1957) (Backus 1978b), (Brainerd 1978).

Textbooks

(Meissner and Organick 1984). The essentials of FORTRAN can be found in (Rosen 1967) and (Sammet 1969).

Implementation Issues

(Gries 1971).

GYPSY

Overview

Gypsy is a language designed for supporting specification, coding, and verification of systems software, with particular emphasis on communications software.

Data Types

Gypsy provides built-in types and constructors. The language does not provide explicit pointer variables. Instead, it has some fully dynamic data types, such as sequences and mappings. A Gypsy unit can contain a type definition, and an access list may specify the legal accesses (see below under "Programming in the Large"). It is thus possible to implement abstract data types.

Control Structures

Gypsy provides Pascal-like control statements. There is no **goto**, but there is a **leave** statement to exit from loops. Unit-level control structures are procedure and function calls, exceptions, and concurrent invocations.

Program Correctness

The language does not provide a **goto** statement. Functions cannot modify actual parameters. There are no global variables or pointers. Most harmful features have thus been excluded. A program verifier is an integral part of the Gypsy system.

Programming in the Large

Program units are routine (procedure, function, or process), type, and constant definition. Units are not nested, and each is provided with an access list that states the access rights to the unit. There are no global variables. Units are verified and compiled separately.

Official Language Definition

(Ambler et al. 1976).

Important Papers

(Ambler et al. 1977), (Good 1977), (Good 1985).

Implementation Issues

(Good et al. 1978)

LISP

Overview

LISP (**Lis**t **P**rocessing) is a symbolic, functional language. It is used in most applications of artificial intelligence. There are several dialects that augment LISP with nonfunctional features.

Data Types

LISP has two types of objects: atoms and lists. It provides functions to operate on lists. LISP programs are uniformly mapped into list structures; the evaluation of a LISP program can be described by an interpreter (function EVAL) that transforms into values a list structure representing a program.

Control Structures

Pure LISP provides neither assignment statements nor GOTO statements. It is a purely functional language, heavily based on recursion. Dialects of LISP provide both assignment and GOTO.

Program Correctness

LISP was the first language to be designed upon a firm mathematical basis (McCarthy 1963**a**), (McCarthy 1963**b**).

Programming in the Large

This is not an issue in pure LISP. Many existing LISP systems support program development with a variety of tools. Common LISP provides modules.

Official Definition

(McCarthy et al. 1965). LISP dialects are described by (Moon 1974), (Teitelman 1975), (Wilensky 1984). (Steele 1984) describes the proposed standard Common LISP.

Important Papers

(McCarthy 1960), (McCarthy 1963a), (McCarthy 1963b), (McCarthy 1978), (Sandewall 1978).

Textbooks

(Allen 1978), (Winston and Horn 1984), (Wilensky 1984), (Steele 1984), (Brooks 1985).

Implementation Issues

(McCarthy et al. 1965), (Henderson 1980), (Steele and Sussman 1980).

MESA

Overview

Mesa is one component of a programming environment aimed at developing and maintaining a wide range of system and application programs.

Data Types

Mesa provides conventional built-in types, enumerations, subranges, and constructors (array, record, record with variant, pointer). Mesa is strongly typed, but the programmer may explicitly disable type checking. The language provides several automatic type conversions. Mesa modules (see below under "Programming in the Large") support the definition of abstract data types.

Control Structures

Statement-level control structures include **if** statement, **select** statement (much like a Pascal **case**), loop statements, loop exit, and **goto**. Unit-level control structures include subprogram calls, coroutine activations, exception conditions, and concurrent activation (interprocess communication is provided by monitors).

Program Correctness

The language provides safe features but allows the use of harmful features, such as **goto** and elimination of type checking. The language is defined in informal English prose and does not address verification issues explicitly.

Programming in the Large

Mesa provides the **module** construct to encapsulate abstractions. Each module has a definition, which specifies the module's interface, and a program, which contains actual data and executable code. Definitions have no existence at run-time, but they allow programs to be compiled separately with full type checking. Programs can be loaded and interconnected to form complete systems, via commands written in the Mesa configuration language.

Official Definition

(Mitchell et al. 1979).

Important Papers

(Geschke and Mitchell 1975), (Lampson et al. 1974), (Geschke et al. 1977), (Sweet 1985). (Teitelman 1985) describes an integration of Mesa and LISP.

MODULA-2

Overview

Modula-2 is a language for programming dedicated computer systems, including process control on smaller machines. The language provides limited visibility of the underlying hardware. The language is based strongly on Pascal. Modula-2 is an evolution of Modula. In many aspects, the two languages differ considerably.

Data Types

Modula-2 adopts most data-type concepts of Pascal. Abstract data types can be defined by the **module** construct.

Control Structures

Modula-2 adopts the Pascal control structures with minor variations. A loop exist construct is provided. Modula-2 provides procedures and functions. Instead of being built into the language, many facilities are provided by predefined system modules. Low-level primitives for process abstraction are provided by the module SYSTEM. Higher-level abstractions can be added on top of them.

Program Correctness

The language is intended to cover applications for which assembly language traditionally is used. Modula-2 considerably improves the readability of such programs and supports a variety of static checks. Wirth (1977) discusses the use of Modula (Modula-2's ancestor) in proving correctness of real-time programs.

Programming in the Large

Modula-2 retains Pascal-like block structure. In addition, it provides the construct **module**. A module is a collection of declarations and an initialization part. A module can explicitly import entities from, and export entities to, the rest of the program.

Official Definition

(Wirth 1982).

Important Papers

(Wirth 1976**b**), (Wirth 1976**c**), (Wirth 1977), (Wirth 1979).

Implementation Issues

(Wirth 1976**d**)—it refers to Modula.

PASCAL

Overview

Pascal was originally designed by N. Wirth as a tool for disciplined programming. The language has met with an enormous success, and there are now implementations on most machines, including microprocessors. Pascal has influenced nearly all recent languages.

Data Types

Pascal provides built-in types, enumeration types, subranges, and constructors (record, record with variants, arrays, file, pointer, and set) to construct new types. Type compatibility was originally not defined rigorously. Pascal does not provide abstract data types.

Control Structures

Pascal provides **if-then-else**, **case**, **while-do**, **repeat-until**, **for** loops, and **goto**. Procedure and function calls are the only unit-level control structures.

Program Correctness

Pascal permits side effects and provides the **goto** statement. The semantics of the language has been defined axiomatically (Hoare and Wirth 1973), but axioms for full Pascal have not been developed.

Programming in the Large

Pascal provides only procedures and functions as abstraction capabilities: Programs are tree-structured and inner modules automatically inherit outer declarations. The official language definition does not specify a standard separate compilation facility.

Official Definition

(Jensen and Wirth 1975) is the official Report. (ISO 1982) is the approved international standard. The Report has been revised consistently with (ISO 1982) in 1985.

Important Papers

(Wirth 1971**a**), (Hoare and Wirth 1973), (Wirth 1975**b**), (Habermann 1973), (Lecarme and Desjardins 1975), (Welsh et al. 1977), (Tennent 1978), (Tanenbaum 1978), (Feuer and Gehani 1982).

Textbooks

(Wirth 1973), (Wirth 1976a), (Findlay and Watt 1978), (Alagić and Arbib 1978), (Moffat 1984).

Implementation Issues

(Wirth 1971**c**), (Ammann 1974), (Nori et al. 1976).

PL/I

Overview

PL/I (Programming Language I) represents an attempt to incorporate into a unique multipurpose language the most notable features of earlier languages (FORTRAN, ALGOL 60, and COBOL).

Data Types

PL/I provides built-in types for which a variety of attributes may be specified (e.g., base, precision). Aggregate constructors include structures (record), arrays, and pointers. Data may be allocated statically (à la FORTRAN), automatically (à la ALGOL 60), or explicitly.

Control Structures

PL/I provides IF_THEN_ELSE, WHILE_DO, counting loop, the case statement (SELECT), and GOTO. Unit-level control structures include subprogram call, exception handling, and multitasking (for concurrent units).

Program Correctness

This is not an express goal of PL/I. The language provides several harmful features. The GOTO is permitted; pointers are not typed and may be left dangling; subprogram calls may generate side-effects; aliasing is permitted. Educational subsets of the language supporting good programming practices have been defined also: PL/C in (Conway and Gries 1979); PLCS in (Conway 1978); and SP/k in (Conway et al. 1977). The language has been defined formally by researchers at the IBM Vienna Laboratory. The method is known as Vienna Definition Language: (Lucas and Walk 1969), (Wegner 1972). PL/C has been defined formally also; a program verifier is described in (Constable and O'Donnell 1978).

Programming in the Large

A program may be structured à la FORTRAN as a set of external subprograms. Each subprogram may be structured à la ALGOL 60 as a set of nested units.

Official Definition

(ANSI 1976).

Important Papers

(Lucas and Walk 1969), (Radin 1978).

Textbooks

(Conway and Gries 1979). The essentials can be found in (Sammet 1969).

Implementation Issues

(Abrahams 1979).

PROLOG

Overview

PROLOG (**Prog**ramming in **Log**ic) is a logic programming language. It was developed by a group headed by A. Colmerauer at the University of Marseilles, France, as a tool for natural-language processing. It is now widely available and used in A.I. applications, especially expert systems.

PROLOG has become very popular in the last few years, in part because of the increasing practical interest in A.I. applications, and in part because of the much-publicized Japanese Fifth Generation Computer Project.

Data Types

PROLOG elementary data types are atoms (i.e., uninterpreted strings of symbols) and numbers. Complex data structures can be constructed using lists and record-like structures. No abstraction and protection mechanisms exist in the language. PROLOG programs are just like any PROLOG data structure and therefore can be manipulated by PROLOG itself.

Control Structures

PROLOG does not provide any control structures in the common sense. Control is built-in into the behavior of the PROLOG interpreter, which performs a depth-first search with backtracking. This built-in strategy can be affected by using extra-logical primitives (**cut** and **fail**).

Program Correctness

A logic programming language is essentially declarative: it specifies a system, rather than describe an algorithmic solution. This makes the correctness problem more manageable. Also, one may use the underlying theory of logic to reason about programs.

Programming in the Large

This is a serious problem, because most currently available PROLOG systems lack modularization mechanisms. M-PROLOG provides a module construct for developing large applications.

Several support environments are currently being designed.

Official Definition

No "official" definition exists yet, but (Clocksin and Mellish 1981) is a *de-facto* standard.

Important papers

(Roussel 1975), (Kowalski 1981), (Colmerauer et al. 1983), (Kowalski 1985).

Textbooks

(Clocksin and Mellish 1981), (Sterling and Shapiro 1986).

SIMULA 67

Overview

SIMULA 67 is a general-purpose language whose main application area has been simulation.

Data Types

Besides built-in types and arrays, SIMULA 67 provides classes for defining abstract data types. Class instances may exist simultaneously at run-time. They can be assigned by reference (:-), and the dot notation provides access to individual components. The class construct has inspired many recent languages for object-oriented programming.

Control Structures

Besides conventional ALGOL-like statement-level control structures and procedure calls, SIMULA 67 provides coroutines to simulate concurrent execution.

Program Correctness

SIMULA 67 provides **goto** statement and side-effects that hamper program readability. The semantics is described in informal English. Program verification was not an issue in the design of SIMULA 67.

Programming in the Large

Procedural abstractions are supported by SIMULA 67. Data abstraction can be implemented (with self-discipline) by classes. Class prefixing allows the definition of hierarchical program structures. Overall, SIMULA 67 preserves the ALGOL-like tree structure of programs. The language does not define an official separate compilation scheme.

Official Definition

(Dahl et al. 1970).

Important Papers

(Ichbiah and Morse 1972), (Dahl and Hoare 1972), (Nygaard and Dahl 1978).

Textbooks

(Birtwistle et al. 1973).

Implementation Issues

(Dahl and Myhrhaug 1969).

SMALLTALK

Overview

Smalltalk is an object-oriented language. Systems are modeled as a set of objects that can communicate with one another by sending messages. The language evolved through several revisions, including Smalltalk-76 and Smalltalk-80, which is the version currently available through Xerox Corp.

Data Types

Besides providing elementary types and aggregate constructors, Smalltalk allows one to build abstract types using the class construct. Classes can be organized hierarchically and instantiated dynamically. Variables are bound to types dynamically, and type checking is done dynamically.

Control Structures

The language provides built-in control structures and can be easily extended with additional control structures via classes.

Program Correctness

This is not a specific issue in Smalltalk. The language and its support environment encourage a highly interactive run-and-modify development style rather than a more systematic development based on formal assessment of correctness.

Programming in the Large

Smalltalk provides modularization facilities through classes. Also, it is highly integrated with a friendly support environment. This results in a powerful workstation for personal use. There is no specific support for large, multiperson projects.

Official language definition and Implementation Issues

(Goldberg and Robson 1980).

Important Papers

(Kay 1977), (Ingalls 1978), and the collection of papers in (BYTE 1981).

SNOBOL4

Overview

SNOBOL4 (**S**tring **O**riented Sym**bo**lic **L**anguage) is a string manipulation language. Its major application lies in areas in which character string data must be processed in complex ways, for example, in processing natural language texts.

Data Types

SNOBOL4 is a dynamically typed language. It provides powerful pattern-matching operations on strings. It also supports the definition of new data types. Through its TABLE data type, it provides for a form of associative retrieval. Strings generated at run-time may be treated as programs and executed.

Control Structures

Statement-level control structures are rather simple. The most complex control structures arise in the control of pattern matching. Subprograms may be called recursively. The language supports the handling of exceptional conditions. Exception handling is basically used for tracing during program debugging.

Program Correctness

Dynamic binding hampers program readability if programs are large. The trace facility helps in program testing. A formal definition of much of the semantics of SNOBOL4 is described in (Tennent 1973).

Programming in the Large

SNOBOL4 programs can be decomposed into subprograms. Subprogram definition, however, is strictly a run-time operation. This is another example of the highly dynamic bindings established by the language. Dynamic binding makes it difficult to produce large programs.

Official Definition

(Griswold et al. 1971).

Important Papers

(Griswold 1978), (Tennent 1973).

Textbooks

(Griswold et al. 1971), (Griswold and Griswold 1973).

Implementation Issues

(Griswold 1972) describes a portable implementation of SNOBOL4.

Bibliography

(ABRAHAMS 1979)
P. Abrahams. "The CIMS PL/I Compiler," **Proceedings SIGPLAN Symp. on Compiler Construction—SIGPLAN Notices 14** 8 (Aug. 1979).

(ACM-Ada 1985)
Proceedings of the Ada International Conference. J. G. P. Barnes and G. A. Fisher, Jr., eds., **Ada Letters 5** 2 (Sept.–Oct. 1985).

(ACM-CS 1974)
ACM Computing Surveys, special issue: **Programming 6** 4 (Dec. 1974).

(ACM-SIGPLAN 1976)
Proceedings of Conference on Data: Abstraction, Definition and Structure. SIGPLAN Notices 8 2 (1976).

(ACM-SIGPLAN 1977)
Proceedings ACM Conference on Language Design for Reliable Software. SIGPLAN Notices 12 3 (March 1977).

(ACM-SIGPLAN 1978)
ACM-SIGPLAN History of Programming Languages Conference. SIGPLAN Notices 13 8 (Aug. 1978).

(ACM-SIGPLAN 1979)
J. D. Ichbiah, J. C. Heliard, O. Roubine, J. G. P. Barnes, B. Krieg-Bruckner, and B. A. Wichmann. "Preliminary Ada Reference Manual" and "Rationale for the Design of the Ada Programming Language." **SIGPLAN Notices 14** 6, Parts A and B (June 1979).

(ACM-SIGPLAN 1980)
Proceedings ACM-SIGPLAN Symposium on the Ada Programming Language. SIGPLAN Notices 15 11 (Nov. 1980).

(ACM-SIGPLAN 1985)
Proceedings of the ACM SIGPLAN '85 Symposium on Language Issues in Programming Environments. SIGPLAN Notices 20 7 (July 1985).

375

(ACM SIGSOFT-SIGPLAN 1984)

Proceedings of a Symposium on Practical Software Development Environments, Pittsburgh, April 1984.

(AHO ET AL. 1985)

A. V. Aho, R. Sethi, J. D. Ullman. **Compilers: Principles, Techniques, and Tools.** Reading, MA.: Addison-Wesley, 1986.

(ALAGIĆ AND ARBIB 1978)

S. Alagić and M. A. Arbib. **The Design of Well-Structured and Correct Programs.** New York: Springer Verlag, 1978.

(ALFORD 1977)

M. W. Alford. "A Requirements Engineering Methodology for Real-Time Processing Requirements." **IEEE Transactions on Software Engineering SE-3** 1 (Jan. 1977): 60–68.

(ALLEN 1978)

J. Allen. **Anatomy of LISP.** New York: McGraw-Hill, 1978.

(AMBLER ET AL. 1976)

A. Ambler, D. I. Good, and W. F. Burger. "Report on the Language Gypsy." Univ. of Texas at Austin, **ICSCA-CMP-1** (Aug. 1976).

(AMBLER ET AL. 1977)

A. L. Ambler, D. I. Good, J. C. Browne, W. F. Burger, R. M. Cohen, C. G. Hoch, and R. E. Wells. "Gypsy: A Language for Specification and Implementation of Verifiable Programs." **Proceedings ACM Conference on Language Design for Reliable Software—SIGPLAN Notices 12** 3 (March 1977): 1–10.

(AMMANN 1974)

U. Ammann. "The Method of Structured Programming Applied to the Development of a Compiler." In **Proceedings ACM Int. Comp. Symp.**, eds. A. Gunther et al. Amsterdam: North-Holland, 1974.

(ANSI 1966)

American National Standard FORTRAN (ANS X3.9-1966). New York: American National Standards Institute, 1966.

(ANSI 1968)

USA Standard COBOL (ANS X3.23-1968). New York: American National Standards Institute, 1968.

(ANSI 1971)

"Clarification of FORTRAN Standard—Second Report." **Comm. ACM 14** 10, (Oct. 1971): 628–642.

(ANSI 1974)

American National Standard Programming Language COBOL (ANSI X3.23-1974). New York: American National Standard Institute, 1974.

(ANSI 1976)

American National Standard Programming Language PL/I (ANS X3.53-1976). New York: American National Standards Institute, 1976.

(ANSI 1978A)

American National Standard Programming Language Basic (ANS X3.60-1978). New York: American National Standards Institute, 1978.

(ANSI 1978B)

American National Standard Programming Language FORTRAN (ANS X3.9-1978). New York: American National Standards Institute, 1978.

(ANSI/MIL 1983)

Reference Manual for the Ada Programming Language. ANSI/MIL-STD-1815A, Washington, D. C.: U.S. Department of Defense. (Jan. 1983).

(ARON 1974)

J. D. Aron. **The Program Development Process, Part I: The Individual Programmer**. Reading, MA.: Addison-Wesley, 1974.

(ASHCROFT AND WADGE 1977)

E. A. Ashcroft and W. W. Wadge. "LUCID: A Nonprocedural Language with Iteration." **Comm. ACM 20** 7 (July 1977): 519–526.

(ASIRELLI ET AL. 1979)

P. Asirelli, P. Degano, G. Levi, A Martelli, U. Montanari, G. Pacini, F. Sirovich, and F. Turini. "A Flexible Environment for Program Development Based on a Symbolic Interpreter." **Proceedings 4th Int. Conference on Software Engineering**. IEEE Cat. No. 79CH1479-5C (Munich, Sept. 1979): 251–263.

(ATKINSON ET AL. 1978)

R. R. Atkinson, B. H. Liskov, and R. W. Scheifler. "Aspects of Implementing CLU." **Proceedings ACM National Conference** 1 (Dec. 1978): 123–129.

(BACKUS 1957)

See (Rosen 1967).

(BACKUS 1973)

J. Backus. "Programming Language Semantics and Closed Applicative Languages." **Conf. Record ACM Symp. on Principles of Programming Languages** (Boston, Oct. 1973): 71–86.

(BACKUS 1978A)

J. Backus. "Can Programming Be Liberated from the von Neumann Style? A Functional Style and Its Algebra of Programs." **Comm. ACM 21** 8 (Aug. 1978): 613–641.

(BACKUS 1978B)

See (ACM-SIGPLAN 1978).

(BAILEY 1985)

R. Bailey. "A HOPE Tutorial." **BYTE 19** 8 (Aug. 1985): 235–258.

(BAKER 1972)

F. T. Baker. "Chief Programmer Team Management of Production Programming." **IBM System Journal** Jan. 1972: 56–73.

(BALZER ET AL. 1983)

R. Balzer, C. Green, and T. Cheatham. "Software Technology in the 1990's Using a New Paradigm." **IEEE Computer 16** 11 (Nov. 1983): 39–45.

(BARNES 1982)

J. P. G. Barnes. **Programming in Ada**. Reading, MA.: Addison-Wesley, 1982.

(BARRETT AND COUCH 1979)

W. A. Barrett and J. D. Couch. **Compiler Construction: Theory and Practice**. Chicago: SRA, 1979.

(BARSTOW ET AL. 1984)

D. Barstow, H. Shrobe, and E. Sandewall, eds. **Interactive Programming Environments**. New York, NY: McGraw-Hill, 1984.

(BAUER AND EICKEL 1976)

F. L. Bauer and J. Eickel, eds. **Compiler Construction: An Advanced Course**, 2nd edition. New York: Springer Verlag, 1976.

(BENTLEY 1982)

J. L. Bentley. **Writing Efficient Programs**. Englewood Cliffs, NJ: Prentice Hall, 1982.

(BENTLEY 1983)

J. Bentley. "Programming Pearls: Writing Correct Programs." **Comm. ACM 26** 12 (Dec. 1983): 1040–1045.

(BENTLEY 1985)

J. Bentley. "Programming Pearls: Confessions of a Coder." **Comm. ACM 28** 7 (July 1985): 671–679.

(BERKLING 1976)

K. J. Berkling. "Reduction Languages for Reduction Machines." ISF-76-8 GMB (Bonn, Sept. 1976).

(BERRY 1979)

See (Wegner 1979).

(BIRTWISTLE ET AL. 1973)

G. M. Birtwistle, O-J. Dahl, B. Myhrhaug, and K. Nygaard. **SIMULA Begin.** New York: Petrocelli/Charter, 1973.

(BIRTWISTLE ET AL. 1976)

G. Birtwistle, L. Enderin, M. Ohlin, and J. Palme. "DEC System-10 SIMULA Language Handbook—Part 1." In **Report N. C8398**. Stockholm: Swedish National Defense Research Institute, March 1976.

(BJØRNER AND JONES 1978)

D. Bjørner and C. B. Jones, eds. **The Vienna Development Method: The Meta Language**. Lecture Notes in Computer Science 61. New York: Springer Verlag, 1978.

(BOBROW 1984)

D. G. Bobrow. "If PROLOG is the Answer, What is the Question?" **Proceedings of Fourth Generation Computer Systems**. OHMSHA Ltd., Tokyo, Japan and North-Holland, Amsterdam, Holland, (1984): 138–148.

(BOBROW AND RAPHAEL 1974)

D. G. Bobrow and B. Raphael. "New Programming Languages for Artificial Intelligence." **ACM Computing Surveys 6**. (1972): 155–174.

(BOBROW AND STEFIK 1983)

D. G. Bobrow and M. Stefik. **The LOOPS Manual**. Palo Alto, CA: Xerox Corp. 1983.

(BOEHM 1976)

B. W. Boehm. "Seven Basic Principles of Software Engineering." In **Infotech State of the Art Report on Software Engineering Techniques**. Maidenhead, U.K.: Infotech International Ltd., 1976.

(BOEHM 1981)

B. W. Boehm. **Software Engineering Economics**. Englewood Cliffs, NJ: Prentice Hall, 1981.

(BÖHM AND JACOPINI 1966)

C. Böhm and G. Jacopini. "Flow-diagrams, Turing Machines, and Languages with Only Two Formation Rules." **Comm. ACM 9** 5 (May 1966): 366–371.

(BRAINERD 1978)

W. Brainerd, ed. "FORTRAN 77." **Comm. ACM 21** 10 (Oct. 1978): 806–820.

(BRANQUART ET AL. 1971)

P. Branquart, J. Lewi, M. Sintzoff, and P. Wodon. "The Composition of Semantics in ALGOL 68." **Comm. ACM 14** 11 (Nov. 1971): 697–708.

(BRANQUART ET AL. 1976)

P. Branquart, J.-P. Cardinael, J. Lewi, J-P. Delescaille, and M. Vanbegin. **An Optimized Translation Process and Its Application to ALGOL 68**. Lecture Notes in Computer Science 38. New York: Springer Verlag, 1976.

(BREED AND LATHWELL 1968)

L. M. Breed and R. H. Lathwell. "The Implementation of APL/360." In **Symposium on Interactive Systems for Experimental and Applied Mathematics**, eds. Klerer and Reinfelds. New York: Academic Press, 1968.

(BRINCH HANSEN 1973)

P. Brinch Hansen. **Operating Systems Principles**. Englewood Cliffs, NJ: Prentice-Hall, 1973.

(BRINCH HANSEN 1975)

P. Brinch Hansen. "The Programming Language Concurrent Pascal." **IEEE Transactions on Software Engineering SE-1** 2 (June 1975): 199–207.

(BRINCH HANSEN 1977)

P. Brinch Hansen. **The Architecture of Concurrent Programs**. Englewood Cliffs, NJ: Prentice-Hall, 1977.

(BRINCH HANSEN 1979)

P. Brinch Hansen. "Distributed Processes: A Concurrent Programming Concept." **Comm. ACM 21** 11 (Nov. 1979): 934–941.

(BRINCH HANSEN 1980A)

P. Brinch Hansen. **Edison—A Multiprocessor Language**. Los Angeles, Cal.: Dept. of Computer Science, Univ. of Southern California, September 1980.

(BRINCH HANSEN 1980B)

P. Brinch Hansen. **The Design of Edison**. Los Angeles, Cal.: Dept. of Computer Science, Univ. of Southern California, September 1980.

(BRINCH HANSEN 1980C)

P. Brinch Hansen, **Edison Programs**. Los Angeles, Cal.: Dept. of Computer Science, Univ. of Southern California, September 1980.

(BROOKS 1975)

F. P. Brooks, Jr. **The Mythical Man-Month—Essays on Software Engineering**. Reading, MA: Addison-Wesley, 1975.

(BROOKS 1985)

R. A. Brooks. **Programming in Common LISP**. New York, NY: Wiley, 1985.

(BROWN 1977)

G. D. Brown. **Advanced ANS COBOL with Structured Programming**. New York, NY: Wiley, 1977.

(BROWNSTON ET AL. 1985)

L. Brownston et al. **Programming Expert Systems in OPS5**. Reading, MA: Addison-Wesley, 1985.

(BURGE 1975)

W. H. Burge. **Recurvise Programming Techniques**. Reading, MA: Addison-Wesley, 1975.

(BURSTALL ET AL. 1980)

R. M. Burstall, D. B. MacQueen, and D. T. Sannella. "HOPE: An Experimental Applicative Language." **Conf. Record of the 1980 LISP Conference** (Aug. 1980): 136–143.

(BUXTON 1980)

J. N. Buxton. "An Informal Bibliography on Programming Support Environments." **ACM SIGPLAN Notices 15** 12 (Dec. 1980): 17–30.

(BUXTON AND DRUFFEL 1980)

See (Hünke 1980).

(BYTE 1981)

Special Issue on Smalltalk, BYTE 6 8 (1981).

(CAMPBELL 1984)

J. A. Campbell. **Implementations of PROLOG**. New York, NY: Wiley, 1984.

(CASHIN ET AL. 1981)

P. M. Cashin, M. L. Joliat, R. F. Kamel, and D. M. Lasker, "Experience with a Modular Typed Language: PROTEL." **Proceedings 5th International Conf. Software Engineering** (March 1981): 136–143.

(CELENTANO ET AL. 1980)

A. Celentano, P. Della Vigna, C. Ghezzi, and D. Mandrioli. "Separate Compilation and Partial Specification in Pascal." **IEEE Transactions on Software Engineering SE-6** 4 (July 1980): 313–319.

(CHEATHAM 1977)

T. E. Cheatham, Jr. "Some New Directions in Program Development Tools." **AICA Proceedings** (Italian Computer Society) 3 (Pisa, Oct. 1977): 3–29.

(CHEATHAM ET AL. 1979)

T. E. Cheatham, Jr., J. A. Townley, and G. H. Holloway. "A System for Program Refinement." **Proceedings 4th Int. Conf. on Software Engineering**. IEEE cat. no. 79CH1479-5C (Munich, Sept. 1979): 53–62.

(CHEATHAM 1980)

See (Hünke 1980).

(CHURCH 1941)

A. Church. **The Calculi of Lambda Conversions**. Princeton, NJ: Princeton University Press, 1941.

(CLARKE ET AL. 1980)

L. A. Clarke, J. C. Wileden, and L. Wolf. "Nesting in Ada Is for the Birds." **Proceedings Symp. on the Ada Programming Language—SIGPLAN Notices 15** 11 (Nov. 1980).

(CLOCKSIN AND MELLISH 1985)

W. F. Clocksin and C. S. Mellish. **Programming in Prolog**. 2nd edition, New York, NY: Springer Verlag, 1985.

(COHEN 1985)

J. Cohen. "Describing PROLOG by its Implementation and Compilation." **Comm. ACM 28** 12 (Dec. 1985): 1311–1324.

(COLMERAUER ET AL. 1983)

A. Colmerauer, H. Kanoui, and M. Van Caneghem. "PROLOG: Theoretical Principles and Current Trends." **Technology Sci. Inf. 2** 4 (1983).

(COLMERAUER 1985)

A. Colmerauer. "PROLOG in Ten Figures." **Comm. ACM 28** 12 (Dec. 1985): 1296–1310.

(CONSTABLE AND O'DONNELL)

R. L. Constable and M. J. O'Donnell. **A Programming Logic with an Introduction to the PL/CV Verifier.** Cambridge, MA: Winthrop, 1978.

(CONWAY 1963)

M. E. Conway. "Design of Separable Transition-Diagram Compiler." **Comm. ACM 6** 7 (July 1963): 396–408.

(CONWAY 1978)

R. Conway. **A Primer on Disciplined Programming.** Cambridge, MA: Winthrop, 1978.

(CONWAY AND GRIES 1979)

R. Conway and D. Gries. **An Introduction to Programming—A Structured Approach Using PL/I and PL/C.** 3rd edition. Cambridge, MA: Winthrop, 1979.

(CONWAY ET AL. 1977)

R. Conway, D. Gries, and D. B. Wortman. **Introduction to Structured Programming Using PL/I and SP/k.** Cambridge, MA: Winthrop, 1977.

(CRESPI-REGHIZZI ET AL. 1980)

S. Crespi-Reghizzi, P. Corti, and A. Daprá. "A Survey of Microprocessor Languages." **IEEE Computer 13** 1 (Jan. 1980): 48–66.

(DAHL AND HOARE 1972)

See (Dahl et al. 1972).

(DAHL AND MYHRHAUG 1969)

O.-J. Dahl and B. Myhrhaug. "SIMULA 67 Implementation Guide." **Publication N. S-9.** Oslo: Norwegian Computing Center, June 1969.

(DAHL ET AL. 1970)

O.-J. Dahl, B. Myhrhaug, and K. Nygaard. "SIMULA 67 Common Base Language." **Publication N. S-22.** Oslo: Norwegian Computing Center, Oct. 1970.

(DAHL ET AL. 1972)

O.-J. Dahl, E. W. Dijkstra, and C. A. R. Hoare. **Structured Programming.** New York: Academic Press, 1972.

(DARLINGTON AND BURSTALL 1976)

J. Darlington and R. M. Burstall. "A System Which Automatically Improves Programs." **Acta Informatica 6** 1 (1976): 41–60.

(DeBAKKER 1980)

J. DeBakker. **Mathematical Theory of Program Correctness.** Englewood Cliffs, NJ: Prentice-Hall, 1980.

(DEMERS AND DONAHUE 1980A)

A. Demers and J. Donahue. "Data Types, Parameters and Type Checking." **Conference Record of the 7th Annual ACM Symp. on Principles of Programming Languages** (Jan. 1980): 12–23.

(DEMERS AND DONAHUE 1980B)

A. Demers and J. Donahue. "Type Completeness as a Language Principle." **Conference Record of the 7th Annual ACM Symp. on Principles of Programming Languages**. (Jan. 1980): 234–244.

(DEMERS AND DONAHUE 1985)

A. Demers and J. Donahue. "Data Types are Values." **ACM Transactions on Programming Languages and Systems 7** 3 (July 1985): 426–445.

(DeMILLO ET AL. 1979)

R. A. DeMillo, R. J. Lipton, and A. J. Perlis, "Social Processes and Proofs of Theorems and Programs." **Comm. ACM 22** 5 (May 1979): 271–280.

(DeREMER AND KRON 1976)

F. DeRemer and H. Kron. "Programming-in-the-Large Versus Programming-in-the-Small." **IEEE Transactions on Software Engineering SE-2** (June 1976): 80–86.

(DEUTSCH AND BOBROW 1976)

L. P. Deutsch and D. G. Bobrow. "An Efficient Incremental Automatic Garbage Collector." **Comm. ACM 19** 9 (Sept. 1976): 522–526.

(DIJKSTRA 1962)

E. W. Dijkstra. **A Primer of ALGOL 60 Programming**. New York: Academic Press, 1962.

(DIJKSTRA 1968A)

E. W. Dijkstra. "Goto Statement Considered Harmful." **Comm. ACM 11** 3 (March 1968): 147–149.

(DIJKSTRA 1968B)

E. W. Dijkstra. "Cooperating Sequential Processes." In **Programming Languages**. ed. F. Genuys. New York: Academic Press, 1968.

(DIJKSTRA 1968C)

E. W. Dijkstra. "The Structure of The Multiprogramming System." **Comm. ACM 11** 5 (May 1968): 341–346.

(DIJKSTRA 1972)

See (Dahl et al. 1972).

(DIJKSTRA 1976)

E. W. Dijkstra. **A Discipline of Programming**. Englewood Clifs, NJ: Prentice-Hall, 1976.

(DIJKSTRA ET AL. 1978)

E. W. Dijkstra, L. Lamport, A. J. Martin, C. S. Scholten, and E. F. M. Steffens. "On-the-Fly Garbage Collection: An Exercise in Cooperation." **Comm. ACM 21** 11 (Nov. 1978): 966–975.

(DOD 1977)

United States Department of Defense. **Requirements for High Order Computer Programming Languages, Revised "Ironman." SIGPLAN Notices 12** 12 (Dec. 1977): 39–54.

(DOD 1978)

United States Department of Defense. **Requirements for High Order Computer Programming Languages, "Steelman,"** June 1978.

(DOD 1980)

United States Department of Defense. **"Stoneman": Requirements for Ada Programming Support Environment.** Feb. 1980.

(ELLIOTT AND BARNARD 1978)

W. D. Elliott and D. T. Barnard, eds. "Notes on Euclid." **SIGPLAN Notices 13** 3 (March 1978): 34–89.

(ELSON 1973)

M. Elson. **Concepts of Programming Languages.** Chicago: SRA, 1973.

(FAIRLEY 1985)

R. E. Fairley. **Software Engineering Concepts.** New York, NY: McGraw-Hill, 1985.

(FALKOFF AND IVERSON 1978)

See (ACM-SIGPLAN 1978).

(FEUER AND GEHANI 1982)

A. Feuer and N. Gehani. "A Comparison of the Programming Languages C and Pascal." **ACM Computing Surveys 14** 1 (March 1982): 73–92.

(FINDLAY AND WATT 1978)

W. Findlay and D. A. Watt. **Pascal: An Introduction to Methodical Programming.** Potomac, MD: Computer Science Press, 1978.

(FILMAN AND FRIEDMAN 1984)

R. Filman and D. P. Friedman. **Coordinated Computing: Tools and Techniques for Distributed Software.** New York, NY: McGraw-Hill, 1984.

(FISHER 1978)

D. A. Fisher "DOD's Common Programming Language Effort.", **IEEE Computer 11** 3 (March 1978): 24–33.

(FISCHER AND LeBLANC 1980)

C. N. Fischer and R. J. LeBlanc. "The Implementation of Run-Time Diagnostics in Pascal." **IEEE Transactions on Software Engineering SE-6** 4 (July 1980): 313–319.

(FLOYD 1967)

R. W. Floyd. "Assigning Meanings to Programs." Proc. Symp. Appl. Math. In **Mathematical Aspects of Computer Science**, ed. J. T. Schwartz. Providence, RI: American Mathematical Society, 1967.

(FOSDICK AND OSTERWEIL 1976)

L. D. Fosdick and L. J. Osterweil. "Data Flow Analysis in Software Reliability." **Computing Surveys** 8 3 (Oct. 1976): 305–330.

(FRANCEZ 1977)

N. Francez. "Another Advantage of Keyword Notation for Parameter Communication with Subprograms." **Comm. ACM 20** 8 (Aug. 1977): 604–605.

(GANNON 1977)

J. D. Gannon. "An Experimental Evaluation of Data Type Conventions." **Comm. ACM** 8 20 (Aug. 1977): 584–595.

(GANNON AND HORNING 1975)

J. D. Gannon and J. J. Horning. "Language Design for Programming Reliability." **IEEE Transactions on Software Engineering SE-1** 2 (1975): 179–191.

(GEHANI 1983)

N. Gehani. **Ada: An Advanced Introduction**. Englewood Cliffs, NJ: Prentice-Hall, 1983.

(GEHANI 1985)

N. Gehani. **C: An Advanced Introduction**. Rockville, MD: Computer Science Press, 1985.

(GENESERETH AND GINSBERG 1985)

M. R. Genesereth and M. L. Ginsberg. "Logic Programming." **Comm. ACM 28** 9 (Sept. 1985): 933–941.

(GESCHKE AND MITCHELL 1975)

C. Geschke and J. Mitchell. "On the Problem of Uniform References to Data Structures." **IEEE Transactions on Software Engineering SE-1** 2 (June 1975): 207–219.

(GESCHKE ET AL. 1977)

C. M. Geschke, J. H. Morris, Jr., and E. H. Satterthwaite, "Early Experience with Mesa." **Comm. ACM 20** 8 (Aug. 1977): 540–553.

(GOGUEN ET AL. 1978)

See (Yeh 1978).

(GOLDBERG AND ROBSON 1983)

A. Goldberg and D. Robson. **Smalltalk-80: The Language and its Implementation**. Reading, Mass.: Addison-Wesley, 1983.

(GOOD 1977)

D. I. Good, ed. **Constructing Verifiably Reliable and Secure Communications Processing Systems**. Univ. of Texas at Austin, ICSCA-CMP-6 (Jan. 1977).

(GOOD ET AL. 1978)

D. I. Good, R. M. Cohen, and L. W. Hunter. "A Report on the Development of Gypsy." **Proceedings ACM National Conference** 1 (Dec. 1978): 116–122.

(GOOD 1985)

See (Hoare and Shepherdson 1985).

(GOODENOUGH 1975)

J. B. Goodenough. "Exception Handling: Issues and a Proposed Notation." **Comm. ACM 16** 12 (Dec. 1975): 683–696.

(GOODENOUGH)

See (Wegner 1979).

(GORDON 1979)

R. Gordon. **The Denotational Description of Programming Languages**, New York: Springer Verlag, 1979.

(GRIES 1971)

D. Gries. **Compiler Construction for Digital Computers**, New York: Wiley, 1971.

(GRIES 1981)

D. Gries **The Science of Programming**. New York, NY: Springer Verlag, 1981.

(GRIES AND GEHANI 1977)

D. Gries and N. Gehani. "Some Ideas on Data Types in High-Level Languages." **Comm. ACM 20** 6 (June 1977); 414–420.

(GRISWOLD 1972)

R. E. Griswold. **The Macro Implementation of SNOBOL4**. San Francisco, CA: W. H. Freeman, 1972.

(GRISWOLD 1978)

See (ACM-SIGPLAN 1978).

(GRISWOLD AND GRISWOLD 1973)

R. E. Griswold and M. T. Griswold. **A SNOBOL4 Primer.** Englewood Cliffs, NJ: Prentice-Hall, 1973.

(GRISWOLD AND GRISWOLD 1983)

R. E. Griswold and M. T. Griswold. **The ICON Programming Language**. Englewood Cliffs, NJ: Prentice Hall, 1983.

(GRISWOLD ET AL. 1971)

R. E. Griswold, J. F. Poage, and I. P. Polonsky. **The SNOBOL4 Programming Language**, 2nd edition, Englewood Cliffs, NJ: Prentice-Hall, 1971.

(GUARINO 1978)

L. R. Guarino. "The Evolution of Abstraction in Programming Languages." Carnegie-Mellon Univ. Dept. of Computer Science **Report CMU-CS-78-120** (May 1978).

(GUTTAG 1977)

J. V. Guttag. "Abstract Data Types and the Development of Data Structures."
Comm. ACM 20 6 (June 1977): 396–404.

(GUTTAG ET AL. 1978)

See (Yeh 1978).

(HABERMANN 1973)

A. N. Habermann. "Critical Comments on the Programming Language Pascal."
Acta Informatica 3 (1973): 47–57.

(HABERMANN 1980)

A. N. Habermann. "An Overview of the Gandalf Project." **Carnegie Mellon University—Computer Science Research Review 1978–79.** 1980.

(HABERMANN AND PERRY 1983)

A. N. Habermann and D. E. Perry. **Ada for Experienced Programmers**. Reading, MA: Addison-Wesley, 1983.

(HARTMANN 1977)

A. C. Hartmann. **A Concurrent Pascal Compiler for Minicomputers**. Lecture Notes in Computer Science 50, New York: Springer Verlag, 1977.

(HECHT 1977)

M. S. Hecht. **Flow Analysis of Computer Programs**. New York: Elsevier North-Holland, 1977.

(HEHNER 1984)

E. Hehner. **The Logic of Programming**. Englewood Cliffs, NJ: Prentice-Hall, 1984.

(HENDERSON 1980)

P. Henderson. **Functional Programming: Application and Implementation**. Englewood Cliffs, NJ: Prentice-Hall, 1980.

(HENDERSON 1986)

P. Henderson. "Functional Programming, Formal Specification, and Rapid Prototyping." **IEEE Transactions on Software Engineering SE-12** 2 (1986): 241–250.

(HEWITT 1969)

C. Hewitt. "PLANNER: A Language for Proving Theorems in Robots." **Proceedings of IJCAI-69**. Washington, D. C.: May 1969.

(HILFINGER 1983)

P. Hilfinger. **Abstraction Mechanisms and Language Design**. Cambridge, MA: The MIT Press, 1983.

(HILL 1976)

See (Bauer and Eickel 1976).

(HOARE 1969)

C. A. R. Hoare. "An Axiomatic Basis of Computer Programming." **Comm. ACM 12** 10 (Oct. 1969): 576–580.

(HOARE 1972A)

See (Dahl et al. 1972).

(HOARE 1972B)

C. A. R. Hoare, "Proof of Correctness of Data Representations." **Acta Informatica 1** (1972): 271–281.

(HOARE 1973)

C. A. R. Hoare. "Hints on Programming Language Design." Keynote address given at the ACM SIGACT/SIGPLAN Conference on Principles of Programming Language. Boston: Oct. 1973. See also Stanford Univ. Computer Science Dept. Tech. of Rep. **STAN-CS-74-403.**

(HOARE 1974)

C. A. R. Hoare. "Monitors: An Operating System Structuring Concept." **Comm. ACM 17** 10 (Oct. 1974): 549–557.

(HOARE 1975A)

C.A. R. Hoare. "Data Reliability." **Proceedings Int. Conf. on Reliable Software—SIGPLAN Notices 10** 6 (June 1975): 528–533.

(HOARE 1975B)

C.A. R. Hoare. "Recurvise Data Structures." **Int. Journal of Comp. and Inf. Sciences 4** 2 (1975): 105–132.

(HOARE 1978)

C. A. R. Hoare, "Communicating Sequential Processes." **Comm. ACM 21** 8 (Aug. 1978): 666–677.

(HOARE 1981)

C. A. R. Hoare. "The Emperor's Old Clothes." **Comm. ACM 24** 2 (Feb. 1981): 75–83.

(HOARE 1985)

C. A. R. Hoare. **Communicating Sequential Processes**. Englewood Cliffs, NJ: Prentice-Hall, 1985.

(HOARE AND SHEPHERDSON 1985)

C. A. R. Hoare and J.C. Shepherdson, eds. **Mathematical Logic and Programming Languages**. Englewood Cliffs, NJ: Prentice-Hall, 1985.

(HOARE AND WIRTH 1973)

C. A. R. Hoare and N. Wirth. "An Axiomatic Definition of the Programming Language Pascal." **Acta Informatica 2** (1973): 335–355.

(HOLT ET AL. 1978A)

R. C. Holt, G. S. Graham, E. D. Lazowska, and M. A. Scott. **Structured Concur-**

rent Programming with Operating System Applications. Reading, MA: Addison-Wesley, 1978.

(HOLT ET AL. 1978B)

R. C. Holt, D. B. Wortman, J. R. Cordy, D. R. Crowe. "The Euclid Language: A Progress Report." **Proceedings of the ACM National Conference** 1 (Dec. 1978): 111–115.

(HOWARD 1976A)

J. H. Howard. "Proving Monitors." **Comm. ACM 15** 5 (May 1976): 273–79.

(HOWARD 1976B)

J. H. Howard "Signaling in Monitors." **Proceedings of the 2nd Intl. Conference on Software Engineering**. IEEE cat. no. 76CH1125-4C (San Francisco, Oct. 1976): 47–52.

(HOWDEN 1982)

W. Howden "Contemporary Software Development Environments." **Comm. ACM 25** 5 (May 1982): 318–329.

(HÜNKE 1980)

H. Hünke, ed., **Software Engineering Environments**. Amsterdam: North Holland Pub. Co., 1980.

(ICHBIAH AND MORSE 1972)

J. D. Ichbiah and S. P. Morse. "General Concepts of the SIMULA 67 Programming Language." **Annual Review of Automatic Programming** 1 (1972): 65–95.

(ICHBIAH ET AL. 1979)

See (ACM-SIGPLAN 1979).

(IEEE-Computer 1981)

Special Issue on Ada, IEEE Computer 14 6 (June 1981).

(IEEE-Software 1985)

Special Issue on Ada Environments and Tools, IEEE Software 2 2 (March 1985).

(IEEE-Software 1986)

Special Issue on Multiparadigm Languages and Environments, IEEE Software 3 1 (Jan. 1986).

(IEEE-TSE 1985)

Special Issue on Artificial Intelligence and Software Engineering, IEEE Transactions on Software Engineering SE-11 11 (Nov. 1985).

(INGALLS 1978)

D. H. Ingalls. "The Smalltalk-76 Programming System Design and Implementation." **Conference Record of the 5th Annual ACM Symp. on Principles of Programming Languages** (Jan. 1978): 9–16.

(INMOS 1984)

INMOS Limited. **OCCAM Programming Manual**, Englewood Cliffs, NJ: Prentice Hall, 1984.

(ISO PASCAL 1982)

International Organization for Standardization. **Specification for Computer Programming Language Pascal**. ISO 7185-1982, 1982.

(IVERSON 1962)

K. E. Iverson **A Programming Language**. New York: Wiley, 1962.

(IVERSON 1979)

K. E. Iverson. "Operators." **ACM Transactions on Programming Languages and Systems** 1 2 (Oct. 1979): 161–176.

(IVERSON 1980)

K. E. Iverson. "Notation as a Tool of Thought." **Comm. ACM 23** 8 (Aug. 1980): 444–465.

(JACKSON 1975)

M. A. Jackson. **Principles of Program Design**. New York: Academic Press, 1975.

(JACKSON 1983)

M. A. Jackson. **System Development**. Englewood Cliffs, NJ: Prentice-Hall, 1983.

(JENSEN AND WIRTH 1985)

K. Jensen and N. Wirth. **Pascal User Manual and Report**. New York: Springer Verlag, 1975. 3rd edition (1985) complies with the ISO Standard.

(JOHNSON 1978)

S. C. Johnson. "A Portable Compiler: Theory and Practice." **Conf. Record of 5th Annual ACM Symp. on Principles of Programming Languages** (Jan. 1978): 97–104.

(JOHNSTON 1971)

J. Johnston. "The Contour Model of Block-Structured Processes." **Proceedings Symp. Data Structures in Programming Languages—SIGPLAN Notices 6** 2 (Feb. 1971): 55–82.

(KAHN ET AL. 1980)

G. Kahn, V. Donzeau-Gouge, and B. Lang. "Formal Definition of the Ada Programming Language." Honeywell-Bull INRIA Report. (Nov. 1980).

(KAY 1977)

A. Kay. "Personal Dynamic Media," **IEEE Computer 10** 3 (March 1977): 31–42.

(KEMENY AND KURTZ 1985)

J. G. Kemeny and T. E. Kurtz. **Back to Basic**. Reading, MA: Addison-Wesley, 1985.

(KENNEDY AND SCHWARTZ 1975)

K. Kennedy and J. Schwartz. "An Introduction to the Set Theoretical Language SETL." **Journal Computer and Math. with Applications** 1 (1975): 97–119.

(KERNIGHAN 1984)

B. W. Kernighan. "The UNIX System and Software Reliability." **IEEE Transactions on Software Engineering SE-1** 5 (Sept. 1984): 513–518.

(KERNIGHAN AND MASHEY 1979)

B. W. Kernighan and J. R. Mashey. "The UNIX Programming Environment." **Software—Practice and Experience 9** 1 (1979): 1–16.

(KERNIGHAN AND PIKE 1984)

B. W. Kernighan and R. Pike. **The UNIX Programming Environment.** Englewood Cliffs, NJ: Prentice-Hall, 1984.

(KERNIGHAN AND PLAUGER 1976)

B. W. Kenighan and P. J. Plauger. **Software Tools.** MA: Addison-Wesley, 1976.

(KERNIGHAN AND RITCHIE 1978)

B. W. Kernigha and D. M. Ritchie. **The C Programming Language.** Englewood Cliffs, NJ: Prentice-Hall, 1978.

(KIEBURTZ 1976)

See (ACM-SIGPLAN 1976).

(KIEBURTZ ET AL. 1978)

R. B. Kieburtz, W. Barabash, and S. R. Hill. "A Type-Checking Program Linkage System for Pascal." **Proceedings 3rd Int. Conf. on Software Eng.** Atlanta, GA: May 10–12, 1978.

(KING 1976)

J. C. King. "Symbolic Execution and Program Testing." **Comm. ACM 19** 7 (July 1976): 385–394.

(KNUTH 1967)

D. E. Knuth. "The Remaining Trouble Spots in ALGOL 60." **Comm. ACM 10** 10 (Oct. 1967): 611–617.

(KNUTH 1973)

D. E. Knuth. **The Art of Computer Programming.** Vol. 1: **Fundamental Algorithms**, 2nd ed. Reading, MA: Addison-Wesley, 1973.

(KNUTH 1974)

D. E. Knuth "Structured Programming with GOTO Statements." **ACM Computing Surveys 6** 4 (Dec. 1974): 261–301.

(KOWALSKI 1979A)

R. A. Kowalaski. "Algorithm = Logic + Control." **Comm. ACM 22** 7 (July 1979): 424–436.

(KOWALSKI 1979B)

R. A. Kowalski. **Logic for Problem Solving.** Amsterdam: North-Holland, 1979.

(KOWALSKI 1981)

R. Kowalski. "PROLOG as a Logic Programming Language." **Proc. AICA Conference**, Pavia, (Sept. 23–25, 1981): 1029–1934.

(KRUTCHEN ET AL. 1984)

P. Krutchen, E. Schonberg, and J. Schwartz. "Software Prototyping Using the SETL Programming Language." **IEEE Software** 1 5 (Oct. 1984): 66–75.

(LAMPSON ET AL. 1974)

B. Lampson, J. Mitchell, and E. Satterthwaite. "On the Transfer of Control between Contexts." **Lecture Notes in Computer Science 19:** 181–203. New York: Springer Verlag, 1974.

(LAMPSON ET AL. 1977)

B. W. Lampson, J. J. Horning, R. L. London, J. G. Mitchell, and G. J. Popek. "Report on the Programming Language Euclid." **SIGPLAN Notices 12** 2 (Feb. 1977). (Revised Report, XEROX PARC Tech. Rep. CSL78-2.)

(LANDIN 1966)

P. J. Landin. "The Next 700 Programming Languages." **Comm. ACM 9** 3 (March 1966): 157–164.

(LASKER 1979)

D. M. Lasker. "Module Structure in an Evolving Family of Real Time Systems." **Proc. 4th Int. Conf. Software Engineering** IEEE cat. no. 79 CHI479-SC (Munich 1979) (Sept. 1979): 22–28.

(LAUER AND SATTERTHWAITE 1979)

H. C. Lauer and E. H. Satterthwaite. "The Impact of Mesa on System Design." **Proc. 4th Int. Conf. Software Engineering.** IEEE cat. no. 79CH1479-5C (Munich 1979): 174–182.

(LeBLANC AND FISCHER 1979)

R. J. LeBlanc and C. N. Fischer. "On Implementing Separate Compilation in Block-Structured Languages." **Proceedings SIGPLAN Symp. on Compiler Construction—SIGPLAN Notices** 14 8 (Aug. 1979): 133–143.

(LECARME AND DESJARDINS 1975)

O. Lecarme and P. Desjardins. "More Comments on the Programming Language Pascal." **Acta Informatica** 4 (1975): 231–243.

(LEVIN 1977)

R. Levin. **Programming Structures for Exceptional Condition Handling.** Ph.D. dissertation. Carnegie-Mellon Univ. Dept. of Computer Science, June 1977.

(LINDSEY 1972)

C. H. Lindsey. "ALGOL 68 with Fewer Tears." **Computer Journal 15** (1972): 176–188.

(LINDSEY AND VAN DER MEULEN 1977)

C. H. Lindsey and S. G. van der Meulen. **Informal Introduction to ALGOL 68.** rev. ed. Amsterdam: North-Holland, 1977.

(LISKOV 1974)

B. H. Liskov. "A Note on CLU." **Computation Structures Group Memo 112.** Cambridge, MA: MIT Project MAC, Nov. 1974.

(LISKOV 1982)

B. Liskov. "On Linguistic Support for Distributed Programs." **IEEE Transactions on Software Engineering SE-8** 3 (May 1982): 203–210.

(LISKOV AND SEIFLER 1983)

B. Liskov and R. Scheifler. "Guardians and Actions: Linguistic Support for Robust, Distributed Programs." **ACM Transactions on Programming Languages and Systems 5** 3 (July 1983): 381–404.

(LISKOV AND SNYDER 1979)

B. H. Liskov and A. Snyder. "Exception Handling in CLU." **IEEE Transactions on Software Engineering SE-5** 6 (Nov. 1979): 547–558.

(LISKOV AND ZILLES 1974)

B. H. Liskov and S. N. Zilles. "Programming with Abstract Data Types." **SIGPLAN Symp. on Very High Level Languages—SIGPLAN Notices 9** 4 (Apr. 1974): 50–59.

(LISKOV AND ZILLES 1975)

B. H. Liskov and S. N. Zilles. "Specification Techniques for Data Abstractions." **IEEE Transactions on Software Engineering SE-1** 1 (1975): 7–19.

(LISKOV ET AL. 1977)

B. H. Liskov, A. Snyder, R. Atkinson, and C. Schaffert. "Abstraction Mechanisms in CLU." **Comm. ACM 20** 8 (Aug. 1977): 564–576.

(LISKOV ET AL. 1978)

B. Liskov, E. Moss, C. Schaffert, R. Scheiffer, and A. Snyder. "CLU Reference Manual." In **Computation Structures Group Memo 161**. Cambridge, MA: Massachusetts Institute of Technology Laboratory for Computer Science, July 1978.

(LISKOV ET AL. 1981)

B. Liskov et al. **CLU Reference Manual**, New York, NY: Springer Verlag, 1981.

(LONDON 1979)

See (Wegner 1979).

(LONDON ET AL. 1978)

R. L. London, J. V. Guttag, J. J. Horning, B. W. Lampson, J. G. Mitchell, and G. J. Popek. "Proof Rules for the Programming Language Euclid." **Acta Informatica 10** (1978): 1–26.

(LUCAS AND WALK 1969)

P. Lucas and K. Walk. "On the Formal Description of PL/I." **Annual Review of Automatic Programming 6** 3 (1969): 105–182.

(LUCKAM AND POLAK 1980)

D. C. Luckam and W. Polak. "Ada Exception Handling: An Axiomatic Approach." **Transactions on Programming Languages and Systems** 2 (April 1980).

(MacLAREN 1977)

D. M. MacLaren. "Exception Handling in PL/I." **Proceedings Conference on**

Language Design for Reliable Software—**SIGPLAN Notices 12** 3 (March 1977): 101–104.

(MAGÓ 1980)

G. A. Magó. "A Network of Microprocessors to Execute Reduction Languages." **Int. J. Computer and Information Sci.** 1980.

(MANDRIOLI AND GHEZZI 1986)

D. Mandrioli and C. Ghezzi. **Theoretical Computer Science**. To appear, New York, NY: Wiley, 1986.

(MANNA 1973)

Z. Manna. **The Mathematical Theory of Computation**. New York: McGraw-Hill, 1973.

(MARLIN 1980)

C. D. Marlin. **Coroutines**. Lecture Notes in Computer Science 95. New York: Springer Velag, 1980.

(MARTELLI AND MONTANARI 1982)

A. Martelli and U. Montanari. "An Efficient Unification Algorithm." **ACM Transactions on Programming Languages and Systems** 2 (April 1982): 258–282.

(MAY 1983)

D. May. "OCCAM." **SIGPLAN Notices 18** 4 (April 1983): 69–79.

(McCARTHY 1960)

J. McCarthy. "Recursive Functions of Symbolic Expressions and Their Computation by Machine." **Comm. ACM 3** 4 (April 1960): 184–195.

(McCARTHY 1963A)

J. McCarthy. "A Basis for a Mathematical Theory of Computation." In **Computer Programming and Formal Systems**, eds. P. Braffort and D. Hirschberg: 33–37. Amsterdam: North-Holland, 1963.

(McCARTHY 1963B)

J. McCarthy. "Towards a Mathematical Science of Computation." **Proceedings of IFIP Congress** (Munich): 21–28. Amsterdam: North-Holland, 1963.

(McCARTHY 1978)

See (ACM-SIGPLAN 1978).

(McCARTHY ET AL. 1965)

J. McCarthy, P. W. Abrahams, D. J. Edwards, T. P. Hart, and M. I. Levin. **LISP 1.5 Programmer's Manual**. 2nd edition. Cambridge, MA: The MIT Press, 1965.

(McCORDUCK 1983)

P. McCorduck. "An Introduction to the 5th Generation." **Comm. ACM 26** 9 (Sept. 1983): 629–630.

(McCORDUCK AND FEIGENBAUM 1983)

P. McCorduck and E. Feignebaum. **The Fifth Generation**. Reading, MA: Addison-Wesley, 1983.

(McDERMOTT 1980)

D. McDermott. "The PROLOG Phenomenon." **SIGART Newsletter no. 71** (July 1980): 16–20.

(McDERMOTT AND SUSSMAN 1973)

D. McDermott and G. J. Sussman. **The CONNIVER Reference Manual. AI Memo 259a**. MIT Artificial Intelligence Laboratory, Cambridge, MA: 1973.

(MEDINA-MORA AND FEILER 1981)

R. Medina-Mora and P. H. Feiler. "An Incremental Programming Environment." **IEEE Transactions on Software Engineering SE-7** 5 (Sept. 1981): 472–482.

(MEISSNER AND ORGANICK 1984)

L. Meissner and E. Organick. **FORTRAN 77—teaching structured progrmming**. Reading, MA: Addison-Wesley, 1984.

(MENDELSON 1964)

E. Mendelson. **Introduction to Mathematical Logic**. New York, NY: Van Nostrand Reinhold, 1964.

(METZGER 1985)

P. W. Metzger. **Managing a Programming Project**. Englewood Cliffs, NJ: Prentice-Hall, 2nd Edition, 1985.

(MITCHELL ET AL. 1979)

J. G. Mitchell, W. Maybury, and R. Sweet. **Mesa Language Manual (Version 5.0)** Xerox Research Center, Palo Alto, Cal.: CSL-79-3 (Apr. 1979).

(MITZE 1980)

See (Hünke 1980).

(MOFFAT 1984)

D.V. Moffat. **Common Algorithms in Pascal**. Englewood Cliffs, NJ: Prentice-Hall, 1984.

(MOON 1974)

D. A. Moon. **MACLISP Reference Manual**. Project MAC Technical Report. Cambridge, MA: Massachusetts Institute of Technology, 1974.

(MYERS 1975)

G. J. Myers. **Reliable Software through Composite Design**. New York: Petrocelli Charter, 1975.

(MYERS 1976)

G. J. Myers. **Software Reliability: Principles and Practices**. New York: Wiley, 1976.

(MYERS 1978)

G. J. Myers. **Composite/Structured Design**. New York: Van Nostrand Reinhold, 1978.

(MYERS 1979)

G. J. Myers. **The Art of Software Testing**. New York: Wiley, 1979.

(NAUR 1963)

P. Naur, ed. "Revised Report on the Algorithmic Language ALGOL 60." **Comm ACM 6** (Jan. 1963) 1–17. See also (Rosen 1967).

(NAUR 1978)

See (ACM-SIGPLAN 1978).

(NORI ET AL. 1976)

K. V. Nori, U. Ammann, K. Jensen, H. H. Nageli, and Ch. Jacobi. **The Pascal "P" Compiler: Implementation Notes**. rev. Edition. Berichte Nr. 10. Zurich: Institut fur Informatik, Eidgenossiche Technische Hochshule, 1976.

(NYGAARD AND DAHL 1978)

See (ACM-SIGPLAN 1978).

(OSTERWEIL 1983)

L.J. Osterweil. "Toolpack—An Experimental Software Development Environment Research Project." **IEEE Transactions on Software Engineering SE-9** 11 (Nov. 1983): 673–685.

(PAGAN 1976)

F. P. Pagan. **Practical Guide to ALGOL 68**. New York: Wiley, 1976.

(PARNAS 1972A)

D. L. Parnas. "A Technique for Module Specification with Examples." **Comm. ACM 15** 5 (May 1972): 330–336.

(PARNAS 1972B)

D. L. Parnas. "On the Criteria to Be Used in Decomposing Systems into Modules." **Comm. ACM 15** 12 (Dec. 1972): 1053–1058.

(PARNAS 1975)

D. L. Parnas. "On the Design and Development of Program Families." **IEEE Transactions on Software Engineering SE-2** 1 (March 1975): 1–9.

(PARNAS 1977)

See (Yeh 1977).

(PARNAS 1984)

D. L. Parnas. Is Ada Too Big? (letter) **Comm ACM 29** 11 (Nov. 1984): 1155–1155.

(PARNAS AND WURGES 1976)

D. L. Parnas and H. Würges. "Response to Undesired Events in Software Systems." **Proceedings 2nd Int. Conference on Software Engineering**. IEEE cat. no. 76CH1125-4C: 437-446 (San Francisco, Cal., 13–15 Oct. 1976).

(PECK 1970)

J. E. L. Peck, ed. **ALGOL 68 Implementation**. Amsterdam: North-Holland, 1970.

(PERLIS 1978)

See (ACM-SIGPLAN 1978).

(PETERSON AND SILBERSHATZ 1985)

J. L. Peterson and A. Silbershatz. **Operating Systems Concepts**. Reading, MA: Addison-Wesley, 1985.

(PLUM 1983)

T. Plum. **Learning to Program in C**. Englewood Cliffs, NJ: Prentice-Hall, 1983.

(POLIVKA AND PAKIN 1975)

R. P. Polivka and S. Pakin. **APL: The Language and Its Usage**. Englewood Cliffs, NJ: Prentice-Hall, 1975.

(POPEK ET AL. 1977)

G. J. Popek, J. J. Horning, B. W. Lampson, J. G. Mitchell, and R. L. London. "Notes on the Design of Euclid." **Proceedings ACM Conference on Language Design for Reliable Software—SIGPLAN Notices 12** 3 (March 1977): 11–18.

(POZEFSKY 1977)

M. Pozefsky. "Programming in Reduction Languages." **Ph.D dissertation**. Univ. of North Carolina Computer Science Dept., 1977.

(PRATT 1984)

T. W. Pratt. **Programming Languages: Design and Implementation**. 2nd edition, Englewood Cliffs, NJ: Prentice-Hall, 1984.

(RADIN 1978)

See (ACM-SIGPLAN 1978).

(RANDELL 1975)

B. Randell. "System Structure for Software Fault Tolerance." **IEEE Transactions on Software Engineering SE-1** 2 (June 1975): 220–232.

(RANDELL AND RUSSELL 1964)

B. Randell and L. Russell. **ALGOL 60 Implementation**. New York: Academic Press, 1964.

(REYNOLDS 1970)

J. C. Reynolds. "GEDANKEN—A Simple Typeless Language Based on the Principle of Completeness and the Reference Concept." **Comm. ACM 13** 5 (May 1970): 305–319.

(REYNOLDS 1979)

J. C. Reynolds. "Syntactic Control of Interference." **Proc. Fifth Annual ACM Symp. on Principles of Programming Languages**. Tucson, AZ: Jan. 23–25, 1979.

(RICHARD AND LEDGARD 1977)

F. Richard and H. F. Ledgard. "A Reminder for Language Designers." **SIGPLAN Notices 12** 12 (Dec. 1977): 73–82.

(RICHARDS 1969)

M. Richards. "BCPL: A Tool for Compiler and System Writing." **Spring Joint Comp. Conference** (1969): 557–566.

(RITCHIE AND THOMPSON 1974)

D. Ritchie and K. Thompson. "The UNIX Time-Sharing System." **Comm. ACM 17** 7 (July 1974): 365–375.

(ROBINSON 1965)

J. A. Robinson. "A Machine-Oriented Logic Based on the Resolution Principle." **J. ACM 12** 1 (Jan. 1965): 23–41.

(ROBINSON 1983)

J. A. Robinson. "Logic Programming–Past, Present, and Future." **New Generation Comp. 1** 2 (1983).

(ROUSSEL 1975)

P. Roussel. **PROLOG: Manuel de Reference et d'Utilisation**. Group d'Intelligence Artificielle, Université de Marseilles, 1975.

(ROSEN 1967)

S. Rosen. **Programming Systems and Languages**. New York: McGraw-Hill, 1967.

(SAMMET 1969)

J. E. Sammet. **Programming Languages: History and Fundamentals**. Englewood Cliffs, NJ: Prentice-Hall, 1969.

(SAMMET 1978)

See (ACM-SIGPLAN 1978).

(SANDEWALL 1978)

E. Sandewall. "Programming in the Interactive Environment: The LISP Experience." **ACM Computing Surveys 10** 1 (March 1978): 35–71.

(SCHORR AND WAITE 1967)

H. Schorr and W. Waite. "An Efficient Machine Independent Procedure for Garbage Collection in Various List Structures." **Comm. ACM 10** 8 (Aug. 1967): 501–506.

(SCHWARTZ 1974)

J. T. Schwartz. **On Programming: An Interim Report on the SETL Project**. New York: Courant Ins. Math. Sci. of New York Univ., 1974.

(SCHWARTZ 1978A)

R. L. Schwartz. "Parallel Compilation: A Design and Its Application to SIMULA 67." **Journal of Computer Languages 3** (1978): 75–94.

(SCHWARTZ 1978B)

R. L. Schwartz. "An Axiomatic Semantic Definition of ALGOL 68." **Ph.D. dissertation**. Univ. of Calif. at Los Angeles Computer Science Dept. Rep. no. UCLA-ENG-7838, July 1978.

(SHAPIRO 1983)

E. Y. Shapiro. The Fifth Generation Project: A Trip Report. **Comm. ACM 26** 9 (Sept. 1983): 637–641.

(SHAW 1981)

M. Shaw, ed., **Alphard: Form and Content**. New York, NY: Springer Verlag, 1981.

(SHAW ET AL. 1977)

M. Shaw, W. A. Wulf, and R. L. London. "Abstraction and Verification in Alphard: Defining and Specifying Iteration and Generation." **Comm. ACM 20** 8 (Aug. 1977): 553–564.

(SMEDEMA ET AL. 1983)

C. H. Smedema et al. **The Programming Languages Pascal, Modula, CHILL, and Ada**. Englewood Cliffs, NJ: Prentice-Hall, 1983.

(SOMMERVILLE 1985)

I. Sommerville. **Software Engineering**. 2nd edition, Reading, MA: Addison-Wesley, 1985.

(STALLMAN 1979)

R. M. Stallman. "EMACS, The Extensible, Customizable, Self-Documenting Display Editor." **AI Lab Memo 419**, Cambridge, MA: MIT Artificial Intelligence Laboratory, 1979.

(STANDISH 1980)

See (Hünke 1980).

(STANDISH AND TAYLOR 1984)

See (ACM SIGSOFT-SIGPLAN 1984).

(STEELE 1975)

G. L. Steele. "Multiprocessing Compactifying Garbage Collection." **Comm. ACM 18** 9 (Sept. 1975): 495–508.

(STEELE 1984)

G. L. Steele, Jr. **Common LISP: The Language**. Burlington, MA: Digital Press, 1984.

(STEELE AND SUSSMAN 1980)

G. L. Steele and G. J. Sussman. "Design of a LISP-Based Microprocessor." **Comm. ACM 23** 11 (Nov. 1980): 628–645.

(STEFIK 1985)

M. Stefik. "Strategic Computing at DARPA." **Comm. ACM 28** 7 (July 1985): 690–707.

(STEFIK ET AL. 1986)

See (IEEE-Software 1986).

(STERLING AND SHAPIRO 1986)

L. Sterling and E. Shapiro. **The Art of PROLOG**. Cambridge, MA: MIT Press, 1986.

(STROM AND YEMINI 1983)

R. Strom and S. Yemini. "NIL: An Integrated Language and System for Distributed Programming." **Proc. SIGPLAN '83 on Programming Language Issues in Software Systems**, June 1983.

(STROUSTRUP 1984)

B. Stroustrup. "Data Abstraction in C." **AT&T BLTJ 63** 8 (Oct. 1984): 1701–1732.

(SUSSMAN ET AL. 1970)

G. J. Sussman, T. Winograd, and E. Charniak. **MICROPLANNER Reference Manual. Al Memo 203**, Cambridge, MA: MIT Artificial Intelligence Laboratory, 1970.

(SWEET 1985)

See (ACM-SIGPLAN 1985).

(TAI 1980)

K.-C. Tai. "Program Testing Complexity and Test Criteria." **IEEE Transactions on Software Engineering SE-6** 6 (Nov. 1980): 531–538.

(TAI 1982)

K.-C. Tai. "A Note on Parameter Passing." **SIGPLAN Notices 17** 2 (Feb. 1982): 24–27.

(TANENBAUM 1976)

A. S. Tanenbaum. "A Tutorial on ALGOL 68." **ACM Computing Surveys 8** 2 (June 1976): 155–190.

(TANENBAUM 1978)

A.S. Tanenbaum. "A Comparison of Pascal and ALGOL 68." **Computer Journal 21** (1978): 316–323.

(TEICHROW AND HERSHEY 1977)

D. Teichrow and E. A. Hershey III. "PSL/PSA: A Computer-Aided Technique for Structured Documentation and Analysis of Information Processing." **IEEE Transactions on Software Engineering SE-3** 1 (Jan. 1977): 41–48.

(TEITELMAN 1975)

W. Teitelman. **INTERLISP Reference Manual**. Palo Alto, CA: Xerox Research Center Technical Report, 1975.

(TEITELMAN 1985)

W. Teitelman. "A Tour Through Cedar." **IEEE Software 1** 2 (April 1984): 44–73.

(TU AND PERLIS 1986)

See (IEEE-Software 1986).

(TEITELMAN AND MASINTER 1981)

W. Teitelman and L. Masinter. "The INTERLISP Programming Environment." **IEEE Computer 14** 4 (April 1981): 25–33.

(TENNENT 1973)

R. D. Tennent. "Mathematical Semantics of SNOBOL4." **Proceedings ACM Symp. on Principles of Programming Languages**. (Boston, 1973): 95–107.

(TENNENT 1976)

R. D. Tennent. "The Denotational Semantics of Programming Languages." **Comm. ACM 19** 8 (Aug. 1976): 437–453.

(TENNENT 1978)

R. D. Tennent. "Another Look at Type Compatibility in Pascal." **Software—Practice and Experience 8** (1978): 429–437.

(TICHY 1979)

W. F. Tichy. "Software Development Based on System Structure Description." **Proceedings 4th Int. Conference on Software Engineering.** IEEE cat. no. 79CH1479-5C (Munich, Sept. 1979): 29–41.

(ULLMAN 1982)

J. D. Ullman. **Principles of Database Systems.** Second edition. Rockville, MD: Computer Science Press, 1982.

(VanEMDEN 1980)

M. H. VanEmden. "McDermott on PROLOG: A Rejoinder." **SIGART Newsletter no. 72** (Aug. 1980): 19–20.

(VALENTINE 1974)

S. H. Valentine. "Comparative Notes on ALGOL 68 and PL/I." **Computer Journal 17** (1974): 325–331.

(van der POEL AND MAARSEN 1974)

W. L. van der Poel and L. A. Maarsen, eds. **Machine Oriented Higher Level Languages.** Amsterdam: North-Holland, 1974.

(van WIJNGAARDEN ET AL. 1976)

A. van Wijngaarden, B. J. Mailloux, J. E. L. Peck, C. H. A. Koster, M. Sintzoff, C. H. Lindsey, L. G. L. T. Meertens, and R. G. Fisker. **Revised Report on the Algorithmic Language ALGOL 68.** New York: Springer-Verlag, 1976.

(WAITE AND GOOS 1984)

W. Waite and G. Goos. **Compiler Construction.** New York, NY: Springer Verlag, 1984.

(WALKER ET AL. 1980)

B. J. Walker, R. A. Kemmerer, and G. J. Popek. "Specification and Verification of the UCLA UNIX Security Kernel." **Comm ACM 23** 2 (Feb. 1980): 118–131.

(WEGNER 1968)

P. Wegner. **Programming Languages, Information Structures, and Machine Organization.** New York: McGraw-Hill, 1968.

(WEGNER 1972)

P. Wegner. "The Vienna Definition Language." **ACM Computing Surveys 4** 1 (1972): 5–63.

(WEGNER 1976)

P. Wegner. "Programming Languages—The First 25 Years." **IEEE Transactions on Computers C-25** 12 (1976): 1207–1225.

(WEGNER 1979)

P. Wegner, ed. **Research Directions in Software Technology**. Cambridge, MA: The MIT Press, 1979.

(WEINBERG 1971)

G. M. Weinberg. **The Psychology of Computer Programming**. New York: Van Nostrand Reinhold, 1971.

(WELSH AND LISTER 1981)

J. Welsh and A. Lister. "A Comparative Study of Task Communication in Ada." **Software Practice and Experience 11** (1981): 257–290.

(WELSH ET AL. 1977)

J. Welsh, M. J. Sneeringer, and C. A. R. Hoare. "Ambiguities and Insecurities in Pascal." **Software—Practice and Experience 7** 6 (Nov. 1977): 685–696.

(WICHMANN 1973)

B. A. Wichmann. **ALGOL 60 Compilation and Assessment**. London: Academic Press, 1973.

(WICHMANN 1984A)

B. A. Wichmann. Is Ada Too Big? Response to Parna's letter." **Comm ACM 27** (Feb. 1984): 98–103.

(WICHMANN 1984B)

B. A. Wichmann. "Is Ada Too Big? A Designer Answers the Critics." **Comm ACM 29** 11 (Nov. 1984): 1155–1156.

(WILENSKY 1984)

R. Wilensky. **LISPCraft**. New York, NY: W.W. Norton and Co., 1984.

(WILLIAMS 1979)

G. Williams. "Program Checking." **Proceedings Symp. on Compiler Construction—SIGPLAN Notices 14** 8 (Aug. 1979).

(WINOGRAD 1979)

T. Winograd. "Beyond Programming Languages." **Comm. ACM 22** 7 (1979): 391–401.

(WINSTON AND HORN 1984)

P. H. Winston and B. K. P. Horn. **LISP**. 2nd edition, Reading, MA: Addison-Wesley, 1984.

(WIRTH 1968)

N. Wirth. "PL360, A Programming Language for the 360 Computers." **J. ACM 15** 1 (Jan. 1968): 37–74.

(WIRTH 1971A)

N. Wirth. "The Programming Language Pascal." **Acta Informatica 1** (1971): 35–63.

(WIRTH 1971B)

N. Wirth. "Program Development by Stepwise Refinement." **Comm. ACM 14** 4 (April 1971): 221–227.

(WIRTH 1971C)

N. Wirth. "The Design of a Pascal Compiler." **Software—Practice and Experience 1** (1971): 309–333.

(WIRTH 1973)

N. Wirth. **Systematic Programming**. Englewood Cliffs, NJ: Prentice-Hall, 1973.

(WIRTH 1974)

N. Wirth. "On the Composition of Well-Structured Programs." **ACM Computing Surveys 6** 4 (Dec. 1974): 247–259.

(WIRTH 1975A)

N. Wirth. "On the Design of Programming Languages." In **Information Processing 74** (Proc. IFIP Congress 74). Amsterdam: North-Holland, 1975.

(WIRTH 1975B)

N. Wirth. "An Assessment of the Programming Language Pascal." **IEEE Transactions on Software Engineering SE-1** 2 (June 1975): 192–198.

(WIRTH 1976A)

N. Wirth. **Algorithms + Data Structures = Programs**. Englewood Cliffs, NJ: Prentice-Hall, 1976.

(WIRTH 1976B)

N. Wirth. "Modula: A Language for Modular Multi-programming." **Software—Practice and Experience 7** (1977): 3–35.

(WIRTH 1976C)

N. Wirth. "The Use of Modula." **Software—Practice and Experience 7** (1977): 37–65.

(WIRTH 1976D)

N. Wirth. "Design and Implementation of Modula." **Software—Practice and Experience 7** (1977): 67–84.

(WIRTH 1977)

N. Wirth. "Toward a Discipline of Real-Time Programming." **Comm. ACM 20** 8 (Aug. 1977): 577–583.

(WIRTH 1978)

N. Wirth. "Modula-2." Tech. Report 27. Zurich: Instit für Informatik, ETH, Dec. 1978.

(WIRTH 1979)

N. Wirth. "The Module: A System Structuring Facility in High-Level Programming Languages." Internal Tech. Report. Zurich: Institut für Informatik, ETH, Sept. 1979.

(WIRTH 1982)

N. Wirth. **Modula-2**. Third edition, New York, NY: Springer Verlag, 1982.

(WORTMAN 1979)

D. B. Wortman. "On Legality Assertions in Euclid." **IEEE Transactions on Software Engineering Se-5** 4 (1979): 359–367.

(WULF 1977)

See (Yeh 1977a).

(WULF AND SHAW 1973)

W. A. Wulf and M. Shaw. "Global Variables Considered Harmful." **SIGPLAN Notices 8** 2 (Feb. 1973): 80–86.

(WULF ET AL. 1971)

W. A. Wulf, D. B. Russell, and A. N. Habermann. "BLISS: A Language for Systems Programming." **Comm. ACM 1** 12 (Dec. 1971): 780–790.

(WULF ET AL. 1972)

W. A. Wulf, et al. **BLISS-11 Programmer's Manual**. Maynard, Mass.: Digital Equipment Corp., 1972.

(WULF ET AL. 1975)

W. A. Wulf, R. K. Johnson, C. B. Weinstock, S. O. Hobbs, and C. M. Geschke. **The Design of An Optimizing Compiler**. New York: American Elsevier, 1975.

(WULF ET AL. 1976)

W. A. Wulf, R. L. London, and M. Shaw. "An Introduction to the Construction and Verification of Alphard Programs." **IEEE Transactions on Software Engineering SE-2** (Dec. 1976): 253–265.

(YEH 1977A)

R. T. Yeh, ed. **Current Trends in Programming Methodology**. Vol. 1, **Software Specification and Design**. Englewood Cliffs., NJ: Prentice-Hall, 1977.

(YEH 1977B)

R. T. Yeh, ed. **Current Trends in Programming Methodology**. Vol. 2, **Program Validation**. Englewood Cliffs, NJ: Prentice-Hall, 1977.

(YEH 1978)

R. T. Yeh, ed. **Current Trends in Programming Methodology**. Vol. 4, **Data Structuring**. Englewood Cliffs, NJ: Prentice-Hall, 1978.

(YOURDON AND CONSTANTINE 1978)

E. Yourdon and L. L. Constantine. **Structured Design**. 2nd edition, New York: Yourdon Press, 1978.

(ZAHN 1974)

C. T. Zahn. "A Control Statement for Natural Top-Down Structured Programming." **Symp. on Programming Languages**. Paris, 1974.

(ZAHN 1979)

C. T. Zahn. **C Notes—A Guide to the C Programming Language**. New York: Yourdon Press, 1979.

(ZAVE AND SCHELL 1986)

P. Zave and W. Schell. "Salient Features of an Executable Specification Language and its Environment." **IEEE Transactions on Software Engineering SE-12** 2 (1986): 312–325.

Index

Printed and bound by KIN KEONG PRINTING CO. PTE. LTD. (Republic of Singapore)